LATIN AMERICAN REVOLUTIONS, 1808–1826

Latin American Revolutions, 1808–1826

Old and New World Origins

EDITED AND WITH AN INTRODUCTION BY

John Lynch

UNIVERSITY OF OKLAHOMA PRESS : NORMAN AND LONDON

BY JOHN LYNCH

Spanish Colonial Administration 1782–1810: The Intendant System in the Viceroyalty of the Río de la Plata (London, 1958)

Spain under the Habsburgs (Oxford, 1964–69, 1991; Barcelona, 1992)

(ed., with R. A. Humphreys) *The Origins of the Latin American Revolutions, 1808–1826* (New York, 1965)

The Spanish American Revolutions 1808–1826 (London, 1973; New York, 1986; Barcelona, 1989)

Argentine Dictator: Juan Manuel de Rosas 1829–1852 (Oxford, 1981; Buenos Aires, 1984)

(ed.) *Andrés Bello: The London Years* (Richmond, 1982)

(ed.) *Past and Present in the Americas: A Compendium of Recent Studies* (Manchester, 1984)

Hispanoamérica 1750–1850: Ensayos sobre la sociedad y el estado (Bogotá, 1987)

Bourbon Spain 1700–1808 (Oxford, 1989; Barcelona, 1991)

Caudillos in Spanish America 1800–1850 (Oxford, 1992)

Latin American Revolutions, 1808–1826: Old and New World Origins (Norman, 1994)

Library of Congress Cataloging-in-Publication Data

Latin American revolutions, 1808–1826 : Old and New World origins / edited and with an introduction by John Lynch.
       p.   cm.
    Rev., updated version of: The origins of the Latin American revolutions, 1808–1826 / edited with an introd. by R. A. Humphreys & John Lynch. New York : Knopf, 1965.
    Includes bibliographical references and index.
    ISBN 0-8061-2661-2.—ISBN 0-8061-2663-9 (pbk.)
    1. Latin America—History—Wars of Independence, 1806–1830—Causes. I. Lynch, John, 1927– . II. Humphreys, R. A. (Robert Arthur), 1907– Origins of the Latin American revolutions, 1808–1826.
F1412.L38   1994
980'.02—dc20   94-16521
                                                                           CIP

Book design by Bill Cason

The paper in this book meets the guidelines for permanence and durability of the Committee on Production Guidelines for Book Longevity of the Council on Library Resources, Inc. ∞

1   2   3   4   5   6   7   8   9   10

To R. A. Humphreys
Teacher, Colleague, Friend

Contents

Maps

Preface

The Origins of the Latin American Revolutions, 1808–1826, edited by R. A. Humphreys and John Lynch, was first published in 1965. The present work, nominally a new edition, is virtually a new book; its contents, structure, introduction, and conclusion are designed to take account of the research and interpretation that have so transformed the subject in the last twenty-five years.

In the body of the text most notes and references have been omitted on the assumption that these can be easily verified in the original. The translations have been made by the editor.

I wish to record my thanks for the help and advice I have received from James Cummins, Frank Safford, Joseph Smith, and Rafael Varón. I am indebted to my daughter Caroline for her assistance in preparing the typescript for publication.

LATIN AMERICAN REVOLUTIONS, 1808–1826

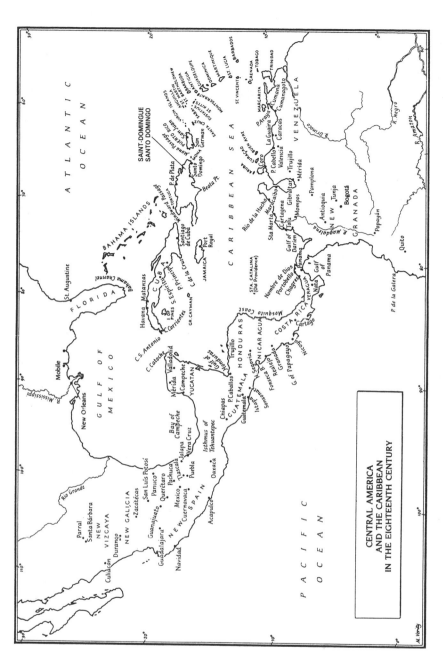

From John Lynch, *Bourbon Spain 1700–1808* (Blackwell: Oxford, 1989), reproduced courtesy of the publisher.

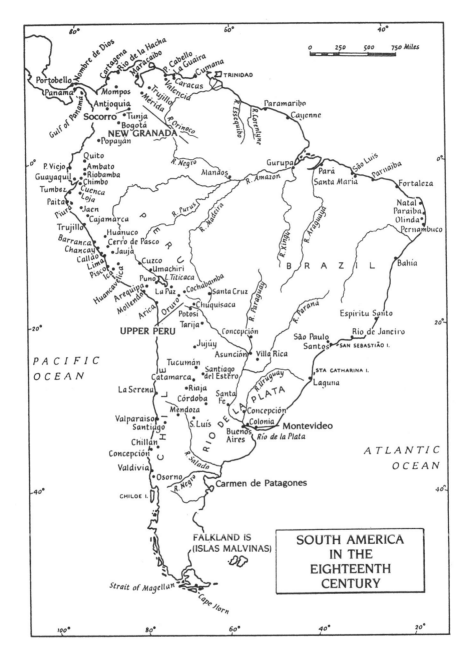

From John Lynch, *Bourbon Spain 1700–1808* (Blackwell: Oxford, 1989), reproduced courtesy of the publisher.

Introduction

The Napoleonic invasion of Portugal and Spain in 1807 to 1808 destroyed the unity of the Iberian world and scattered its rulers. The flight of the Braganzas and the fall of the Bourbons left government in disarray. Once the metropolis had lost its authority, who ruled in America? And who should be obeyed? As legitimacy and loyalty were disputed, argument gave way to violence, and resistance escalated into revolution. But if the war of independence was sudden and apparently unplanned, it had a long prehistory, during which colonial economies underwent growth, societies developed identity, and ideas advanced to new positions. Demands were now made for autonomy in government and a free economy. The Portuguese court met these expectations by adopting them; moving temporarily to Brazil, the monarchy itself led the colony peacefully into independence with its own crown and a minimum of social change. Spain, on the other hand, fought fiercely for its freedom in Europe and for its empire in America. Spanish American independence recoiled, regrouped, and struck back on two fronts. The southern revolution advanced across the pampas from Buenos Aires and was carried by the Army of the Andes under José de San Martín to Chile and beyond; the northern revolution, more closely monitored by Spain, was led by Simón Bolívar from Venezuela to New Granada, back to its birthplace and on to Quito and Guayaquil. Both movements converged on Peru, the last stronghold of Spain in America, where independence was won at the battle of Ayacucho in 1824. In the north, Mexican insurgency took a different route—frustrated social revolution, prolonged royalist reaction, and finally political independence. By 1826 Spain had lost an empire, salvaging only the two islands of Cuba and Puerto Rico, while Portugal retained nothing.

In Spanish America most of the independence movements began as the revolt of one minority against a smaller minority, of *criollos* (Span-

iards born in America) against *peninsulares* (Spaniards born in Spain).
Some creoles were royalists, and the conflict often assumed the appearance of a civil war; but many simply stayed at home and awaited the
outcome. Around 1800, in a total population of over 13.5 million, there
were 3.2 million whites, of whom only some 30,000 were peninsulares.
In demographic terms political change was overdue, not an accident of
1808. The aim of the revolutionaries was self-government for creoles,
not necessarily for Indians, blacks, or mixed races, who together comprised some 80 percent of the population of Spanish America. The
imbalance reflected the existing distribution of wealth and power. The
newly aware creole groups of the late colonial period were indispensable for independence—to administer its institutions, defend its gains,
and conduct its trade. Were creoles, then, the conscious authors of
independence? And were creole interests its "cause"?

IMPERIAL RENEWAL

The history of creole America was not a featureless desert. It was alive
with change and movement, gains and losses, all distinct from those of
imperial history. Creole disquiet was not the accompaniment of three
centuries of oppression; rather it was a relatively recent reaction to
Spanish policy. Creoles in the late eighteenth century were the heirs of
a powerful tradition, and recalled a time, roughly 1650 to 1750, when
their families had broken through imperial barriers, gained access to
the bureaucracy, bargained over taxes, and become part of the various
interest groups disputing royal policy. Political participation was accompanied by economic autonomy: Americans had developed a thriving internal market, producing agricultural and manufactured goods
and selling them from region to region in a vital demonstration of self-
sufficiency—and they bypassed the Spanish monopoly to engage in
direct trade with foreigners. In this way, imperial government and economic relations proceeded by compromise, and Americans reached a
kind of colonial consensus with their metropolis. As they advanced
into the regional oligarchy to become senior partners in the colonial
compact, the creoles were living proof of Montesquieu's dictum that
while the Indies and Spain were two powers under the same master,
"the Indies are the principal one, and Spain is only secondary."[1]

Bourbon planners led by José de Gálvez, visitor-general of New Spain
and minister of the Indies, decided to bring the creole age to an end and
turn the clock back to more primitive political times. The object was
to restore Spain to imperial greatness, and the conditions seemed right
for recovery. Spanish America underwent a triple expansion in the

eighteenth century: in population, mining, and trade. Even as Spanish policy favored growth, it also exploited it to control the economy and increase revenue, goals that were thought to require an exclusively Spanish administration. Americans soon noticed the unusual pressure because they felt it in their pockets and in the uncompromising hand of the state. The answer to new and non-negotiable taxation was opposition. From about 1765 resistance to taxation was constant and sometimes violent; and as from 1779 Spain began to dig deeper into American resources to finance war with Britain, so defiance mounted. But there was no relief. Extension of state monopolies such as tobacco and spirits remained a comprehensive grievance; in the case of tobacco, the monopoly not only hurt consumers but also producers, restricting cultivation to high quality areas and depriving marginal farmers of a livelihood.[2] The increase in *alcabala* (sales tax) rates weighed heavily on peasants as well as landowners, on workers as well as merchants. Revenue from Mexico mounted spectacularly in 1750 to 1810, as the colonial state imposed unprecedented levels of taxation and monopoly in a desperate effort to defray defense costs in America and retain some profits of empire for Spain. The thirty years after 1780 yielded an increase of 155 percent in alcabala revenue over the thirty years before, an increase not derived from economic growth but from pure fiscal extortion.[3] Bourbon policy culminated in the Consolidation Decree of 26 December 1804, which ordered the sequestration of charitable funds in America and their remission to Spain. As applied to Mexico this arbitrary expedient forced the Church to withdraw its money from creditors and deliver it to the state, accepting a reduced rate of interest. The transfer affected merchants, miners, and landowners, who suddenly had to redeem the capital value of their church loans and encumbrances and contemplate a life without investment funds. The clergy too were losers: Miguel Hidalgo, the *cura* of Dolores and rebel leader in the making, forfeited his two haciendas for refusing to comply. Tax excess in itself did not turn Americans into revolutionaries, but it fostered a climate of resentment and a desire to return to colonial consensus or, more ominously, to advance to a greater autonomy.

Could the Spanish American economy take the strain? The Spanish planners believed it could, if its growth were encouraged. Between 1765 and 1776 they dismantled the traditional framework of colonial trade, lowered tariffs, abolished the monopoly of Cadiz and Seville, opened free communications between the ports of the peninsula and the Caribbean and its mainland, and authorized intercolonial trade. And in 1778 "a free and protected trade" between Spain and America was extended to include Buenos Aires, Chile, and Peru. There was another spurt of reform in the years 1788 to 1796 when the secretary of state, the count of Floridablanca, undertook a further review of *comercio libre*, as it was called. In 1789 Venezuela and Mexico were brought into the system, more inter-American trade was authorized, and taxes on colonial trade were reduced. Comercio libre, which was "free" only for Spaniards not for foreigners, greatly expanded trade and navigation in the Spanish Atlantic. To Spanish America it brought both revival and recession. During 1782 to 1796 the average annual value of American exports to Spain was more than ten times greater than that of 1778.[4] For Mexico and Peru free trade promoted commercial growth and agricultural and mining development, to the satisfaction of Crown and creole alike.[5] Precious metals continued to dominate the trade: treasure returns to Spain in 1781 to 1804 were 47 percent higher than those of 1756 to 1780.[6] But agricultural exports were also stimulated: marginal regions such as the Río de la Plata and Venezuela, and neglected products such as agropastoral goods, were brought into the mainstream of the imperial economy. New frontiers of settlement appeared, notably in the pampas of the Río de la Plata and the valleys and plains of Venezuela, where growth in population and production created incipient export economies and added to wealth and employment.

Was the late colonial period, then, a golden age of growth, prosperity, and reform that raised the expectations of the creoles once more? Or was it an age of shortage, famine, and epidemics that revealed the privileges and monopolies of the Spaniards in yet more glaring light? Standpoint is all. Peasants suffered misery, or at best bare subsistence, as haciendas ate into their land and inflation cut their real income. Even among the elites there were losers as well as gainers, manufacturers who were unable to compete as well as merchants and miners who improved their incomes. In any case they all knew that they were still subject to a monopoly, still deprived of market options, still dependent on Spanish-controlled imports. And just as they were inhibited politically, so they were virtually excluded from overseas, as distinct from internal, trade.

They also learned that their own industries were left unprotected and open to freer competition from European imports. Did this destroy colonial industry and with it another legacy of autonomy? In Mexico production of woollen cloth, no longer sheltered from the world market, was unable to compete with cheaper foreign cottons. Local output was challenged from 1790 not only by British contraband but also by Catalan calicoes, profiting from comercio libre; thus, the Mexican *obrajes* (textile workshops) were already slipping into decline before they succumbed to even greater shock during the years of revolution.[7]

The obrajes of Cuzco, on the other hand, producing woollen cloth for colonial markets were victims of new trading conditions rather than imports alone; competition from other forms of colonial production such as domestic textile manufacture in the *chorrillos* meant that Peru's industry underwent change rather than decline. In New Granada the textile industry of Socorro survived to sustain a large artisan population. In the Río de la Plata, too, the textile production of the interior managed to adjust to new competition. Yet Americans were probably more conscious of policy decisions than of long-term trends in the economy, and they knew that Spanish policy remained implacably hostile to colonial industry, sometimes effectively, sometimes not. In Peru, Viceroy Francisco Gil de Taboada warned the government that local factories survived through lack of competition from European manufactures and were damaging to Spanish interests: "only a highly protected trade will suffice to destroy them."[8] After 1796, when war with Britain imposed blockade, it was colonial industry that enjoyed a kind of protection, but this was overtaken by contraband and neutral trade which revived European competition.

Whatever the fate of industry, agriculture sought greater export outlets than Spain would allow. America was still denied direct access to international markets, was forced to trade only with Spain, and was deprived of commercial stimulus for production. In Venezuela, creole landowners, producers of cacao, indigo, and hides, were critical of the Spanish monopolists—and their Venezuelan associates—who controlled the import-export trade and had a record of paying low for exports and charging high for imports. The intendant of Caracas, José Abalos, concluded that "if His Majesty does not grant them the freedom of trade which they desire, then he cannot count on their loyalty."[9] In 1781 the Caracas Company lost its contract, and in 1789 free trade was extended to Venezuela. But commercialized agriculture of goods such as cacao and hides, having little sale within the colony, still depended on export outlets, many of them in the hands of foreigners beyond the control of the colonial oligarchy. In the 1790s cacao exports plunged owing to the fall in Mexican demand and Spain's inability to absorb the surplus.[10] So the Caracas planters began to substitute coffee for cacao. They still demanded more trade with foreigners and in 1797 to 1798 denounced the monopolists as "oppressors," attacked the idea that commerce existed "solely for the benefit of the metropolis," and agitated against what they called "the spirit of monopoly under which this province groans."[11] Not all these protestations need be taken at their face value. In 1797 most of Venezuela's producers and exporters favored free trade, beyond the authorized neutral trade. Their fear was that the monopolists were trying to stage a comeback. But this did not happen; the monopoly in practice was dead, killed off by the war with Britain and the demise of the monopolists. The Caracas elite was accustomed to adjusting to circumstances and surviving economic crises; in the years 1797 to 1808 they were nervous, but they were probably more worried about social order than economic survival.

The Río de la Plata, like Venezuela, underwent its first economic development in the eighteenth century, when an incipient cattle interest emerged, responding to comercio libre and ready to expand the export of hides to Europe and salted meat to Brazil and Cuba. From 1778 the Cadiz merchant houses with capital and contacts secured firm control of the Buenos Aires trade and interposed themselves between the Río de la Plata and Europe. But in the 1790s these were challenged by independent porteño merchants, who procured slave concessions and with them permission to export hides. They employed their own capital and shipping and offered better prices for hides than did the Cadiz merchants, freeing the estancieros from the grip of monopoly.[12] The normal estancia was a small or medium size cattle ranch, capital investment was low, and the life-style of its owner was austere.[13] The estancieros were not yet a political elite, but they formed a third pressure group, allies of the creole merchants against Spanish monopolists. These porteño interests had spokesmen in Manuel Belgrano, Hipólito Vieytes, and Manuel José Lavardén. Belgrano was secretary of the consulado, or merchant guild, which he made a focus of new economic thinking.[14] Lavardén—son of a colonial official, man of letters, and successful estanciero—reduced the economic demands of porteño reformers to four freedoms: to trade directly with all countries and obtain imports from the cheapest source; to own an independent merchant marine; to export the products of the country without restrictions; to expand livestock and agriculture by land distribution on condition that the recipient worked the grant.[15]

Economic interests in America were not as coherent as this program suggests: There was conflict between and within the various colonies as market forces collided with protected groups. Independence was more than a simple movement for free trade. Many freedoms had already been won: the further expansion of free trade from 1778 to 1789, the gradual extension of a freer trade in slaves from 1789, and permission to trade with foreign colonies from 1795. Concessions such as these made the economic argument appear less urgent—but not less relevant. Americans had experienced the possibilities of economic growth within an imperial framework during the years of trade-induced prosperity from 1776 to 1796. Now, in an age of Atlantic warfare, Spain's imperial world was collapsing; as the trade routes were cut by the British navy, interlopers came and went at will.[16]

In the course of 1797 American ports—Havana, Cartagena, La Guaira, and Buenos Aires—with the connivance of local officials traded directly with foreign ports. Spain responded by offering a legal and heavily taxed trade with Spanish America in neutral vessels, though with the obligation to return to Spain. This condition could not be observed because of the blockade, and in the following years trade was free and for United States vessels virtually unrestricted. Under pressure from the monopolists of Cadiz the Spanish government revoked the concession in 1799, but this was a further blow to imperial authority, for it was found that the reversal could not be enforced. To retain a place for itself and earn revenue, Spain was reduced to selling licenses to various European and North American companies and to individual Spaniards to trade with Veracruz, Havana, Venezuela, and the Río de la Plata, and the cargoes were often British manufactures. In 1805 neutral trade was again authorized, this time without the obligation of returning to Spain, and it seemed that Spanish Americans at last had an outlet to the world market, bypassing their own metropolis. In 1807 Spain did not receive a single shipment of American treasure and to all appearances was no longer an Atlantic power.[17] Yet Spaniards did not abandon their claims; Spanish Americans knew, and had it confirmed by experience in 1810, that no matter how unrealistic these claims were, the monopolists of Cadiz would never concede a full free trade and the Crown would never grant one. Only independence could destroy monopoly.

THE DECONSTRUCTION OF THE CREOLE STATE

Conflict of economic interests did not exactly follow the lines of social division between peninsulares and creoles. Some creoles were associates of the monopolists, others sought alliance with royal officials. But there was a rough alignment of society according to interests, and interests were one of the ingredients of the Spanish–creole dichotomy. A number of leading Americans were convinced that the conflict between Spaniards and creoles was the cause of the revolution. Lucas Alamán, Mexican statesman and historian, said so explicitly.[18] So did Miguel de Lardizábal y Uribe, a Mexican creole and ultra-conservative who became Ferdinand VII's minister of the Indies in 1814. He attributed the insurgency to rivalry between *gachupines* (Europeans) and creoles; although the Mexican nobility were loyal, he claimed, low-born creole merchants and artisans were revolutionaries. Manuel Abad y Queipo, bishop elect of Michoacán, disagreed, arguing that "this is no conflict between brothers" but a desire for independence, originating among those who were confident that Spain was finished and wanted to occupy the vacant space.[19]

Rivalry between creoles and peninsulares was a fact of colonial life. In many parts of America the creoles had become powerful elites of landowners, officeholders, and cabildo members, who further profited from trade expansion under the Bourbons to improve their production and prospects. But growth also brought to the colonies more tax officials and new immigrants—Basques, Catalans, Canarians, and others from poor but ambitious families, who often moved into the American end of the transatlantic trade and the traffic with the interior. In Venezuela there was a division between creole hacendados and peninsular merchants, no doubt exaggerated in the rival propaganda of the time but nonetheless real. In Buenos Aires the merchant community itself split along Spanish–creole lines, the creoles offering better prices to local ranchers, demanding freedom to trade with all countries, and in 1809 urging that Buenos Aires be opened to British trade. The animosity of the porteños towards peninsulares can be read in the words of Mariano Moreno, radical lawyer and political activist, once the May Revolution had stripped away pretence:

> The European Spaniard who set foot in these lands became noble as soon as he arrived, and was rich within a few years, master of all employment and thereby all powerful over subordinates, with the arrogance typical of those who are in command far from home. . . . And although they were well aware that, lacking the immediate presence of their country, supporters, and family, they were entirely dependent on the good will of their so-called brothers, they still shouted at them with contempt: "Americans, keep your distance, you are not our equals, spare us that degradation, for nature has created you to vegetate in obscurity and depression."[20]

The new wave of peninsulares after 1760 encroached on the political space of the creoles as well as on their economic position. The policy of the later Bourbons was to increase the power of the state and apply to America closer imperial control. The clergy were pressured, their *fueros* (privileges) curtailed, the Jesuits expelled, taxes extended and raised, and creoles demoted. This was a reversal of previous trends and took from Americans gains they had already made. Thus the great age of creole America, when the local elites bought their way into treasury, audiencia, and other offices, and secured an apparently permanent role in colonial administration, was followed from 1760 by a new order, when the government of Charles III began to reduce creole participation and to restore Spanish supremacy. Higher office in the audiencias, the army, the treasury, and the Church was now assigned almost exclusively to peninsulares, at the same time as new opportunities in the transatlantic trade were made their special preserve.

Alexander von Humboldt suggested that the prejudice against creoles was not a policy of distrust but a question of money, as the Crown benefited from sale of office and Spaniards from the fruits of empire.[21] But in fact there was a strong element of distrust, as well as a conviction that the time had come to restore Spanish America to Spain. The antipathy of José de Gálvez towards creoles was not simply a personal phobia but represented a basic shift of policy. Juan Pablo Viscardo, the Jesuit émigré and advocate of independence, indicted Gálvez, but above all he blamed the system. As one who had been a direct observer of policy trends in Peru, he bore witness to the fact that the Bourbons moved from consensus to confrontation, alienated the creole elite, and eventually drove them towards independence. "From the seventeenth century creoles were appointed to important positions as churchmen, officials, and military, both in Spain and America." But now Spain had reverted to a policy of preference for peninsular Spaniards, "to the permanent exclusion of those who alone know their own country, whose individual interest is closely bound to it, and who have a sublime and unique right to guard its welfare." And he concluded that "the Spanish New World has become for its own inhabitants an immense prison, where only the agents of despotism and monopoly have the freedom to come and go."[22]

The chronology of change was not the same for all regions. In Venezuela cacao production and export created a prosperous economy and a regional elite, which in the seventeenth and early eighteenth centuries were largely ignored by the Crown and found their economic metropolis in Mexico rather than Spain. From about 1730, however, the Crown began to look more closely at Venezuela as a source of revenue for Spain and cacao for Europe. The agent of change was the Caracas Company, a Basque enterprise that was given a monopoly of trade and, indirectly, of administration. Aggressive and novel trading policies, allowing fewer returns for struggling immigrant planters and even for the traditional elite, outraged local interests and provoked a popular rebellion in 1749. This was quickly crushed and Caracas then had to endure a series of military governors, increased taxation, and a greater royal presence than it had previously experienced. The highest among the elite were offered capital stock in the reformed Caracas Company, a palliative to secure their collaboration and detach them from their inferiors. Thus the new imperialism was given its first practical application in Venezuela. The Caracas model of regional growth, elite autonomy, and royal reaction provided perhaps the earliest evidence of the great divide in colonial history, between the creole state and the Bourbon state, between compromise and absolutism, and the division can be located in the years around 1750.[23]

In Mexico the break came with the visitation conducted by José de Gálvez in 1765 to 1771, when many of the economic, fiscal, and administrative changes that, as minister of the Indies, he later imposed on the whole of America, were first applied or conceived. When creoles reacted against demotion and taxation, they were told in effect that Mexico obtained advantages from the new policies. But even the government-sponsored mining boom exposed unpalatable truths. Mining generated three things that were potentially in conflict: creole profits, government revenue, and inflation. Silver paid not only for luxury imports but also for Mexico's taxes in the imperial system. Creoles could see that mining not only promoted growth but also induced the colonial state to siphon more money from the economy in taxation, monopoly profits, and war loans; yet, had it not done so, inflationary pressures could well have become intolerable. The Mexican elites did not necessarily have answers to these dilemmas, but, from a position of wealth, they wanted power and with it the means of controlling appointments, taxation, and remittances to Spain and the Americas. Protestation gained nothing and colonial government remained beyond their grasp. When, in the years after 1810, Mexico lapsed into revolution and counterrevolution, the mining industry was one of the first victims. And as the silver boom came to an end, so did belief in the efficacy of the colonial state.

In Peru the financial, commercial, and administrative changes introduced during the visitations of José Antonio de Areche and Jorge Escobedo (1777–1785)—when the new formula of royal monopolies, tax increases, and stronger agencies was applied—produced positive results, especially for Spain. Legal commerce was expanded, mining output improved, and following the introduction of the intendant system in 1784, royal revenues rose. But there was protest: Local hacendados and obrajeros objected to paying a higher (6 percent) alcabala tax, and creoles resented the new bias towards peninsular officeholders.[24] Resistance grew into rebellion in 1780 to 1783—first creole, then Indian. This was the dividing line in Peru between traditional consensus and new colonialism. The colonial state recovered and renewed the instruments of control, to keep Peru loyal for the rest of the century. When in 1810 to 1814 radical movements made their appearance in the context of American independence, the Lima elite held aloof, fearful of these movements' regional and Indian character.

The shift from compromise to control was not a clean break. Spanish America still bore marks of the character given it in the age of consensus; so economic habits endured, contraband trade reappeared, bargaining continued. As old ways survived from one age to the other, so did memories of a different time. In 1772, Viceroy Pedro Messía de la Cerda warned his successor in New Granada that it was often necessary to bow to circumstances: "The obedience of the inhabitants has no other guarantee, outside the military garrisons, than the free will and choice with which they comply with orders, for without their consent there is no force, weapon, or power which their superiors can use to impose respect and obedience; hence authority is very uncertain. . . . "[25] But the visitor-general, Juan Francisco Gutiérrez de Piñeres, had no such doubts and he imposed the new system, not by consultation but by dictates, replacing creole officeholders by Spaniards, reorganizing revenue collection, and raising taxes and royal monopoly prices. He had to run for his life in 1781 when resentment spawned rebellion, but the colonial state recovered its authority through a mixture of conciliation and coercion; if the viceroys never completely overcame disobedience or eliminated contraband, that was partly because they did not expect too much from New Granada as a source of revenue and trade.

The Río de la Plata, however, was too important to overlook. A new viceroyalty, it soon became a model of the new empire. Buenos Aires was at the leading edge of Spanish imperial strategy, for Spain was alerted by the growing power of Britain in the Americas, its encroachment on Spanish territorial and trading positions, and its new interest in the southern seas. As Pedro de Cevallos, the colony's first viceroy, pointed out, the Río de la Plata "is the true and only defensive wall in this part of America, and its development must be vigorously promoted . . . for it is the one point where South America will be retained or lost."[26] The arrival of more bureaucrats, military officers, and churchmen increased the Spanish presence in Buenos Aires and sharpened the division between peninsulares and creoles. Previously the minor strategic role of the port had created less need for imperial controls; creoles in the cabildo handled many matters of routine administration, while Spanish governors and officials were agents of inertia not of change. But the establishment of the viceroyalty and the appointment of intendants ended the creole age. While Spanish judges, intendants, commanders, and clerks usurped the best offices, creoles were confined to minor positions. The effect of Bourbon innovation in Buenos Aires was to increase the power of the colonial state—now unmistakably a Spanish state—reminding creoles of their colonial status and making them more conscious that they were different from peninsulares. Of the eleven viceroys between 1776 and 1810 only one, Juan José de Vértiz, was an American, though not from the Río de la Plata. Of the thirty-five ministers of the audiencia of Buenos Aires in 1783 to 1810, twenty-six were born in Spain, six were creoles from other parts of America, and only three were creoles of Buenos Aires.[27] No native of the Río de la Plata managed to obtain a confirmed royal appointment as an intendant in the viceroyalty. The bureaucracy of Buenos Aires was dominated by peninsulares; in the period 1776 to 1810 they held 64 percent of appointments, natives of Buenos Aires 29 percent, and other Americans 7 percent.[28]

By 1810 Buenos Aires was home to a Spanish party and a revolutionary party. The Spanish party consisted of peninsular officials and monopoly merchants, but also included some creole merchants who profited from trading links with Spain. The revolutionary party comprised creole bureaucrats and military who were critical of Spanish rule, creole merchants who specialized in neutral and other non-monopoly trade, smaller retail merchants, and a few Spanish merchants of similar exporting interests. In other words, division between privileged and marginal merchants, between higher and lower bureaucracy, was also, though not absolutely, a division between Spaniards and creoles. The roots of independence, it is sometimes argued, are to be found in economic interests and social perceptions, or in an ideological division between conformists and dissidents, rather than in a simple Spanish–Creole dichotomy. Nevertheless, Americans were becoming conscious of their identity and interests, and aware that these were different from those of Spaniards. The viceroyalty brought the age of absolutism to Buenos Aires; it provided a new bureaucracy, more trade, an improved infrastructure. But it also brought a heavier burden of government, greater exploitation, a more peremptory policy. Did it also bring *better* government?

The results of the new imperialism were not uniform throughout the Americas. There were still officials who married locally, further examples of interest networks, continuing signs of nepotism, inefficiency, and even corruption. Everywhere new institutions clashed with old, and Spanish divisiveness reasserted itself. In Mexico, where wealth was at stake, the Crown closely monitored the new administration. In Chile, where resources were less obvious, the bureaucracy remained an ally—even a captive—of the local elite, and the Crown appeared unconcerned. In Buenos Aires, where pre-viceregal government and society had been weak, the new bureaucracy grew up in isolation from local pressure but also, in the crisis of 1810, from local support.[29] In general the Crown acquired a more professional administration, less bound to local interests, and a keener instrument of imperial control. But the cost was high: frustration among Americans mounted as their claims were ignored, their expectations denied, and the new policy further disturbed the balance of interests on which colonial government had traditionally rested. Standards appeared to be falling. In 1804 the consolidation and remittance to Spain of church wealth, the epitome of fiscal extortion in the last decades of empire, was administered in Mexico by a corrupt viceroy who made a fortune out of the operation. In his Representation of 1771 Antonio Joaquín de Rivadeneira had strongly hinted that peninsular officials were corrupt.[30] Simón Bolívar did not doubt it. Thus, in the decades after 1750, Spanish Americans saw their hard-won and often costly advances reversed by a new colonial state that was more ruthless than its predecessor but not more respected. This government was deaf to representations; none received a favorable response, and their only result was to underline the futility of protest. In De Tocqueville's classic theory it is not when conditions are deteriorating but when they are improving that a society falls into revolution. Spanish America demonstrates a different truth: A society is more likely to accept the absence of rights it has never experienced than the loss of rights it has already secured. If this is true, and the historian wishes to personalize events, then José de Gálvez was the author of the Spanish American revolutions, as many Spaniards at the time believed. But history is more complicated.

IMPERIAL DEFENSE

The de-Americanization of the colonial state did not apply completely to its military arm. By 1800 to 1810 the army of America was dominated by creole officers, who constituted 60 percent of the veteran officer corps.[31] This was the regular army. The shift of power was even more noticeable in the militia. Spain had accumulated more empire than it could defend, and it depended on colonial militias for imperial defense and internal security. From 1763, following defeat in the Seven Years' War, these were expanded, reorganized, and endowed with privileges; as an aid to recruitment militia service was opened not only to creoles but also to the mixed races, and these too were granted the privilege of the *fuero militar*.[32] Over 90 percent of the militia officers were American-born, sons of merchant and landed families; virtually all the soldiers were Americans. Thus Spain fashioned one of the main instruments by which the American elites retained some leverage in the last decades of empire.

Did Spain compromise its security in entrusting the defense of

America to Americans? Did the new empire arm potential rebels? The evidence is mixed, though it suggests that the Spanish authorities were concerned enough to take steps, if unsuccessfully, to halt the process of Americanization. In New Granada and Peru the elites came to dominate the colonial armed forces after 1750, though with different results. In 1781 the *comuneros* of New Granada appropriated the militia system to organize the rebel army, and the Crown had to turn to the regular army to reassert control. The militia remained the traditional stronghold of the landed upper class and urban merchants, but the Crown reduced the strength of the militia and renewed its officer corps, at least in Bogotá, to ensure the predominance of peninsulares. In Peru, although the authorities sought to extend royal reforms and jurisdiction in the wake of the Túpac Amaru rebellion, they still needed the hacendados of the sierra and their peon militiamen to keep the peace in the Andes, while these in turn looked to the Crown for privilege and support. Elsewhere the officer corps of the regular army, though initially dominated by Europeans, also succumbed to American majorities as powerful creoles deployed their economic and political influence to secure appointments for their sons. Inevitably, by 1810 militias and regulars alike responded to local rather than imperial needs. In Peru the two coincided; conservatives of the sierra supported the royal army with manpower and money in the years after 1810, fearful of popular mobilization. But the Crown was to be less fortunate in other areas, where the local military forces it had created were often turned against Spain. The Americanization of the military, therefore, varied in its consequences according to place and people. In northern South America and the Río de la Plata, Spain soon, or relatively soon, lost its army and its military control. In Mexico and Peru the creole-dominated Spanish army stayed loyal for over a decade, in default of alternative security.

POPULAR PROTEST

Granted the numbers of the creoles and the strength of their grievances, why did they not form a movement, a party, or an opposition? In the first place, there were no institutions outside the bureaucracy where they could assemble and debate. The cabildos, it is true, represented creole interests and from 1782 were encouraged by the intendants to play a more active role in local government. They were by no means silent on matters of public policy, but they were small and not entirely elective bodies and remained, at least until 1810, administrative agencies rather than political assemblies. Second, to some extent there *was* a fusion of creoles and peninsulares to form a white ruling class, united in their economic activities and in defense against the popular sectors. Peru provides an example. In the second half of the eighteenth century new immigrants moved successfully into the commercial life of Lima; soon they dominated the Atlantic and Pacific trades and, in collusion with Spanish officials, established their control over the internal market. Such was their dominance that they were not averse to co-opting eligible Peruvians, and thus the Lima elite came together in solidarity against Indians and blacks and in loyalty to Spain.[33] But it would be wrong to imagine that all creoles were of the elites: They could be poor, propertyless, traditionalist—an amorphous group conscious of failures as well as successes. Finally, aware of their own numerical inferiority to Indians, blacks, and mixed races, the creoles never lowered their guard against the popular sectors.

In parts of Spanish America slave revolt was so fearful a prospect that creoles were loathe to leave the shelter of imperial government and break ranks with the dominant whites unless there was a viable alternative; this was one of the reasons why Cuba did not embrace the cause of independence at this time. But creoles were not entirely reassured by Bourbon policy. The government appeared to accept some social mobility, and Spanish officials, unlike creoles, did not have to spend the whole of their lives in colonial society. So the *pardos* (mulattos) were allowed into the militia. They could also buy legal whiteness through purchase of *cédulas de gracias al sacar*. By law of 10 February 1795 the pardos were offered dispensation from the status of *infame:* successful applicants were authorized to receive an education, marry whites, hold public office, and enter the priesthood. In this way the imperial government recognized the growth of the pardo population and sought to mitigate the grosser forms of discrimination. The concession did not have great resonance in the colonies: Whites were indifferent, pardos apathetic, and officials unenthusiastic. But in Caracas some whites reacted sharply.[34] And throughout the Americas, in New Granada and the Río de la Plata as well as in Venezuela, the numerical increase of the *castas* (blacks, mestizos, and mulattos), together with growing social mobility, alarmed the whites and bred in them a new awareness of race and a determination to preserve discrimination.

In other parts of Spanish America race tension took the form of direct confrontation between the white elites and the Indian masses, and here too creoles looked to their own defenses. In Peru the creoles had no reason to doubt that Spain possessed the will to keep Indians in subordination and to support creole control of social and economic life in the Andes. But there were questions. Did the colonial state have the ability to contain Indian discontent? And were new forms of exploitation accompanied by appropriate levels of security? After the great rebellion of Túpac Amaru, when creole-led militias were in action in defense of the existing order, they noticed the way in which *repartos* (forced sale of goods to Indians) were abolished, creole militias were reduced, and peninsular officials sought to apply the pro-Indian sentiments of the ordinance of intendants. The creoles of the sierra were interested parties in the subsequent struggle between Spanish reformers and local officials for control of the Indian economy.[35] In Mexico, too, the social situation was explosive, and the whites were always aware of the simmering resentment of the Indians and castas. Here, too, the reparto returned, justified by colonial interests as the only way to make the Indians work and consume. Traditionally the elite looked to Spain to defend them; property owners depended upon the Spanish authorities against threats from laborers and workers, and the military and militia were frequently deployed in defense of law and order. The critical moment arrived in 1810 when Mexico erupted in violent social revolution—proof, if proof were needed, that the creoles were the ultimate guardians of social order and the colonial state.

Many creoles turned the argument concerning security against Spain, caught as they were between the colonial government and the mass of the people. They pointed out that without creole support Spain could not govern America, yet they were given neither the autonomy nor the status they deserved. They themselves were sometimes tempted to mobilize support among the popular classes in the hope of shaking government complacency and adding force to their protests. Most creoles regarded this as a dangerous game, but the more daring, or more desperate, among them were prepared to play it.

Movements of popular resistance to authority increased in frequency in the eighteenth century, a response to growing pressure from the new colonial state. If the economic argument for rebellion was not in itself decisive, there was usually a backward linkage from extortionate officials to higher taxes and deteriorating material conditions. Do revolutions occur in the midst of poverty or plenty? In Mexico prices of local commodities, though not of imports, rose strongly and to some extent inexplicably after 1780; maize prices soared dramatically from 1800, while wages remained stagnant and the great estates extended their control over production. High prices for Mexico's basic staple had a crushing effect on peasants and workers, causing new levels of famine, disease, and mortality. A dry summer in 1809 severely reduced maize output and caused prices to quadruple. So the violence of Mexico's first revolution in 1810 had its origins in the hunger and despair of the rural poor.[36] The revolts of Túpac Amaru and Tomás Catari (1780–1783), on the other hand, occurred in the midst of agricultural growth in Peru, characteristic of the whole period 1760 to 1790. But this was a growth in hacienda production by extension of territory, to some extent at the expense of common land and Indian resources. Agricultural growth meant an oversupplied market and low prices, which made it difficult for Indian producers to earn sufficient surplus to pay their tribute and purchase repartos.[37] On top of this, they were now subject to unprecedented alcabalas in new internal customs houses. These factors gave the rebellion of Túpac Amaru a decidedly fiscal origin. In Buenos Aires wages moved up strongly in the late colonial period, and in 1810 were 70 percent higher than in 1776. But there was also a long-term upward trend in prices, a consequence of rapid population growth and, after 1802, of drought, the British invasions, and the resultant militarization. In times of emergency and dearth Buenos Aires could not feed its own population, for agriculture was starved of investment and profit levels were depressed by imports. The conjunction of dearth and disease, prices and wages, was not in itself an immediate cause of independence, but the loss of purchasing power of many wage earners through inflation of basic staples helps to explain the popular support for revolution in 1810.[38]

Popular rebellion anticipated the revolutions for independence in many parts of Spanish America, and continued throughout the revolutionary period and beyond without limitation by political chronology. The insurrection in the city of Quito in 1765 was a major urban rebellion precipitated by changes in taxation. The attempt of the viceroy of New Granada to extend the royal liquor monopoly and later the sales tax in Quito united different social groups in a common reaction to royal policy.[39] In Mexico the focus of rebellion was rural rather than urban. It is true that hunger and grievance could bring mobs on to the streets, and urban riots, a recurring feature of colonial—and later of republican—life, were a constant fear of authorities and elites. But normally an urban mob in Mexico was not revolutionary; and being less structured than rural communities the popular sectors of the towns were less easily mobilized for mass action, as the insurgents learned to their cost in 1810.[40]

In Peru, creole protest against Bourbon fiscal and administrative policy was overtaken by a great Indian rebellion. The violent scenes in the southern highlands were the culmination of endemic grievance centered on tribute and reparto (legalized in 1754), and now aggravated by new alcabalas and customs posts. With repercussions in the northern sierras and rebellion too in Upper Peru, the events of 1780 to 1782 represented a basic defiance of authority and a critical challenge to the colonial state.[41] Although the Indian policy of Bourbon reformers overtly corrected abuses, abolishing repartos in 1780 to 1781 and gradually replacing *alcaldes mayores* and *corregidores* by intendants and subdelegates, these measures had little effect on the lives and liabilities of the Indians. They simply meant that the colonial state now transferred to itself some of the surplus from Indian production previously taken by the corregidores and monopoly merchants. The alcabala was extended and increased, and tribute collection rigorously enforced. In Cuzco tribute revenue in the decade 1780 to 1789 increased by 171 percent over that of 1770 to 1779, while in Potosí it increased by 72 percent. In Cuzco alcabala revenue in the quinquennium 1780 to 1784 increased by 81 percent over that of 1775 to 1779, in Potosí by 24 percent.[42] Thus did new royal officials compete with old interest groups in exploitation of the Indians and seizure of their surplus.

The standard model of colonial rebellion was exemplified in New Granada. There the rebellion of the comuneros was a creole-dominated protest against tax innovation and bias in appointments. Local power groups particularly resented the hordes of new and ill-bred tax officials who operated outside the accepted norms of law and custom to terrorize, extort, and insult, and who brought fiscal despotism to the doorstep.[43] The rebellion also incorporated grievances of mestizos and Indians, and these sectors were useful to the movement in adding to its numbers and frightening the authorities. But they also frightened the creoles, who eventually lost their nerve and abandoned the struggle—a characteristic pattern. Movements of protest were overtly resistance to Bourbon innovation, anti-tax riots, and risings against specific abuses. In creole perceptions they were not designed to be more; they took place within the framework of colonial institutions and did not challenge the social structure. But not all rebels accepted these rules. Andean insurrection contained elements of neo-Inca ideology and cultural renaissance, which had a powerful, if not universal, appeal among Indian *kurakas*. In a cultural context the rebellion of Túpac Amaru was ambiguous, the leader apparently claiming legitimacy both from an alleged royal commission and from his Inca past. But whatever its messianic message, the rebellion went farther than creole-inspired movements and became a more basic revolution, projecting a new order of society and provoking a hostile reaction from all the colonial elites.[44]

Throughout Spanish America popular rebellions raised to the surface deeply rooted social and racial tensions, which normally lay silent and only exploded when exceptional tax pressure and other grievances brought together different social groups in alliance against the administration and gave the poorer sectors an opportunity to voice their dissent. They reveal the interests, values, and politics of the common people, their insistence on traditional rights and natural justice, and their determination to defend the customs of the community. While the temporary alliance of patricians and people alarmed the Spanish authorities, the creoles soon became aware of the social dangers and returned to the fold, usually to a more lenient reception than that awaiting the other rebels. Popular rebellion, insofar as it had an ideology, tended to look to past utopias or an age of consensus, rather than to a future of national independence.

New Granada, like Peru, was overtly pacified in the period after 1781, but anger was never far below the surface. Antonio Nariño, a leading creole dissident, reported in 1797 on popular unrest in the villages to the north of Bogotá. And in 1803 the viceroy himself drew attention to peasant grievances caused by low wages and rising prices:

> I understand that the same wages are paid now as were paid fifty or more years ago, despite the fact that prices of all essential goods have risen. . . . This is an injustice that cannot be tolerated much longer, and without predicting likely events I am convinced that the day will come when the laborers will dictate to the landowners and these will be obliged to admit to a share in the profits those who have helped to produce them.

The same viceroy warned of the danger of introducing new taxes, "which are almost never received without irritation, resistance, and even unrest among the people."[45] Popular grievances in New Granada had local roots and did not suddenly disappear in 1810 or indeed after the war of independence. Many social and regional conflicts—tax protests, land disputes, Indian grievances, and slave rebellions—were inherited from the colonial period and then intensified during the war. Regional elites sought power bases among the popular sectors, sometimes for insurgency, sometimes—as in the south—for royalism, and usually with some circumspection.[46] This was also true of Mexico. Whatever the political objectives of the elites, popular insurgency was essentially social and agrarian, a part of the revolution but not necessarily a cause or a beneficiary of it.

Social protest in Andean America was not confined to massive Indian movements, as in 1780 and 1814, but had a continuous existence among free bandits and fugitive slaves. These are sometimes measured against the model of the social bandit: the pre-political rebel born of social division, deprivation, and injustice, denounced as a criminal by rulers and proprietors, but defended as a hero and fighter for justice by

peasant communities. Social banditry had no ideology and looked back
to a traditional social order, not forward to a revolutionary one. Peruvian bandits had some affinity with this social type, but were not
identical.[47] The bandits in the environs of Lima came unmistakably
from the popular sectors, from blacks, mulattos, zambos, mestizos,
and poor whites, operating between the coastal valleys and the viceregal capital. The bands were held together by group cohesion and
personalist loyalties, and were totally lacking in ideology or class consciousness. It is true that they were nurtured and sustained by popular
discontent; as one local official reported in 1808, it was difficult to
capture bandits "because as they are related to the blacks of all the
haciendas it is impossible to get any tip-offs on their movements"—an
Indian hacienda worker told the court that he had taken to banditry
because a laborer could not earn enough to sustain his family.[48] But the
bands tended to reproduce the forms and values of the colonial hierarchy, and they were just as capable of terrorizing their own people
as they were of attacking the rich, or as a law officer said of a hacienda slave turned bandit leader, "he robbed without distinction of
persons or classes."[49] In the absence of any political allies they remained addicted to plunder rather than protest. This did not prevent
their passing from bandits to guerrillas to patriots during the revolution, a sequence followed by many such groups in Spanish America;
and the transition was effected without changing style or relinquishing
their life of plunder.

Some of the guerrilla leaders in central Peru during the war of independence were creoles and mestizos whose families and property had
suffered at the hands of the royalists and who now sought vengeance.
Others were genuinely populist, pursuing advantage for their communities and their right to collaborate or not collaborate. Others were
Indian kurakas, moved by a mixture of personal and communal motives, and not normally friendly towards whites of any political variety.
Some communities in guerrilla territory, putting their agricultural
interests first, refused to support the cause of independence, which
appeared to them to serve foreign and elite priorities. The bands themselves, like the colonial bandits, lacked cohesion; interest and motivation differed widely between men and between groups. Dissension
between guerrilla chiefs, or between these and patriot officers, often
arose out of regional, racial, or political rivalries. The fact remained
that Indian suspicion of whites went too deep to transform popular
guerrillas into instant patriots.[50]

RACE AND RESISTANCE IN BRAZIL

Brazil too was divided by hierarchy, but in other respects was unique in the Iberian world. Portuguese America underwent none of the great informal shifts of power—from primitive dependence to creole state to renewed imperialism—characteristic of Spanish America. Brazil was always more colonial and less Americanized than its Spanish neighbors, and although it was not so institutionalized as the rest of America its ruling groups held firm to the metropolis through good times and bad. In the first two centuries of colonization the dominant division was between whites and non-whites; most of the whites, Americans as well as Europeans, identified with Portugal, were conscious of race and status, and were anxious to keep the large population of Indians and Africans at a distance.[51] Solidarity of this kind did not prevent the emergence of a Brazilian identity, and from about 1700 the hostility of Brazilian Portuguese towards those born in Portugal became another point of contention in colonial society. To some extent this coincided with rivalry of interests between native landowners with a power base in the plantations and Portuguese merchants who relied on the favor of the Crown, and could be seen too in American competition for public office and ecclesiastical preferment.

The metropolis aggravated tension. In Brazil, as in Spanish America, the eighteenth century saw renewed royal control over colonial government and society, partly in response to rapid population growth, partly to make Brazil work more directly for Portugal. The new policy was evident in the Crown intervention in the mining industry, the increase of taxation and control of commerce, the greater power of the Portuguese bureaucracy, the intrusion of royal officials in municipal affairs, and the expulsion of the Jesuits.[52] Resentment was exacerbated in Brazil, as in Spanish America, by the Crown's tendency to underestimate Americans and to favor Europeans in appointments to offices. Absolutism reached its peak in the policy of the marquis of Pombal, whose attempt to free Portugal from dependence on England involved reducing Brazil to greater dependence on Portugal. The Brazil trade was placed in the hands of Portuguese monopoly companies, the colony was taxed for higher revenue, the Church was reduced to yet greater compliance, and the administration was strengthened to meet its new role. Socially the results were not impressive—Brazilians were alienated and reminded, in effect, that they were colonists. And the attempt to acculturate and integrate the Indians into Portuguese economic life was more profitable to the Portuguese than to the Indians, whose true interests were gravely damaged by forced labor and production. Pombal did little to alleviate the economic depression engulfing Brazil around 1770, though later his reforms bore some fruit; from 1780, in combination with changing patterns of supply and demand for tropical products in the Atlantic world and the development of new agricultural commodities, the colonial economy expanded, accompanied by higher levels of slave importations.

Portugal could increase imperial pressure without danger to itself because the white elite in Brazil needed slavery and social hierarchy more than it wanted freedom. Brazilians might have resented discrimination and denial of free trade—and expressed their anger in conspiracy and rebellion—but they stopped short of independence, just as their intellectuals drew back from equality. The rebellion in Minas Gerais in 1788 to 1789 was an amalgam of tax revolt, intellectual stirring, and political agitation by white dissidents, and posed little real threat to the colonial state. More significant, though even weaker in impact, was the mainly mulatto conspiracy in Bahia in 1798, which stood for equality as well as liberty, and frightened white Brazilians as well as the Portuguese authorities.[53] The metropolis was aware that social tensions in the colony were a guarantee of elite loyalty. After suppressing the movement of 1798, the governor of Bahia wrote to the Crown that there was no need for concern, for the upper classes had remained aloof. "That which is always most dreaded in colonies is the slaves, on account of their condition, and because they compose the greater number of inhabitants. [It is therefore] not natural for men employed and established in goods and property to join a conspiracy which would result in awful consequences to themselves, being exposed to assassination by their own slaves."[54]

Slavery was an inherent part of the economy and social structure of Brazil. The mines no less than the sugar and cotton plantations were dependent on slaves for their labor supply, and at least 5 million were imported from Africa before 1800. Around 1800, in a population of something over 2 million, two-thirds were of African origin (blacks and mulattos), and there were more free persons of color than whites. Miscegenation became a characteristic feature of Brazilian society but not a means of racial harmony; the free mulattos suffered hardly less prejudice than the slaves. The demographic growth of free blacks and mulattos, accompanied by legal, economic, and social discrimination, increased the potential for conflict in Brazilian society. This had the effect of keeping the local oligarchy loyal to the Crown and dependent on Portuguese protection at a time when revolution in Saint-Domingue

(1791) frightened whites and slave owners in Brazil no less than in Venezuela and the Spanish Caribbean. For these reasons, in spite of their growing hostility to Portugal, the Brazilian elites were willing to compromise their politics to maintain their society and did so until 1821.

THE AGE OF REVOLUTION

The Spanish American revolutions responded first to interests, and interests invoked ideas. The deconstruction of the creole state, its replacement by a new imperial state, the alienation of the American elites—these were the roots of independence. Creole resentment was accompanied by popular unrest, with potential for social revolution rather than political independence. This was a continuing challenge to authority during colony, revolution, and republic. In this sequence, ideology does not occupy prime position and is not seen as a "cause" of independence. Nevertheless, this was the age of democratic revolution when ideas appeared to cross frontiers and leave no society untouched. In Spanish America too the language of liberty was heard in the last decades of empire. Then, after 1810, as Spanish Americans began to win rights, freedom, and independence, ideology was used to defend, to legitimize, and to clarify the revolution.

The second half of the eighteenth century was an age of revolutionary change in Europe and America, a time of struggle between the aristocratic and the democratic concept of society, between monarchical and republican systems of government. Reformers everywhere put their faith in the philosophy of natural rights, proclaimed ideas of popular sovereignty, and demanded written constitutions based on the principle of the "separation" of powers. To what extent was Latin America influenced by the ideas of the eighteenth century and a participant in the movement of democratic revolution? The political and intellectual movements of the time were marked by diversity rather than unity. The concept of a single Atlantic revolution inspired by democracy and nurtured on the Enlightenment does not do justice to the complexity of the period, nor does it discriminate sufficiently between minor currents of revolution and the great wave of change unleashed by the most powerful and radical movements of all. The age of revolution was primarily that of the Industrial Revolution and the French Revolution, a "dual revolution" in which Britain provided the economic model to change the world, while France provided the ideas.[55] Yet even this conceptual framework does not accommodate all the liberation movements of the time, and it cannot provide a precise place for those in Latin American.[56]

The Latin American revolutions did not conform exactly to political trends in Europe. Even the most liberal thinkers were guarded towards the French Revolution. As Francisco de Miranda observed in 1799, affected no doubt by his own tribulations in France, "We have before our eyes two great examples, the American and the French Revolutions. Let us prudently imitate the first and carefully shun the second."[57] First impressions, it is true, raised greater expectations, and many young creoles were fascinated by the ideas of liberty and equality and by the war against tyrants.[58] But liberty was a dangerous call in Spanish America, a project without power. The French Revolution drew from the colonial authorities a fierce reaction that caused creole radicals to run for cover and enlightened ideas to go into hiding. Equality too was an illusion. The more radical the French Revolution became the less it appealed to the creole elite. They saw it as a monster of extreme democracy, which, if admitted into America, would destroy the social order they knew, as it had destroyed the slave colony of Saint-Domingue. During the course of the May Revolution in Buenos Aires Mariano Moreno was regarded by the moderates led by Cornelio de Saavedra as an extremist, a "malvado de Robespierre" who would reproduce all that was worst in the French Revolution; they therefore moved quickly to marginalize him and protect the revolution from his influence. This was a characteristic response. Nevertheless the French Revolution in its imperial phase continued to cast its spell. Indirectly, in terms of military and strategic consequences, events in France had a resounding impact in Latin America, first from 1796 by drawing the hostility of Britain on France's ally Spain and thus isolating the metropolis from its colonies, then in 1808 when France invaded the Iberian peninsula and deposed the Bourbons, thereby precipitating in America a crisis of legitimacy and a struggle for power.

The influence of Britain was forceful but finite. It was from 1780 to 1800 that the industrial revolution began to bear fruit and Britain experienced an unprecedented growth of trade, based mainly upon factory production in textiles. Virtually the only limit on the expansion of British exports was the purchasing power of their customers, and this too depended on export earnings. These factors help to explain the particular attraction of the Spanish American market. As there was little possibility of rival industrialization in the underdeveloped Hispanic world, it was a captive market and one that had a vital medium of trade, silver. Britain therefore valued its trade with Spanish America and sought to expand it, either via Spain and the Caribbean or by more direct routes. During times of war with Spain, while the British navy blockaded Cadiz, British exports supplied the consequent shortages in the

Spanish colonies—a new economic metropolis was displacing Spain in America. It would be an exaggeration to say that British trade undermined the Spanish empire, or made revolutionaries out of opponents of monopoly; but the stark contrast between Britain and Spain, between growth and depression, left a powerful impression on Spanish Americans. And there was a further twist to the argument: if a power like Britain could be evicted from America, by what right did Spain remain?

The alliance of Spain with the North American revolution was a blow for national interests not for colonial freedom. But American independence returned to mock Spain and to give a clear if distant signal to the peoples of the subcontinent. In the years around 1800 the influence of the United States was exerted by its mere existence, and the example of liberty and republicanism remained an enduring inspiration in Spanish America.[59] The proclamations of the Continental Congress, the works of Thomas Paine, the speeches of John Adams, Jefferson, and Washington all circulated among creoles, and many of the precursors and leaders of independence visited the United States and observed free institutions in action. They were impressed more by the practical achievements of the American Revolution than by the concept of democracy emanating from France. But Spanish American independence was not a mere projection of the American Revolution, nor was there a specific influence from one to the other. North American government, especially federalism, drew a mixed response from the new republics, admired by some, repudiated by others; and to a leader like Bolívar, struggling to govern heterogeneous peoples, it was anathema. Yet simply to know other systems was to question that of Spain. In the Río de la Plata, Viceroy Avilés observed in 1800 "signs of a spirit of independence," which he attributed precisely to excessive contact with foreigners.[60] Many of these were undoubtedly citizens of the United States.

THE ENLIGHTENMENT AND INDEPENDENCE

Spanish Americans, unlike the North American colonists, did not enjoy a free press, a liberal tradition going back to the seventeenth century, or local assemblies where freedom could be practiced. But they were not isolated from the world of ideas or from the political thought of the Enlightenment. Leading creoles were familiar with theories of natural rights and social contract. From these they could follow the arguments in favor of liberty and equality, and accept the assumption that these rights could be discerned by reason. The object of government, they would agree, was the greatest happiness of the greatest number, and many of them would define happiness in terms of material progress. Hobbes and Locke, Montesquieu and Rousseau, Paine and Raynal, all left their imprint on the discourse of independence. But did these thinkers exert a precise or exclusive influence? An alternative interpretation insists that the *doctrinas populistas* of Francisco Suárez and the Spanish neo-scholastics provided the ideological basis of the Spanish American revolutions, with the corollary that Spain not only conquered America but also supplied the argument for its liberation. A variant of this suggests that neo-Thomism was a vital component of Hispanic political culture, the basis of the patrimonial state and an ideological accompaniment of independence.[61] Yet doubts remain. In the early nineteenth century Catholic thought did not sit easily with liberty. Could tradition welcome revolution? Authority embrace independence? The Enlightenment would appear a more immediate influence, and one that was perceived by Americans themselves. But what kind of influence was it?

Americans, or some of them, read widely in order to educate themselves, to acquire knowledge in general rather than a specific program. In the case of Bolívar, it is true that his reading of the philosophers of the seventeenth and eighteenth centuries was a major and probably a preferred part of his education; but it seems more likely to have confirmed his scepticism than have created it, to have enlarged his liberalism than have implanted it. And from time to time he became disillusioned with the *effective* power of European ideas and North American example. Where are they now, when we need them? he asked in the Jamaica Letter.[62] Ideas were a means to action, and the actions of the liberators were based on many imperatives, political, military, and financial, as well as intellectual. The basic objectives were liberation and independence, but liberty did not mean simply freedom from the absolutist state of the eighteenth century, as it did for the Enlightenment, but freedom from a colonial power, to be followed by true independence under a liberal constitution.

The texts of liberty were read by many and were significant to some. John Locke on natural rights and social contract was known at first or second hand. Citing Acosta, Locke argued that the original inhabitants of the Americas were free and equal and placed themselves under government by their own consent. He also argued that people lose the freedom and independence gained by contract "whenever they are given up into the power of another."[63] This was an argument for freedom but not specifically for freedom from colonial power. Montesquieu was a favorite source for Spanish American intellectuals, and most of them were familiar with his statement that "The Indies and

Spain are two powers under the same master, but the Indies are the principal one, and Spain is only secondary. In vain policy wants to reduce the principal one to a secondary one; the Indies continue to attract Spain to themselves."[64] Montesquieu seemed not unsympathetic to the idea of a nation establishing colonies abroad, as long as it was a free nation and exported its own commercial and government systems. But this did not deter Bolívar, who drew on Montesquieu throughout his political life. In the Jamaica Letter he used Montesquieu's concept of oriental despotism to define the Spanish empire, and his entire political thought was imbued with the conviction that theory should follow reality, that legislation should reflect climate, character, and customs, and that different peoples required different laws. Rousseau, too, had his followers, who found in his political thought an instrument of revolution. In Buenos Aires Mariano Moreno was clearly indebted to Rousseau for an answer to the question, Is the meeting of a congress legitimate?

> The bonds which unite the people to the king are different from those which unite men to each other: a people is a people before giving itself to a king, and therefore although social relations between people and king may be dissolved or suspended by the captivity of the monarch, the bonds which unite one man to another in society remain in existence because they do not depend upon the former. The people do not have to form themselves into a people, because that is what they already are; they simply have to chose a ruler or rule themselves.[65]

But liberty was not enough. Liberty could be an end in itself and stop short of liberation. This was the belief of the Spanish liberals in the Cortes of Cadiz, who subscribed to the freedoms of the Enlightenment and offered them to Spanish Americans, but with equal determination refused them independence. The Enlightenment, in other words, could be invoked to grant greater freedom within a Hispanic framework, to justify reformed imperialism. Spanish Americans saw the distinction and some accepted it. In 1814 the creole leader of the rebellion in Cuzco, José Angulo, welcomed the Constitution of 1812 as valid for Peru and simply demanded that it should be strictly applied, against the opposition of the viceroy. "Although systematically retarded in our industry and mechanical skills, Americans have been advancing in political awareness, which everyone derives from the natural law and the impluse to liberty and independence inspired by the very author of our being; and of these only independence is renounced, not liberty."[66] But for the revolutionaries liberty was not enough.

Was the Enlightenment, then, a source for independence as well as

for liberty? European intellectuals and statesmen of the eighteenth
century were blind to the existence of nationality as a historical force.
The cosmopolitanism of the *philosophes* was inimical to national aspirations; the majority of these thinkers disliked national differences and
ignored national sentiment. They seem to have been totally unaware of
the possibility of new and embryonic nationalities, of the need to apply
ideas of freedom and equality to relations between peoples, or of any
right of colonial independence. The British conservative theorist Ed-
mund Burke came close to developing a theory of national self-determination, but he was far from admitting that colonists had rights to
independence as a separate nation. Theory of nationality was taken
farther by Rousseau, who argued that if a nation did not have a national
character it must be given one by appropriate institutions and education. Rousseau, moreover, was the leading intellectual defender of political freedom against the despotic monarchies of the eighteenth century. But Rousseau did not pause to apply his ideas to colonial peoples.
And the fact remains that few of the eighteenth-century progressives
were revolutionaries. Neither Montesquieu, nor Voltaire, nor Diderot
went to the logical conclusion of advocating revolution; even Rousseau
stopped short of sanctioning violent political change.

The leading exceptions were Thomas Paine and the Abbé Raynal.
Paine's *Common Sense* (1776) was an outright justification for colonial
rebellion, defending American independence as a "true interest," on
account of miseries endured, redress denied, and the right to resist
oppression: "there is something absurd in supposing a continent to be
perpetually governed by an island."[67] This impressed Spanish Americans as an exact statement of their own case, as did his later conclusions: "What were formerly called revolutions were little more than a
change of persons or an alteration of local circumstances. . . . But what
we see now in the world, from the revolutions of America and France,
are a renovation of the natural order of things. . . ."[68] Paine was cited
and paraphrased by Viscardo, and read by many more. In 1811 a Venezuelan enthusiast published in the United States an anthology of
Paine's works translated into Spanish, which circulated from hand to
hand in Venezuela and was an influence on the constitutional thinking
of the republic.[69]

Paine was also cited by Raynal, who in the third edition of his *Histo-
ire des deux Indes* (1781) described the American Revolution and praised
the struggle of the colonists for liberty against the abuses of the British
Crown. Spanish Americans were impressed by his paraphrase of Paine:
"By the rule of quantity and distance, America can belong only to
itself." They noticed too his implicit comparison between Spain and

Britain, between despotism in Spanish America and freedom in North America. And his comment that colonists were forced to acquire the enemies of their metropolis only confirmed their own experience.[70] Raynal was significant too for his influence on Dominique de Pradt, a French cleric and servant of Napoleon, who took the Enlightenment closer to Spanish America. He was the first European to call for the absolute independence of the Spanish colonies, made inevitable, he argued, by the example of the United States, political movements in Europe, and the ideas of the age—influences that Spain was impotent to stop and that hastened the tendency inherent in colonies to grow to maturity and break away.[71]

Independence, therefore, as distinct from liberty, engaged the attention of only a minority of Enlightenment thinkers. It needed the makers of North American and Spanish American independence to develop a concept of colonial liberation, as Bolívar did in his *Jamaica Letter*.[72] In most parts of the Atlantic world post-Enlightenment liberalism was not in itself an effective agent of emancipation. Jeremy Bentham was one of the few reformist thinkers of the time to apply his ideas to colonies, to advocate independence as a general principle, and to expose the contradiction inherent in regimes that professed liberalism at home and practiced imperialism abroad. But Bentham was exceptional, and most liberals remained no less imperialist than conservatives. The contradiction is not surprising: liberal political ideas found a constituency in new social groups, many of whom were involved in trade and industry, and—like the Spanish constitutionalists in Cadiz—were ready to promote formal or informal empire in order to secure captive markets.

If it was not a "cause" of independence, the Enlightenment was an indispensable source from which leaders drew to justify, defend, and legitimize their actions, before, during, and after the revolution. As a working ideology its impact was late, and there is little or no trace of it in the rebellions of 1780 to 1781. During the next thirty years it entered the political consciousness of creoles, but in the interests of their own safety they were more likely to invoke its ideas after than before 1810. In the course of this year Mariano Moreno turned from moderate to radical policies, and was soon described by his enemies as a Jacobin because of his political aggression, egalitarianism, pretensions to absolutism, and terrorism against the revolution's enemies. It is true that the essential idiom of the May Revolution was that of 1789: liberty, equality, fraternity, popular sovereignty, and natural rights. But influence is not to be judged by language alone.[73] In practice the terms of revolution did not have the same meaning in Buenos Aires as they did in France. The two revolutions were twenty years apart, and while in Buenos Aires democratic principles were debated and proclaimed, political procedure was more cautious and less "popular" than the discourse of the time. The *morenistas* were ready to propagate revolutionary ideas among the popular sectors, but they saw the revolution as a controlled and guided force, not a spontaneous movement.[74] The balance between tradition and innovation is seen in the decision of Moreno to suppress from his translation of Rousseau's *Social Contract* the chapter on religion, while at the same time he ordered two hundred copies to be printed for use as a textbook to teach students "the inalienable rights of man."

AMERICAN IDENTITY

Americans did not spend the last fifty years of empire waiting for liberation. It would be anachronistic to judge all Spanish policy and every American response as a prologue to independence. But there was a sense in which political consciousness was changing. Political power, economic freedom, social order, these were the basic requirements of the creoles. Even had Spain been able and willing to guarantee their needs, would they have been satisfied for long? Reform was not enough; Andrés Bello, in acknowledging the "new order of prosperity" brought to Venezuela by the Spanish Caracas Company, also added wryly, "if such institutions may be regarded as useful when societies in passing from infancy no longer need the leading strings with which they made their first steps towards greatness."[75] This was the silent factor, the metamorphosis ignored by Spain: the maturing of colonial societies, the development of distinct identity, the new age of America. Colonial societies do not stand still; they have within them the seeds of their own progress and, ultimately, of independence. Amid the mountains of paper passing between officials, imperial policy makers did not pause to consider the rate of growth of the American colonies. Yet the signs were there; the demands for equality, for office, and for opportunities expressed a deeper awareness, an increasing sense of nationality, a conviction that Americans were not Spaniards. Creole nationality was nurtured on conditions within the colonial world: Spanish administrative divisions, regional economies and their rivalries, access to offices and demands for more, pride in local resources and environments—a pride typically expressed in the writings of Jesuits and creole chroniclers—these were the components of identity developing over three centuries and only to be satisfied in independence.[76] Individuals began to identify themselves with a group, and these groups possessed some of the qualifications of a nation: common descent, language, religion, territory, customs, and traditions. Recent experience sharpened these perceptions. Since 1750 creoles had observed a growing Hispanization of American government; by 1780 they were aware that their political space was shrinking and they had no redress. Identity fed on frustration. If Americans had once gained access to office, bargained over taxation, and traded with other nations, if they had already experienced intimations of independence and savored its benefits, would not this in itself increase their awareness of *patria,* consciousness of identity, and desire for further freedoms? And would not a reversion to dependency be regarded with a sense of loss and as a betrayal, not only of their material interests, but of their pride as Americans?

At the same time as Americans became estranged from Spanish nationality, they were also aware of differences among themselves. Even in their pre-national state the various colonies rivaled each other in their assets and interests. Regional identity was nourished on regional opportunities, employment, and resources, to be guarded and developed against the encroachments of outsiders. America was too vast and diverse a continent to claim individual allegiance. Some of the liberators, it is true, had a vision of a greater America and a single community transcending particular nations, but the majority of their followers were primarily Venezuelans, Mexicans, Chileans, and porteños. And it was in their own country, not America, that they found their national home, there developing a higher degree of communication with each other than with neighbors and foreigners.[77]

The colonial origins of national identity also prescribed its limits. National perceptions were confined to creoles, while those with a lesser stake in colonial society had less regard for the *patria;* so the pardos had only an obscure sense of the nation, and the blacks and slaves none at all. Indian leaders, on the other hand, had an alternative concept of nationality. Túpac Amaru hailed his *paisanos* and *compatriotas,* meaning Peruvians as distinct from European Spaniards. In his proclamation of 16 November 1780, offering freedom to the slaves, he called on the *Gente Peruana* to help him confront the *Gente Europea,* on behalf of the "common good of this kingdom." The Gente Peruana, whom he also called the *gente nacional,* consisted of creoles, mestizos, zambos, Indians, all the natives of Peru, excluding only European Spaniards whom he regarded as foreigners.[78] But the attempts of Túpac Amaru to attract creoles and mestizos to an Andean movement and even to project a greater American identity were rebuffed; as the killing increased, it became clear that Inca nationalism had nothing in common with creole interests, and that the real division was not between Americans and Europeans but between insurgents and royalists. After 1810 those Indians who joined patriot armies or guerrilla bands usually did so without strong political convictions, and they changed sides without compunction. They might act under duress, or from habit, or to acquire arms, but rarely did they act on individual initiative. A guerrilla leader in Upper Peru admonished royalist Indians:

> "The *patria* is the place where we live; the *patria* is the true cause which we ought to defend at all costs; for the *patria* we ought to sacrifice our interests and even our life." Proclamations of this kind were issued on all sides, but for the moment we did not have a single Indian. We were speaking to thin air, as though it were a foreign country which we had to conquer.[79]

The Indians of Upper Peru were more aware of traditional and communal allegiances, and the guerrillas could make no impression on those who had taken the king's medal, the *amedallados*:

> They said it was for their king and lord that they were going to die, and not as rebels, nor for the *patria*; they did not know what this *patria* was, nor what it meant, nor what it looked like; they said that no one knew if the *patria* was a man or a woman. As for the king, they knew him, his government was well established, his laws were respected and duly observed. So they were put to death, all eleven of them.[80]

Incipient nationalism, therefore, was a predominantly creole nationalism. It was the nationalism expressed by Viscardo, who used the language of the eighteenth century, that of "inalienable rights," "liberty," and "natural rights," and invoked Montesquieu to deny the right of the lesser power (Spain) to rule the greater (America). Viscardo put his own gloss on Paine's concept of natural independence conferred by distance: "The distance of places which proclaims our natural independence is less than the distance of interests." But Viscardo also relied on native American texts and creole grievances to justify his argument that Americans had a right to govern their own country to the exclusion of foreigners, and to defend themselves against the abuses of Bourbon absolutism. Viscardo presented access to office and political control as matters of national interest: "The interests of our country are precisely our interests . . . and we alone have the right to exercise the functions of government, to the benefit of the *patria* and of ourselves." This was the argument of his *Lettre aux Espagnols-Américains*, published in 1799 and quickly recognized as a classic statement of colonial grievance and national independence. "The New World is our homeland, and its history is ours, and it is in this history that duty and interest alike oblige us to seek the causes of our present situation, to make us determined thereby to take the necessary action to save our proper rights and those of our successors."[81]

Grievance in itself is not sufficient to make a revolution. Popular rebellion tended to flare, explode, and recede. Creole demands for office, trade, and tax cuts were normally bought off or ignored. Americans, it seemed, could not generate their own progress. In order that grievances should become demands, patriotism grow into nationalism, and resentment turn to revolution, Spanish Americans needed a favorable conjuncture in which to seize the initiative. The opportunity for action is sometimes located in the events of 1808 to 1810, when the French invasion of Spain, the fall of the Spanish Bourbons, and the isolation of the colonies from their metropolis created a crisis of government that quickly became a war of independence. But this was not a chance event, or a sudden emergency, or an unexpected crisis. Spain had been living dangerously since 1796, and from that date lost economic control of America. War with Britain, a prolonged naval blockade, an outcry from colonial producers, widespread defiance of the laws of trade by colonists and officials, and dependence on other nations for shipping forced Spain to divert trade to neutral carriers and even to tolerate trade with the enemy. In this testing time the American empire virtually left the Spanish system of comercio libre and entered world trade as an independent economy, while remaining aware that should Spain ever recover it would certainly revert to monopoly. But economic anxiety was not enough in itself to stir the creoles. Their real fears lay elsewhere, in the growth of social and racial instability over which they had no political control. If government failed at the center, disobedience became a habit of life, security forces remained weak, and the local ruling class simply waited on events, then authority on the street and in the countryside would be fatally impaired and the result would be anarchy.

The tension between imperial power and American interests was mounting. Economic issues were serious but not necessarily decisive. Americans could see that when Spain was subject to severe pressure on its trade and revenue, as it was from Britain after 1796, then it would yield in order to survive. But there was no external pressure on Spain to contemplate political submission; this was an option that Britain was even less likely to canvass following the failure of the British invasions of the Río de la Plata in 1806 to 1807 and the onset of the Anglo-Spanish alliance in 1808. For political change, therefore, Americans would have to rely on their own resources. In this period, from 1795, creoles entered a new stage of alienation; they were casualties of panic reaction to the French Revolution, disillusioned with the prospects of reform falsely promised and never fulfilled, and convinced that collaboration with Bourbon absolutism would never overcome the invincible monopoly of trade and office. Vargas, Nariño, Belgrano, creoles in Mexico and Peru, all had tried and failed, and now they saw their failure. Abandoned by Spain, creoles were still conscious of the more radical demands of the popular sectors, and the race divisions of which they might become victims. Peasants and populace in Mexico and Peru, Indians and castas in the Andes, these could not be left without a supreme authority. The revolt of slaves and blacks in Coro in 1795, fired by slave revolution in Saint-Domingue and proclaiming "the law of the French," was followed by the conspiracy of Manuel Gual and José María España in La Guaira in 1797. This demanded equality as well as liberty, a republic as well as reform; such demands were echoed by the mulatto agitation in Bahia in 1798. And they persuaded not only the Venezuelan elite but many others in the Americas that the time was coming when they would have to preempt revolution in order to save themselves.

PART ONE

IMPERIAL RECOVERY: FROM CONSENSUS TO CONTROL

1

Bourbon Innovation, American Responses

John Leddy Phelan

Habsburg government in America avoided confrontation. Colonial officials sought to persuade rather than dictate, taking into account the interests of the local elites and the needs of weaker groups. Viceroys acted as brokers between the imperial government and its American subjects and preferred to compromise with creoles and to avoid popular protest. Bourbon government took a different view. From about 1750 Spanish ministers began to strengthen the colonial state and to attack local interest groups. Taxes were increased, creoles were denied access to office, Indian rights were eroded, and senior officials from Spain arrived to impose the new regime. In New Granada fiscal pressure, state monopolies, expropriation of Indian lands, and unpopular officials created resentment across the whole of society which eventually erupted into rebellion. John Leddy Phelan (1924–1976), who was Professor of History at the University of Wisconsin-Madison, studies the comunero movement of 1781 as a response to the new ideas and methods of the colonial bureaucracy and a demand for a return to the older procedure of bargain and compromise. The model he establishes for New Granada may be applied to other regions of Spanish America and tested for local variations and results.

The Caroline administrators were embryonic technocrats; the viceroys were politicians, who traditionally followed the policy that the aspirations of the local creole elites should be taken into account and reconciled to some extent with a program of paternalistic protection for the nonelites. It was this tradition, of Habsburg origin, that José de Gálvez [minister of the Indies] wanted to eliminate. The viceroys should no

Reprinted from John Leddy Phelan, *The People and the King: The Comunero Revolution in Colombia, 1781* (Madison, Wisconsin, The University of Wisconsin Press, 1978), pp. 7–9, 29–30, 81–88, by permission of the publisher.

longer act as brokers between the central authorities in Spain and the regional elites and other classes. The creoles had too much power, Gálvez argued. He condemned their ascendancy in the audiencias and in the exchequer, for they were "too bound by ties of family and faction in the New World to provide disinterested and impartial government."

Although the overwhelming majority of viceroys in the eighteenth century were Spanish-born, some 90 percent of those appointed between 1746 and 1813 were career military officers, nearly one-half of whom had previous military experience in the New World. Hence, many viceroys were apt to lend a sympathetic ear to creole points of view. The career of Manuel Antonio Flores (1723–99), who served as viceroy both in New Granada and Mexico, is not atypical. Born in Seville, Flores entered the naval service in 1763. He spent some ten years in Peru exploring the disputed boundaries with the Portuguese empire. He also did tours of duty in Havana and Buenos Aires before being appointed viceroy of New Granada in 1776. His wife was a creole from Buenos Aires, and several of his children were born in America. It becomes clear why viceroys, with their previous American experience, were suspect in the circle of José de Gálvez, with its pronounced bias against creoles. . . .

New Granada was then a relatively poor land with a modest if somewhat primitive economy. Any increase in taxation, however moderate, would be felt. The tax and administrative changes hit every group in that society, suddenly and simultaneously. The tobacco and aguardiente increase affected a large number of consumers, the overwhelming majority of the population, who regarded these luxuries as necessities. The small farmers in the province of Tunja, who had only recently been accustomed to having tobacco as a cash crop, resented the prohibition against cultivation in most of the province.

While the rates of the sales taxes were not much increased, direct collection meant that more and more people were paying more of the taxes, of which only a fraction of the legal amount due had been collected in the past. The slaveowners and the clergy were not happy with the visitor general's zeal in eliminating some of their customary if extralegal tax exemptions. The Indians were bitterly restless over the expropriations of their community lands, the resguardos. Everyone's pocket was affected by the changes. All classes and ethnic groups had some cause for irritation. The creole elite families in Bogotá were alarmed at the loss of their traditional "rights" to high office. The local creole elites in the provincial towns such as Socorro and San Gil saw their political and social roles undercut, as the new fiscal administration imposed a host of new officials, usually European Spaniards who responded to the dictates of Bogotá rather than those of the localities where they were temporarily stationed. The lower classes were deeply alienated by the abrasive enforcement of the taxes and monopolies. The instinctive hatred of the plebeians toward the *chapetones*, as the European Spaniards were derisively called, became intensified.

New Granada, in fact, had been accustomed to a loose and decentralized administration in which the viceroy and the audiencia acted as brokers between local interests and the mandates of the central authorities in Madrid. Change did occur, but its pace was slow. The viceroys courted public opinion by enlisting the support of the parish clergy and the local elites, whose institutional strongholds were the cabildos, and sought to balance regional pressures with the demands of the central bureaucracy. No better example of this system can be found than the conduct of Viceroy Flores, who managed to accomplish a great deal to centralize the tobacco and aguardiente monopolies without arousing militant opposition.

Juan Francisco Gutiérrez de Piñeres [regent of the audiencia and visitor general] was certainly intransigent and uncompromising about implementing the fiscal program of Charles III, but he could be remarkably flexible and responsive to local interests on matters not directly affecting the royal treasury. He provided some paternalistic protection to the Indians in their desperate struggle to resist the land and labor hunger of the creoles and mestizos. In the heated controversy involving changes in the curriculum of higher education the regent visitor general also demonstrated a willingness to listen to local vested interests. He was, indeed, quite capable of practicing coalition politics in almost every sphere excepting the fiscal. His instructions from José de Gálvez were to increase the royal revenues immediately, and he adamantly refused to consider any accommodation that might have reduced the initial intake of the royal treasury but might also have avoided the violent confrontation of 1781. He was not, like Viceroy Flores, a political conciliator, but a technocrat who wanted results immediately. . . .

The apparently ambivalent position of the Comunero chieftains in reaffirming loyalty to the king while tenaciously resisting his minister's specific policies had several antecedents in the history of New Granada. There were three "tax revolts" before 1781. Each one was basically a constitutional crisis, for which the tax issue constituted the tip of the iceberg. They occurred in Tunja in 1592, when Philip II sought to extend the alcabala to New Granada, again in Tunja in 1641 with the establishment of the armada de Barlovento sales tax, and in 1740 in Puente Real de Vélez when Viceroy Sebastián de Eslava sought to raise a forced loan to defray the expenses of the war with Great Britain.

The sales tax revolts of 1592 and 1641 made substantial contribution to the evolution of the "unwritten constitution" of New Granada. While the crown's ultimate right to impose new taxes was preserved, the manner in which they were to be imposed was subject to significant restraints. First, king's subjects had the right to petition the Crown to reconsider. Second, the bureaucracy had to mount a sustained effort to persuade public opinion in favor of the new measures, thus implying some form of consent from those who were being taxed. Third, new taxes were subject to negotiation, with the Crown informally committed to the principle of making concessions to regional interests. During the crisis of 1778–81 the regent visitor general violated every one of these powerful, if informal, traditional procedures.

The Spanish monarchy was absolute only in the original medieval sense. The king recognized no superior inside or outside his kingdoms. He was the ultimate source of all justice and all legislation. The late medieval phrase was "The king is emperor in his realm." The laws that bore the royal signature, however, were not the arbitrary expression of the king's personal wishes. Legislation, and the extent to which it was enforced, reflected the complex and diverse aspirations of all or, at least, several groups in that corporate, multi-ethnic society. The monarchy was representative and decentralized to a degree seldom suspected. Although there were no formal representative assemblies or cortes in the Indies, each one of the major corporations, such as the cabildos, the various ecclesiastical groups, the universities, and the craft guilds, all of which enjoyed a large measure of self-government, could and did speak for their respective constituents. Their views reached the king and the council of the Indies, transmitted directly by their accredited representatives or indirectly through the viceroys and the audiencias, and their aspirations profoundly shaped the character of the ultimate decisions.

The most influential of these corporations were apt to be the city councils in the larger cities and towns overseas. Having purchased their positions from the Crown as status symbols in a status-dominated society, the aldermen were the leading citizens both in social prestige and often but not always in wealth. In the second half of the seventeenth century and during the reigns of the first two Bourbons, the town councils were strongholds of the well-to-do creoles, although some wealthy European Spaniards were in their ranks. The cabildos were not reluctant from time to time to defend their own more selfish vested interests as well as to act as spokesmen for the interests of the larger community.

The views of the rising creole elites, institutionalized in the cabildos, influenced decision-making in the imperial bureaucracy through the application of the suspensive veto. In those situations where royal mandates sharply conflicted with local conditions or where enforcement might create an injustice, the viceroys and the audiencias possessed discretionary authority to suspend the execution of a law. In a picturesque ceremony in which the chief magistrate kissed the royal cedula, he invoked the celebrated "I obey but do not execute" formula. Upon applying the formula, the viceroy and the audiencia were required to submit to the council of the Indies concrete proposals by which the suspended legislation might be improved or modified so that it would not create an injustice or be in sharp conflict with local conditions. In making recommendations to the king, the viceroy and the audiencia usually took into account not only the views of the creole elites, but also the interests of the plebeians. What finally emerged was an accommodation between the initial directives from the central authorities in Spain, and the pressures generated by the regions involved. The difficult and complex responsibility of the viceroys and the audiencias was to act as brokers between what the central authorities wanted and what local conditions would permit. Everyone usually got something, perhaps not as much as each initially wanted. What emerged was a workable compromise that all could live with. The Spanish system of bureaucratic administration had a built-in flexibility in which local interests were able to influence significantly the outcome of events.

The primary mechanism of bureaucratic decentralization was the "I obey but do not execute" formula. The phrase "I obey" denoted the respect enshrined in Roman law for the legitimacy of royal authority, which, if properly informed, would never will an injustice. Cementing the loyalty of all groups to the Crown was the powerful myth of the king as the fountain-head of all justice. The phrase "I do not execute" represented the discretionary authority of subordinates, one of whose major responsibilities was to accommodate themselves to the pressures generated by both the central authorities and local conditions.

During the reigns of the first two Bourbon kings, Philip V and Ferdinand VI, the voice and influence of the creoles greatly increased. Under such circumstances the viceroys and the audiencias perforce pursued policies that enjoyed the positive acceptance of local interest groups. When in the 1760's orders came from Spain to organize the tobacco monopoly on the Mexican model, the viceroys [of New Granada] interpreted these directives in the spirit of the "I obey but do not execute" formula. The tobacco monopoly was introduced gradually and piecemeal. During the 1770's, the viceroys and the audiencia, in effect, bowed to the pressure generated by demographic change and the land hunger of the creoles and the mestizos, when they sanctioned a wholesale reduction of the community lands of the Indians in the province of Tunja.

Until the arrival of the regent visitor general, Gutiérrez de Piñeres, the creoles were accustomed to a government of compromise, conciliation, and accommodation in which some creoles actively participated in the decision-making process. The basic goal of Charles III was to create a unitary and centralized state in which directives emanating from Madrid would be enforced without being diluted by any kind of compromise with local conditions and influences. In 1781 the Comunero leaders were frantically searching for a formula by which they could return to the kind of decentralized government which had evolved out of the tradition of municipal government in medieval Castile and the Habsburg system with its complex blending of centralization and decentralization. In seeking to abolish or, at least, to modify the fiscal program of Charles III, the Comunero leaders sought not to overthrow the Crown, but to persuade the king to return to the traditional system of negotiating with his subjects. In organizing the march on the capital, they were, in effect, engaging in a campaign of massive civil disobedience in order to persuade the king to change the policies of his ministers.

The goals of the populace and the nobles must be carefully distinguished. Both groups were in a revolutionary state of mind in that they totally rejected the present, i.e., the innovations of Charles III, and both yearned for a return to a golden age of the past. In economic terms, the utopia of the plebeians was the abolition of the abrasively collected new and old taxes. Politically, it meant a return to the days of the early viceroys. If the people's utopia was tied to bread and butter issues, the central concern of the nobles was the distribution of political power.

The creoles took their point of departure in a utopian past—the Habsburg system of bureaucratic decentralization. Yet, when it came time for them to articulate their political and constitutional aspirations in the capitulations of Zipaquirá, they reacted to Charles III's political revolution with a revolution of their own. The concept of "counterrevolution" is loaded in the context of the Comunero Revolution. Its use would imply that Charles III was "progressive" and the Comuneros were "reactionary". Such name-calling is both tendentious and ahistorical.

It is inappropriate to label the political and fiscal innovations of Charles III as "reforms." These were indeed changes, but they were differently perceived by different groups. To cite one outstanding example: the tobacco monopoly may have been a "reform" for the king's ministers in that royal revenues spectacularly increased. But the small farmers in the regions of Socorro, who suddenly found themselves deprived of a cash crop, scarcely viewed the monopoly as a change for the better. For this reason, I have consistently preferred to use more neutral phraseology by referring to the "reforms" of Charles III as changes or innovations.

Equally, it was unthinkable in 1781 for the creoles, still deeply attached to the myth and mystique of the Crown, to repudiate the monarchy as an institution. From our vantage point, the men of Zipaquirá may loom as precursors of nineteenth-century federalism, but the spirit and the tone of the capitulations of Zipaquirá conjure up the golden age of the Habsburgs, and their rhetoric employs key concepts of sixteenth- and seventeenth-century Spanish political theory. There is little evidence that the Comuneros had access to the political thought of the European Enlightenment that nourished the North American and French revolutions. Instead, they had another ideological tradition from which they drew inspiration.

Considerable controversy exists as to whether the ideology of the classic Spanish political theorists influenced the thinking of the generation of 1810. Some have claimed that the classic Spanish theologians were as influential as, if not more so than, the political philosophers of the Enlightenment—an assertion that has been hotly disputed. What is incontrovertible is that a generation before in New Granada there was a profound coincidence between the implicit political theory of the Comunero Revolution and the rich body of classical Spanish political theory whose outstanding figure was Francisco Suárez (1548–1617). Among the notable sixteenth-century Spanish political theorists were Martín de Azpilcueta, Diego de Covarrubias, Domingo de Soto, Francisco de Vitoria, Domingo Báñez, Alfonso de Castro, Luis de Molina, and Juan de Mariana. The outstanding figures of the seventeenth century were Diego de Saavedra y Fajardo, Pedro Fernández de Navarrete, Francisco de Quevedo y Villegas, and Jerónimo de Castillo de Bobadilla.

While there were several copies of works by these men in a few libraries in Bogotá, one cannot automatically assume that these books were read or that they directly influenced the thinking of the generation of 1781. All the copies were printed in Europe, since Bogotá had no functioning printing press until the late 1770's. Tracing the paternity of ideas is a risky business at best. There is, for example, no hard evidence that the author of "our royal decree" or the framers of the capitulations of Zipaquirá had ever read these weighty tomes of political theory. It is nonetheless apparent that some of the basic doctrines of classical Spanish political theory coincided not only with the political posture of the Comunero leaders in 1781 but also with the "unwritten constitution" that had evolved in New Granada prior to 1778. The Spanish political theorists stressed the popular origin of sovereignty, limitations on political power, a social contract between the governors and the governed, resistance to tyranny, the invalidity of an unjust war, popular consent to new taxes, the primacy of the common good of the whole community, and the rule of natural law.

In eighteenth-century Bourbon Spain these doctrines had gone out of style, to be replaced with notions of French absolutism from the France of Louis XIV and Louis XV. No clearer expression of Bourbon centralism can be found than *El vasallo instruido*, by Friar Joaquín de Finestrad. In his denunciation of the Comunero Revolution, he seldom cited the classic Spanish political theorists of the sixteenth and seventeenth centuries. He preached the gospel of blind obedience to constitutional authorities, and assailed all rebellions, even those against a blatantly tyrannical government.

The most influential of the classic Spanish political theorists was the Jesuit, Francisco Suárez, whose major political treatises were *De legibus ac deo legislatore* and *Defensio fidei*. His works and those of many other Jesuit authors were banned from the curriculum of all Spanish universities in a royal cedula on May 23, 1767, shortly after the expulsion of the Jesuit order from all the Spanish dominions. Suárez's cautious admission that tyrannicide might be justified under certain carefully prescribed conditions was a doctrine associated with the Jesuits that aroused the ire of the governing circles around Charles III.

Suárez was the heir of the tradition of Aristotle and Thomas Aquinas. His ontological formulation of the origin of the political community and civil power rested on the premise of the natural sociability of man. The end of all society is to achieve the common good, *bonum commune*, of all those who compose it, not as individuals but as members of the community. When a group of people decide to become a political society, they cease to be a mere collection of individuals, and become a *corpus mysticum politicum*, a political mystical body. God is the ultimate author, the efficient cause, of political authority, in that man's sociability made political society a dialectical necessity. Yet political power comes into being by a social contract either explicit or implicit between the people and the sovereign. Thus, Suárez stresses the popular origin and contractual nature of sovereignty. . . . Although emphasizing the popular origin of sovereignty, Suárez argues that the granting of power to the prince is not a delegation, but a quasi-alienation. . . . Yet Suárez's defense of monarchical power did not exclude people's right to depose a legitimate king who had so grossly abused his power that he had become a tyrant. . . .

The Comunero Revolution produced no self-conscious political theorists. The men of 1781 were seeking the redress of specific political, constitutional, and fiscal grievances. In the public proclamations of the leadership, in "our royal decree," and in the text of the capitulations of Zipaquirá there hovers a spirit of diluted and popularized Suárecismo. There is clearly implicit the notion that New Granada constituted a *corpus mysticum politicum* with its own traditions, whose end was to achieve the common good of the whole community. That common good, according to the men of 1781, was being grossly violated by the innovations of Charles III's ministers. The men of 1781 never appealed to the *nación* or the *patria*. The community, *el común*, a term that the leaders invariably used in their public proclamations, had the right to protest—hence the phrase that came to describe the movement, the Comuneros. Deeply embedded in the documents of the time is the notion of classical Spanish political theory, that the spirit of the *corpus mysticum politicum* of New Granada required some form of popular approval for new taxation and that unjust laws were invalid. . . .

Monarchical sentiments had deep roots. The king was still the fountain-head of justice. But though the king was just, his ministers, in particular the regent visitor general, were tyrants against whom it was licit to offer armed resistance. Their policies were a flagrant violation of the common good of the community. Whether some of the Comunero leaders had read the texts of the classical political theorists of Spain is unprovable. That they were indirectly influenced by these doctrines is highly probable. The political theorists of Old Spain, on the level of high abstraction, and the generation of 1781 in New Granada, on the level of political activism, both came to grips with a central issue of political theory and practice: how to reconcile reverence for constituted political authority with the right of subjects to resist injustice.

2

Creole Participation, Spanish Reaction

Mark A. Burkholder and D. S. Chandler

Spain did not trust Americans with exercise of power; peninsular Spaniards were still preferred in higher office. Some creoles, owners of land and mines, had wealth enough to be classed with peninsulares among the elite; these wanted office to protect their interests. But the majority had only modest expectations, and to these, struggling with mortgages and household expenses, or living on the meager income of the professions, office was a need not an honor. They wanted not only equality of opportunity with peninsulares or a majority of appointments, they wanted them above all as "native sons" in their own regions because they regarded creoles from other countries as outsiders. During the period 1650 to 1750 the financial needs of the Crown caused it to sell offices to creoles, and thus they became treasury officials and corregidores; by the 1760s the majority of judges in the audiencias of Lima, Santiago, and Mexico were creoles. Most of the creole judges were linked by kinship or interest to the local elites, and the audiencias became a preserve of the rich and powerful families of their region. From 1750 the crown began to recover control. The government of Charles III and José de Gálvez in particular sought to reduce creole participation, and to break the links between bureaucrats and local families. Sale of audiencia office was ended, the creole share of places was reduced, and creoles were now rarely appointed in their own regions. The research of Mark A. Burkholder, Professor of History at the University of Missouri-St. Louis, and D. S. Chandler, Professor of History at Miami University, Oxford, Ohio, for the first time quantifies the shift from creole representation to Spanish dominance and lays open to closer inspection the last phase of colonial government.

Reprinted from Mark A. Burkholder and D. S. Chandler, *From Impotence to Authority: The Spanish Crown and the American Audiencias, 1687–1808* (Columbia, Missouri, University of Missouri Press, 1977), pp. 115–19, 134–35, 140–41, by permission of the authors.

The royal concern with native-son strength and the limited number of peninsulares serving on the audiencias can be further seen by an examination of the new appointments made from 1751 to 1775. Appointments during these years differed markedly from those of the preceding two decades. They demonstrated explicitly the crown's return to its traditional policy of naming far more peninsulares than creoles and exercising great restraint toward native sons. Also, the surplus of ministers at midcentury meant few new appointments. In the first twelve years of this period the crown named only twenty new men, including but one native son among the four Americans. In the following thirteen years it named over twice as many new men, but not a single native son appeared among the five creoles. . . . The inevitable consequence was an increasingly obvious decline in native sons and other American ministers as those named before midcentury died or retired. . . .

Americans' irritation over the limiting of indirect access to the audiencias [promotion through the ranks] complements the better-known anger they displayed over the lack of direct representation [as a first appointment]. While more native sons and other Americans gained appointments from 1778 to 1808 than had from 1751 to 1777, the number was still a small minority of the total. Such discrimination had provoked protests in the past; in the midst of demographic expansion and an increased number of graduates from American law schools there was greater pressure on creole aspirants than ever before, and resentment again surfaced.

The population of Spanish America grew dramatically in the second half of the eighteenth century. Among the urban centers that exhibited marked increases were Buenos Aires, which rose from about ten thousand inhabitants in 1744 to roughly forty thousand by the end of the century, and Caracas, which increased by perhaps a third from 1778 to 1800. The traditionally populous capital of Mexico City also showed impressive growth. While the percentage of growth that arose from the creole population is unknown, there can be no doubt that whites participated in the expansion. Their number in New Spain expanded from 565,000 in 1742 to nearly 800,000 in 1772 and to over a million in 1793.

The growing creole population created rising pressure for government employment, and mounting frustration over the inadequate number of positions going to native sons was visible. While the total number of positions increased from the 1760s to the 1790s, the appointment of peninsulares to a majority of the most desirable ones bred resentment among native sons. The creation of forty-two positions of intendant from 1764 to 1790 highlighted their problem. Powerful and prestigious, these new posts also paid well, a not unimportant consideration. But by 1808 no American, let alone a native son, had obtained a confirmed royal appointment as intendant in Peru or the Río de la Plata, and few if any had appeared elsewhere. The steady appearance of peninsulares in new offices provoked native sons to a new awareness of the discrimination they faced.

The number of native sons eligible for appointment to the audiencias was also rising in the late eighteenth century. Protest by and in behalf of this limited group formed part of the more widespread unhappiness over appointments that was visible during the closing decades of the Age of Authority. In any region eligibility for a *plaza* was limited to a small part of white society. Not only were legitimacy and social requirements considered; an aspirant needed university training in the law, preferably training that culminated in an advanced degree of licentiate or doctor in laws or canons. Fragmentary evidence suggests that the number of men with legal training rose after 1750 and expanded greatly in the final quarter of the eighteenth century. These numbers reflect both the establishment of new universities and the consequent increase in opportunity and a general resurgence of university enrollment in the Spanish world. Previously Chileans had needed to travel abroad, usually to Lima, for legal education. After 1758 those unable to afford such expenses could study at the University of San Felipe in Santiago. In Caracas the impact of the university founded in 1725 on the legal profession was profound. For the first time a substantial group of locally born lawyers became prominent. The establishment of an audiencia in 1783 was the crowning step in this region, for it obviated the need for any travel to become an abogado. In Guatemala the University of San Carlos graduated more men with legal degrees from 1775 to 1799 than during the preceding fifty years. That the increased numbers reflected the overall growth of enrollments at the institution as a result of a reinvigorated intellectual climate does not detract from the implications of a growing group of letrados within the region.

The rising number of men with degrees in law produced an expansion of the number of attorneys authorized to practice before the audiencias (abogados). By 1808 the total number of abogados in America was probably around a thousand. New Spain had the most, with roughly four hundred, but scarcely half of them (210) were practicing. The city of Lima counted 91 in 1790, but the remainder of Peru did not seem to be proportionately as well represented. The Audiencia of Buenos Aires had admitted fewer than 100 abogados to practice by 1802, while the captaincy general of Caracas boasted 105 by 1805. Whatever the precise total, the crown suspected that the Indies harbored an excess. Its conviction produced a cédula in 1784 that ordered the Audiencia of Cuba not to examine aspirants for abogado, since Havana had too many attorneys already. Five years later the regent of the audiencia recommended the continuation of this order in full vigor and, moreover, tightening of the requirements for entry into the legal profession.

Concern over the number of lawyers surfaced again in 1802 when Charles IV ordered an investigation to determine if surpluses of attorneys required the establishment of quotas. The lawyers guild (colegio) in Mexico City reported that although the region had over 200 practicing attorneys, some areas of the viceroyalty lacked any, and certainly (as the audiencia later agreed) there was no excess. In contrast, by 1796 the lawyers' guild in Caracas had already decided to take steps to prevent a surplus and moved to establish a limit of fifty in the capital. Looking ahead, it proposed not to limit entry into the profession, but rather to place a ceiling on the number allowed to practice in the capital (thereby securing its members' livelihoods) and thus force newcomers to establish offices in less favorable locations.

Upon examination, then, the "abogado problem" was not excessive numbers but imbalanced distribution. Most of these well-educated men preferred the amenities of urban life in the capitals to the humdrum existence of the provinces. They probably believed that the possibility of notable economic and professional success was greater in the capitals than elsewhere. While awaiting fortune, however, the lot of most was unenviable. The solution to the problem, from the attorneys' perspective, was simple: appointment to office. The lawyers' guild in Mexico City proposed that one answer to the dearth of abogados in the countryside and the poverty of those in the city was for the crown to select men from its number to hold half or at least one-third of the corregimientos and alcaldías mayores of New Spain. In addition, the guild advocated that men who served in these posts for fifteen years should then be given preference by the crown for one-third of the togado posts in America and Spain. While Charles was apparently convinced that the total number of attorneys did not call for reduction or even mandatory stabilization in 1804, he refused to accede to the plea for, in essence, guaranteeing American advocates a fixed proportion of the positions. The king's refusal faithfully mirrored the royal attitude for the entire period. Earlier calls for native-son appointments had already revealed Americans' resentment at the intensified discrimination they faced. Uniformly, however, the crown responded negatively to creole protests.

In the course of the comunero revolt in New Granada in 1781, the rebels enumerated their grievances. Although opposition to an increase in taxation had been the immediate stimulus for the rising, one of the complaints focused on offices. Responding to the diminution of local influence that took place in the late 1770s as a result of the visita of Gutiérrez de Piñeres, the comuneros called for preference for creoles in filling posts in New Granada. With both direct and indirect representation on the Audiencia of Santa Fe de Bogotá and in other important offices largely excised, this article can best be interpreted as a call for the immediate return of native sons to office. The failing revolt did not elicit sympathy for this demand, and but two native sons entered the audiencia before 1808.

In New Spain the dilution of local strength that had accompanied the Gálvez visita had already drawn cries of anguish in the 1770s. Failure to obtain redress, however, prompted yet another effort in 1792 when the City Council of Mexico resubmitted its 1771 petition almost verbatim. This repeated call for almost total native-son appointments brought a promise that creoles would receive half of the positions in the choirs (coros) in the cathedrals of New Spain but no similar assurance for civil posts.

At almost the same time the City Council of Lima composed a set of instructions for its agent to follow at court. While the Audiencia of Mexico had no more than one native son serving from the early 1770s and had enjoyed only a brief overlap of nine years when two had served simultaneously since the late 1730s, Lima had grown accustomed to extensive direct representation from the late seventeenth century. Never less than five native sons served in Lima from the mid-1690s, and this number had peaked at midcentury when thirteen native sons held appointments. It had declined to six in 1780 and to only four at the end of 1792. The trend was obvious; no Peruvian had been appointed since Melchor de Santiago Concha gained promotion from Santiago in 1777. Moreover, the remaining native sons were old and appeared to be close to the grave. In the face of this deterioration the city council asked its agent to request that Peruvians be given one-third of the positions in both Lima and Cuzco. In addition he was to seek explicit assurance that no objection would be made to ministers serving in their home districts. Unlike the Mexico city council, which had requested a condition never previously enjoyed, the Lima cabildo sought, in effect, a return to the "good old days." Its protest, like that from Mexico, brought no satisfaction.

The Lima instructions represented a retreat from previous creole claims that only native sons should govern; nonetheless they requested an augmentation of local representation. The specific demand for Peruvian rather than "American" ministers reflected limeño recognition of the nature of appointments since royal control had triumphed. Evidently realizing that the crown would consider even their plaintive call an extreme demand, however, six years later the cabildo advised a new agent to use discretion in even mentioning the request. Not until 1809 would it again press the issue, and then it joined a widespread clamor for more native-son appointments. . . .

The state of the audiencias in 1808 was a tribute to the success of the tenaciously followed policy of control initiated at mid-eighteenth century. Only six native sons and nineteen "outsider" creoles were among the ninety-nine men serving when Charles IV and Ferdinand VII abdicated in May 1808. On the other hand, every tribunal but Manila and Quito had at least one American present, a token representative of the crown's willingness to reward a moderate number of qualified creoles. Only in the relatively unimportant tribunal of Chile had the crown allowed significant direct representation. Radicado ministers plus native sons were a slight majority of the men serving in the empire in 1808, but their number was less than in 1785, 1795, or 1800, to say nothing of 1750. Moreover, the implications of radicados' tenure were not as grave as earlier for, in addition to tighter enforcement of the marriage laws, the crown demanded routine reports on the ministers from the president of each tribunal and knew their local ties, length of service, capabilities, and vices. Reprimands were forthcoming for men who abused their positions or conducted themselves in a manner inappropriate to their station.

The control over the audiencias present at the time of the abdications stands in contrast to the disruption and the relative lack of prompt information that characterized much of the Age of Impotence. The continued smooth functioning of the audiencias is all the more impressive in light of the almost continual state of war since 1793. The "crisis of administration" perceived in other spheres had not affected the audiencias significantly.

It is impossible to explain with certainty why a breakdown in the audiencias did not occur between 1793 and 1808. Several important differences from the last lengthy period of war (that of Jenkins' Ear), however, are apparent. The colonies at the close of the eighteenth century were far more valuable sources of revenue than they had been earlier. Mexico, the principal source of bullion, was minting roughly three times as much silver and gold in the 1790s as it had in the 1740s. Taxable trade, too, had increased greatly during the intervening years, and the Spanish economy itself enjoyed unprecedented prosperity in the late eighteenth century. The crown had no desire to alienate any part of the vast sums at stake. Moreover, the great increase in overall royal revenue meant that selling appointments would provide a far smaller percentage of the total than previously. When pressed to secure new funds the crown turned to bonds, loans, "voluntary contributions" and eventually *consolidación*. Unlike the sale of appointments, which always brought distasteful results that extended for decades, the crown conceived consolidación (erroneously for America) as both of immediate financial benefit and lasting social value. Finally, throughout these years, the Council of the Indies had more ministro togados with personal experience in America than ever before. Some of these men, a majority of the council, had personally witnessed the abuses and thwarting of the royal will that the previous sales had brought and showed no interest in relaxing the grip the crown had finally achieved over the audiencias. When one anachronistic limeño sought to purchase an appointment in 1798, he quickly learned how much had changed since 1750.

The Age of Authority ended with local influence on the courts far less than in 1750. The crown had successfully reestablished its control by appointing new men, almost uniformly "outsiders," and limiting their co-optation by local families. Yet the cost of success was high. The visible decline in native-son strength on the courts gave substance to the creoles' belief that they faced systematic discrimination. Of equal and perhaps greater importance, the attack on local indirect influence on the tribunals had removed an important safety valve. Even without native sons serving, local families traditionally had enjoyed social relationships with the ministers and found them receptive to their concerns. In 1808 the ministers' few local ties underscored that they were tools of Spain's will rather than representatives of local interests. As the Age of Authority yielded to the Crisis of Independence, the courts often became the focus for attack by supporters of de facto if not de jure home rule. Rather than leaders or mirrors of local opinion, ministers became its victims. . . .

Both contemporaries and many later historians have argued that Spain's virtual exclusion of creoles from high positions in the colonies was an important, perhaps the most important, "cause" of the Wars of Independence. Although the demand for more native-son appointments clearly occupied a prominent place in Americans' lists of grievances, caution is required to avoid overestimating its significance. The leading families in each region sought continued or expanded access to political and economic power. The placement of native sons in office provided the most obvious and direct way in which this desire could be realized; this was only one route, however, and historically its importance had varied widely by region. From an empire-wide viewpoint, the reduction and restraints placed on radicado ministers were more important than the reduction in native sons serving on the tribunals.

Seen from the American perspective of 1750, the Hispanic-American world in 1808 was "upside down."[1] To right it meant to return to the flaccid administration and extensive indirect access to power that had characterized the Age of Impotence. As most means of indirect access to the audiencias violated restrictive statutes, however, and since the courts themselves now competed with additional rival institutions, Americans found it easier to call directly for the legally justifiable appointment of native sons to a variety of posts. The events of 1808 provided an unexpected forum for American grievances, including native-son appointments; yet without the Napoleonic invasion of Spain, local frustration over limited access to political power might have simmered indefinitely. Perhaps more important than any of the celebrated background "causes" of the Wars of Independence were the events after 1808.

3

America for the Americans

Antonio Joaquín de Rivadeneira

The shift towards appointment of peninsular Spaniards, quickened by Gálvez's prejudice against creoles, was resented by the creole elite. Among the many voices of protest, that of Mexico City council in 1771 has retained an enduring interest. Stung by a report that questioned the creoles' qualifications for high office and by suspicions that a new policy in favor of peninsular Spaniards was in place, the council argued that civil and ecclesiastical appointments in America should be reserved for Americans to the exclusion of peninsulares; and it requested an explicit policy statement to this effect. The author of the paper was Antonio Joaquín de Rivadeneira y Barrientos, a native of Mexico City who had practised law in Madrid and in 1771 was a judge of the audiencia of Mexico. His creole credentials and his erudition had already been displayed in two books and were now eloquently employed in Mexico City's petition. Rivadeneira took the argument into his opponent's camp and maintained that creole rights were based not only on natural justice but also on the law of Spain and the Church. He expressed a strong sense of American identity in language that assumed that Spanish America in general and Mexico in particular had reached a high degree of nationhood. As for Spaniards, he had no inhibitions in calling them foreigners. At the same time the document reveals an ambiguity concerning creole identity: Americans were Spaniards, yet not Spaniards. And they were certainly not Indians; the author shed few tears over Indian degradation, and his hostility towards intermarriage was characteristic of the creole elite. The petition for rights to office was presented as a major creole grievance—perhaps the most critical griev-

Translated by John Lynch from "Representacion que hizo la ciudad de México al rey D. Carlos III en 1771 sobre que los criollos deben ser preferidos á los europeos en la distribucion de empleos y beneficios de estos reinos," *Colección de documentos para la independencia de México de 1808 a 1821*. Ed. J. E. Hernández y Dávalos (6 vols., Mexico, 1877–82, Kraus reprint 1968), I, 427–55.

ance of all, for the situation was getting worse. Yet it appears to have made not the slightest impression in Spain. Appointment of Mexicans to the audiencias of Mexico declined in the years after 1770, and creoles learned that the issue would not be resolved by reason or request.

The reason for this protest is the circulation among Americans of the news that some minister or prelate here has written a Report to Your Majesty in the following or similar terms: "The spirit of the Americans is submissive and docile, and reflects well their depressed state. But if they are raised to authority or office, they are prone to the greatest errors; so it is best to keep them in subjection, though with positions of middle rank. Neither humanity nor my own feelings propose that they should be deprived of all preferment, but I know from experience that it is far better that our Europeans be placed at the head, for they nobly seek the good of our native land and the tranquillity of our beloved monarch." We have recently reflected with some dismay on the fact that favors and grants from Your Majesty to American Spaniards have become rarer than ever, not only in the secular but also in the ecclesiastical field where hitherto we had received some recognition. . . .

It is not the first time that the reputation of Americans has been maliciously attacked and that they have been regarded as unsuitable for honors of any kind. This is a war we have suffered since the discovery of America. The Indians, the natives born and originating in America, have even had their rationality questioned, against all the evidence. With equal injustice it is also claimed that those of us born here of European ancestry lack enough reason to be really men. We have been depicted as suspicious creatures, full of our own opinions, resentful of reproof, and—the ultimate insult—it has been alleged that Mexico is apparently moribund. . . .

The object of the Report is to persuade Your Majesty that provision should not be made for American Spaniards except in appointments of middle rank, while Europeans are preferred for the highest positions. In other words, in ecclesiastical appointments we should be excluded from bishoprics and the highest offices in the Church, and in secular appointments from the senior ranks of the military, the administration, and the judiciary. This is to seek to overturn the law of peoples. It will lead not only to the loss of America but to the ruin of the state. In a word, it is the greatest and most monstrous injustice. . . . We must not exhaust Your Majesty's patience, but we have to declare the rights of the native inhabitants to be appointed to offices in their own countries, not only in preference to foreigners but to their exclusion.

This is a principle founded on such useful and necessary reasons, political and religious, that there is no law which has not adopted and upheld it. It derives its origin from even before the law of the gospel; God himself implanted it in the hearts of his people. To violate this principle has been regarded as an odious abuse, and its defense has moved all governments to vigilance, not least those of Your Majesty and your glorious ancestors, ever attentive to the happiness of their subjects. A striking example of this is the law of King Henry III in the Cortes of Madrid, 24 September 1396, which strictly prohibits foreigners from obtaining any benefices in Spain. The Law Codes of Castile, laws 4 and 5, section 3, book 1 were made for the same purpose; presentations to benefices made by the court of Rome in favor of foreigners are withheld by the royal council, the income of the benefice is confiscated, and the incumbent is subject to other penalties. . . .

Reasons of equal weight to those advanced in the case of ecclesiastical preferment insist also that all secular appointments be granted to natives. We will discuss these when dealing with the general principles in favor of Americans. For the moment we simply wish to establish that the appointment of natives to the exclusion of foreigners is a rule supported by the laws of all kingdoms, adopted by all nations, dictated by obvious principles conforming to natural reason, and imprinted in the hearts and desires of men. It is a right that, if we cannot class it as a natural right, is certainly common to all peoples and therefore deserving of the most sacred observance.

In violation of this, the Report argues (if we are not mistaken) that here in America the native inhabitants should be excluded from all higher ecclesiastical benefices and secular appointments of the first rank, seeking perhaps to justify this infringement of countervailing rights by the argument that Europeans are not strictly foreigners in America, for they readily recognize the authority of Your Majesty. According to this, the New World was incorporated into the Kingdoms of Castile and León without becoming a separate Crown but simply a new jewel in the Crown bequeathed by the Catholic Monarchs, Ferdinand and Isabella, and now fittingly adorning Your Majesty. Under this single head European and American Spaniards form one body politic, and thus the former cannot be considered foreigners in America.

This is true inasmuch as the subjects of both Spains must recognize the same sovereign. But as for appointments, European Spaniards must be regarded as foreigners, for the same reasons work against them, namely that all peoples have always resisted the appointment of foreigners. They are foreigners by nature, if not by law. Nature rightly recognizes the love that men bear their native soil and their dislike of elsewhere, and these two reasons are the basis for reserving posts to native sons and denying them to foreigners. Appointments to secular and ecclesiastical positions are not made primarily to reward the recipient but to secure good administration and serve the public interest. Service to the people of a city, a bishopric, a province, or a kingdom is better provided by a native who loves the place of his birth than by a person whose native land is two thousand leagues away and who regards his appointment as an exile and a burden. The first naturally serves the public interest; the second lacks commitment. These considerations have always favored the employment of native sons, and in America too they reinforce our determination not to appoint Europeans.

The truth is that while these people may not be considered foreigners in the Indies from a constitutional point of view, in fact they do not derive their identity from the Indies. They have their homes, their parents, their brothers and sisters, and all their ties in Old Spain, not in New Spain. When they are exiled to a post at this distance they do not change their nature, or lose the instincts they were born with, or cease to regard the interests of their family. On the contrary, they seek to support or even enrich them, and so they regard themselves as transients in America whose prime purpose is to return wealthy to their own home and their native land. We see this every day, and it is bound to be the case if posts are granted to those who are not born in the regions where they serve. . . .

There are other reasons why European Spaniards appointed to posts in America fail to serve the public good. They have to defray the high costs of transport, raised even higher when they feel obliged to travel in style and comfort, accompanied by a retinue of servants and relatives, not only those whom they need but others whom they cannot refuse. For an appointment in America is the occasion for many other Europeans without a career to seek their fortune there by pressing themselves on the new appointee and importuning him to take them in his entourage. Again, we see this practice every day, and its pernicious results. The last two archbishops of Mexico paid a total of 45,000 pesos for their transport; the cost for the present incumbent was 20,000, as he has often admitted, and that for his predecessor D.D. Manuel Rubio y Salinas 25,000 pesos. This is only the cost of the sea passage. Add to this the journey from port to destination over hundreds of leagues of neglected roads, where the travellers have to be accompanied by a mule train led by hordes of retainers, and the whole operation becomes extremely expensive. Then the appointee has to set up home and furnish it, and he has to employ a staff corresponding to his status. All this without counting his postal and office expenses (which are no greater than those for Americans). Taking into account too the premiums for life and travel insurance, even if kept to a minimum, then the total cost cannot be less than 30,000 to 40,000 pesos.

The European appointee to the Indies as often as not arrives to take up his job heavily in debt. If he has a secular appointment, apart from the office of viceroy, he receives an income sufficient to maintain a standard of living commensurate with the appointment and no more. There are even posts, such as all the *alcaldías mayores* in New Spain, which do not carry any salary for the incumbents. How then will these repay the heavy debts with which they entered office? Will they perhaps cease to repay their creditors? While not the worst option, this would be bad enough to bring dishonor and disgrace on ministers, contempt on their offices, and discredit on their decisions. What benefit to the public could we expect from their administration? But in fact they do not stop repaying their debts, because that would close the door to further benefits from their creditors. The creditors themselves are not so indifferent to the loss of their interest that they cease to pursue, harass, and embarrass their debtors until they obtain satisfaction. The debtors cannot endure harassment by the creditor, and they are not without means of paying him. But what are they? Slice off a portion of salary to cover the debt? This is impossible, for the salary is designed only to maintain a decent subsistence and there is nothing left to satisfy debts. The Indies are rich in gold and silver for those equipped to acquire them and not scrupulous about the means; and those driven by necessity, pressed by creditors, and arraigned perhaps before the judge, are not in a position to be too scrupulous when they see that they have frequent opportunities to escape from financial embarrassment. They will give gifts, soon to pass into blatant bribes, they will sell justice, and they will concentrate their minds on their own interests at the expense of their duties to the public.

Would that these were mere suspicions and possibilities, and not events to lament every day. This is what we see, men appointed to offices in these kingdoms and arriving burdened with need and debt; yet within a few years they have paid off their debts and can return home bursting with wealth. Once there they claim that there are plenty of legal ways to amass gold in America. But we Americans can see that public office yields only what is paid by Your Majesty or the income allocated to each post, and that there would be nothing left after meeting the subsistence of the office holder. . . .

This is not the end of the harm done by the appointment of Europeans to public office in the Indies. These countries have their own laws of government, ordinances, judicial decrees, royal *cédulas*, court procedures, in short a whole legal system, which needs a lifetime's study beyond the attainment of the European, for in his country this would be totally pointless. So he comes to govern a people he does not know, to administer laws he has not studied, to encounter customs he does not understand, to deal with people he has never met. And to help him he usually arrives surrounded by an entourage equally ignorant; he comes full of European ideas which do not apply in these parts. Even if American and European Spaniards are not totally distinguishable from each other, the miserable Indians are another matter. These are the weakest and neediest of the kingdom, its majority and core. They are a subject of concern for Your Majesty's government, and are certainly of a distinct condition, needing quite different rules from those prescribed for Spaniards. Yet the newly arrived seek to introduce their ideas and to establish their rules, until bitter experience opens their eyes; meanwhile their efforts have been a complete waste of time. . . .

[For over two centuries the welfare of the Indians has been a prime preoccupation of the royal government.] Yet we sadly see that the Indians are far from advancing: the longer the time since the conquest, the more their culture declines, their condition deteriorates, their misery increases, and even their numbers diminish, so much so that in whole areas not a single Indian is to be found, while in the rest of the kingdom they are likely to disappear in a few years. Much effort is spent in seeking the cause of this state of affairs, but the effort must be in vain as long as the principal reason is ignored, namely direct government by the Europeans. What does it matter that Your Majesty's laws are the most blessed and useful possible for these regions and their native inhabitants if the governor or prelate charged with their observance is not trained in their application? This, Sir, is the true reason for the backwardness and depopulation of the Indies. There is no point in searching for other reasons as long as native sons are excluded from appointments to secular and clerical office; these are the people who are brought up here, who are trained for what the administration needs, who are rooted in their region and not preoccupied with leaving it loaded with gold. Otherwise the evils will continue and there is no prospect of the improvement which we have a right to expect for these countries. . . .

What encouragement will American Spaniards have either for investing in their education, or for service to the state, or for fulfilling their duty to Your Majesty, when they realize that they will never be rewarded for their services with appointments of the first rank? They will lose heart, tire of futile and pointless study, and lapse into idleness or inertia; their conduct will decline, leaving them without culture or refinement, and Your Majesty will be left with a crowd of deadweights in the Indies, useless to state and society. Government is sustained by two incentives among its servants: one is the glory of honor, a natural desire of the human spirit; the other is the advancement of fortune, which appeals to our self esteem. Americans have neither of these incentives, seeing themselves excluded from high office and knowing that at the most they can only expect to reach the middle rank, which will satisfy neither their material nor their spiritual aspirations. Thus the government of the Indies will lose one of its vital supports.

Yet American Spaniards are qualified for the highest ranks. In talents, application, conduct, and honor, they cede nothing to any of the other nations of the world. This has been confirmed by impartial and respected authors. And it has been proved by experience, at least to those with open eyes and minds. American Spaniards are ever hopeful; they are useful, worthy, eager to make good, yet dejected, abandoned, and "destined to be kept in subjection, the despised servants of foreigners."[1]

The disregard for Americans will be judged even more severely. It is not that they will be unemployed; they will simply be absent, for the depopulation of America will be a consequence of their exclusion. The Indians, as has been noticed, have already undergone a decline in numbers which has to be seen to be believed. And this would be experienced even more among American Spaniards. Their innate sense of honor prevents them from entering into marriage while they cannot provide a decent subsistence to cover their costs; and being excluded from office, they see themselves deprived of the one thing that would assure their upkeep. The Americans have no other resource. Commerce is closed to them; as this is based in Europe, it is normally undertaken by the Europeans. The mechanical crafts are neither fitting for their status nor in the Indies do they yield an adequate subsistence; as the best manufactures are imported from Europe at a price Americans can afford, artisans in the Indies cannot compete. In the Indies wealth is less regular and stable than elsewhere in the world, a fact that is well known here but whose causes are not relevant to our present discussion. Suffice it to say that the principal funds available to American Spaniards to enable us to pay our way are the income or salaries provided by appointments to office. If these are closed to us then our prospects will be gloomy indeed; unable to make good marriages, we will have children fit only to join the common people. Alternatively we will be forced into celibacy, and perhaps obliged to join a religious order or the secular priesthood and rely on Mass donations; this will prevent the increase, or even the proper preservation, of the population of America. . . .

[It may be argued that Americans can obtain posts in Spain; in theory

this is possible, though the practical difficulties of obtaining and holding such appointments are almost insuperable.] We would be perfectly
satisfied if European Spaniards took the numerous appointments that
are open to them in Spain and left to us the few jobs available in
America. We have always regarded ourselves just as much subjects of
Your Majesty as the natives of Old Spain. Old and New Spain are two
states and as such are like two wives of Your Majesty: each has her own
dowry in the form of public offices, which are paid from the revenues
of each. We will never complain that the children of Old Spain enjoy
the dowry of their mother, but equally the dowry of our mother should
be left for us.

The argument so far has shown that all public offices in America
without exception ought to be conferred only on American Spaniards
to the exclusion of Europeans. But everything has its drawbacks, and it
has to be admitted that these would be considerable in the case of the
entire removal of Europeans. Justice has to be done to the many in
major appointments who have served with due zeal, commitment, and
disinterestedness; and we cannot ignore the fact that the necessary
bonds which the government of Spain has to preserve with that of the
Indies, and the dependence which America has to maintain with respect to Spain indicate that we cannot cut out the Europeans altogether. This would mean seeking to maintain two separate and independent bodies under one head, something of a political monstrosity.
Americans are not so dedicated to their own interest over that of the
state that they would ignore or underestimate these considerations.
Whatever harm is done by the appointment of Europeans to America,
with or without blame to themselves, even greater harm could be
feared were no appointees to come from Old Spain. But these fears will
not be realized, for Your Majesty can rely on the loyalty of Americans
no less than that of Europeans in maintaining the security of these
provinces; nevertheless, our separation from natives of Spain would
foster some distrust of the state, and this distrust in itself is a serious
political danger, and one to be avoided.

Thus it is essential that some officials come here from Spain. But do
they have to receive all the higher appointments? Do all the governors
Your Majesty has in the provinces and cities of this part of North
America [i.e., Mexico] have to be born and reared in Old Spain, as they
are at present? Are we never to have in the whole continent a single
archbishop or bishop who was born here, as this kingdom does not have
at present? Have the majority of higher legal officials in these parts
always to come from Europe, as they do now? Are the natives of the
Americas never to occupy more than half the cathedral canonries here?

Among the many officials in the administration of the royal revenue in New Spain are we never to see, except rarely, one from our own country? In the case of military appointments, are we always to be confined to the militia, and discriminated against in the regular reserve, admitted for wartime service but denied the promotion offered Europeans?[. . . .]

To promote such great injustice against American Spaniards and justify it to Your Majesty, the Report needed to depict us as unworthy of office and to propagate against us the blackest slanders that hatred could produce. Of course they say that we are humble and submissive in spirit; while this could be a compliment to our qualities, in fact it is spitefully turned against us, and we are represented as abject and contemptible in character. . . .

Let us be clear that we are not speaking of Indians, conquered as individuals or under their leaders by our arms. We are speaking of Spaniards born in these regions, tracing our descent in a clear line from the first conquerors and colonists from Spain, or from those who came to trade or to occupy government positions. The Indians, victims of their race, or divine punishment, or conquest, or lack of culture, still after two centuries of conquest are born to poverty, bred in destitution, and controlled through punishment: they survive by work of the hardest kind, and live without shame, honor, or hope. Sunk in squalor and misery, degradation is their very nature. Authors who have observed the Indians and whose judgement can be trusted describe them as degraded. By an error of interpretation or carelessness in reading, these descriptions have been applied to American Spaniards without justification, and they need to be corrected.

We do not wish to bore Your Majesty or waste your time, but we have to make it clear that America consists of a large number of Spaniards whose blood is as pure as that of Spaniards from Old Spain. There are many among our rivals who spend their time asserting that in America we are all Indians, or at least that there are hardly any who do not have some Indian mixture from one branch of the family. It is not our object today to dispel so gross a prejudice; anyone who cannot see the truth for himself is beyond convincing. Who does not know that after the conquest one of the first concerns of our monarchs was the colonization of these dominions, and for this they arranged for many noble families drawn from the purest provinces of the crown of Castile to cross the sea? Who is ignorant of the care that was taken to ensure the purity of this population, forbidding the immigration not only of foreigners but also of Spaniards marked with any stain of disgrace either in themselves, their parents, or grandparents? Who has not seen the many concessions granted by the crown to encourage the increase of settlers? And who, finally, is unaware of the many inhabitants of Spain who have crossed to New Spain, to the point of causing concern over Spain's depopulation? According to a leading politician of this century, the number of European Spaniards emigrating to America each year amounts to more than ten thousand. Thus from the conquest onwards hardly less than two million five hundred thousand Spaniards have come to these parts; and even if no more than one-sixth of these have settled permanently, it is still sufficient to have caused a vast multiplication of Spaniards. . . .[2] [And what families have settled here? Among the best in Spain. American Spaniards are descendants of the nobility of Castile, holders of *mayorazgos* and *señoríos*. America is full of native-born Spaniards with purity of blood and titles of nobility.]

The miscegenation that is attributed to the Spanish colonists to discredit their purity of blood is subject to a number of objections and these are not easy to ignore. Miscegenation does not occur except through physical or natural attraction, or by desire for wealth or honor, and none of these things have persuaded the Spanish colonists to intermarry with Indian women. These are generally, and with only rare exceptions, positively ugly, with very bad color, coarse features, notorious slovenliness when they are not completely naked, no cleanliness, and even less culture and rationality. They have a great aversion to Spaniards and even resist communication with them. They are poverty-stricken and live in mud or wooden huts with straw roofs and earth floors. They eat in the greatest squalor and filthiness, and their food is worse than their dress. They have no beds and only palms or animal skins for blankets. And the little they need for such a miserable subsistence they earn with the most gruelling work imaginable. Above all, a Spaniard who intermarried with an Indian woman would see his children denied the status of a Spaniard, and even excluded from enjoying the privileges conceded to the Indians. It has to be said, and with greater emphasis, that the same would apply to miscegenation with negroes, mulattos, and other castas descended from them; so such intermarriages are far from normal and certainly not as common as malicious rumor has it.

It is true that at the time of the conquest, when the drawbacks to which we have referred did not apply, there were a number of unions between Spaniards and Indian women; but these were unions with the Indian royal families and were not despised even by some of the first grandees of Spain. Intermarriages of this kind have not debased in any way the character of their offspring, and they do not affect the fourth generation either privately or publicly; a person who has only one Indian among sixteen grandparents is unexceptional, and is regarded for all civil purposes as pure Spanish and free of mixed blood. . . . Thus there are many American Spaniards born of European parents, grandparents, and great grandparents, all without mixed blood and of proven nobility. Many trace their origin from the leading nobility of Spain, and others no less reputable from royal blood in America. Purity of blood, nobility of birth, distinction of character, none of this bears out the assertion that their modesty and mildness are signs of a debased nature, for their nature is that of their ancestors who were born in Spain, and it has been matured and improved by education and by America's favorable climate. . . .

The final section of the Report alleges that American Spaniards must always be subordinate to the Europeans in appointments to offices, because the Europeans nobly consult the welfare of the state and the interests of our beloved sovereign. That is indeed what the Europeans do, and we will never seek to question it. But what does it prove? Would not American Spaniards do as much? The Report assumes we would not, and that this is the reason why in our own native land the Europeans should take preference over us. They are superior to us (so it is argued) in zeal for the service of the state and devotion to the sovereign, and in the loyalty and respect we owe him as God's representative in the government of the kingdom. But what is the justification for underrating our loyalty and other political virtues? Who are these American Spaniards who have failed in their loyalty and duty to the king and the state, and where are the proofs? There are none. In two and a half centuries of European wars, American Spaniards have never failed in their duties to the king or given any reason to doubt their loyalty. Let us take only this century, when American Spaniards could already be numbered in their thousands. At the beginning of the century, in the critical circumstances of the accession of your father Philip V, of glorious memory, and the hostility of Austria and Britain, the loyalty of some of the regions of Old Spain was shaken and people of first rank vacillated, while some turned their back on their sovereign. Was there any unrest in America? Did anyone by word or deed challenge the just rights of the great house of Bourbon? On the contrary. Our loyalty and allegiance to our legitimate sovereign were much admired. In spite of false propaganda, disinformation, and British attempts to distort news of events and subvert our allegiance, the only effect was to stimulate our loyalty. Thus, while in Europe there were those who abandoned the cause of our sovereign, two thousand leagues away we Americans supported his interests, and as far as our situation permitted we made ready to resist invasion by his enemies.

The policy of the state everywhere has always been to preserve its military forces, not only to ensure respect from the monarch's neighbors but also to maintain his authority among his own subjects and hold them to their duty and allegiance. Only America has failed to observe these sound rules, and magnificently so. Without troops, and without the consequent burden on the royal treasury, America has voluntarily maintained its loyalty and allegiance to the sovereign, and it has prevented other states from attempting to invade these extensive dominions. Up to seven years ago there had never been an entire regiment of soldiers stationed here. At the beginning of the last century three infantry companies were formed in Mexico City. Even so feeble a force, incapable of resisting any public upheaval, was an offense to our loyalty and we requested the dissolution of any such military unit as insulting and superfluous among subjects ready to volunteer their lives in the service of Your Majesty, and your viceroy and ministers agreed. . . .

[In the sixteenth and seventeenth centuries there were numerous examples of American loyalty and voluntary military service for internal and external security. Then in 1763, at the end of the war with Britain, the crown began to organize militia forces in Mexico.]

At the end of the war Your Majesty saw fit to send troops to this kingdom and to form urban and provincial militias. When the project was proposed in Mexico City a *cabildo abierto* (expanded town meeting) was called for all the patricians and these attended in large numbers. They generously offered their persons and resources for the royal service, and so the militias were promptly organized with the support of Americans, the most distinguished of whom earnestly requested promotion to higher rank, as a European had been given the rank of colonel. We made a strong claim to the viceroy that this rank should be given to a patrician, and so it was, to the Count of Santiago. Thus, with the leading nobility of Mexico, we raised a Regiment of Spanish Militias; we paid for the uniforms, arms, quarters, bivouacs, and utensils. We also raised, clothed, and provisioned a Militia Battalion of Mulattos.

Hardly had the militias been raised than they were called into service. The expulsion of the Jesuits, a serious measure which at this distance might be expected to cause disastrous disturbances, was entrusted to the militia, which accomplished the task to the complete satisfaction of the government. We remained under arms for two consecutive years performing full military duties and alternating in mounting guards and other tasks with the regular troops, without receiving either the periods of leave prescribed by the Ordinance or the pay corresponding to the duration of service. . . . As we had not joined for the money but out of duty and allegiance, we served without complaint and were indistinguishable from the regular troops in training and discipline, and when we were ordered to stand down we were reluctant to abandon arms, though we had neglected our interests and left our houses to serve in the militia. We have recently returned to duty to face the threat of war with Britain. Even our artisans have demonstrated their loyalty, requesting permission to form urban militias to do garrison duty in Mexico City, as the regular troops and provincial militias have left for the coast and for further display of American loyalty. . . .

We hope that this time Your Majesty will be pleased to listen to our complaints and extend your goodwill towards us. But royal intentions are diluted by distance, and Your Majesty's wishes are not always reflected in the actions of those who govern us. Let us conclude with a specific example of this truth. The Renta de Tabaco [Royal Tobacco Monopoly] was recently established, and one of its principal promoters was undoubtedly Judge Sebastian de Calvo, an American. Among the hordes of officials employed in the administrative offices of the monopoly hardly one-twentieth are Americans. The same thing, with the same disproportion or even total exclusion of Americans, occurs here in many other positions in the royal service in which European Spaniards are employed. . . .

We ask Your Majesty to make it clear to the person who has reported against our reputation in the terms we have expressed, or similar terms, that it is not to your liking that the honor of a whole nation such as America should be so impugned. And in order that Americans may be allowed to serve you and these kingdoms fulfil their great prospects, let it please Your Majesty to order that high offices in Church and state here be assigned to American Spaniards, and while an occasional official from Spain may be admitted in order to maintain government links, in general the offices in the Indies should be barred to natives of Spain, just as Americans are absolutely excluded from offices in Spain. . . .

If we appear to ask too much, this is not so, for what we are seeking is justice, and we are confident that Your Majesty can and will dispense justice, relief, and happiness to your subjects in these vast dominions, who, removed as they are by distance from your person, simply want the satisfaction of working for the royal service in every kind of office.

4

Military and Society

Allan J. Kuethe

The Spanish empire in America was not a military empire. It was governed by civil laws, administered by civilian officials, and defended by a minimum of soldiers. Defence costs ate into the profits of empire, argument enough against excessive militarization. In the second half of the eighteenth century, however, Spain had to strengthen its imperial defenses. Increasing British pressure in the Americas demanded greater attention to external defense, while rebellion within caused a reappraisal of internal security. The regular army was strengthened and garrisons improved, but in the absence of money and manpower, Spain relied chiefly on colonial militias, which from the mid-eighteenth century were expanded and reorganized. To encourage recruits, they were admitted to the *fuero militar*, thus giving creoles, and also mixed races, the privileges enjoyed by the Spanish military and the regular army. These consisted of the right to be tried by military law before military tribunals rather than by ordinary royal courts; they also included certain fiscal exemptions. These developments were destabilizing in some respects, and thus raise problems of interpretation. First they appeared to contradict another principle of Bourbon policy: opposition to corporate bodies—the Church, for example—enjoying special status and privilege, as these were now regarded as obstacles to the absolutist state. Second, they tended to undermine the existing social structure by admitting hitherto nonprivileged groups to military privilege and to equality with the colonial elite; at the same time, against the trend of Spanish policy, they gave more opportunities to creoles. Third, they shifted imperial defense from the exclusive control of the metropolis and the regular army and shared it with the colonial mili-

Reprinted from Allan J. Kuethe, *Military Reform and Society in New Granada, 1773–1808* (Gainesville: University Presses of Florida, 1978), Latin American Monographs 22, Center for Latin American Studies, pp. 27–32, 37–38, 41–43, 185–86, by permission of the author and publisher.

tias. Allan Kuethe, Professor of History at Texas Tech University, guides the student through these minefields and interprets the reforms as they applied to New Granada. The works of Archer and Campbell (see Bibliography) perform a similar task for Mexico, where the Crown was reluctant to advance creoles to the highest military ranks, and for Peru, where Indian rebellion caused a reappraisal of the role of creole militias.

The implantation of privileges of this magnitude, enjoyed by so many, severely strained existing political and social institutions. Politically, by exempting large portions of the most active citizenry from ordinary justice, the fuero militar tended to undermine the authority of the cabildos, or municipal governments. Socially, many of those excepted as members of the new military organization came from the lower classes. This circumstance worked to subvert the traditional order of society, because the fuero removed militiamen from the authority of the cabildos—normally comprised of members of the creole aristocracy—and placed them under officers who might be inclined to regard military interests first and social origins second. Indeed, those pleading cases often sought, and sometimes received, preferential treatment at the hands of military justices who were more concerned with promoting the *esprit de corps* of their units than with dispensing impartial justice. These factors were additionally important because reformed militia units tended to exist in the principal population and administrative centers, where the institutional impact of their status was greatest. Furthermore, because the militiamen were in effect citizen soldiers, they carried the influence of military privileges with them into daily community life. Consequently, as the military reform entered the provinces of Cartagena and Panama, local authorities resented, and at times bitterly contested, the intrusion of military privileges into their jurisdictions. The most visible consequence of this confrontation was a series of civil-military conflicts, which raged throughout the early period of the reform.

During the first years of the military reorganization, the most sensitive point in the emerging crisis over military privileges was the status of black militiamen. During the formation of the disciplined militia, Pérez Dávila and Martínez Malo had enlisted large numbers of free blacks and mulattoes into what were euphemistically called *pardo* and *moreno* companies.[1] The latter term referred to the free offspring of purely Negro parents; the former encompassed the various types of mulattoes. For all intents and purposes, however, the same laws applied to both kinds of units, and most colonial officials ignored the distinction, referring to both as pardos. . . . Nearly half of the disciplined militia of Panama and Cartagena was of the pardo category; the total included three battalions, one from Cartagena and two from Panama, as well as twenty-one separate companies and a brigade.

Given the demography of the coastal areas, the enlistment of pardos was more a matter of necessity than of choice. Originally, colonists had imported large numbers of Negro slaves as agricultural workers, domestic servants, and laborers for the mines. The government itself had increased the Negro population by employing significant numbers of slaves for the construction of the massive fortification complex at Cartagena. Because manumission was a relatively simple process in the Spanish Empire, many blacks soon won the status of freemen, and eventually far outnumbered slaves. One fairly reliable authority places the number of free Negroes and mulattoes in New Granada in 1810 at 182,000, compared to merely 78,000 slaves. This free population remained largely clustered in the tropical lowlands and in some places comprised a majority of the inhabitants. Moreover, miscegenation, a common feature of the colonial social scene, had reached an advanced stage by the end of the eighteenth century, with few people clearly able to claim the more prestigious white social position. Given these circumstances, the military reformers could ill afford to ignore the black and mulatto populations.

Policies regarding the Indian further contributed to the importance of the pardo. Socially, the Indian constituted what amounted to a separate estate in the empire. Legally, he was in effect a perpetual minor and, as an expression of this status, was barred from service in the military. A question arose on this point in New Granada, however, when Pérez Dávila, Cartagena's special commander, enlisted Indians in Turbaco, a small town near the provincial capital. He based his action on a special provision in the Cuban reglamento which allowed the enlistment of Indians to complete the white battalions of Cuba and Bayamo. Upon hearing of Pérez Dávila's action, Commandant General Roque de Quiroga became concerned, because he suspected that such recruitment was inconsistent with "the privileges and exemptions conceded to this group of people." Finding nothing in the regulations specifically prohibiting the practice, but believing that the Cuban example was an exception due to extenuating local circumstances rather than a precedent, he asked Viceroy Manuel Guirior for a ruling. Guirior confirmed Quiroga's suspicions and ordered the immediate termination of Indian enlistment.

Although prized as a laborer and accepted as a soldier, the Negro held a most unfavorable place in the colonial social structure. Colonists credited him with few redeeming qualities and commonly condemned him as stupid, degenerate, and untrustworthy. The "taint" of Negro blood, or the suspicion of illegitimate parentage, placed a man in the lowest estate of society, the *castas* (literally "castes"), where for all intents and purposes he lived under a separate legal code with harsher punishments and tighter controls. Colonial law went so far as to impose limitations on his form of dress and his right to possess horses. He paid tribute and found himself barred from entering most honorable professions.

In the strategic Caribbean, however, military reformers keenly appreciated the crucial role that the Negro would have to play in any successful defense system. Thus O'Reilly, then organizing the disciplined militia of Cuba, not only recruited significant numbers of pardos, but in order to increase morale, loyalty, and dignity, he extended the fuero militar to pardo militiamen on the same basis as for whites.[2] This concession was a significant instance where a functional corporation cut across the stratified classes in Spanish society, granting an equal juridical status to both whites and pardos, at least so far as their relations with the outside world were concerned. Under this parity of privilege, both white and black soldiers presented their causes before the same tribunals and enjoyed the same immunities from ordinary justice.

Some evidence suggests that the social tolerance displayed in the military reform may have stemmed partly from the egalitarian spirit of the Enlightenment, which, during the closing decades of the century, brought about some improvement in the status of those with Negro parentage. In 1784, for example, the monarchy ordered a halt to slave branding, and in 1789 it furthered this humanitarian spirit through the promulgation of a new code intended to improve the treatment of slaves. Moreover, a 1795 *cédula* formalized the fee structure and the legal procedure to be used by mulatto subjects petitioning for a dispensation from the stigma of slave ancestry and, thus, for the acquisition of the rights of whites. Yet the apparent willingness to smooth over social differences, while enlightened in tone, was principally a response to demographic reality. In the Province of Cartagena, members of the white estate were not only few in number but also widely scattered. The 1778 census, for example, recorded only 6,860 white males, excluding clergymen.

The extensive miscegenation in coastal New Granada, combined with the judicial parity, gave rise to still another intriguing development—the creation of companies "of all colors." These were integrated units formed in those areas where no single social grouping was sufficient to permit the establishment of a full company. . . . These units contained varying mixtures of men listed as morenos, pardos, *ter-cerones* (quadroons), *cuarterones* (octeroons), *zambos* (of Indian and Negro parents), mestizos, whites, and even an occasional Indian, although as indicated earlier this class legally could not serve in the militia.

A word of caution is in order concerning the classification *blanco*, or white, for it cannot be presumed that all members of that group derived from purely white racial stock. Companies labeled as "white" could fill out their enlistment quotas with mestizos and cuarterones, although both groups also could and did serve in pardo units. Moreover, culture was important in determining social status. Those who behaved like Spaniards were usually taken for Spaniards and, as indicated earlier, if they possessed sufficient wealth they could purchase a certificate of whiteness in Spain. As Viceroy Pedro Mendinueta (1797–1803) commented some years later, "those enlisted in the militia [of Cartagena] are at best from the ones known as local whites [*blancos de la tierra*], who in reality are mulattoes [but] somewhat closer to our race, and in that contingency only the circumstance of engaging in labors less demanding than those of agriculture lightens the color [*hace disimular el color*]."

So blurred were racial distinctions in New Granada that in some instances the military leadership itself differed concerning the proper classification of companies. Governor Juan Pimiento, for example, labeled five of the companies of Mompós as white, two as pardo, and six as all colors, while Lieutenant Colonel Anastasio Zejudo classified five as white, three as pardo, one as zambo-moreno, and four as all colors. Even greater variation occurred in the companies of Lorica, where Governor Pimiento pronounced nine companies as white and nineteen as all colors; Zejudo found eleven companies white, four zambo, two pardo, one pardo-zambo, two cuarterón, one moreno, and seven all colors!

The critical question regarding the status of the pardo within the military corporation was whether, in the interest of achieving military objectives, the white leadership would uphold pardo privileges against cabildo opposition or whether social loyalties and affiliations from civilian stratified society would penetrate the military corporation. Coastal cabildos chafed at the prospect of losing authority over much of the pardo population, which they viewed as inherently vicious and untrustworthy. Moreover, pardo overreaction to the newly acquired immunities exacerbated the crisis. Long subject to the control of the superior classes, men of color, once freed from the restraints of ordi-

nary justice, responded with pent-up resentment and boldly defied and
harassed local magistrates. To the cabildos this development placed a
special, alarming emphasis on what was already an obvious erosion of
their authority, and they challenged the issue of pardo and military
privilege at every opportunity. Yet throughout the history of the reform, military objectives normally prevailed over civilian social allegiances. From company captains to the viceroys as captains general,
military officers typically reacted first as loyal members of the military
corporation and willingly defended even the lowliest soldier from civilian authority. . . .

The fundamental arguments recurred with monotony. Ordinary justices contended that the exemption of so many individuals from their
authority diminished their power, and they complained that they were
humiliated by the contempt and arrogance displayed by the immune
lower classes, as well as by a general military disregard and disrespect
for the dignity of their offices. Conversely, the military jealously defended its fuero as just compensation for the highest order of service to
the state and regarded any incursion by ordinary justice into its domain
as a menace to the promotion of pride and dedication to duty. The
result was a withering of respect for justice, an undermining of the
prestige and credibility of local government, and the establishment of
the military as a dominant force in the provinces of Cartagena and
Panama.

[The privilege of the pardo was not the only issue. Even more significant was the role of the creole. The reform of the colonial state by
Charles III and Gálvez involved a diminution of opportunities for creoles, which in turn exacerbated tensions between them and peninsular
Spaniards.] One indispensable tool for the implementation of enlightened reforms was the military, which, in the final analysis, provided
the power that underpinned royal initiatives. The military was reorganized and strengthened not only to defend the empire from foreign
aggression but to maintain order and to support the government as
well; in the long run, the latter proved the more compelling objective.
Thus, given the tension between the creole aristocracy and the enlightened despotism of the government of Charles III with its dependence
upon Europeans, the relationship of the military to the social structure—and in particular to the various elements of the white estate—
was a critical question, especially as the tensions generated by reform
increased.

The creole, historically, was not a significant participant in the defense system. Rotating battalions, which shouldered much of the defense burden before the expansion of the veteran colonial army, were

Spanish. Moreover, even the early Fijo of Cartagena, although mainly comprised of the native-born in the ranks, possessed a predominantly Spanish officer corps.[3] The 1741 battle, in which the army of Cartagena defeated the British invasion under Admiral Edward Vernon, has frequently been characterized as a creole-Spanish victory. Yet close examination reveals that most of the fighting was done by marines and troops from the battalions of Aragón and Spain, while the Fijo played a secondary role. In any event, by conservative estimate, half of its officers were Spanish. The first set of service records for the Fijo, year 1749, indicates a four-to-one Spanish-to-creole ratio, with most of the latter serving in the lower levels. This percentage remained stable up to the Seven Years' War, after which the gap gradually narrowed to just under a two-to-one margin on the eve of the reform, still a considerable edge in favor of Europeans. In the old Fixed Infantry Battalion of Panama, the difference was even more substantial. Spanish officers outnumbered creoles six to one in 1751, and although that margin eventually shrank too, Spaniards still held nearly a three-to-one superiority in the years following the Seven Years' War.

There is a temptation to explain the preponderance of Spanish officers as either a systematic exclusion of the native-born or, perhaps, a manifestation of creole reluctance to enter the military. While there is probably some validity to both contentions, neither is adequate in itself because of built-in limitations on creole opportunity. The principal and most convenient source of experienced officers was the rotating battalions returning to Spain, from which officers could easily be recruited, usually with the incentive of a promotion of one rank. Thus, the battalions of Spain and Aragón, which returned to Europe in 1748, left behind in Cartagena a large number of young officers, a process repeated by other units after the Seven Years' War. In Panama, the early fixed battalion was formed directly from the Battalion of Granada; there could hardly, therefore, have been many creole officers in it. On the other hand, during the 1750s and 1760s young creoles began embracing military service in significant numbers as cadets. In Cartagena most of these men claimed noble status, which indicated a willingness to make the military a career by those sons of families who had to find outside outlets and support. In Panama, these cadets were nearly all sons of Spanish officers who had joined the fixed battalion and who obviously found the military one of the few honorable professions available on the isthmus. Thus, while few openings existed for creoles in the early army, the monarchy did display a willingness to train creoles as officers, an opportunity that many sought. . . .

The increased size of the reformed military placed new pressure upon the human resources of Panama and Cartagena and made the enlistment of significant numbers of creoles inevitable. In the ranks of the white militia there were various kinds of storekeepers, craftsmen, artisans, and small farmers who comprised the nucleus of the coastal creole population. These people it should be remembered, were in the main "blancos de la tierra," ethnic mulattoes who through occupational status and social reputation passed as white. In Panama, which had only a small European population, creoles dominated the volunteer officer corps nearly four to one. Presumably creoles also dominated officerships in the backlands of Cartagena, because of the lack of Spanish-born competition. . . . [By the end of the eighteenth century creoles dominated the junior ranks of the officer corps not only in the militia but also in the regular army and were already moving to more senior positions.]

In final analysis, the military reform made substantial progress toward achieving its original objective of strengthening New Granada's external defenses. The regular army was expanded considerably in size, and, as a result of better leadership and organization, also seems to have improved in quality. The disciplined militia system, despite nagging problems such as empty companies, lazy officers, and weapon shortages, was clearly superior to what preceded it. Through a systematic training program, it acquainted large numbers of coastal subjects with the rudiments of the military art, thereby making them a creditable reserve force. Furthermore, the quality of the militia improved as the viceroyalty gained in experience and as it developed a coordinated system of supervision. . . .

Less clear-cut were the results of the attempt to use the army to strengthen the domestic authority of royal government, which to the viceregal leadership became an important, and at times the paramount, objective of the reform. Certainly the reformed army, which did much to contain the Comunero Rebellion, was a major force in the reestablishment of royal authority during the nullification of the Capitulations and during Caballero y Góngora's administration in the strained aftermath of that action. Moreover, the archbishop-viceroy, confident of the military force supporting him, made extensive advances in revenue reform during his administration. In the long run, nevertheless, the reformed military proved an uncertain pillar of royal authority. First, the machinations of Gil y Lemos in 1789 led to the dissolution of the upland militia establishment.[4] Then, during the 1790s and after, Spain's preoccupation with the nearly constant warfare in Europe denied New Granada's regular army the Spanish reinforcements it so desperately needed, while Spanish enlistment also dwindled in the militia. The result was a strong shift toward creole domination of the officer corps of both the regular army and the militia at the very time that the native population was increasingly influenced by the revolutionary currents unleashed in France. The Auxiliary Battalion stood as a vivid exception to this rule, but even it could not guarantee domestic security as the foundation of Spanish dominion in New Granada slowly crumbled.

Of comparable, perhaps superior, significance were the social and political side effects of the military reform. Throughout its history, the reformed army acted at a number of levels as an important vehicle for social mobility in the colony. The personal immunities and the extensive judicial prerogatives attached to military service elevated the social status of thousands of militiamen, many of them pardos, who in return accepted the drudgery of Sunday drills and risked the danger of possible mobilization. Although creoles suffered discrimination in competition for officerships both in the militia and in the regular army, many were able to validate or reinforce claims of honor by the acquisition of commissions, often through purchase, especially during the latter period of the reform. The social impact of the military reorganization was uneven, however. Its smallest effect came in the uplands, where the militia's duration was brief; its greatest effect occurred on the coast, where the militia was largest and where it enjoyed a continuous existence.

5

Bourbon Taxes, Indian Resistance

Scarlett O'Phelan Godoy

Bourbon policy was not accepted passively in Spanish America. Discrimination in appointments and increase in taxation were burning issues; they led to protest and in some cases to violence. The precise relationship between Bourbon innovation and armed insurrection is an interesting exercise in interpretation. The reactions of the creoles anticipated the dilemmas of the revolutions for independence. After an initial involvement in purely fiscal agitation, they usually saw the danger of more violent protest from below, directed not only against administrative authority but against all oppressors. The creoles then united with the forces of law and order to suppress the more radical rebels. This happened in Peru, where creole tax revolt was overtaken by Indian rebellion; the majority of creoles then held back or withdrew from the movement, which was left to the leadership of Túpac Amaru. Indian grievances were more profound, stemming as they did from long-term conditions: from the tyranny of the corregidores, simultaneously officials, judges, and merchants to the Indians; from the historic demands upon them for tribute and tithe; from the *reparto*, or imposition of goods; and from the *mita* system with its inhuman conditions of forced labor, especially in the mines of Potosí. These are often listed indiscriminately as "causes" of rebellion. But Scarlett O'Phelan, of the Pontificia Universidad Católica, Lima, who has made a comprehensive study of agrarian protest in eighteenth-century Peru, focuses more precisely on two particular Bourbon expedients, the raising of the *alcabala* and the establishment of internal customs posts to ensure collection.

Reprinted from Scarlett O'Phelan Godoy, *Rebellions and Revolts in Eighteenth-Century Peru and Upper Peru* (Cologne, Böhlau Verlag, 1985), pp. 161–73, 206–07, by permission of the author and publisher.

The alcabala tax was a sales tax initially introduced [in Peru] in 1591 under the government of Viceroy García Hurtado de Mendoza. It stipulated that goods in the colonies should be taxed at two per cent of their value at each commercial transaction. . . . As with most of the tax policies some products and institutions were not subject to alcabala. For instance, wheat, corn and bread were free from the alcabala tax; the clergy and the Indian communities were, as social groups, exempt.

The Bourbon Reforms were carried out within the Spanish colonies during the reign of King Charles III of Spain, who sought to increase the royal revenue by reforming the various branches of the treasury. These measures were comprised in the *Informe y Plan de Intendencias*, which was specially prepared in 1768 by Visitor José María de Gálvez together with the Marquis de Croix, Viceroy of New Spain. In the case of the Viceroyalty of Peru, the economic programme was implemented under the guidance of Visitor Antonio de Areche, whose constant complaints against Viceroy Guirior induced the Crown to replace him by Viceroy Agustín de Jaúregui (Captain General of Chile) on 22nd July 1780, just a few months before the Great Rebellion broke out.

From 1770 onwards, the taxation measures included within the Bourbon economic programme were gradually introduced into the colonies. The new taxes, as well as the reparto, were both related to a specific economic policy. In the case of the reparto, the Crown hoped to stimulate and control the development of an internal market. Small producers who owned *chorrillos* and *chacras* as well as the artisans became involved in the economic expansion which coincided with a rise in mining activity. It is not surprising, therefore, that the alcabala was increased so as to incorporate the middle sector of the population who were profiting from the commercial expansion. The effect of the economic reforms was in fact to drain the Viceroyalty of more of its surplus through taxation and royal monopolies. . . .

On 30th March 1772, a royal cedula established a general increase in the alcabala tax, from 2 to 4%, on "colonial articles and imported goods." However, in October 1773 some authorities were still reluctant to collect the increased tax, arguing that they had not been clearly informed exactly which commodities were to carry the new charge. Moreover, there is some evidence to suggest that during the late '70s, the hacendados from Arequipa were still paying only 2%, ignoring the increase to 4% established by Viceroy Amat in 1772.

In some provinces, the alcabala revenue increased more rapidly than in others, because direct tax collection began to replace tax farming with the establishment of Customs Houses (Aduanas). Such was the

case of the Cochabamba Customs House, which began operating in
Arque and Tapacarí in 1774 provoking protests and riots.

In effect, on 2nd August 1774, an upheaval took place in Cochabamba
in protest against the new method of the alcabala collection through
the recently established Aduana. As a precautionary measure, some
local merchants removed their goods during the night and deposited
them at La Merced Convent, "to ensure they will be saved." The artisans were also restless as they suspected the Aduana system was to be
applied to their sales too. Indeed, the authorities sought to calm their
fears by stressing that the Guilds were already subject to the alcabala
payment and therefore that this was not a new tax imposed upon them.
However, it is not clear if the artisans were actually paying the alcabala
prior to the introduction of the Aduana system.

On the other hand, Indian traders were suspicious of the new system
and reluctant to submit their products to it because they thought the
alcabala would be charged on them regardless of existing legal exemptions. The law stipulated that the Indians had the privilege of not
paying the alcabala on commodities *"de la tierra"* which they grew on
their land, or that they produced by themselves. However, they were
liable to pay alcabala on *"de Castilla"* goods which they produced or
traded in.

As a result of the evident resentment created by the Cochabamba
Customs House, Dr. Miguel Josef de Allende y Maldonado, *procurador*
of the village of Cochabamba, declared that, "the cause of the unrest
was due to the new tax laws to be enforced, charging the guilds of
tocuyeros, tailors, shoemakers, blacksmiths, soapmakers with alcabala
tax, which had only recently also been imposed on wheat and corn,
commodities produced by the local hacendados." In view of this last
measure, it is not surprising to find that grain traders and pack drivers
were also involved in the revolts. In order to bring local clashes to an
end, Dr. Allende y Maldonado recommended that the collection of the
new tax be suspended forthwith. Since Cochabamba's principal products were grain and *tocuyos*, their motives for avoiding payment of the
new tax must have been particularly strong.

The revolt against the Aduana was followed by enquiries regarding
the nature of the new taxation system. The majority of the queries
concerned the proposed extent of Indian involvement in the reformed
system, and whether products such as dried potatoes (*chuño*), potatoes,
chili, corn flour, cheese and *boquillas* fish, which had previously been
exempt for Indian traders, were to become subject to the new charge.
The documents reflect the doubts and lack of confidence which those
involved in production and trade had in the new economic measures.

Therefore, the protests against the Cochabamba Customs House could
be seen as the first sign of the struggle which developed between the
colonial population and the Crown in consequence of the new taxation
policy. It was the Cochabamba Customs House experiment which became a sounding board for the full range of local feelings, clearly demonstrating that it would be virtually impossible to implement the tax
reforms without generating discontent and social unrest.

A turning point in colonial administration took place two years later.
During 1776 the Viceroyalty of the Río de la Plata was created, and
Upper Peru, which, since the beginning of the colonial period had been
part of the Viceroyalty of Peru, was suddenly incorporated into the new
Viceroyalty. Numerous accounts point out that this division gravely
altered the previously well defined trade routes which had developed
between Lower and Upper Peru over the past two centuries. In commercial terms, Buenos Aires was undoubtedly better placed to control
the Upper Peru's regional market. More importantly, the income of the
Viceroyalty of Peru was severely affected by the division, since the
important mines, like Potosí and Oruro, were transferred to the new
Viceroyalty.

It must be pointed out that not only creole and mestizo producers
and traders, but also caciques and wealthy Indians were involved in the
South Andean trading system. Such was the case of the caciques of
Pacajes, Sicasica and Paria, who maintained an early and lively trade
with the Desaguadero region in Lower Peru. Even the rebel cacique,
José Gabriel Túpac Amaru, was able to develop an important muleteer
enterprise covering the Cuzco-Potosí trade route.

According to the available evidence, it is possible to detect a notable
increase in "the Indian trading of local products such as coca, textiles,
cotton, chili and other items" from the 1750s onwards. This expansion
in Indian commercial activities may have been a result of the reparto
requirements, especially as the Indian population was in a position to
avoid paying the alcabala tax, and therefore make some profit. Most of
the colonial products handled by the Indian escaped the initial rise in
the alcabala to 4% in 1772, but were later affected by the new increase
to 6% in 1776. At the same time, Customs Houses were being established at important cities along the Potosí main trade route, such as
Arequipa, Cuzco and La Paz, in order to secure stricter control over the
economic transactions between Lower and Upper Peru.

It is my belief that 1776 was, for many reasons, a crucial year in the
growth of social unrest which reached its climax in 1780. In the first
place, during that year Upper Peru was formally brought under the
control of the Viceroyalty of Río de la Plata. At the same time, on 6th

July, a royal decree established a new increase in the alcabala tax from 4 to 6%, and yet another, issued on 26th July, ordered the establishment of a Customs House at La Paz (Upper Peru). Furthermore, it was during 1776 that Visitor Antonio de Areche set sail for the colonies for the purpose of personally supervising the implementation of the economic measures ordered by the Crown.

However, although these measures were promulgated during 1776, their full impact was not felt until the years immediately following that date. In the case of Visitador Areche, he did not arrive in the Viceroyalty until 1777, whereupon he immediately set about the supervision of the collection of the new alcabala tax. In August of that year, a circular was distributed to the corregidores at Chayanta, Paria, Oruro, Pacajes and La Paz, requesting them to apply greater pressure to ensure the efficient collection of the alcabala. From 1777 onwards, then, the corregidores were not only involved in the distribution of goods, but also in the collection of the alcabala. Thus, their presence was in direct conflict not only with the economic interests of the Indian peasants, who were affected by the reparto, but also with those of the mestizo and creole land tenants and merchants who were affected by the collection of the alcabala.

Although in 1777 the proposal to impose a tax of 12.5% on the aguardiente was issued, in Viceroy Guirior's words "because that spirit was dangerous to the Indian's health," the royal decree was not actually approved until 1778. Chronologically, this measure coincided with a powerful campaign, led by Guirior and supported by Areche, to put a stop to the notorious contraband in silver and gold which was rife in the Viceroyalty.

All these measures were potential sources of unrest and disappointment within different sectors of the colonial population. Hacendados, obrajeros and traders must have been affected by the alcabala increase to 6%, especially when it began being systematically collected. The high rate of tax imposed on aguardiente affected not only the producers, but also the mine owners, whose laborers were the principal consumers. Therefore, mining centres such as Cailloma (Arequipa), Condoroma (Cuzco), Oruro and Potosí (in Upper Peru), must have had to adjust their demand to the new tax. In addition, mine owners were also affected by the steps taken by Guirior to restrict contraband and avoid the circulation of silver and gold that had not been previously taxed and smelted. It is not surprising, therefore, to find that mining profits increased from 1778 onwards reaching a peak in 1780. This striking rise in mining production may, however, have been due more to better administrative control rather than to any real increase in physical output.

It appears that the new taxation policy increased the pressure on producers and traders alike. In 1779 even coca was included among the commodities liable to pay the alcabala. As consumers and traders this measure more directly affected the Indian population, but indirectly it also affected mine owners and *obrajeros* since coca was one of the items included in the "payment in kind" allotted to the laborers. The inclusion of grain within the scope of the alcabala from 1780 onwards must have produced a similar effect. The figures concerning Arequipa, Cuzco, Cochabamba, La Paz and Potosí clearly indicate a dramatic increase in alcabala tax revenue from 1775 onwards, 1779 being recorded as the peak year for Potosí and La Paz, and 1780 for Arequipa and Cuzco.

It is important to bear in mind that up to 1779, Customs Houses had only been established in Upper Peru: first in Cochabamba and subsequently in La Paz. Nevertheless by 1780 Customs Houses had begun to operate in Lower Peru and it seems to me that this was a crucial factor in encouraging an increase in social unrest, because it meant that both extremes of the South Andean trade circuit were blockaded by Aduanas. On 1st January a Customs House was created at Arequipa, provoking several riots and clashes with the authorities. According to contemporary sources, the rebels, "attacked the recently established Customs House, destroying its offices, burning the official papers and stealing three thousand pesos kept there."

As Arequipa had close commercial links with Cuzco, the news of the intention to open a Customs House at Cuzco also spread rapidly. On 14th and 26th January respectively, a series of lampoons appeared in Cuzco calling for a revolt against the *aduaneros* "who were coming to impose their taxes on the city of Cuzco." However, the rebels' conspiracy was uncovered and the principal culprits were tried and condemned.

Nevertheless, as a result of Lower Peru's open resistance against the Customs Houses, an uprising took place at La Paz's Customs House in March. As in the case of the Arequipa revolt, the Indians and mestizos of La Paz, who worked as muleteers and traders, were the principal participants in the uprising. Their main complaint was against the Customs House authorities (*aduaneros*), who were charging the alcabala twice and for items that were usually tax free, and were even confiscating their products when the traders were unable to meet the alcabala demands.

However, despite the obvious social unrest that the Bourbon economic reforms were causing among the colonial population, yet another royal cedula was issued this time affecting the artisans. On 31st July 1780 instructions were issued obliging all artisans to belong to a guild and to be properly registered, so as to ensure the proper collection of the alcabala on their transactions. Furthermore, there is evidence which suggests that *chorrillo* textiles, which were normally exempt from the alcabala, were included in 1780, as were those produced by the *obrajes*.

Therefore, not only hacendados, *obrajeros*, mine owners and traders, but also petty landowners, *chorrillo* owners, retailers, muleteers and artisans were affected in one way or another by the tax reforms. Nevertheless, obviously the middle element of the population was more likely to be adversely affected by the alcabala and the Customs Houses since they were small producers and therefore earned less money to cope with the new taxes. . . .

[This was in the southern Andes.] Revolts against the alcabala in the central and northern highlands. . . . did not develop into far reaching movements. Why this should have been the case was probably because, firstly, the central and northern regions did not possess any well developed trade routes like those in the South Andean region, and secondly, because other circumstances in the South Andean region encouraged the spread of a more general social unrest. In particular, it should be remembered that the South Andean provinces were still subject to the *mita* of Potosí, and also to a massive tribute payment since the Indian population was higher there than in other regions. Moreover, the incorporation of Upper Peru into the recently established Viceroyalty of the Río de la Plata may well have made the region more sensitive to economic pressure, and hence, to social instability.

In brief, when the reparto was added to the tribute payments, the Indians from the South Andean region were obliged to expand their trading activities out of sheer necessity. Such was the case of the numerous Indian traders who travelled, at least once a year, to trade in native commodities, mainly those exempted from the alcabala tax. However, in order to make some profit from their trade, they turned to more devious methods which would guarantee them the necessary surplus needed to meet the payment of the tribute, repartos, and ecclesiastical taxes. They found that a good way of increasing their profits was to declare less goods than they were actually carrying. In purely economic terms, then, it seems that the reparto was able, on the one hand, to incorporate itself into the colonial economy, helping it to function normally, and on the other, it acted to some extent as a stimulus to the Indian economy, by obliging the peasants to expand their commercial relations. Even so, in social terms the reparto constituted a heavy burden for many Indian communities.

Strangely enough, the economic imbalance only became evident after the establishment of the Customs Houses, when the peasants' fraudulent practices were disclosed. Moreover, their economic stability could have already been threatened from 1779 onwards, when the goods which they had been in the habit of buying and selling, such as coca, grains, dried potatoes and *chorrillos* textiles, became subject to the new alcabala tax.

In the case of the South Andean hacendados, it appears that they were actually using Indians as pack drivers and itinerant traders, in order to avoid taxation and thus increase their own profits. Perhaps this malpractice enabled them to accumulate a surplus. Most of the rich South Andean hacendados were involved in the production of aguardiente, grain and coca and so it was probably more profitable for them to assume the Indian taxes and reparto payments and avoid the alcabala tax. Moreover, particularly in the case of Arequipa, it was discovered that in 1780 the hacendados were still only paying alcabala tax at the old rate of 2% which had been increased to 4% in 1774, and to 6% in 1778. This seems to prove that in the colonial system, tax evasion enabled a considerable number of people to retain profits which they would otherwise have had to forfeit. As this proved to be a source of self-enrichment it is hardly surprising to find that taxes were openly resisted.

PART TWO

THE COLONIAL ECONOMY: GROWTH AND CRISIS

6

The Mexican Mining Boom

D. A. Brading

Mexican silver production rose from 5 million pesos in 1702, to 18 million pesos in the boom of the 1770s, and a peak of 27 million in 1804. Growth was spasmodic rather than continuous, with particular spurts in the 1720s, 1740s, and 1770s, but each new plateau was a gain for production. The preconditions for growth in silver mining were a quadruple increase of mercury output at Almadén in Spain, indispensable for the amalgamation process, and population increase in Mexico which provided more labor for the industry. The boom itself was the result of state intervention and private enterprise. Fiscal concessions encouraged mining entrepreneurs and merchant houses to invest in expansion, and the results could be seen in the great increase of profits, the creation of private fortunes, and the stimulus to agriculture, industry, and foreign trade. They could also be seen in the increase of revenue for Spain; Mexico was a profitable colony in which both the Spanish state and peninsular exporters had a vital stake. Yet the mining industry did not entirely serve imperial or Mexican interests. First, the metropolis was placed under more urgent pressure by the colony to maintain vital supplies of mercury and equipment, which it was patently incapable of doing during wartime; so the mining boom slowed down in the last years of the eighteenth century and Spain itself was seen not only as a fiscal predator but also as an obstacle to growth. Second, state intervention could not resolve all the problems of the industry; failure to innovate technically or to increase the scale of operations prevented significant reduction of costs. There were premonitions of recession already before the end of the colonial period. The modern historian of eighteenth-century mining is David Brading,

Reprinted from D. A. Brading, *Miners and Merchants in Bourbon Mexico 1763–1810* (Cambridge, 1971), Copyright Cambridge University Press, 1971, pp. 28–30, 143–52, 156–58, reprinted with the permission of Cambridge University Press and the author.

Reader in Latin American History in the University of Cambridge, who
has placed it in a framework of government reform and social change
and assessed its significance as a factor in colonial stability.

i

The visitor-general, José de Gálvez, declared: "Since mining is the
origin and unique source of the metals which give spirit and movement
to all human occupations and to the universal commerce of this globe,
in justice it demands the principal attention of the government." He
therefore organized the miners into a guild which possessed its own
courts and exercised jurisdiction over all mining litigation. To the
concession of this new fuero was added the entire battery of current
economic policy. His object, apart from increasing silver production,
was to liberate the mining industry from mercantile control. For Gálvez, following Campillo, was determined to destroy the economic
dominance of the great Mexico City import houses. In 1778 the famous
decree of *comercio libre* terminated the old Cadiz monopoly: henceforth all the chief ports of the Peninsula could trade freely with the
American colonies. Somewhat later, new independent merchant guilds
were established at Veracruz and Guadalajara. This attack upon the old
monopolists proved largely successful: both the silver miners and the
provincial merchants obtained financial independence. More importantly, silver production, as measured by annual mintage, augmented
from under twelve million pesos in 1762 to a peak of over twenty-seven
million pesos in 1804. The less complete figures for transatlantic commerce indicate an equally dramatic expansion.

If Gálvez devoted much energy and thought to the restructuring and
expansion of the export economy, he paid little attention to Mexican
industry and agriculture. Landowners did not have any legal privilege,
nor did they receive much encouragement, fiscal or otherwise, from the
new regime. As for native manufacturers, their very existence was condemned. Gálvez asserted that colonial industries damaged Spain, "whose
interest consists in that the inhabitants of the Indies do not become
accustomed to live independently of this monarchy for the supply of
necessities." Years later that enlightened viceroy, the second Count of
Revillagigedo, reiterated this opinion: "It must not be forgotten that
this [country] is a colony which ought to depend upon its origin, Spain,
and to yield some profit in return from the benefits of protection. But
great prudence is required to arrange the dependency and to make the
interest mutual and reciprocal, for this relation would cease the moment European manufactures and produce are no longer needed here."

The "profit" to which Revillagigedo referred was by no means small. Whereas in 1712 royal revenue from Mexico amounted to no more than three million pesos, by the last decade of the century annual tax and monopoly receipts averaged over twenty million pesos. This revenue can be divided into four broad categories. First, there were the various taxes raised from the mining industry—the tithe on production and the monopoly profits on mercury, gunpowder and mintage. The vast tobacco monopoly formed a class in itself. Then there was a variegated range of customs and excise duties levied on all produce sold on the open market, including under this head taxes charged on pulque and salt. The final category was formed by the capitation tribute paid by Indians and mulattoes, by this time far less important than the other types of taxation. The principal innovation introduced by the Bourbons consisted in the establishment of Crown monopolies in tobacco, playing cards and gunpowder and in the utilisation of salaried officials to administer these monopolies and to collect excise duties. After 1776 the Habsburg practice of farming out revenue collection to private individuals or institutions was terminated. A small army of officials, clerks and guards, stationed in all the chief towns of New Spain, administered these taxes, new and old, with unparalleled vigour and efficiency. The drive to revitalise and expand the bureaucracy was crowned in 1786 with the appointment of some twelve intendants.

This revolution in government undoubtedly paid off. In all the Crown obtained nearly fourteen million pesos a year from New Spain. Of this sum four million were required to support the civil administration, the law courts, the fiscal bureaucracy, the military, and to protect the northern frontiers. The remainder, some ten million pesos, were shipped out of Mexico. Four million went to subsidise a wide circle of forts and garrisons that stretched from Trinidad to Louisiana, from California to the Philippines. The other six million—the monopoly profits—went straight to the royal chest in Madrid. For the monarchy only raised thirty-five million pesos in taxes from the Peninsula. It therefore relied upon its American possessions to finance their own administration and defense. In addition, the Crown received from America a surplus of eight million pesos, of which three-quarters came from Mexico. Clearly, by the close of the century New Spain had emerged as a source of revenue second only to the metropolis itself.

For Mexico, as for most of Spanish America, the decades following the Seven Years War constituted a distinct epoch in its colonial history Far from being the culmination of two hundred years' settlement, however, this so-called golden age of the late eighteenth century sprang from a profound regeneration of the New World's hispanic society. In some sense, the Bourbon dynasty reconquered America. It entirely transformed the system of government, the structure of the economy and the order of society which had prevailed in the colonies since the days of the Habsburgs. At the same time, a more numerous Spanish immigration invaded the continent. Many arrived to occupy the newly created posts in government and the army, but the great majority entered commerce to profit from the great economic expansion of these years. Whereas in 1689 only 1,182 peninsular Spaniards resided in Mexico City, by 1792 that number had just about doubled. Bourbon Mexico, if such we may style the period 1763–1810, took its origin from the successful collaboration of a despotic but enlightened administration with a vigorous group of merchant-capitalists and silver millionaires. The success of the government's economic reforms in large measure depended upon the enterprise and capital of these businessmen. . . .

ii

A significant change in the burden of taxation occurred in the decades that followed 1769. In that year Gálvez, to encourage José de la Borda to go to Zacatecas to drain the Quebradilla mine, granted the famous miner a complete exemption from the silver tithe until the initial cost of restoration was reimbursed, to be followed by a 50 per cent exemption for the subsequent 15 years. For the entire period Borda was also supplied mercury at the cost price of 30 ps. per cwt. At much the same time two other miners, José de Moya at Pachuca and Cayetano Núñez de Ibarra at Temascaltepec, were conceded similar tax exemptions. Thereafter such fiscal backing to miners who attempted to renovate old, waterlogged mines became quite common. By 1810 three of the major mines in Zacatecas—the Vetagrande, the Quebradilla and the San Francisco—all enjoyed these tax rebates. The Fagoagas at Sombrerete and Juan Sierra Uruñuela at Bolaños were also encouraged by such benefits. On the other hand, in Guanajuato and Catorce, the industry's most successful camps, such exemptions were not to be found: it was only in the older more marginal camps with waterlogged mines that the Crown granted these fiscal subsidies to production. Naturally it still retained the profits of mintage.

After taxation the treasury despatched all silver bar by mule-train to Mexico City. There, the royal mint cut 69 rls. from every mark of silver, of which 65 rls., the legal price, were returned to the owner. At the beginning of the century mintage was a lengthy process, the more especially since the Crown had rented the office to private individuals who lacked funds to purchase the bar as it arrived in the capital. Most miners, therefore, preferred to sell their silver to merchants or silver banks resident in Mexico City at a discount of a real in every mark exchanged. This unsatisfactory system was terminated in 1729 when the Crown appointed salaried officials, housed the mint in a magnificent new edifice, and set up a revolving fund of half a million pesos for immediate purchase of all silver. In 1732, the quality or grade of the silver in the coinage was reduced from 11 dineros 4 granos (268 grains) to a straight 11 dineros. In effect this meant that 69³/₁₀ rls. could be cut from a mark. Yet at the same time the price paid by the mint to the public was reduced from 65 rls. to 64 rls. 2 maravedis. The remainder went to the Crown. A further devaluation in the fineness of the coinage occurred in 1772 when the silver quality fell to 10 ds. 20 grs. (260 grains) and again in 1786 when the grade was stabilised at 10 ds. 18 grs. Profits from this debasement, although great, were of course occasional and in no sense approached the annual yield. . . .

The Crown's monopoly of the third stage of Mexico's national industry weighed heavily upon the producers of the raw material. For the northern mines especially the cost in time was high: at Catorce or Durango miners might have to wait six months for the return of their silver in specie. The tardy development of the Sonoran minefields in part sprang from the Crown's insistence that silver could only be minted in Mexico City. It was only during the 1790s that this burden was lightened. In that decade each treasury established a revolving fund of specie with which to purchase silver directly when the miners presented it for taxation. Discounts on this exchange still varied according to proximity to Mexico City. In Guanajuato miners received 62 rls. 25 ms., whereas in Durango the treasury paid 62 rls. 17 ms.

The Crown's new-found efficiency and flexibility further benefited the industry when during his Visitation Gálvez installed salaried officials to manage the production and sale of gunpowder, hitherto farmed out to private individuals. He reduced the price from 8 rls. to 6 rls. a pound. A large factory was constructed outside Mexico City, which employed 80 workers, and which in 1801 produced over 786,000 pounds of gunpowder. It was in that same year that the price was further lowered to 4 rls. a pound.

Finally, miners were exempted from paying the alcabalas, or sales tax, upon their raw materials and supplies. The new customs department, established in 1776, first tried to collect a 6 per cent duty on nearly all the materials used by both miners and refiners. But in 1781 in response to the industry's vigorous protest, the viceroy, Mayorga decreed that all mining instruments should be relieved of the excise. Four years later this exemption was extended to all raw materials needed for smelting and amalgamation. The excise officials protested against the concessions, and controversy between government departments as to the precise extension of these alcabala exemptions persisted until 1810. Dispute especially centered upon the maize brought into camps to feed the mules and workers employed by the industry. To encourage important discoveries, moreover, the Crown frequently granted temporary relief from all excise duties. Both Catorce in 1779 and Guarisamey in 1787 enjoyed total exemption from these imposts for periods of up to four years.

In general, therefore, in the decades that followed the Gálvez Visitation, royal policy towards the Mexican silver mining industry became more flexible and more intelligent. Old burdens were lightened or eliminated, and a series of extraordinary fiscal subsidies were extended to individual miners and particular camps. These concessions, general and particular alike, were justified in the official mind by the argument that all tax or monopoly price reductions had resulted in an increased production of such proportion that overall tax yield and monopoly profits, instead of declining, almost immediately augmented. Moreover, mintage profits rose steadily. In all the Spanish Crown gained [in 1789 a net revenue of 4,569,973 pesos] from the Mexican silver industry.

It is estimated that taxation and mintage charges absorbed 16⅔ per cent of all silver produced. But since part of the mint profits were gained by a slight debasement of the coinage the actual total levy upon the miner was closer to 13 per cent.

iii

Mexican mine-workers, far from being the oppressed peons of legend, constituted a free, well-paid, geographically mobile labor force which in many areas acted as the virtual partners of the owners. . . . The rapidity with which new discoveries such as Bolaños and Catorce were able within a few years to attract and sustain populations of 12,000 and 20,000 persons indicates the mobility of the northern mine-worker. These men were largely mulattoes and mestizos. . . .

The vast majority of Mexican miners—they did not number more than 45,000 individuals—worked voluntarily. Draft Indian labor was still recruited, however, especially in camps such as Real del Monte and Pachuca that lay near to Mexico City. The Count of Regla obtained a levy of 4 per cent of the male labor force from all villages that lay within a 30-mile radius of Real del Monte. But the alcaldes mayores, the hacendados, and the parish priests of the area all resisted his demands, arguing that their Indians were best suited for agriculture. Elsewhere other miners appealed for these levies. But even where such Indians were recruited they served as little more than auxiliary workers. Within the Mexican mining industry at large the role of drafted Indian labor dwindled to insignificant proportions during the course of the eighteenth century. . . .

The system of payment for free labor varied from camp to camp. The most common practice was to give all workers, be they pick and blast men . . . or porters and whim-minders, a standard 4 rls. a day. This rate may be compared to the earnings of hacienda peons who earned 1½ to 2 rls. a day together with food and land. But what attracted men to mining was not their daily wage but a share in the ore. The size of these *partidos*, as the shares were called, also varied greatly. In Guanajuato and Real del Monte, once the worker finished a fixed daily quota of ore, he could split the remainder cut during that day on equal terms with the owner. It was the foreman's task to ensure that neither party was ill-done by the division. In other camps workers took a percentage on all the mineral they produced. At Zacatecas and further north this amounted to a quarter of the total, but at Tlalpujahua José de la Borda only paid a twelfth. In the early days at Catorce this proportion rose to as much as a third, and even a half. But when partidos became so large the workers did not usually receive a wage; at Bolaños, for example, all they were paid was a third of the ore. This latter arrangement resembled the practice common throughout the industry whereby impoverished owners took their workers into partnership, granting them half the mineral and paying little more than overhead costs, such as drainage. But this could easily ruin a mine, since the pickmen, *buscones* as they were called, were soon tempted to destroy the ore-bearing pillars which alone prevented the collapse of the work tunnels. Whatever the method of payment most Mexican mine-workers expected a share of the product, and at all times tried to hide the richest ore in their own bags. Several efforts were made to reform the system but without success, since the miners were notoriously unruly and riot-prone. Many owners, therefore, suffered the mortification of seeing their mines' best mineral sold by their employees to independent refiners.

In the sphere of labor relations, as elsewhere, the Gálvez Visitation inaugurated a new stage. The ruthless suppression of the revolts in San Luis Potosí and Guanajuato, combined with the subsequent enrollment of the respectable classes into regiments of militia, strengthened the power of the mine-owners over their workers. In general, discipline became more stringent and in some camps earnings were reduced. At Real del Monte, for example, the Count of Regla attempted both to cut the daily wages of the peons from 4 to 3 rls. and to reduce the share of ore received by the pickmen. But in response, his men went on strike, closed down the Veta Vizcaína mines, and murdered the local magistrate. Francisco Javier de Gamboa, at that time a judge in the Mexican audiencia, was sent to arbitrate. He restored much of the old order, since he stipulated that all employees, peons as well as pickmen, should be paid 4 rls. a day. As before, foremen were to assign variable quotas according to the type of mineral, especial care being taken to prevent workers reserving for themselves the richest ore. Both the porters and the laborers who repaired the tunnel and shaft supports were entitled to cut up to a bag of ore, subject, however, to division with their employer. Clearly a Mexican mine operated as much for the benefit of its workers as for the owner.

In Guanajuato, on the other hand, the Rayas mine successfully suppressed the payment of all partidos. But other mines only slowly followed this example. It was not until the early 1790s that the great Valenciana mine terminated the practice, being then obliged to more than double the wages of the pickmen. By 1803 they received 10 rls. a day instead of their former 4 rls. and partido. In Zacatecas a similar movement to reduce labor costs occurred. When in 1767 José de la Borda went to that town he took advantage of the current unemployment to reduce the daily wage from the former 6 rls. to the more standard 4 rls. He also lowered the workers' share in all ore produced from a quarter to an eighth. Later, during the first decade of the next century, the new owners of the Quebradilla finally succeeded in eliminating payment of all partidos. The workers in vain petitioned the viceroy to restore the old system. It appears, therefore, that in the years following the Gálvez Visitation Mexican mine-owners launched a concerted attack upon what they considered to be the excessively high earnings of their labor force. Nevertheless in most camps, especially in the north, workers still received a large share of ore and acted as virtual partners if not active rivals of the mine owners.

iv

Within the Mexican mining industry a great variety prevailed, both in the size of enterprises and in the degree of vertical integration. It was the great mines, however, such as the Veta Vizcaína and the Valenciana, which attracted travellers' attention. Yet not all these mines refined their own mineral. True, Regla at Real del Monte and the Fagoagas at Sombrerete operated vertically integrated concerns, but at Guanajuato and Catorce the great mines frequently sold a considerable part of their ore to independent refiners. In Zacatecas most mines also possessed refining mills, but even there the partners of the Quebradilla shared out the mine's ore among themselves for individual refining.

In addition to these great enterprises the industry contained a host of small mines, in the same camps or on isolated lodes, whose owners were frequently obliged to sell their metal at once in order to obtain cash to meet their operating costs. Then again workers always sold their *partidos*. So a natural component of the industry was the independent refiner, or *rescatador*. These men bought at the pithead, after merely handling the ore. The prices they paid depended upon competition and their own informal valuation but were in general sufficiently low for them to make considerable profits. Clearly at times if his guess proved wrong, the refiner lost money, but his losses, unlike those of the miner were marginal and cumulative, never total. An English observer stated: "The great mine-owners of Mexico generally speaking, formerly gained more by the haciendas [refining mills] than by their mines."

Simple miners, refiners and integrated enterprises all required financial backers or *aviadores*. In 1772 a knowledgeable report claimed that only twelve miners could finance their own operations. Similarly, since independent refiners had to pay cash for all ore, then they too were obliged either to sell their silver at once or to find an aviador. Miners especially suffered from lack of support; most merchants preferred to back refiners, and when they did support miners they demanded payment every eight to fifteen days, and were quick to cut off credit if a mine ceased to produce. It was for this reason that many miners were forced to sell their ore as soon as it was produced.

The aviador, therefore, usually a local merchant, was an indispensable third agent in the industry. He supplied miners with iron, wood, leather and mules, and refiners with salt, copper pyrites, lime, maize and mercury. He charged these commodities upon account at current market price; upon European goods he added 25 per cent to invoice cost upon landing. In addition the aviador paid the libranzas drawn upon him when the refiner or miner bought his own material. He also advanced the refiner the necessary cash with which to buy ore. In return for this financial backing all silver produced was sold to the aviador at a discount. Formal contracts were rare, balances were struck at infrequent intervals, and nothing was more common than for miners or refiners to overdraw their account. Many an aviador by progressive foreclosure found himself the owner of first a refining mill and then a mine. In mining, as distinct from refining, some aviadores took shares in mines from the outset. They then participated in overall profits rather than charging a discount on the silver. They still, however, received the normal commercial profit on the materials they supplied. . . .

In general Mexican mining suffered from a chronic lack of both credit for operating costs and capital for fixed investments. Whereas the industry had reached a stage where heavy fixed capital investment in the form of deep shafts, long adits and massive refining mills were all necessary, the merchant-aviadores upon whom the majority of miners depended preferred to supply only short-term credit to meet operating costs. Many merchants took no risk at all but simply purchased silver on the open market. Clearly the effects of the *comercio libre* decree of 1778 were all important: it drove mercantile capital into Mexican silver mining precisely at a time when the industry most needed it and when, moreover, it could justify such investments by the increased rate of profitability which the several tax and monopoly price reductions conceded by Gálvez had promoted. Mining profits rose and commercial profits fell. Former aviadores and silver merchants then directly entered the industry's productive stages which hitherto they had eschewed.

V

Any explanation for the great Mexican boom must be tentative. Let us record two contemporary opinions. In 1793 Viceroy Revillagigedo wrote; "The causes of this increase are not that there have been greater bonanzas, nor that the ore is of higher quality: it is caused chiefly by the greater number of persons who have devoted themselves to mining, to the small advance made in the manner of working them, to the conveniences in the price of mercury, the reduction in gunpowder and the exemptions from salestax." He also pointed to the formation of mercantile companies to exploit some older mines.

In 1803 Humboldt largely agreed with Revillagigedo.

> The enormous expansion in the produce of the mines observable in latter years is to be attributed to a great number of causes all acting at the same time, and among which the first place assigned must be to the growth in population on the tableland of Mexico, the progress of knowledge and national industry, the freedom of trade conceded to America in 1778, the facility of procuring at a cheaper rate the iron and steel necessary for the mines, the fall in the price of mercury, the discovery of the mines of Catorce and Valenciana, and the establishment of the *tribunal de minería.*

Clearly, in this hunt for causes, the Mexican viceroy scored over the Prussian traveller. Several of Humboldt's agents were simply concurrent phenomena. At best, the growth in population formed but a prerequisite; and as for *comercio libre* its success may well have been the effect of the rise in silver output. Revillagigedo pointed more precisely to the question of costs and the entrance of capital and entrepreneurs into the industry. Now it is necessary to be quite clear about what one is trying to explain.

There are, in this context, three facts which demand explanation. The first is the century-long upward curve in silver production: in each succeeding decade, with the single exception of the 1760s, more silver was minted. Secondly, the great spurt forward of the 1770s, in which production leapt from 12 million to 18 million pesos a year. Thirdly, the maintenance of this new level, followed by another slow rise. We here ignore the yearly fluctuations, in large part caused by British naval blockades, and drought. It is the continuous upward curve which offers the greatest difficulty and which in part works to refute several possible lines of argument. It especially illumines the danger of the *post hoc propter hoc* fallacy. The efficacy of any particular measure, be it *comercio libre* or the Jesuit expulsion, could always be proved by the subsequent increase in silver production. This, needless to say, was a favorite manner of argument among both statesmen and miners of the period, wishing to laud a favored measure or to secure further concessions. Clearly it is absurd to invoke one cause to explain a century-long process. At different times different agents worked to produce the same effect.

Granted these difficulties, it seems best to concentrate upon the boom of the 1770s which followed the recession of the 1760s. Here we can perceive several factors at work which combined to create a significant lowering of production costs sufficient to increase profits quite considerably. In mining itself, owners gained a greater control over their workers, and in some cases were able to reduce their partidos and wages. Then the more extensive use of gunpowder was encouraged by a cut in price and a more efficient supply. Finally, several risky enterprises were encouraged by tax exemptions. The refining industry benefited equally. The cheaper and more abundant supply of mercury led to a greater reliance upon amalgamation as against smelting. At the same time the local price of silver bar rose appreciably. Here again, individual exemptions included a further reduction in mercury to 30 ps. By contrast the industry's merchant-aviadores experienced a setback. Trading profits in general and premiums on silver in particular both fell during the 1780s. Here, then, is a possible causal sequence. The great boom of the 1770s sprang both from general cost reductions affecting all the industry and from a remarkable series of concurrent bonanzas in particular mines. Then, in the 1780s this boom was sustained and pushed still further by the widespread entrance of mercantile capital into the industry and matched by a greater willingness to plough back mining profits. Moreover, an increasing number of miners and companies in the older camps obtained tax exemptions. Now all these cost reductions may well have acted as so much bait; quite possibly it was the entrance of investment capital which made the difference. Proofs, however, are lacking. In the last resort until long-term account books are discovered and studied, any explanation must remain, at best, hypothetical.

7

The Rural Economy

Eric Van Young

Agriculture for local or regional markets continued to ebb and flow in response to demands from urban, mining, or intercolonial markets, or remained at a subsistence level. The silver mine and the rural estate were closely related. Agriculture supplied the mines, fed their workers, and provided horsepower and transport. Successful mineowners invested their profits in large estates, thereby acquiring social prestige and alternative products. Both were linked to the export sector, which generated further profits, not only for buying imports but also for investing in mining and agriculture. Landed estates produced primarily for colonial markets. For most colonial people, producing for the domestic market and consuming American products constituted the whole of their economic life. Population growth among Indians and mestizos meant not only more labor but also more mouths to feed and greater pressure on the land. Many Indian villages still possessed sufficient land to support themselves and even to produce a surplus; and in regions like the Bajío of Mexico smallholders survived. Most rural laborers, however, were tenants or sharecroppers, tied to the hacienda in one form or another and subject to the pressures of prices, profits, and periodic crises of subsistence. The performance of agriculture, the profits of hacendados, and the living conditions of campesinos are known for particular regions, but Eric Van Young, Professor of History at the University of California, San Diego, the historian of late colonial Guadalajara, here takes a synoptic view of Mexican agriculture and assesses its place in the background to independence.

Reprinted from Eric Van Young, "The Age of Paradox: Mexican Agriculture at the End of the Colonial Period," Nils Jacobsen and Hans-Jürgen Puhle (eds.), *The Economies of Mexico and Peru during the Late Colonial Period, 1760–1810* (Colloquium Verlag, Berlin, 1986), pp. 64–65, 67–70, 71–83, by permission of the author and editors.

i

The eighteenth century was, for Mexico, an age of paradox. . . . In no
aspect of Mexican life of the period was this characteristic more
marked than in rural economic structure. Thus, for example, while
absolute levels of agricultural and livestock production seem to have
risen considerably, productivity—that is, the relative capacity to produce of a given unit of capital, land, or labor—seems to have stagnated or grown little. Rising prices for agricultural and livestock
products made large-scale agriculture more profitable, while declining real wages for farm labor helped produce a general scenario of
rural impoverishment and proletarianization. Large landholdings
seem to have grown more valuable and effectively larger, and small
ones smaller. While agricultural surpluses grew and commercialization spread through the countryside, crises of death and famine
seemed to come more frequently and to be of greater magnitude.
Rural population grew precipitously, but poverty was ever more
widespread. . . .

Agriculture was the step-child in the age of enlightened despotism—
it was almost totally neglected by the Bourbon reformers, both in a
philosophical and a practical way. Compared with the perceptible restructuring of activity that occurred under the impact of the Bourbon
reforms in bureaucratic organization, fiscal policy, international and
domestic commerce, and to some degree in the mining sector, state-
induced change in agriculture was minimal. The agricultural economy
was thus the passive recipient of effects produced in other sectors of
the colonial economy which were directly affected. David Brading has
suggested, for example, that one result of reduced trade restrictions
within the Empire beginning in the 1770s was to drive mercantile capital out of international commerce, where it had enjoyed strongly monopolistic advantages and concomitantly high profits, and into large-
scale landownership. Other investigators, on the other hand, have
pointed to the continuing functional links between large-scale commerce and landownership to the very end of the colonial period, since
the business of agriculture often required a constant injection of capital
to yield its unspectacular but steady profits. The relationship suggested by the latter situation, then, would be one not so much of
capital flight or self-liquidation as of constant symbiosis. Whatever
interpretation one elects, it seems clear that the late colonial commercial boom was stimulated by population growth and imperial
trade reform, and that commercial capital in turn was made available
to finance agriculture.

ii

Although it would be difficult, if not impossible, to construct figures regarding productivity in agriculture for the last half-century of the colonial era, it seems reasonable to say that overall increases in production can be ascribed to higher levels of capital investment and labor inputs, rather than technological improvements or new production arrangements. . . . Capital investment in market-orientated agriculture, especially among large and middling haciendas, seems to have moved up and in; that is to say, from the mass of the rural population towards large landowners, and from the countryside to the city. Low rural wages partially underwrote the profitability of investment in large-scale agriculture, and in turn fed the burgeoning cities of the realm. Under such circumstances, the landholding elite, new and old, exacted a kind of brokerage fee in the transfer of resources from country to city in the form of profits on agricultural investment. Wages lagged behind prices for agricultural commodities and manufactured goods, creating an available surplus for a form of primitive accumulation which fueled some forms of economic development, albeit in a truncated way.

Capital investment in commercial agriculture apparently tended to assume the form of land acquisition, where possible; or of *mise-en-valeur* of land previously underutilized; or of the expansion of a technology already basically in place. One common form of the latter process was the pattern of crop successions and displacements typical of areas of commercial agriculture. In the valley of Mexico, for example, Tutino has noted the northward displacement of stock raising in the late eighteenth century in favor of *pulque* production and other more intensive activities which grew up in response to the expanding market of Mexico City. Similarly, in the Guadalajara region and Bajío tillage expanded at the expense of livestock raising, and wheat cultivation at the expense of maize, while in large parts of Michoacán, considerable capital was invested in irrigation works. Land values rose, particularly in the commercial agricultural sector, not just owing to the passive processes of population growth and the limitation of resources, but also due to active capital investment, much of it supported by landowner borrowing from the church. In the case of the Guadalajara region increases of several hundred percent in the value of major grain-producing haciendas were not uncommon. For example, the important Hacienda de Atequiza, near Lake Chapala, grew 800 percent in value between 1725 and 1821, and the great Hacienda del Cabezón, further to the west, increased in value by 300 per cent in the thirty years between 1763 and 1793. By way of contrast, rural wages remained virtually stable during the eighteenth century, while maize prices barely doubled between 1700 and 1810. Capital continued to flow into large-scale agriculture, as we have noted above, from the mining and commercial sectors of the colonial economy, supporting traditional elite status aspirations and the optimizing strategy of economic diversification so characteristic of late colonial family enterprises. The late colonial rise in production levels was created principally by capital investment in dams, irrigation works, storage facilities, etc.; by the intensification of existing technologies; and by increased labor inputs. Productivity increases ascribable to the natural fertility of previously unworked lands being brought into production were probably offset by the fact that most prime arable land in the more heavily populated parts of Mexico had already long since been occupied. The development or application of new technologies—of new multipliers of human effort—in late colonial agriculture, such as the fallowing practices, fertilizers, or crop rotations which characterized the "new husbandry" in northern Europe, were scarcely to be found in New Spain or elsewhere in Latin America. At the end of the colonial period contemporary observers, such as Baron von Humboldt, noted the relative backwardness of Mexican agricultural technology even within the commercial sector. Attempts at state-directed innovation in agriculture were not particularly successful. Even capital-intensive, specialized agricultural industries, such as sugar production, tended to experience improvement in very small increments, if at all. In the specific case of sugar there were technological innovations, especially in the milling processes but these seem to have been zealously guarded and remained of local impact only. . . .

iii

The growth of population in eighteenth-century New Spain seems to have fueled a certain amount of economic expansion while at the same time imposing limits on that very expansion. The increase of rural population in particular, through the process of migration, contributed to the growth of Mexican cities at rates considerably in excess of the natural, thus stimulating the economic division of labor within the country while providing larger markets of agricultural products. This was notably the case with the viceregal capital, which grew from a population of about 100,000 in around 1742, to nearly double that number in 1810, but it also occurred in other regional capitals. For example, Guadalajara, which had a population of about 5,000 in 1700, had increased to some 35–40,000 by 1800, or roughly double the size one would expect to see assuming a natural rate of increase in the 1700 population of even 4 percent annually. Moreover, the growth of this provincial capital was concentrated most strongly in the period after 1750, during which the city nearly quadrupled in size. Much of this growth was the result of migration from the countryside around the city. Other provincial cities, if they experienced less dramatic rates of growth during the later eighteenth century, nonetheless increased in size substantially, such as Guanajuato, which tripled in size to reach some 90,000 between 1742 and 1809, and Querétaro, which doubled its population (from about 25,000 to 50,000 inhabitants) between 1750 and 1800. Intra-regional migration, then, played an important part in the creation of market opportunities—even though the market thus created may have possessed a relatively low consumer power—by achieving a partial horizontal shift in population.

There is evidence, however, that the same demographic expansion which helped to stimulate the colonial economy by depressing wage levels and contributing to urban growth was flagging by the end of the colonial period as a result of Malthusian pressures. To cite the case of the Guadalajara region once again, the rate of aggregate population growth, combining a recovery in the Indian population (after its nadir in the seventeenth century) with increase of non-Indian groups, hit well over 2 percent by the early eighteenth century, but lost its momentum by the close of the colonial period, dropping to 0.7 per cent in the decade 1800–1810, and recovering only slightly in the following decade. Other areas in New Spain showed the same general upsurge during the seventeenth and eighteenth centuries, and the same tendency to reduce their rates of growth in the last decades of the colonial era. Demographic analyses for San Luis de la Paz and León, both in the Bajío, corroborate this overall trend in population movement, as do those for parts of Oaxaca. Within the overall trend of increasing population, but with a decline in the rate of increase setting in at the end of the colonial era, shifts also occurred in the ethnic composition of the Mexican population, though with strong regional variations. The valley of Oaxaca, for example, remained heavily Indian to the end of the period despite major demographic strides by non-Indian groups in the population. In the middling case, the population of the Guadalajara region was divided almost equally between Indians and white and mixed-blood groups by the close of the colonial period, while that of large parts of the Bajío was becoming predominantly mestizo. This would have important implications for regional agrarian structures, particularly for the resilience of Indian landholding communities, the degree of commercialization in agriculture, and the extent of rural proletarianization and proto-industrialization.

The reasons for the slackening in Mexican population growth toward the end of the colonial period are not altogether clear as yet.
David Brading and Elsa Malvido, among others, have suggested that
variations in the death rate, especially in the Indian segment of the
population, rather than changes in fertility or other factors account for
the characteristic "old regime" demographic movements one sees during the last century of colonial rule. These patterns include periodically sharp increases in mortality—e.g., 1690s, 1730s, 1760s, 1780s
(though unevenly distributed among the major ethnic components of
the general population)—linked to epidemic disease and subsistence
crises, and an equally marked tendency for high birth rates and the
ability for the population to reestablish relatively rapid rates of growth
after each crisis. Although changes in mortality do account convin-
cingly for general population movements during the period, it is impossible to explain the demographic retrogression of the late eighteenth
century by reference to the inherent severity of disease and famine
alone. Indeed, it is difficult to see that the incidence of disease and
famine increased significantly during the late eighteenth century over
the early part of the century, or even over the seventeenth. What *did*
change during the period, however, were the relative relationships of
different sectors of the population to the means of production, and the
relationship of the Mexican population as a whole to environmental
resources. Contemporaries certainly noted the demographic effects of
recurrent disease and famine. . . . Alexander von Humboldt, on his part,
ascribed much of the social malaise of New Spain, despite the country's abundant resources, to the highly skewed distribution of wealth.

It is with reference to distributional factors, then, that one must seek
to explain the severe effects of late colonial subsistence crises and
epidemic disease on the Mexican population.[1] Enrique Florescano has
mapped and traced these episodes for the eighteenth century. In addition to describing the dislocative effects of recurrent subsistence crises
linked to occurrences of epidemic disease—rising incidence of vaga-
bondage and crime, labor problems, disruptions in mining, manufacturing, and agricultural activities—he emphasizes the periodicity of
such crises, the increasingly wild fluctuations in maize production and
prices which characterized them, and the secular trend of rising maize
prices which set in after 1790 or so. The most serious and so far the best
studied of these late colonial breakdowns was that of the famous *año
de hambre* of 1785–1786, in which agricultural dearth combined with
epidemic disease produced truly lethal effects over much of New
Spain. It is true that such cycles in New Spain tended during the late
colonial period to correspond with those in Europe, lending some

weight to the argument that meteorological and other factors extrinsic to the Mexican economy were in part responsible for the demographic slow-down visible after 1760 or so. Nonetheless, it is important to note that such mortal episodes were frequent in the era before the population break-down, that they demonstrated a relative intensity on occasion equal to or greater than those of the later period, and that after them population still continued its rapid upward climb. What had changed by the late eighteenth century, and what aggravated the effects of dearth and disease, was the economic situation of the mass of the Mexican population, especially in rural areas. Increasing rural proletarianization, declining real wages, growing concentration of property in land, and a number of related socio-economic factors combined to make the popular classes even more vulnerable to the effects of epidemic and subsistence crises. . . .

iv

The most important key to the late colonial situation seems to have been the growth of population in many regions of New Spain relative to available land resources—that is, an increasing concentration in land-ownership. . . . By the time the [Indian] population recovery of the period 1650–1750 began to put significant pressure on agricultural resources, most readily cultivable land had been pre-empted by Indian communities themselves and by non-Indian estates. As the eighteenth century progressed, and with it an increasing development of large-scale capitalist agriculture, the chafing between growing numbers of peasant villagers and estate-owners became even more notable. Litigation, violence, land invasions, and enclosure seem to have increased in frequency in a number of major agricultural regions of New Spain. Minor adjustments were made in the boundaries of already-existing haciendas in many areas of the country, but remarkably few new properties were created by agglomeration of smaller parcels or by large scale expropriation of Indian lands, as studies of the valley of Mexico, the Puebla-Tlaxcala area, the Bajío, and the Guadalajara region have all shown. More specifically, the ownership histories of individual rural estates indicate that major land acquisitions for the most part preceded 1750, or even 1700. . . . What occurred during the growth phase of large-scale Mexican agriculture in the latter part of the eighteenth century was a process of internal colonization of estates already established during the preceding centuries, and not the creation of a land-hungry, aggressive commercial agriculture out of whole cloth.

Rural agrarian structure, at the end of the colonial period, demon-

strated a more complex distribution of types of production units than
just large haciendas and Indian villages. Particularly in the north-
central and western-central parts of New Spain—in the Bajío, in Michoacán, and in New Galicia—smallholdings survived in considerable
numbers in the countryside on the margins of the large hacienda, often
enjoying independent juridical status as individually owned *ranchos*.
But also in the valley of Oaxaca, where Indian landholding remained
relatively more important in the total land tenure picture than elsewhere, small non-Indian owned properties were numerous, and may
even have increased in number, if not in aggregate size, during the
eighteenth century. Indeed, such small properties, sandwiched in
socio-economically along with small provincial merchants and other
rural middlemen between landholding Indian communities and large,
commercially oriented estates, served to articulate peasant and capitalist modes of production in important ways. In some areas renting and
sharecropping arrangements abounded, so that even where legal title to
agricultural lands had already been preempted by the owners of large
estates, effective units of production were more numerous than might
be expected. In fact, as has been demonstrated for parts of the Bajío and
Michoacán, while hacendados often worked their *demesne* farms, income from rentals and sharecropping formed important parts of overall
hacienda revenues, with the terms of such arrangements generally
shifting in favor of large landowners towards the close of the colonial
period. . . .

v

For purposes of the present essay, the most important questions to be
answered about the late colonial rural labor system are two. First, to
what degree was it dominated by the institution of debt peonage, and
how widespread and exploitative was the practice? Second, in what
way did labor, considered as a component of the agricultural production process, contribute to late colonial agrarian development?

   Viewed as a whole the evidence on debt peonage suggests that where
labor was in short supply, either because of a manpower scarcity or
because of a strong peasant subsistence sector which offered viable
economic alternatives to large numbers of potential rural laborers,
peonage could be relatively harsh. Where manpower was plentiful, on
the other hand, the logistics of maintaining a permanent estate labor
might necessitate some degree of debt peonage, but on the whole the
institution was likely to be less pervasive and less harsh. . . .

   Much of the most recent research on rural labor during the colonial period tends to the view that debt peonage was neither as widespread nor as harsh as historians had previously believed, subject, of course, to the qualifications stated above regarding regional differences. There are two major reasons for this. In the first place . . . debt represented not so much a coercive mechanism on the part of labor-recruiting land-owners, as a reflection of a strong bargaining position on the part of rural laborers, growing out of the labor-scarce conditions of the seventeenth century. Thus, debt levels would logically vary directly with the strength of labor's bargaining power, the major determinant of which would be the availability of labor. Under such conditions, one would expect to see a decline in overall indebtedness when labor became more abundant and a concomitant weakening of the laborers' positions. This is precisely what happened in many areas in the late colonial period, when population increased relative to the land base of independent peasant farming and the needs of expanding commercial agriculture, as in the Guadalajara region in western central Mexico. The resultant conditions for rural wage labor might indeed be harsh, but as a result of the weakening of debt peonage, not its health. In the second place, many researchers have noted the increasing relative importance of temporary wage labor, drawn in large measure from Indian peasant villages where shortages of land prevailed at the end of the eighteenth century. In many areas such laborers were at a disadvantage compared to resident debt peons, since they enjoyed no perquisites on rural estates, no protection, and sometimes no regular rations as part of their wages.

The preceding discussion provides the rudiments of an answer to the second question regarding the late colonial rural labor system, that of its role in the commercial agricultural expansion of the period. Put simply, the growth of rural population and the static land base of peasant farmers and villages increased the available labor pool during the late colonial years and insured that rural wages did not rise in money terms, thereby effectively depressing real wages. The evidence for such a trend is unequivocal and comes from all over New Spain, and even parts of the north and near north, where labor remained in relatively less abundance. Cheap labor thus supported the expansion of commercialized large-scale agriculture and largely eliminated the need for technological innovation. Productivity may have remained low, but so did wages, even though labor costs made up a high percentage of overall production costs. These conditions, in the evocative phrase of Charles Harris, created a situation in which "the peon pretended to work and the master pretended to pay him."

vi

If eighteenth-century haciendas were frequently sprawling, under-utilized properties with markedly patriarchal social structures, they nonetheless typically demonstrated a high degree of market participation. Sidestepping here the issue of whether such characteristics made the late colonial rural estate capitalist or feudal in nature (or both), we can still assert that the earning of profits through the maximization of their market position seems to have been uppermost in the minds of hacendados. . . . The apparent "feudalization" of much of Mexican agriculture which set in during the seventeenth century in response to population shrinkage and economic decline was simply an adaptive response to prevailing conditions, rather than the acting out of seigneurial ideals on a Mexican *tabula rasa.* When a favorable conjunction of circumstances offered itself in the last century of colonial rule—a mining resurgence, increased availability of investment capital, population growth, and expansion of markets—large-scale agriculture responded appropriately.

The late colonial trade in agricultural products and livestock is difficult to trace with any precision, but it is clear that it could extend both to regional and inter-regional markets, as well as the more familiar trans-oceanic markets for dyestuffs and other rarefied products. . . . One would normally expect that Mexico City, given its size and pre-eminence within New Spain, would be the center of a far-flung hinterland and the crystallization point for a developing commercial agriculture. . . . By the same token, one would naturally expect to see mining centers, with their specialized non-agricultural work forces, emerge as important markets for the products of the countryside. What is less well studied, though hardly surprising, is the structure of major intra-regional markets centered on provincial capitals and other cities, which grew considerably, albeit unsteadily, as the pace of urbanization advanced in the period after 1750 or so. Cities such as Guanajuato, Valladolid, San Miguel, Querétaro, and Guadalajara consumed substantial amounts of maize, wheat, and livestock products annually, not to mention the garden crops typically supplied by Indian and other peasant farmers. An important provincial urban market tended to function as the central place around which the internal socio-economic integration of an entire region might crystallize, and with it regional political and cultural identity. Furthermore the structure of local market demand tended to have a strong influence on the structure of production and landholding, typically exerting pressure in the direction of production and land concentration. Smaller producers, among them the Indian farmers of communal villages and other, non-Indian independent peasants, tended to be at a definite disadvantage *vis-a-vis* the bigger urban markets, though they sold surprisingly large quantities of grain in provincial cities and towns, particularly maize. Larger producers enjoyed advantages perhaps out of all proportion to the economic efficiency of their farming, since they commonly were able to exercise control over the market by holding back their produce until prices rose, and interfered with the structure of urban supply through their political power. . . .

vii

The latter part of the eighteenth century in Mexico, then, was one of contradiction. A considerable degree of economic expansion and prosperity was present, but also an increasing amount of rural proletarianization and impoverishment. . . . Gross indicators of agricultural prosperity—rising prices, rising tithe collections, increasing stability of ownership of large estates, rising levels of profits and investment in large-scale agriculture—pointed to economic growth, but signs of rural impoverishment and a fall in living standards for the rural masses in many parts of New Spain attested to how that growth was achieved. In terms of the two distributional variables—vertical (class/ethnic) and horizontal (geographical)—the period saw an ever-increasing skewing in the social distribution of wealth in favor of large landowners and their allies; a probable transfer of economic resources from the countryside to the city; and a northward shift in the economic center of gravity of New Spain as a whole. What is not clear as yet is the relationship of these developments to the situation of Mexico after Independence. On the whole, the conditions of the country until the later nineteenth century—economic decline and stagnation, slow demographic growth, ruralization, political Balkanization and instability—lend weight to the view that a prolonged crisis had begun under cover of the prosperity of the late colonial era, and continued for the first half-century of the republican period.

At the end of the period under discussion we have the Mexican Wars for Independence. Given the evolution of the Mexican rural economy during the last half-century of colonial rule, it seems impossible to view that prolonged violent episode as a mere political epiphenomenon floating freely on the socio-economic substrate of New Spain. The social redistribution of wealth noted by so many historians of the eighteenth century must surely have played a role in creating pre-conditions for the rural rebellion which was such a prominent component of the wars of Independence. The strains attendant upon changes in agrarian structure in many parts of the country have been noted often. More particularly, the embattled status of the independent, landholding Indian village and its tendency to assume a hostile posture with regard to outsiders becomes increasingly apparent at the close of the eighteenth century. It seems probable, then, that secular changes in agrarian structure contributed something to the motive force behind rebellion against the colonial regime. But it must also be noted that agrarian issues— land reform, for example—played very little explicit role in the ideological and programmatic expressions of the rebels. To make the connection between long-term agrarian conditions and revolt, therefore, one must look to intervening variables, and the code of symbolic expression, in order to decipher the relationship between the way rural people thought and the way they lived.

8

The Era of Free Trade

John Fisher

Comercio libre has a special meaning in Spanish imperial history, indicating not the free trade of Adam Smith but the protectionist policy of Bourbon planners. Their aim was to expand the colonial market, tax it, and control it. With this in mind they reorganized colonial trade to free it for Spaniards and close it to foreigners. Between 1765 and 1776 they lowered taxes, abolished the monopoly of Cádiz and Seville, opened free communications between the ports of the peninsula and the Caribbean and its mainland, and authorized inter-colonial trade. In 1778 the new system was extended to include Buenos Aires, Chile, and Peru, and in 1789 Venezuela and Mexico. The purpose of *comercio libre* was the development of Spain rather than America, yet it was America rather than Spain that responded most to the new opportunities for exports. This is the conclusion of John Fisher, Professor of Latin American History and Director of the Institute of Latin American Studies in the University of Liverpool, who not only measures the value, distribution, and nature of the trade between Spain and Spanish America in the last quarter of the eighteenth century, but also assesses the results of free trade for the economies of both. The aim of the following section is to evaluate the imperial response to free trade "by means of an examination of American exports to Spain in the period up to 1796." The study can also be read for an understanding of the colonial economies behind the transatlantic trade. The author suggests that the economic growth of Spanish America released by free trade was capable of even further extension, until from 1797 Spain's international difficulties and internal divisions halted the new policy and made Spanish Americans aware that the prospect of further growth could not

Reprinted from John Fisher, *Commercial Relations between Spain and Spanish America in the Era of Free Trade, 1778–1796* (Institute of Latin American Studies, University of Liverpool, Monograph Series, No. 13, 1985), pp. 9–10, 13–15, 73–83, 87–89, by permission of the author.

be realized within the imperial framework. Moreover, American growth enhanced the opportunities and privileges of Spanish immigrants and merchants rather than those of their creole rivals.

i

It is clear from an examination of the origins of American goods shipped to Spain in the late eighteenth century that the viceroyalty of New Spain was the richest and most productive region in the empire. The port of Vera Cruz alone provided the mother country with 16.6% of all its imports between 1782 and 1796, and in combination with other ports (Havana, Puerto Rico, La Guaira, and Campeche) with a further 15.5%. Campeche, Guatemala, and Honduras were responsible together for 3.9%, thus giving an overall total for New Spain of 36%. The viceroyalty's trade was primarily with two Spanish ports: Cádiz, which it provided with 39.3% of all its imports, and Barcelona (35.8% of all imports); the other enfranchised Spanish ports, by contrast, drew only 8.6% of their imports from New Spain.

The range of products exported from New Spain in the period after 1778 was extensive. Virtually every vessel which arrived in Spain from Vera Cruz carried hides, cochineal, spices, and dye-wood, and the last of these items was dominant in trade between Campeche and Spain. The fundamental explanation for the viceroyalty's dominant role in imperial commerce derives, however, not from its agricultural activities—vibrant and diversified though they were—but from the dramatic growth of its mining industry, "the showpiece of the Bourbon age." The output of the mines expanded almost fivefold in the course of the eighteenth century—from 5 million pesos a year in the 1690s to 24 million in 1798, when Mexico was producing two-thirds of all American silver—with a particularly significant increase in the 1770s, partly as a consequence of new discoveries and partly through fiscal incentives. Reductions in the price of mercury, that essential amalgamating ingredient, and institutional reforms in the 1780s, when a new mining code was introduced and a mining tribunal was established, were of considerable importance in promoting mining development, but the essential factors which explain the resurgence derive from the internal dynamics of the viceregal economy: the growth of its population by 2.5 million between 1742 and 1793 (from 3.3 to 5.8 million) provided an adequate supply of labor. More significant still was the willingness of merchant-capitalists in Mexico City to invest large sums in the development of the mines. . . . It has been argued authoritatively that the extension of free trade to New Spain in the 1780s promoted economic growth in an unintended way by persuading the great merchant families of Mexico City, whose profits from trade dwindled with the loss of their monopoly, to turn away from commerce and invest in mining and agriculture. The vacuum which they left in the commercial sector was filled by ambitious, hard-headed immigrants from northern Spain, prepared to work long hours for smaller profits, and now able to bypass the old monopoly and enjoy virtually unlimited access to the markets of the interior of the viceroyalty.

It has often been assumed that the price paid by the colonists for agricultural prosperity and an easing of commercial restrictions in the late colonial period was not only this unwelcome influx of avaricious immigrants but also the destruction of colonial industry, unable to compete with cheap, high quality European manufactures. The evidence available for the viceroyalty of New Spain does not entirely substantiate this assumption, at least for the period prior to the introduction of neutral commerce in 1797. It is true that the number of woollen factories in Puebla, Mexico City, and Coyoacán declined sharply in the course of the eighteenth century, but to a certain extent this trend was compensated—and perhaps provoked—by the growth of the woollen industry in Querétaro. By the late eighteenth century, this major commercial, agricultural and manufacturing centre, strategically located in the Bajío region, with easy access to the markets of both Mexico City and the mines of the north, and ample supplies of wool and labor, had some 20 woollen factories, with over 200 looms, in production.

Like textile manufacture everywhere, the woollen industry here was subject to often sharp fluctuations in its fortunes. A serious slump in production and sales began in 1785 (its effect continued to be felt until 1792), but it was caused less by excessive imports than by the severe agricultural crisis of that year, which, with its associated epidemics hit the Bajío particularly hard. The human population declined by 20%, and the number of sheep fell by a similar proportion (from 5 million to 4 million), causing shortages of both consumers and wool, and the prices of mules and horses doubled, factors which, in their turn, led to higher prices and poorer quality products. External trade, like domestic industry, was a victim of this crisis, as exports to and imports from Spain fell in 1786–1787 to their lowest levels since 1778. The Querétaro woollen industry, like commerce, recovered, however, from the crisis by the early 1790s to survive a further trough in 1805–1808, and even the dislocation caused by the wars of independence. Overall, it "expanded in the late eighteenth and early nineteenth century, but"—and this is an important qualification—"not in the dramatic or spectacular way usually associated with the late Bourbon period." Other trends, of general application, which need to be taken into account when assessing the state of the woollen industry are a shift in consumer preference from woollens to cottons, a factor which, in the case of New Spain, benefitted Puebla, and the decline of traditional *obrajes*, relics of the period of *repartimiento* labor, in the face of competition from smaller establishments known as *trapiches*, which, although less conspicuous, made an important contribution to cloth production.

Exports from the Spanish islands in the Caribbean, excluding those carried by ships which had begun their voyages in mainland ports, accounted for 23.2% of imports into Spain. They included shipments from Santo Domingo and Puerto Rico, which were worth a total of 101 million reales, but were dominated by those from Cuba, "the phoenix of the late Bourbon period," which added up to 2,753 million reales between 1782 and 1796. . . . The statistics relating to Cuba's economic growth in the late eighteenth century are almost overwhelming: for example, the number of sugar mills tripled from 89 to 277 between 1759 and 1789, and the average production of each mill rose 165 tons a year in 1760 to over 400 tons during a similar period: the island's slave population rose from 86,000 in 1792, the year in which the crown made permanent the temporary permission granted in 1789 for foreign ships to freely supply the island with Negroes, to 286,000 in 1827. The white population also grew significantly, partly as a result of an influx of French settlers from St. Domingue in the 1790s, and partly because of the phenomenon already noted for New Spain, the new wave of peninsular migration. There is less evidence from Cuba, however, that the new arrivals were regarded as parasites, partly because the scale of economic growth was sufficient in this period to satisfy traditional residents and newcomers alike, and partly because of the extraordinary generosity of crown policy towards the island. Although some rather ineffectual attempts were made in the early 1790s to protect the interests of Cádiz merchants by imposing restrictions upon the growth of inter-colonial trade between Havana and Vera Cruz, the general trend of crown policy was to grant Cubans all the commercial privileges that they sought, including virtual free trade with the United States from 1793, in the hope, which was fulfilled, that the grateful "sugarocracy" would shoulder the burden of imperial defense in the Caribbean. . . .

Venezuela enjoyed a sustained export boom, particularly in the 1790s when restrictions on its participation in the free trade system had been removed. Ninety-one percent of its 1,181 million reales of exports, consisting mainly of cacao, indigo, hides, and other agricultural products, reached Spain through the port of La Guaira. The remainder were shipped, in descending order of importance, from Cumaná, Maracaibo,

Guayana, and Trinidad. Together they were worth on average 51 million reales a year in the period 1782–1789, and 110 million a year in 1790–1796. Total imports from Venezuela were worth 9.6% of all American products brought into Spain between 1782 and 1796. The captaincy-general was thus of tertiary importance to New Spain and Cuba, but its contribution to the 76% of all imports received in Spain from the circum-Caribbean region as a whole was substantial. With no traditional manufacturing industry to protect, Venezuela was immune from one of the harmful effects of its closer incorporation into the imperial economic system, but the gratitude of its great creole landowners for the new opportunities provided for the production and export of agricultural goods was qualified by resentment of the continuing monopoly of trade enjoyed by Spanish merchants. Their complaint in 1797 that commerce existed "solely for the benefit of the metropolis" was an unwitting acknowledgement of the success of the free trade legislation within the terms of reference designed by the Spanish crown.

The destruction of colonial industry which might compete with that of the metropolis was also a clear aim of crown policy, specifically after 1778 and generally throughout the colonial period. Despite this policy, articulated in the late Bourbon period by the oft-cited order to viceroy Ozana "procurad la destrucción de ellos," the *obrajes* of colonial Quito survived to the end of the colonial period, as did the smaller establishments producing coarser cloth in Cundinamarca, Boyacá, Pasto, and Socorro. There is no doubt whatsoever that the liberalization of trade in 1778 had harmful effects for a textile industry which had developed in the seventeenth century in response to the chronic incapacity of the Hapsbsurg commercial system to supply the colonial market with manufactured goods. It is most important to stress, however, that in the case of Quito this industrial decline had begun much earlier, as a reflection in part of internal factors, including major epidemics and high mortality in the centres of textile production in the 1690s, a series of major earthquakes, and a rise in the price of dyes; external factors included the gradual increase in foreign competition from 1700 as a result of both contraband and the introduction of register ships to the Pacific, and the restructuring of trade routes which followed the abandonment of the Portobello fairs. It has also been suggested by one scholar that the growing European demand in the period after 1778 for cacao, and official attempts to promote the mining industry, led the mercantile capitalists of Quito and other New Granadan cities to withdraw their investments from the risky textile industry in favor of agricultural and mining enterprises. Mining production, primarily of gold, certainly expanded substantially in New Granada in this period—

mintage at Bogotá reached 1 million pesos by the early 1790s, and that at Popayán attained a similar level by 1800—to provide the viceroyalty with the bullion to pay for imports from the metropolis: according to one estimate, in the decade 1784–1793 imports from Spain were worth 19.5 million pesos, but exports reached 21 million, of which all but 1.8 million consisted of gold. However, despite the local importance of this trade, it was relatively insignificant in overall imperial terms. The registers of the 222 ships known to have entered Spanish ports from New Granada between 1782 and 1796 (216 from Cartagena and 6 from Santa Marta) show the total value of imports as 388 million reales, a figure a little lower than that cited above. This represented only 3.2% of total imports into Spain from America, a share which confirms the generally held view that New Granada was relatively unimportant in terms of its registered external trade.

Imports from the Río de la Plata, which, like Venezuela, enjoyed an impressive and new-found prosperity in the last quarter of the eighteenth century, totalled 1,489 million reales, or 12.2% of all imports. All but 52 of the 631 registers of imports from this region show Montevideo rather than Buenos Aires as the port of departure, despite the fact that the latter had its own customs house from 1778. A further 44 refer to Montevideo-Buenos Aires, 7 to Buenos Aires alone, and 1 to Maldonado. The pastoral economy was a major beneficiary of the opening of these ports to direct trade with Spain, as the export of hides increased from 150,000 in 1778 to 875,000 in 1796. Other animal and farm products helped to give agriculture a share of between one fifth and one third of total trade; the export of salted beef to Cuba to feed the slave population also grew substantially in this period. The principal export, however, was silver from Potosí, which after 1778 looked south to Buenos Aires rather than north to Lima for its principal outlet to the peninsula. There had always been a semi-legal seepage, even in the seventeenth century, but between 1776 and 1783 the combination of administrative, economic, and strategic factors combined to turn this into a torrent. They included not only the formal opening of the Plate ports but also the ban imposed by the first viceroy of the Río de la Plata upon the export of unminted bullion to Peru, the disruption of the traditional Potosí-Lima links during the rebellion of Túpac Amaru, and the virtual suspension of Spanish trade with the Pacific ports during the 1779–1783 war with England. During these years, however, the bullion exports to Spain from the Río de la Plata, primarily through Montevideo and in navy ships, were worth 11.7 million pesos, thereby establishing a pattern of trade which was to persist when peace was restored.

The lure of commercial growth attracted Cádiz firms and their agents to Buenos Aires, where there were large profits to be made after 1778 from the importation of manufactured goods for distribution to the interior provinces of the viceroyalty in return for silver. Potosí itself also experienced an influx of poor Spaniards in the late eighteenth century, hoping to make their fortunes from trade. Some of their more enterprising representatives, of whom the most important were Antonio Zabaleta, Luis de Orueta, and Pedro Antonio Azcárate, realizing that the very growth of commercial competition had hit profit margins, turned instead to the mining industry itself, taking advantage of the willingness of creole *azogueros* to both marry off their daughters with large dowries, and to rent their mills to newcomers. Between 1780 and 1805 these three men alone sold 7 million pesos of silver to the Bank of San Carlos. Their fellow immigrants, who stayed behind in Buenos Aires, including the founders of the Anchorena and Martínez de Hoz dynasties, made their fortunes in a somewhat less ostentatious fashion, but in the long run their prosperity, based upon commerce and, subsequently, the expansion of the *estancia,* was to prove more enduring than that based upon the production of silver in Upper Peru.

The truncated viceroyalty of Peru and its port of Callao inevitably suffered from the expansion of Spanish trade with the Río de la Plata despite the fact that its nominal monopoly of South American trade had ceased in reality decades earlier. However, the gloomy prophecy of the *consulado* of Lima in 1779 that free trade with the Río de la Plata and with Pacific ports other than Callao (Valparaiso, Concepción, Arica, and Guayaquil) would reduce the volume of Lima's trade to little more than a third of its pre-1778 level was not borne out. Callao continued in the 1780s to import European manufactures for re-export to Guayaquil in return for its cacao, despite earlier fears that this commodity would begin to be exported directly to Spain from the northern port. Only 9 of the 72 ships which reached Spain from the Pacific showed Guayaquil as a port of departure, and in each case they had also visited Callao; a further 2 came from Callao-Valparaiso, and 3 from Callao-Montevideo. Between them these 14 ships brought to Spain imports valued at 171 million reales, the bulk of which consisted, in any case, of Peruvian silver. The 58 further ships whose sole port of origin was Callao carried cargoes worth a total of 1,515 million reales (an average of 26 million reales per vessel). No case has been found of any arrival from the Pacific which did not list Callao as at least one of its ports of origin. During the period as a whole imports into Spain from Callao alone were worth an average of 101 million reales (5,051,062 pesos) a year; when those from combinations of ports involving Callao are included the figure rises to 112 million reales a year. From 1787 actual annual imports were usually very close to this mean. In other words Peru's trade with Spain attained a certain level once post-war irregularity had been overcome, and tended to stay there. It was enabled to do so by the fact that silver production within the viceroyalty—notably at Cerro de Pasco—expanded sufficiently to compensate for the loss of Potosí to the new viceroyalty of the Río de la Plata. Between 1779 and 1788 registered production of silver at Potosí exceeded that of all Lower Peruvian mining centres; thereafter, the output of Lower Peru surged ahead, while that at Potosí stagnated and then declined. By 1802 production at Potosí, 205,000 marks, was only 40% of that of Lower Peru: 505,000 marks, of which Cerro de Pasco alone was responsible for 283,000 marks. This year, moreover, was one in which a shortage of mercury, provoked by external factors, caused a decline in Peruvian production, which had reached a high point of 637,000 marks (more than double the 1778 figure) in 1799.

There is little direct evidence for Peru of a causal relationship between the introduction of free trade and the growth of the mining industry in the late colonial period. The Lima capitalists, unlike their Mexican counterparts, showed little inclination for long-term investment in silver production, although they were closely involved in the industry, sometimes as owners of pits, and more commonly through the provision of short-term credit and supplies to local silver-merchants (*aviadores*). There is clear evidence, however, of a dynamic relationship between the increase in silver production at Cerro de Pasco and the transmission there from Lima of imported European goods: as mining expanded, Peruvian regional economies benefited from increased demand for the cloth of Huamanga, the *coca* of Huánuco, the sugar and *aguardiente* of Jauja and Huaylas, the *aguardiente* of Ica, and the chilli of Chiquián. By far the greatest beneficiary, however, was Lima, whose exports to Cerro de Pasco quadrupled—from 101,000 to 417,000 pesos—between 1786 and 1795. In this latter year "efectos de Europa" accounted for 49% of the merchandise despatched to the mining centre by merchants in the viceregal capital. The same pattern emerges from an analysis of trade with Hualgayoc, the second mining centre of Peru in the late colonial period. . . . The mining sector was thus a major consumer of the large volume of manufactured goods imported into Peru from Spain (between 1785 and 1796 Peru absorbed 22% of all exports from Cádiz to America), and the source of the commodity, silver, which enabled the viceroyalty, with a 13.8% share of American exports to Cádiz and Barcelona in 1782–1796, to retain its position as Spain's most important trading partner in South America.

Peruvian commentators were divided in the 1780s and 1790s over the question of whether the introduction of free trade in 1778 had detrimental effects upon the viceregal economy. The *consulado* of Lima had no doubt that the repercussions had been disastrous: it complained bitterly in 1787 of a saturated market and the drain of circulating capital, and demanded a complete ban upon trade between Buenos Aires and Peru, and a two year moratorium on imports through the viceroyalty's own ports. . . . However, influential writers in the *Mercurio Peruano* believed that the fundamental grievance of the *consulado* was that the loss of its monopoly had reduced the easy profits of the large merchants who dominated the corporation, but that trade as a whole had expanded through the efforts of smaller firms, prepared to work for reduced margins. Moreover, despite initial difficulties caused by the loss of Upper Peru, trade between the two viceroyalties still showed by 1790 a balance in Peru's favor of 1,170,190 pesos, thus providing the viceroyalty with a net balance on all inter-colonial trade of 725,190 pesos, without taking into account the invisible earnings of 400,000 pesos a year of shipowners and muleteers. There is some evidence to suggest that in Peru, as in other viceroyalties, the profits of this vigorous local trade began to be diverted in the 1780s from established merchants to recent peninsular immigrants. . . .

Throughout Peru, the greater availability and lower prices of imported manufactures in the 1780s stimulated commercial activity—the number of retail shops in Lima grew by a third, for example—and the production of foodstuffs for the increasingly affluent urban middle and lower classes. But what of the impact of free trade upon domestic industry? The *consulado* again was quite convinced that after 1778 the supply of manufactures through Buenos Aires had not only drastically reduced the Upper Peruvian market for Peruvian cloth, but had also undermined it within Lower Peru by encouraging a tendency for agricultural exports from Arequipa and Cuzco to be paid for in part by European textiles, which were cheaper and of better quality than those produced by local *obrajes*. There is no doubt, in fact, that its basic observation was accurate: the traditional *obrajes* of the Cuzco region, producing woollen cloth for local consumption and for export to Upper Peru did, indeed, experience a period of decline in the last quarter of the eighteenth century, although textiles still accounted in 1790 for 60% of exports to the Río de la Plata (and sugar from Abancay for a further 16%). It is also clear that competition from imports was a significant factor in this decline. However, internal factors were probably of greater significance: they included the destruction of *obrajes* during the Túpac Amaru rising, a change in patterns of commercial activity as Peruvian capitalists shifted their attention from Upper Peru to the expanding mining zones of the centre and north of the vice-royalty, and the abolition of the *repartimiento* system. A further factor which has received less attention than it deserves is that in Peru, as in other parts of Spanish America, there was a tendency for the old-style *obraje*, the large establishment with 200–300 workers, to decline in the face of not only competition from imports but also from smaller local establishments, *chorrillos*, producing cheaper cloth for an expanding popular market. [Evidence for new trends can be found from Huamanga and from Arequipa, where textiles survived by aiming at the poorer end of the market.]

The hiatus between the era of Hispanic "free trade" 1778–1796, and the genuine free trade of the post-independence era, was a period of contradictory trends when American industry first developed more quickly in response to the sudden reduction in the supply of manufactures through normal channels in 1797, but subsequently suffered from the increased supply of European manufactures through contraband and neutral channels. It should be stressed, however, that on balance in the period 1778–1796 American industry gained more from the economic and commercial expansion generated by free trade than it lost from the influx of European manufactures. There was never any doubt that agricultural and mining exports multiplied many times in the same period, to the satisfaction of the crown and creole producers alike. The only disadvantages of this process for Americans were first, that the pace of expansion was limited by the continuing exclusion of non-Spaniards from international trade, and second, that those enterprising Spanish merchants who migrated to America on the tide of the commercial growth which did occur were more privileged and more successful businessmen than their American counterparts.

ii

The era of genuine free trade in the Hispanic world as envisaged by the economic theorists of Bourbon Spain was short-lived. It was introduced hesitantly, like so many other aspects of the reform programme of Charles III, in the 1760s as part of the reconstruction of imperial policy which followed Spain's humiliation at the hands of Britain in the Seven Years War; it collapsed in 1797, an early casualty of Spain's alliance with revolutionary France, with the introduction of neutral commerce as a desperate expedient to maintain some imperial trade in the face of the British blockade of the Atlantic ports. The intervening Anglo-Spanish conflict of 1779–1783, the only one of the three from which Spain emerged as a victor, did less permanent damage than that which began in 1796 to commercial relations between Spain and America, but, by paralyzing trade for three years, it did frustrate the expansionist aims enshrined in the 1778 reglamento of free trade. Even when the conflict ended in 1783, and merchants became free for the first time since early 1779 to organize their trade with America in response to purely commercial considerations, restrictions remained upon the application of the 1778 legislation to Venezuela and New Spain. These restrictions remained in force, at least in theory, until 1789, thereby limiting the period of full imperial free trade to less than a decade. In practice, however, they tended to be cumbersome irritants rather than major obstacles to trade with the excluded regions, and one is justified in regarding the coherent chronological framework for the analysis of the impact of free trade upon the commercial relations between Spain and America as not 1789–1796, but that extending from 1782, when trade began to recover from the collapse of 1779–81, to 1796.

During this period, 1782–1796, free trade promoted a massive expansion in the value of exports from Spain to America. The rise was uneven, partly because of commercial and economic factors, partly because of the effects of the 1793–1795 war between Spain and France, but the average annual value of exports, expressed in terms of constant prices was four times higher than in 1778. The share of registered Spanish products in these exports rose from a minority share of 38 percent in 1778 to an average of 52 percent in 1782–1796, thereby fulfilling in part the hope of the commercial reformers that freer trade with America would stimulate production in Spain and reduce the reliance of her merchants exporting to America upon foreign suppliers. As a result of the decision of the customs officials in Cádiz, unlike those in other ports, not to record in ships' registers the separate values of individual commodities despatched to America, it is impossible to measure with precision the relative importance of Spanish manufactures and agricultural goods in exports. There is considerable evidence, however, for concluding that agricultural producers were more responsive than industrialists to the wider opportunities in the American market offered in 1778 by the introduction of free trade. Commercial reform thus failed in its prime aim of promoting a significant alteration in the structure of the peninsular economy by means of an industrial regeneration: instead it consolidated the traditional pattern, whereby Spain supplied the American market from her own production with wines, spirits and agricultural goods, but continued, despite some industrial growth in this period, to meet some of its demand for manufacture by re-exporting foreign products. . . .

Although impressive in relation to the low level of trade established by 1778, the fourfold expansion in exports from Spain to America in 1782–1796 may be considered modest in the context of the potential for growth in Spanish America and the actual economic growth achieved in this period by Britain, Spain's principal territorial and commercial rival in the Americas. There are no such reservations arising from an analysis of the much more spectacular results of the new commercial system for Spanish-American exports to Spain. In 1782–1796 their average value was more than ten times greater than in 1778. An overwhelming 84% of them were landed in Cádiz for distribution throughout Spain and to the rest of Europe; Barcelona, which is sometimes wrongly depicted as a major beneficiary of free trade, came a poor third, with a mere 3.8%, behind La Coruña. An examination of the commodities imported into Cádiz and Barcelona confirms the success of free trade in promoting the exploitation of formerly neglected natural resources, for imports into Spain of tobacco, cacao, sugar, cochineal, indigo, hides, and other agricultural products accounted for 44% of the total. They continued to be overshadowed, nevertheless, by the productions of the American mines, which made up the remaining 56%. Approximately one quarter of the treasure imports consisted of crown revenues remitted to Spain, the bulk of them during the latter years, when it was making a strenuous effort to increase its profits from the empire. The viceroyalty of New Spain, as the most important producer of silver in America, was responsible for remitting no less than 36% of all the imperial products imported into Spain. The major islands of the Caribbean, led by Cuba, were in second place with 23%, followed by Peru (14%), the Río de la Plata (12%), and Venezuela (10%). The traditional bulwarks of the imperial structure, New Spain and Peru, and areas of secondary importance such as Quito and the interior provinces of the Río de la Plata paid in part for their new prosperity after 1778 with a relative decline of their domestic industries, although even the industrial sector felt some benefits from the general economic expansion of the last quarter of the eighteenth century. A clearer grievance, affecting both the old viceroyalties and the peripheral regions, was that the very success of free trade encouraged the migration to America of large numbers of peninsular Spaniards, whose privileged positions in both the bureaucracy and commerce, coupled with their dynamism, enabled them to profit at the expense of creole producers and displaced local merchants.

9

Buenos Aires and Commercial Expansion

Tulio Halperín Donghi

From the middle of the eighteenth century Buenos Aires began to emerge from its long stagnation and enter a period of enhanced imperial role, commercial growth, and demographic increase. The resurgence of Buenos Aires was due in part to realization of its economic potential, but even more perhaps to its strategic importance. It was now seen to be an essential base in the South Atlantic, the most effective guard over the route to the Pacific, and the best point of penetration into the interior of South America. Defense depended upon reformed institutions and new officials. It also needed a sound economy. In the second half of the eighteenth century the Río de la Plata became a true frontier of settlement, where new immigrants could find land, export opportunities, or alternative activities in the newly incorporated mining sector. But opportunities were not evenly shared between imperial and local interests; nor, as the following study shows, were they effectively maintained by Spain. Tulio Halperín, Professor of History in the University of California, Berkeley, has patented a number of original themes in the historiography of independence. (1) The Buenos Aires economy was based on commerce and precious metals, not yet on livestock, though estancias were in the process of formation, and their owners, as the following passage suggests, took a more hostile view of commercial monopoly than did those merchants who profited from it. (2) The course of independence can only be understood by reference to the pressures of war and the increasing burden of the state. (3) While the traditional social structure survived, there were two groups close to the revolution—merchants and bureaucrats. The emergence of the career revolutionary, of a new group of bureaucrats and

Reprinted from Tulio Halperín Donghi, *Politics, Economics and Society in Argentina in the Revolutionary Period* (Cambridge, 1975), Copyright Cambridge University Press, 1975, pp. 29–40, reprinted with the permission of Cambridge University Press and the author.

military personnel whose only power base was their function, is also a Halperín theme. Many of these developments have their origins in the late colonial period.

Buenos Aires was the capital of the rising Littoral, the seat since 1776 of a Viceroyalty, and the protagonist since the early years of the eighteenth century of a progress that was never to be arrested. In the last years of that century Buenos Aires was already comparable to a Spanish city of the second rank and was very different, therefore, from the village of straw and adobe that it had been half a century before. This growth—accompanied as it was by a rapid increase in population—was not based solely on the economic rise of the Littoral; it was a consequence of the promotion of Buenos Aires as the principal centre for overseas trade for the extreme South of the Spanish empire. Thus the prosperity of the port was more closely connected with the maintenance of the Imperial structure than its beneficiaries realised.

Buenos Aires was at the time, fundamentally, a commercial and bureaucratic city, with complementary economic activities (both craft and primary) geared to satisfying the demand created, above all, by those engaged in administration and commerce. The commercial importance of Buenos Aires dated from before the reforms of the 1770s, which established exemption from duty for goods shipped to Chile and Peru, and free trade with the most important ports of Spain. . . . But there is no doubt that the reforms consolidated and accelerated the commercial rise of Buenos Aires. They facilitated the establishment of a nucleus of powerful merchants which was soon to acquire a position of hegemony in the economic system of the entire Viceroyalty.

In the course of the second half of the eighteenth century the representatives of a reinvigorated Spain made their appearance in Buenos Aires: the Catalans Larrea and Mateu, the Basque-Navarrese Anchorena, Alzaga, Santa Coloma, Lezica, Belaútegui, Azcuénaga, and the Galicians Llavallol and Rivadavia. Their rise to fortune had been comparatively recent: the list of the richest citizens of Buenos Aires in 1766 includes only two of their names—Lezica and Rivadavia; but by the end of the century the Anchorena fortune was already almost legendary, partly owing to the precautions which its owner took to conceal it. This fortune had been made by exercising a form of commerce that owed nothing to innovation and was reluctant to take big risks. Most of the Buenos Aires merchants were agents for Spanish firms, and in more than one instance were relatives of the Spanish businessmen whom they represented or with whom they maintained close commercial ties. An example of this was Domingo Mateu, who established himself in Buenos Aires and represented his brothers who had settled in Guatemala and Manila, all of them maintaining ties with the parent firm in Barcelona. But even those who did not limit their operations to acting as agents for Spanish business houses engaged in business transactions without difficulties or risks.

This routine-bound commercial way of life was bitterly denounced by Argentine economists of the Enlightenment. According to one famous characterisation, for these merchants who set the tone of Buenos Aires life business was just a matter of "buying for two and selling for four." In more modern terms, this pejorative characterisation has been repeated in recent times: in so far as they were merely acting on a commission basis for Spanish businessmen, the Buenos Aires merchants linked to the Cádiz route played no important part in the process of capital-accumulation which was to be the indispensable basis for the subsequent development of the local economy. However, this assertion is somewhat dubious. Indeed in spite of the lack of detailed studies of this matter, it is safe to assert that this agency business was a source of high profits to the local agents concerned. Their rapid enrichment is a ready proof of it, and it is not difficult to give an explanation of the process. Sheer distance, and the ignorance as to the movements of the local market which this necessarily provoked, put the Spanish principals at the mercy of their local agents. Even a small-scale merchant such as Santa Coloma was in a position to give only vague answers to the specific and urgent questions raised by the Spanish owners of the goods he held in his shop: sales had fallen, and prices had been cut, because times were bad; anyone not satisfied with this reply could simply try to find another agent, without any guarantee of finding a better one.

This free-and-easy relationship with the Spanish principals coincided with a much stricter control over the commercial agents in the Interior. In this case contacts were much more frequent, and more complex types of association made possible a more effective vigilance. This was especially true of the biggest Buenos Aires business houses: the Anchorenas, for example, had agents established in the cities of the hinterland, from Santa Fe as far as Peru, and also had itinerant salesmen working on commission, who would set off with a fleet of wagons to sell goods on behalf of the Buenos Aires parent firm. Both sources supplied, independently, information as to the state of the market. In this way, the distribution of commercial profits favored the Buenos Aires firms both at the expense of their Spanish principals and at the expense of the smaller commercial firms of the hinterland. This process was also self-sustaining: the possession of capital allowed the

Buenos Aires merchants to complement their agencies for Spanish goods with direct purchases, not to mention extremely varied intermediate forms of transaction, and thus achieve an increasing autonomy *vis-à-vis* their original Spanish headquarters. Similarly, this capital made it possible to give credit in the hinterland, and occasionally to effect cash purchases from producers, by-passing the local distributors, as happened, for example, in the case of the purchase of hides in Corrientes and Entre Ríos.

Thus the big business firms of Buenos Aires had greater freedom of manoeuvre than their function as local agents of the Cádiz merchants would lead one to suppose, and they enjoyed the high profits which that freedom made possible. But this prosperity was not accompanied by the fulfilment of any dynamic function in the local economy. True, the merchants established in Buenos Aires did not, of course, disdain to engage in the export of hides, by means of which they channelled into their pockets a good part of the profits of the most dynamic sector of the Viceregal economy. The greater part of their business, however, consisted of the distribution of European imports which were paid for in cash. In neither field do the Buenos Aires merchants appear to have discovered the advantages of a progressive increase in throughput at the cost of a small decrease in profit-margins. On the contrary, their business dealings, not unjustly accused of being routine-bound, were maintained at a low level and guaranteed high profits. . . . The greater part of the hinterland of Buenos Aires, including the Interior and Upper Peru, from which the greatest return in money was expected, was sharply divided between the small sector of *gente decente* (the rich), who were consumers, and a lower class which a cheapening of products by the sacrifice of the high profits of the importers could not possibly incorporate into the market. It is, therefore, probable that, in insisting on high profits and refusing to expand the market, the Buenos Aires merchants showed more knowledge of their business than did their subsequent critics. But, whoever was at fault, the fact is that this commercial sector, the hegemony of which over the Viceregal economy became ever more solidly established, did not fulfil a dynamic role; its success was due to the fact that it satisfied a demand which it believed to be irremediably static. . . .

But it was not only commerce with the Interior and Upper Peru, which consisted of the sale of fine and medium quality textiles and some hardware, for payment in cash, that took place in conditions which made dynamic expansion impossible. Even in the commercial relations between Buenos Aires and its immediate zone of influence in the Littoral one observes trends which had the same effect. Of course,

the export of hides, which was for three quarters of a century the
principal contribution of the River Plate region to the world market,
did not encounter in the limitations imposed by world consumption
any brake on its expansion. But the production of hides was not the
only rural activity of the Littoral. In Santa Fe, Western Entre Ríos and
Buenos Aires mule-breeding received a fresh stimulus, whilst in
Buenos Aires, with the presence of a strongly consumption-orientated
urban centre, meat for human consumption played an important part
in the development of cattle-raising, which was comparatively slow in
this part of the River Plate region. Both types of stock-raising were
orientated towards somewhat inelastic markets. One of the causes of
the prosperity of the mule-trade consisted in the limitations placed on
dispatches of droves towards the North, which kept prices at a high
level. As for the consumer market, it was a well known fact that those
who controlled it were more afraid of abundance than of scarcity.

But even the production of hides failed to play a dynamic role. Of
course, exports rose, and very swiftly, but this rise was not continuous.
For an excessively long period overseas exports suffered the consequences of the world war situation, and the oscillation between years
of stagnation and brief flurries of frenzied exporting continued. In the
case of the hides, too, the immediate search for high profits, guaranteed
by purchasing at low prices, and the storing of the hides in expectation
of better times, was of more interest to the merchants than was the
encouragement of a regular growth of production by increasing the
profits of the stock-raisers. . . .

The basic principles of this method of doing business, which implied
a resigned acceptance of a fundamentally static situation and an ability
to take advantage of it, were not affected by the expansion of stock-
raising, orientated towards the export of hides, which appears in retro-
spect to be the most potentially lucrative innovation of the Viceregal
era. They were more directly affected by the war and the confusion
which this provoked in commerce. The continually changing circumstances favored those who were prepared to abandon the routine-bound
practices to which the commerce of Buenos Aires owed its first phase
of prosperity and instead display audacity and versatility. Besides the
merchants concerned with the trade-route from Cádiz, the war raised
to a level of prosperity others who were prepared to use varied routes:
those via Cuba, Brazil and the United States, that of neutral Northern
Europe, which opened the door to France, which was an ally but semi-
isolated, and to Britain, which was an enemy. . . .

This new commercial sector, which had come to the fore all of a
sudden, naturally displayed an increasing impatience with the legal

restrictions with which its commercial practices were hedged round. During the final years of Spanish rule it came out, together with the landowners, in favor of the liberalisation of trade undertaken by the Crown. This was not enough to give it a modernising role in the strictly economic field; or, to put it more exactly, one fails to recognise in its attitudes the style of modernisation which the new economic theory propounded, even though this sector was beginning to hint at innovations which independent Argentine was to know only too well.

What in fact happened was that this new sector replaced the routine exploitation of a privileged position in business with a tendency towards sheer speculation, and this tendency was, of course, represented, with some pride, as progressive in comparison with the previous situation. . . . The commercial expansion which they brought to Buenos Aires was, in fact, ephemeral, and when the cycle was completed, they showed even less ability than the merchants accustomed to using the Cádiz trade-route to survive the changes brought about by free trade with overseas and by the Revolution. The fragility of their fortunes was a direct result of the situation from which they arose; the creation of a centre of autonomous commercial life in Buenos Aires was due to the simultaneous decline in the ascendancy of the European centres on which Buenos Aires depended. At war first with France and then with Britain, Spain saw threatened and later destroyed its ties with its overseas territories. A whole corpus of emergency legislation arose, designed to find palliatives for this situation, conceding commercial liberties that previously had been stubbornly denied. This legislation implied a recognition of the swift disintegration which was afflicting the economic unity of the Empire. These concessions—which were by no means spontaneous gestures of liberalisation—included authorisation to import slaves in ships owned by Buenos Aires merchants (1791), authorisation to accord naturalisation papers to ships with the same objective (1793), authorisation of exports to and imports from other nations' colonies (1795), authorisation for River Plate ships and merchants to intervene actively in trade with the Peninsula (1796) and authorisation of trade with neutral countries (1797). They were rescinded as soon as they ceased to be unavoidable, as was the case with the most important concession, regarding trade with neutrals. These measures were, undoubtedly, less influential in the rise of an autonomous commercial nucleus in the River Plate region than was the existence of an international situation which obliged the metropolis to follow this new policy because the commercial structure of the entire world had been dislocated.

The crisis not only diminished the pressure from Spain, but it also removed from the River Plate scene the most solidly established commercial powers, which were replaced by others which took advantage of a situation favorable to them. Buenos Aires was now to see the merchant ships of the United States, the Hanseatic cities and the Scandinavian countries, and even Turkey. But these new powers were a poor substitute for those which were no longer able to fulfil their traditional role, and Buenos Aires was to build up its own merchant fleet by the seizure of ships lying at anchor in the port when war broke out, and also by means of shipbuilding in the Corrientes and Paraguay yards, accustomed to building smaller craft for river trade. By this means, the Buenos Aires merchants reached the new markets of Europe, North America, Africa, and the sugar islands of the Indian ocean. For a city used to thinking of itself as being in the uttermost part of the earth, this was a heady experience. Normally cautious observers spoke of the city as being the "centre of the commercial world." And in that world transformed by the semi-withdrawal of its European centre Buenos Aires came to occupy, if not the centre, at least an important place. [The process was accelerated because of the vacuum of naval, commercial, and financial power.]

But the autonomous commercial development arising from this vacuum was of necessity ephemeral. Before the conclusion of the cycle of wars of Europe, the peace between Spain and Britain was to give the Americas a commercial and financial metropolis fully capable of fulfilling its functions. The repercussions of this new arrangement were to reach the river Plate as early as 1809, when commerce with the new ally was authorised. From then on, Buenos Aires would again be relegated to the periphery of the commercial world, and years were to go by before the full consequences of this new position were to be recognisable.

Is it possible to make a quantitative analysis of this frenzied commercial development?. . . . In the first place, and despite the expansion of stock-raising in the Littoral, the principal export during this period was still precious metals. The proportion of total exports constituted by these varied, and in any case are not exactly known. In 1796, out of total exports of 5,058,882 pesos, gold accounted for 1,425,701 and silver for 2,556,304; that is, precious metals constituted 80 per cent by value of total exports. It would, of course, be wrong to extrapolate the figures valid for that year, in which exports of all products reached exceptional levels, to the period as a whole. But it is enough to bear in mind that the principal export item of the Littoral stock-raising industry— hides—only in exceptional years reached a total of one million units (of fluctuating value, but very roughly calculable as one peso per unit), to realise that the data for 1797 were in no way anomalous. The other export items were much less important than hides: the value of dried and salted meat can be calculated for the quinquennium 1792–96, at around sixty thousand pesos a year; ten years later, the export of those products had increased markedly—in the second half of 1803 they were over 120,000 quintals, with a value that could be calculated as between 150 and 180 thousand pesos; in the following years, no figures as high as this were recorded; the figure for the whole of 1804 was 70,000 quintals, and for 1805, 60,000. The average annual values were under $100,000. In any case, the expanding salted meat industry only accounted for a very minor part of the River Plate's exports. Agricultural exports accounted for even less, and only occurred in exceptional years.

The primacy of precious metals among exports was, therefore, unquestioned. Through Buenos Aires there passed every year a quantity of silver that equalled the total amount minted in Potosí. Of course, a high proportion of Upper Peru's silver never found its way to the mint, but even so the rôle of Buenos Aires as the South American extreme of a mechanism for sucking precious metals out of the Americas is quite evident. How was Buenos Aires able to fulfil this rôle? A part of the silver that passed through the port was outside the commercial process altogether: this was the Crown's share of mined and minted silver. But the latter was comparatively small, and most of Upper Peru's precious metals, and of those of Lower Peru attracted to the Potosí mint, had to be attracted to Buenos Aires by the functioning of certain commercial mechanisms. This functioning is even more difficult to understand if one bears in mind that during the early phase of the Viceregal period the trade of the River Plate was certainly not in deficit. How, therefore, was it possible to extract from that region, as happened in the period 1792–96, four million pesos per year by value, of which at least two-thirds consisted of precious metals, in exchange for goods to the value of around two million pesos? Only the existence of an exceptionally expensive commercial system could guarantee an equilibrium. Such a system had the effect of levelling out in the centres of production, above all Upper Peru, what in Buenos Aires appeared to be in such pronounced imbalance. . . .

The prosperity of Buenos Aires, and that of the more modest of the centres of commerce and transport on the Peru route, was fundamentally derived from its participation, although in a subordinate position, in the advantages which the Colonial order gave to the marketers—the local emissaries of Spain's economy—over the producers. Here we find one of the reasons for the suspicion with which the mercantile sectors were to face the Revolutionary crisis. Denunciations of the monopoly of Cádiz not only aroused misgivings owing to the ties of economic dependence which they maintained by means of that monopoly. The mercantile hegemony of Cádiz was only one aspect of a system of commerce which included the hegemony of Buenos Aires as a secondary metropolis, a position which was guaranteed, less by any gravitational impulse, than by political decisions taken by the Crown. The biggest business in the River Plate area—the export of Spanish products to Tucumán, Cuyo and Upper Peru, to be exchanged for precious metals—presupposed the maintenance of the Colonial order. The business of exporting hides and jerked beef might well be an attractive complement to the former business, but as a substitute it would be ruinous.

The exports of precious metals were valued in millions, and those of the products of the Littoral stock-raising industry were around one million pesos a year. If we leave aside these two dominant nuclei of the Viceregal economy, and consider the nuclei subordinate to them, we find much more modest figures.

Tucumán was importing annually goods to a value of 140,000 pesos, of which two-thirds were products of Castile, textiles which found consumers not only among the upper sectors but also, in this exceptionally prosperous region, even among the people of the countryside, who "kept Castilian cloths and linens for the days when they dressed up." Imports from Chile and Peru were of the order of ten thousand pesos; from the Andean area twenty-four thousand pesos. As an importing centre Tucumán was more closely tied to the metropolis than to the neighbouring and poorer regions.

Its exports were more complex: the principal item was the carrier business, which brought in seventy thousand pesos; the principal destination of goods was the Littoral. The second most important item was cattle on the hoof, to the value of 53,000 pesos, exported to Upper and Lower Peru. Thirdly, there were tanned shoe-soles and hides, to the value of thirty thousand pesos, which found a consumer-market in the Littoral and Córdoba. There was a more widely dispersed consumer-market for rice (seventeen thousand pesos), finished wooden goods (nine thousand pesos) and saddlery (three thousand pesos). Here too, however, the most important items were orientated towards the economically dominant zones, Buenos Aires and Upper Peru. Orientated as it was towards the more prosperous zones, the commerce of Tucumán was also linked to the socially dominant sectors; it was the satisfaction of their needs that accounted for the greater part of imports. In this respect, it is enough to compare the ninety thousand pesos' worth imported from Castile with the six thousand pesos' worth of ordinary textiles (raw cotton from Catamarca, to the value of 4,000 pesos, and coarse cloth from Cochabamba to the value of 2,000 pesos) to recognise to what extent luxury goods enjoyed a dominant share of imports. . . .

The Colonial order was characterised by the rigid separation between a very small sector incorporated into a large-scale economic system, and much bigger sectors with an economic life carried on a more reduced scale. As arbiter between one and the other there were those who dominated the marketing processes and used them to maintain this differentiated structure, which guaranteed them an exceptionally high proportion of the profits.

The period of dislocation of world trade, therefore, did not betoken any fresh prosperity for Buenos Aires. The prospects of commercial independence that were opened were not a valid substitute for the guaranteed profits assured by its enjoyment of a privileged position in the Imperial commercial structure, reformed for Buenos Aires's benefit. The new trade was a welcome complement; it was, above all, the result of necessity. But even though these prospects were in the long run deceptive, they contributed to weakening the resistance of the dominant commercial sector to the possibility of more far-reaching changes, towards which they were impelled, in the first place by outside pressures, and secondly by those exercised by the producers of the expanding Littoral, who were prepared to open up a broader road towards the overseas consumer markets. Even though, around 1810, Buenos Aires was still basically a silver port, the fluctuations in fortune caused by the world war situation were no less important for being ephemeral. Because of them Buenos Aires was able to face lightheartedly the crises which the Revolution necessarily was to bring in its train, and renounce the advantages which the Colonial order guaranteed it, with the conviction which the new situation had implanted in the heads of her wiser sons: placed there in the "centre of the commercial world," the Tyre of the New World did not need the protection which the Imperial order provided. By gaining independence from this decrepit order, it hoped to embark on a new phase of life marked by unbounded prosperity.

10

Free Trade versus Monopoly

Mariano Moreno

Mariano Moreno's *Representación de los hacendados* was written in 1809, at a time when, because of the Napoleonic wars and the collapse of Spanish power, trade between Buenos Aires and Spain was practically suspended. Two British merchants had petitioned for leave to dispose of goods recently brought from England, and a newly-arrived viceroy referred their petition to the cabildo and the consulado for study and advice. The attorney for the merchants of Cádiz argued that such innovation would harm not only Spanish interests but also colonial industries: "Our interior provinces are going to suffer intensely from the entry of English goods into our ports." The landowners of the Río de la Plata commissioned Mariano Moreno, a young creole lawyer, to put the case for open trade. Moreno went beyond the argument of immediate fiscal advantage and presented freedom of trade as an obvious truth and vital for the welfare of the people of the Río de la Plata. He was an eloquent and enlightened advocate. Born in 1778 and educated at the University of Chuquisaca, Moreno became secretary of the first independent junta in Buenos Aires in May 1810; sent on a mission to England, he died at sea in March 1811. The influence of the *Representación* has been much debated. The ideas of economic liberalism which it expressed had long been current in creole circles, especially in the writings of Manuel Belgrano. But this was the most forthright and least ambiguous statement of the argument for free trade—not so much an appeal to the crown as an expression of rights, an affirmation of regional interest and landed power.

Translated by John Lynch from "Representación de los Hacendados, por el Apoderado de los Labradores y Hacendados de la Banda Oriental y Occidental del Río de la Plata," in Diego Luis Molinari, *La Representación de los Hacendados de Mariano Moreno* (2nd ed., Buenos Aires, 1939), pp. 280–377.

As the funds and resources of the royal treasury were exhausted by the enormous expenditure recently experienced, Your Excellency began his government without the necessary means to provide for our security. The only way of remedying this unhappy situation appeared to be to grant permission to the English merchants to introduce their goods into this city, and to export therefrom the products of our country, thus giving an impetus to our declining trade and increasing the treasury's income from duties on this double transaction. Although Your Excellency possesses ample powers to apply any measures that the safety of the country may require, a natural anxiety to ensure the success of such measures by improving your knowledge of the province led Your Excellency to consult the cabildo and consulado of this city. [But these two institutions do not fully represent the landowners and farmers of our country; they too deserve to be consulted.]

The decision of Your Excellency had hardly been made known when several merchants displayed their anger and discontent. Groups of shopkeepers throughout Buenos Aires stirred up complaints and protests; they sought to disguise their personal interest and clandestine dealings, though they were given the lie by their previous conduct. Some of them gathered to deplore the mortal blow which the interests and rights of the metropolis were about to receive. Others announced the ruin of this country and the total destruction of its trade. Others predicted the poverty which the free export of our money would bring upon us. And yet others discovered a new zeal for the welfare of our artisans, whom they normally despised, lamenting their fate and pretending to enlist in their cause the sacred name of religion and the defence of our way of life.

America has never been in a more critical situation, and never has a leader been more entitled to dispense with old rules; for if in times less dangerous than these the laws have been allowed to remain dormant, because their application was obstructing policy necessary for the welfare of the country, surely Your Excellency cannot be blamed for a decision vital to the very survival of the Monarchy. The dangers that threaten us are too serious to ignore and too imminent not to take measures to remove them.

Those who maintain that to open trade to the English under present circumstances is harmful to Spain and to this province must be totally discredited. But even if it were true, it is a necessary evil, and since it cannot be avoided it ought at least to be used for the general good in order to derive some advantage from it and direct it to the security of the state. Ever since the English expedition of 1806 appeared on our shores the merchants of that nation have not lost sight of the Río de la

Plata in their speculations. A continual series of commercial ventures have followed, and these have supplied almost the entire consumption of the country; this huge importation, pursued in defiance of the laws and repeated prohibitions, has encountered no other obstacles than those necessary to deprive the treasury of its dues and the country of the advantage which it would have received from a free export of its own products in return.

The result of this situation has been to place the English in the exclusive position of providing the country with all the merchandise it requires, while the treasury has lost the immense revenues which these imports ought to produce, together with corresponding exports, and simply because of exaggerated respect for laws which have never been more scandalously ignored and violated than now, when their observance is demanded. For what, Sir, can be more ridiculous than to see a merchant loudly demanding the observance of laws against foreign trade, at the very door of his shop whose only contents are English contraband goods?

There are truths so obvious that it insults the intelligence to attempt to prove them. Such is the proposition that this country should freely import the goods which it does not produce or possess and export its own abundant products which are being wasted for lack of outlet. Those who believe that an abundance of foreign goods is bad for a country are ignorant of the first principles of political economy. Nothing is more advantageous for a country than an abundance of the goods which it does not itself produce, for this lowers value and price, to the benefit of the consumers and harmful only to the importers. If an excessive importation of English cloths were to produce oversupply in this line of goods, these prices would fall and the trade would turn to other lines. Is it not better for the country that its inhabitants can buy for three pesos a cloth which previously cost eight, or obtain two pairs of pants for the price of one?

To the advantage of importing foreign goods may be added the benefit the country will derive from exporting its own produce. This province is fortunate in having agricultural products which are much esteemed, reliable, and essential. How rapidly our agriculture would grow if the ports were open to all our exportable products and the farmer could rely on a profitable sale! Those who now hesitated to undertake farming because of the uncertainty of the market would then work with the vigor inspired by certain profit, so increasing the wealth of the producers and the revenue of the royal treasury.

These plains produce annually a million hides, without counting other skins, tallow, and grains, all of which are valuable to the foreign merchant. But our warehouses are full, for there is no opportunity of an active export; the result is an immense stock which ties up the capital of our merchants and prevents them from making new purchases. So the landowners are left with produce which they cannot sell at a good price for lack of export or buyers; in this way they are reduced to their present sorry state and forced to abandon an occupation which does not repay them for their labor and costs. Freedom to export will generate a rapid turnover, activate production, and bring new products into the market; profits will improve, agriculture will flourish, and trade will pick up as the wealth of producers increases, for these are the people who sustain the principal and exclusive business of the province. We have seen the way agricultural production regains strength following a war, when exports can begin again. But this time only a new policy can restore our fortunes; peace with Great Britain has not brought us the expected rewards, because the commerce of our metropolis is in ruins. Once our contact with the metropolis was broken during the last war, we were deprived of essential imports and had no outlets for our own products, the inevitable result of going to war against a powerful nation which is mistress of the seas and able to cut all communication with the metropolis.

Freedom of trade in America has been proscribed not as a real evil but as a sacrifice which the metropolis demands of its colonies. Well known is the history of that exclusive commerce and its development until it degenerated into a total monopoly of the Cádiz merchants. Enlightened opinion denounced a system so weak, so ruinous, and so ill-judged; but deep-seated evils cannot be cured in an instant. Minor reforms were preparing the way for a new system founded on sounder principles when the recent extraordinary events undermined the political state of Spain and destroyed by unforeseen blows all the pretexts on which the prohibitory laws had been based. The new order of things which the metropolis has proclaimed as the happy beginning of national regeneration and prosperity has completely overturned the old reasons for the prohibitory system and revealed in their fullest extent the advantages that will result to the country from a free trade. So the political objective of applying a remedy to urgent needs is converted into a question of justice which the first magistrate cannot in duty ignore.

Is it just that the valuable products of our agriculture should perish and waste because the unfortunate provinces of Spain cannot consume them? Is it just that the abundant produce of the country should lie rotting in warehouses because we no longer have the ships to export them? Is it just that we should increase the distress of our metropolis by the news of our own critical and unstable situation, when we are offered the means to consolidate our security on solid foundations? Is it right that when the subjects of a friendly and generous nation appear in our ports and offer at a cheap rate the goods that we need and which Spain cannot supply we should reject the proposal and allow a few enterprising merchants to capture the market by means of a contraband trade? Is it right that when we are urged to sell the accumulated produce that we cannot consume we should decree the country's ruin and harm both treasury and society? Enlightened English merchants, who are observing us closely, will return to Europe confirmed in their view of our barbarism, if these claims simply reveal the obstinacy of men unrepentant in their errors.

If Your Excellency wishes to avoid the excessive extraction of specie such as has taken place in recent times, then there is no alternative to opening the ports to the English merchants so that they can extend their trade to the whole range of exports. It is one of the fatal consequences of contraband that the importer is compelled to take payment in cash. It is true that his real interest lies in taking the returns in goods, which can lead to further business, but the risks involved in ignoring so strict a prohibition force him to sacrifice these advantages in preference to the greater security which exports in money afford over the exports of bulky commodities. So the merchant is deprived of further profit and the country of opportunities to export its products.

"Agriculture will reach its nadir." This was the special discovery of the agent of the Cádiz monopolists. The free export of agricultural products is described as the ruin of agriculture. What then shall be its support? According to the ideas of our merchants, agricultural products should be allowed to accumulate, and purchasers are to be deterred by the difficulty of exporting these products to likely markets; then after ruining the farmer by preventing him from recovering his costs, the superfluous crops are to be used to fill up the ditches and marshes of the capital. Yes, Sir, this is the depressed state to which our agriculture has been reduced in the last few years: the marshes around the city have actually been filled with wheat. But this miserable situation, which depresses all patriots and scandalizes all people, is the inevitable fate of a country which, in trying to apply a remedy to these great evils, has merchants who cry "agriculture will be ruined if its products are allowed a market price and a ready export."

"The provinces of the interior will be ruined." The agent of the consulado makes this dire prediction, going so far as to suggest that their ties with us are at risk. But in imagining that the coarse cottons of Cochabamba are consumed in Chile he reveals his ignorance of the countries he is discussing. The textiles of our provinces will not decline through free trade, because the English will never supply cloths as cheap and as serviceable. Therefore, the demand that clothing, furniture, coaches, and other articles be prohibited is an unacceptable constraint. A country that is beginning to prosper cannot be deprived of fine and elegant furniture, for which there will be increasing demand. If our artisans were able to make articles as good, they ought to be preferred, even though the foreigner would be unable to compete. But it would not be right to deprive the consumer of choice of good furniture simply because our artisans are not committed to excellence. It is scandalous that in Buenos Aires a pair of well-made boots costs twenty pesos. Fine furniture and other manufactures should all be allowed importation. If they are inferior to local manufactures then no harm is done; if they are superior they will invite comparison and force our artisans to improve their work and offer competition. In any case prices will come down, to the benefit of artisans as well as consumers.

The interests whom I represent make the following requests: that free trade be granted for a term of two years, with possibility of renewal by the supreme junta; that the right of export be open to anyone by the simple fact of being a native of the kingdom, together with free choice of sales methods; and that all importers be obliged to take half their returns in agricultural products of the country.

These, Your Excellency, are the wishes of 20,000 landowners whom I represent, and the only way to ensure the revival of our fortunes and the recovery of the treasury. Buenos Aires, 30 September 1809.

11

Chile: Poverty by Default

Manuel de Salas

The Spanish empire in the eighteenth century was home to various economies. Some, such as Mexico and Peru, were sources of precious metals, profits, and revenue. Others, such as Venezuela and the Río de la Plata, were new frontiers of agricultural settlement, hitherto marginalized, now more valued. And other colonies, such as Chile (and perhaps Central America), existed simply by conquest, to occupy imperial space and keep at bay hostile Indians and intrusive foreigners. They were given a minimum of attention and protection compatible with their role, and their economies were not expected to deliver large remittances to the metropolis. In the case of Chile, remote from the major shipping routes, minimalism degenerated into inertia and neglect. Yet this did not prevent the growth of regional identity, creole patriotism, consciousness of wrongs. Grievance was heightened in the second half of the eighteenth century when a modest restructuring of administrative and fiscal institutions still left Chile behind in the priorities of empire, while across the Andes Buenos Aires and its hinterland were promoted to higher roles. Colonial monopoly was relaxed under the later Bourbons; access to international markets was easier and foreign manufactures were in greater supply. Chile's difficulty was to earn a surplus to pay for expanding imports; failure meant that the market was glutted—bankruptcies followed, local industry declined, and precious metals flowed out of the country. At the close of empire Chileans believed that their economy needed freedom—not necessarily free trade but freedom to impose its own protection, to arrange its own taxes, to control its own growth. Above all, in accordance with the

Translated by John Lynch from "Representación hecha al Ministro de Hacienda don Diego de Gardoqui por el Síndico del Real Consulado de Santiago, sobre el estado de la agricultura, industria y comercio del reino de Chile," 10 January 1796, Manuel de Salas, *Escritos de don Manuel de Salas y documentos relativos a el y a su familia* (3 vols., Santiago, 1910–14), I, 152–94.

political economy of the Enlightenment, it wanted freedom to expand, to develop resources neglected by the metropolis, and to earn more by producing more. This seems to have been the thinking behind the following extract. Manuel de Salas, a creole intellectual and administrator, was educated in Lima and later exposed to Spanish reformism during his residence in the peninsula. He was appointed treasurer of the consulado of Chile in 1795, shortly after its creation, an appropriate position for one who believed in economic growth, public welfare, and education reform, all under the beneficent influence of the state. But the state to which Salas deferred was the colonial state, and the trade he sought to expand was Spain's monopoly trade. While his thought did not overtly extend to free trade or economic independence, it was nevertheless important as a source of independence. He painted a grim picture of the poverty, stagnation, and hopelessness inherent in Chile's colonial condition, and he singled out the small and restricted consumer market as a major obstacle to growth.

The kingdom of Chile is without doubt the most fertile in America and the most propitious for human happiness; yet in fact it is the most wretched of all the Spanish dominions. With scope for everything, it lacks the essentials, and imports products that it could easily export to others.

In spite of its resources, the population is estimated at no higher than 400,000; and while it is capable of sustaining at least 1,000 persons per square league, the kingdom has at most only a twentieth of the population it could hold. This astonishing lack of people, a true gauge of the state of a country, will give an accurate idea of Chile's poverty. It is truly amazing that a country should be such a desert when it responds generously to cultivation, its women are highly fertile, it is always open to immigrants, rarely sees its own people emigrating, and loses men neither to the army nor the navy. But it is even more extraordinary that among the inhabitants of such a country, whose modest production is exported to feed other places, there are many people near to poverty, very few free from it, and even fewer who enjoy a good living. Nothing is more common than to see in the same fields that have just produced bumper crops, people with their arms outstretched begging bread, the same arms that have just gathered the crops, and perhaps in the same place where a *fanega* of wheat has just been sold at a ridiculously low price.

At first sight the observer may resolve the contradiction by concluding that the basic cause is the innate idleness attributed to the Indians, from which all those born in this continent have been contaminated, and which has been increased and encouraged by nature's abundance; or, more tolerantly, it may be attributed to the climate. But no one bothers to analyse the situation or takes the trouble to seek more direct and realistic reasons. The laziness and soft living attributed to these peoples is an error, but it is an error I have often noticed even among broadminded men. Every day in the squares and streets you see sturdy laborers offering their services, underselling themselves in exchange for payment in kind, much of it useless and overpriced. You see them early in a morning at the doors of country houses begging for work, while unfortunately the owners have to dismiss them. I see this all the time in the public works of the capital, where swarms of wretches arrive to request work, begging a chance, and so insistently that it is difficult to refuse them or to increase their misery by sending them away. So in the winter one offers them a silver real a day, half a real for the children, although the lowest rate is one and a half reales, rising to twice that amount in some works. In this way as many people gain work as the funds allow, and there are always more waiting; the accounts prove it. No one can say that projects or works remain incomplete for lack of labor: as soon as something is announced hundreds of people arrive. Wheat harvests, which need numerous laborers all at once, are always gathered in time, no matter how abundant; the wine harvests, which require more workers than those in Spain because of the particular processes used here, are all completed at the same time, employing human labor alone; the mines, which involve harsh working conditions, are never short of labor. Therefore, it is not idleness that creates the problem; it is lack of work which makes people idle, some of them for most of the year, others for most of their lives.

If, as some indolent politicians have argued, agriculture and mining constitute sufficient work for all, people would not wait to be told; they would be drawn to work by need and expectation. But land is only cultivated in proportion to consumption; otherwise dearth or decline result. [Chile's lack of population reduces consumption. But export to adjacent regions such as Peru and Paraguay could conform to a useful division of labor and mean that we were not deprived] of that exchange of goods and free trade that the Author of creation has instituted in giving us different lands, climates, and talents. . . . The consulado will seek to argue the case for establishing that fraternity which creates common interests, as of a single people, to extend these ideas to include the metropolis, and to open the door to its products. Convinced that what is to the advantage of the metropolis is also ours, the consulado will provide preferential opportunities for profits, which will flow back to these countries in the protection, support, and security that the metropolis provides; for while we should always have held these convictions out of rational economic motives, now we ought to hold them for this reason and from gratitude. . . .

The trade of Chile with the rest of America is almost all in agricultural products and only a small part in industrial goods. Wheat is the leading export: 220,000 fanegas are sent each year to Lima, 170,000 of them from the main port of Valparaiso where they are purchased by the owners of 26 ships engaged in this trade, all inhabitants of Lima, and three from Concepción whose port takes larger vessels. Bound by common interest, they buy at the lowest possible price, leaving only a small profit for the producers who are badly rewarded for their land and labor. Measures taken to avoid this harm are defeated by the fraudulent practices of the warehouses; instead of holding the products for the owners, who pay them one real per fanega for the service, they sell directly to the ships and so deprive the owners of the advantages to be gained from fixing prices according to the state of the market. In Valparaiso the system of monopoly means that the warehouses, which are situated at great distance from the producers, know the prices in the countryside and at the port, and without risking any money can buy and sell, and hold on to the profits of the owners, who in ignorance of what has been done finally order the warehouses to sell off cheaply. All the measures that have been taken to end these abuses have been useless. . . . The basic reason is that a country is at the mercy of its resources. Those that are limited to livestock, wheat, and minerals are poor and always subject to the law of the buyers, especially when the market is fixed and limited and they have no other activity to compensate. Here we only have Lima; there is no possibility of holding back, or selling elsewhere, or producing another product.

The trade in European goods is subject to the vagaries of war and other eventualities, and their importation is therefore difficult to list. On the other hand it can be measured, because it corresponds to the export of precious metals, which are the only means of payment. It is known with certainty that of the 1,300,000 pesos in gold, silver, and copper which are exported every year 250,000 pesos can be deducted: this is used to buy 100,000 arrobas of yerba in Buenos Aires. The rest pays for European goods. There is no doubt that much more could be bought if we had the means of paying, and that Spanish ships would come more frequently to these ports if we had the cargoes to fill them. There is no point in opening ports and lowering prices if the peninsula does not consume more and take more of our products. It will simply mean that Chile is filled with more than it can digest, and has more commerce than it needs and can sustain; that the continual extraction of money, which the internal market needs just as a machine needs oil, will obstruct and weaken its economy, depriving it not only of coinage but also of commodities, and of a resource that the country ought to conserve.

The state of our population and trade will give a good idea of the state of industry. Only vital necessities are produced. Even those that have been long established still fall far short of perfection; they lack the first essentials for their improvement—design, technology, investment—the mother of invention and wealth, which it is not to the advantage of the metropolis to oppose, and which should be directed to making men industrious and active. Crude metalworkers, tasteless silversmiths, carpenters without ideas, masons ignorant of architecture, painters oblivious of design, tailors who can only imitate, vulgar tinsmiths, dishonest shoemakers, this is the rabble who pass for artisans here, people who owe more to inclination than to acquired skill or formal training. Ignorance, poor earnings, and other defects often cause them to abandon their trade, take up another, and end by mastering none. An academy or society might inspire them and improve their knowledge, so that at least they would have clear objectives and the means of reaching them.

In agriculture nature has responded generously to the efforts of men. The products of an equable climate, and those too of its variations, all sprout and grow under the hands of its cultivators; nothing has been tried that has not been successful, and progress has been halted only by lack of demand. The number of consumers never changes, which limits production to a modest level and acts as a disincentive. Wine is the only expanding product in the countryside, in spite of the stationary or even diminishing population, gaining ground at the expense of public health and morals. The wine of Concepción and Coquimbo has hitherto had only a limited cultivation; now it is going to be developed by a company that enjoys tax exemption and plans to export aguardiente to the archbishopric of Charcas. If they manage to resist the competition of the producers who have previously supplied that market, then they should make a profit; otherwise they will only have increased the glut of aguardiente created by excessive planting and undue expectations. Some is sold to the garrisons, but the regular drinkers are to be found in the ports and mining camps. If total production could be ascertained, people would be surprised how much is consumed by so few drinkers.

Cattle breeding is a major activity. An animal on the hoof fetches up to ten pesos, and in salt meat, tallow, fat, and hides it will yield the same price, while a sheep will sell for seven or eight reales and a ewe for three and a half. These prices, the result of a favorable conjunction of circumstances, led to an increase in production, which in turn reduced prices to almost half the old level.

Enduring custom, lack of options, and reluctance to abandon work already begun cause landowners to continue developing the same crops, cattle, and sales. Once their wealth is exhausted, owners keep up a pretense, trying to hide their decline, without deceiving anyone and only making matters worse. They never calculate expenditure and income, fearing to face the evil day; when this arrives, only too soon, and they are overtaken by mortgage or bankruptcy, they realise they have been living on their capital, and see their property illegally foreclosed into mortmain and their children reduced to a state of poverty and distress.

The deplorable state of Chile, far from inducing despair for its remedy, ought to be a stimulus to seeking it. The country itself contains the resources to restore its population, industry, trade, and agriculture, and to become as useful to the metropolis as it has hitherto been a burden. Spain needs consumers of its products and manufactures; Chile needs to consume and pay for them. The first needs a large market, the second the means to meet its imports. And the happiness of both countries would be complete if the goods that Chile sent in return were not those produced in Spain but had to be bought from other nations. Thus with its exports unhindered and its due dependence on the mother country preserved, Chile would be free of its afflictions. Where man finds the means to satisfy the wants with which he was born, to subsist, to live in comfort, to make his way, there he increases and multiplies. He finds satisfaction where he has steady work, open to whatever improvement he cares to give it, and sufficient to occupy a quarter of the people who form society and who ought to sustain the other three quarters. This kingdom has the capacity to provide occupation not only for a quarter of its actual inhabitants but for seventeen times more than it actually contains.

[To achieve this it is only necessary to diversify and exploit the resources which Chile possesses, to increase their range, and enlarge their production. These should include medicinal verdigris, alum, ammonia, potash and other forest products, zinc, platinum, cobalt, bismuth, tanned leather, hemp, rigging and other naval stores, and last but not least flax for the Spanish linen industry.] If private companies are unable or unwilling to take risks and overcome obstacles in order to develop these resources, revenue from the royal treasury could be employed in the expectation if not of great profit at least of great advantage for the revenue, population, shipping, and inhabitants of this kingdom. The success of these projects and their stimulus to job creation will give birth to other commercial enterprises, which will provide cargoes for Spanish shipping and bring more to our ports. People will settle in towns to undertake new employment, and the king will have more subjects producing for exports to the peninsula. The increase of population will surpass the usual one percent, for marriages will become more common as the means to undertake them and to support families improve. Land will be divided naturally and in proportions suitable to the demands of cultivation, as happens in the valley of Aconcagua, which is fertile in wheat and close to a port, and generally in the vicinity of the capital and the major towns. This can be done without resorting to the violent methods of those who denounce the great landowners and attribute to them the depopulation of our country, mistaking cause for effect. Crimes will cease, for these are the consequences of idleness and neglect, which here as elsewhere are more common in provinces where there is less employment. Decisions will be taken to supply Buenos Aires by sea with the flour it needs in times of dearth, and Panama too, which at the moment is supplied by speculators in the produce of our country, and perhaps Havana and Cartagena, hitherto supplied by Jamaica and other English colonies.

PART THREE

COLONIAL SOCIETY: CONTINUITY AND CONFLICT

12

Aristocracy and People

Alberto Flores Galindo

Colonial government and society were scenes of intense competition. Rivalries between jealous officials, disputes between landowners and merchants, tension between proprietors and peons, and between whites and castas—these were the routines of colonial life, and they complicate the thesis of peninsular-creole antipathy. In Peru there were linked groups of landed, merchant, municipal and bureaucratic oligarchies, in which peninsulares and creoles merged as a white ruling class. In this way functions, interests, and kinship are seen as more significant than the peninsular-creole dichotomy. Alberto Flores Galindo (1949–1990), who was Professor of History in the Pontificia Universidad Católica, Lima, reopened and revised many aspects of the social history of Peru during the period of colony and republic. In his book *Aristocracia y plebe* (Lima, 1984), on which the following extract is based, he shows that in the last decades of the eighteenth century new waves of immigration to Peru reshaped the local ruling class into one dominated by recently arrived peninsulares who quickly came to control commerce, forge links with the bureaucracy, acquire titles of nobility, and constitute for Spain a loyal support but also a demanding one. As they were all first or second generation peninsulares, they left no room at the top for creole competition or even resentment; rather, it was they who absorbed the eligible Peruvians. Thus the Lima elite came to be characterized by solidarity against the popular sectors and by loyalty towards Spain.

During the eighteenth century, reflecting the movement of shipping into and out of the port of Callao, the dominant colonial class was

Translated by John Lynch from Alberto Flores Galindo, "Independencia y clases sociales," *Independencia y revolucion (1780–1840)*, Compilador Alberto Flores Galindo (2 vols., Instituto Nacional de Cultura, Lima, 1987), I, 125–44, and printed by permission of Cecilia Rivera.

restructured: the basic component became the great merchants of Lima, linked to the bureaucracy and even admitted to the orders of nobility. Not all the wealthy belonged to an order, but all aristocrats had to be wealthy; as well as nobility the other indispensable qualification was affluence, especially for the new order of Charles III. Between 1761 and 1810 349 titles of nobility were granted.

Lima's wholesale trade was based on commercial exchanges with the peninsula and control over neighboring colonial areas, Quito and Valparaiso. Possession of the major merchant marine in the Pacific, consisting in 1818 of 81 frigates, 76 brigs, 13 schooners, and 34 lesser vessels enabled the monopoly to be exercised by a number of merchants who were also shipowners and owners of warehouses in the port of Callao. In addition to the profits they obtained in the external market, they also expanded their activities in the internal sector, ranging from itinerant traders, to the compulsory commerce of the corregidores, and the construction of a network of trade by a system of credit. They came together in the consulado, the business guild of the time, which enabled them to operate coherently, above the divisions which could develop between greater and lesser merchants.

Tensions between Spaniards and creoles occupied a secondary place. The majority were peninsulares or alternatively, as sons of immigrants, considered themselves as such, so much so that they regarded the very name of creole as offensive and pejorative. Not even José de la Riva Agüero—one of the so-called precursors of independence—could accept a term that had originated in the Caribbean to define the shameful mixture, as he saw it, of whites and blacks. These men were strongly marked by a combination of racism and feeling of supposed superiority in being considered European. The merchant aristocracy shared with a number of large mineowners and landowners, and with the Church, a conception of society as one of estates: as in the human body, each single organ could fulfil only one function. Just as the head was destined to think and the feet to walk, and it was impossible to switch them, so peasants and slaves could not possibly hope to become masters. Apart from noble title, public office, and Spanish status, education was the other privilege that set the boundaries between aristocracy and common people, if we may employ two terms of the time.

One example among many could be Domingo Ramírez de Arellano. Born in 1742 in Logroño, Navarre, he came to America as the heir to an uncle, Andrés Ramírez de Arellano. There the newcomer took possession of the ship "Nuestra Señora de la Mercedes," one of the frigates trading between Callao and Valparaiso. His interests diversified with the acquisition of a hacienda in Magdalena. He belonged to the Order of Calatrava, was prior of the consulado (1783–94) and captain of the halberdiers. Following the tendency of the colonial aristocracy to inbreed, he married Catalina de Baquíjano y Carillo de Córdoba, daughter of Juan Bautista Baquíjano, a recent (first third of the century) arrival in Peru who had ships, houses in Lima, and haciendas in Cañete and Jauja. His daughter also bought the hacienda Pando and the farm Aguilar in Maranga. The marriage to Domingo Ramírez de Arellano produced a daughter, Maria Josefa, who married Gaspar Antonio de Osma, judge and member of the Council of His Majesty.

Apart from marriage alliances, the Lima aristocracy found its cohesion in taking up the defense of the colonial order. In its origins it had benefited from the commercial monopoly and hegemony assigned to Lima. From then onwards its members understood that their future as a class depended on staying with the *pacto colonial*. This conviction held firm in spite of the fact that the Bourbon reforms, in creating the viceroyalty of the Río de la Plata and freedom of trade, directly harmed their interests. But these setbacks were bearable compared to what could occur with a victory for the patriots. The outbreak of the wars of independence had the effect of binding the future of the aristocracy even closer to Spain. A report of the consulado (about 1810) argued that "the Americas are an integral and major part of the Spanish monarchy. Closely bound to it and always collaborating for its greater glory and prosperity, it makes it extremely difficult for any foreign power ever to overthrow it. . . . So the Americas are the same thing as Spain, for they are a constituent and major part of Spain."

The consequences of these assumptions are undeniable, and they are demonstrated too in the less publicized activity of the merchant, namely the payments and donations towards the maintenance of the armies. Some of them may be briefly listed. In 1780 the consulado undertook to support 1,000 armed men and a further 1,000 with uniforms to confront "the great rebellion" of Túpac Amaru; in 1810 they granted a donation of 1,000 pesos, and in the following year 21,000 pesos for the Concordia regiment; in 1812 they granted a total of 496,000 pesos to maintain the troops in Upper Peru; there followed donations of 45,285 pesos and others of 100,000 to "recover" Quito; in 1814 the aid reached 1,000,000 pesos, not to mention a loan of 40,000; in the following year they granted a loan of half a million, and in 1821 a grant of 100,000 pesos. All this without counting private contributions. Just a few months before San Martin's entry into Lima the consulado was still offering compensations to all deserters from the rebel army. At no time did the merchants cast doubt on their royalist position, their alignment with Spain, and loyalty to the monarch, but in the end their obstinacy would be one of the causes of their ruin as a social class, not only because of the victory of the patriots, but also because of the immediate consequences of the military conflict, namely loss of markets like Chile and Quito, destruction of Lima's merchant marine, and sacking of haciendas.

If Peru was one of the foci of royalist resistance, this was not due exclusively to the personality of the viceroy, Fernando de Abascal, as traditional historiography insists on repeating, but on the presence in Lima of a colonial aristocracy which was the most numerous in the whole of Spanish America. Although the last third of the eighteenth century did not provide a favorable conjuncture for their business, the economic power they retained was enough to support the campaigns against all the efforts of subversion.

Every social revolution enters its first stage with the division of the ruling class: this is a sign of that class's breakdown and of its inability to maintain itself at the head of society. This did not happen in Peru, either in 1780, or 1810, or 1821. While the colonial aristocracy was not devoid of internal differences—in the elections of priors of the consulado, for example—it was a stable structure, without significant cracks, in spite of the many social conflicts of the time. Therefore, like rigid buildings in an earthquake, it came to an end amidst a catastrophic collapse. This general picture could only be made more precise with particular cases, like that of the conde de la Vega del Rhen, an unsuccessful conspirator from the time of Abascal onwards. In 1821 there were few aristocrats ready to collaborate with San Martín. Some had emigrated to Spain, like the marqués de Valle-Umbroso, others disappeared to take refuge in the monasteries of Lima, or made their way to the castles of Callao to avoid the patriots and a rising of the common people of Lima. Among those who collaborated with the new regime, some like Torre Tagle soon regretted it. The anti-Spanish campaign unleashed by Bernardo de Monteagudo frightened them: for them it was a reproduction of the Jacobin terror in Lima itself.

In this way the war of independence, perhaps in spite of some of its leaders, ended by producing a change of scene in the social landscape of Peru: the collapse as a class of the colonial aristocracy. This event, which is now ignored by many historians, did not go unnoticed at the time by shrewd observers such as Córdoba y Urrutia, who remarked at the end of the 1830s: "The war of independence has removed the American capitalists; and their wealth is now reduced to whatever property they have, to rural and urban estates whose earnings sustain their families." The complaints of Doña Grimanesa de la Puente, obliged to support an extensive family following the loss of a ship and the plundering of her hacienda of Chuquitanta, exemplify the fate of a social class alien to the country and incapable of noticing the almost inevitable course of political events in the continent. In the final analysis the problem is not that the aristocracy were obsequiously royalist but that they were totally incapable of proposing an alternative, of trying a different road which in accord with their interests would not involve their economic and social collapse.

The outcome of a revolution is decided within the popular classes rather than at the level of the dominant class. The banditry that ravaged the roads and valleys of the coast, the frequent rural revolts in the sierra, the persistence of the rebellion of Juan Santos Atahualpa are signs not only of a social malaise but of a deep unrest, a refusal to submit, which spread to a variety of places and over the whole eighteenth century. Was this popular violence, however, capable of producing any alternative to colonialism and the Lima aristocracy?

Independence begins in 1780. The Tupamarist uprising surprises any student of peasant movements by the sheer extension of the rebellion, from Cuzco to the altiplano, fanning out to Huarochirí, in the sierra of Lima, and Salta, Jujuy and Tarapacá in the south. . . . Events began in Cuzco in November 1780 and did not end with the execution of Túpac Amaru in the following April but lasted until 1782 after the siege of La Paz by Catari. In short the whole of the Quechua and Aymara speaking territory was in turmoil. . . .

Perhaps the complexity of the Tupamarist movement lies in the fact that it was not only a peasant rising, nor was it a spontaneous or unforeseen outbreak. From the beginning it had an organization, a specific group of leaders, and a program of action. In this sense the conscious intention, the historic will, played a decisive role. In confrontation with colonialism and the Lima aristocracy, Túpac Amaru outlined a program that could be reduced to three central points. (a) The expulsion of the Spaniards, or *chapetones* as they were scornfully called. It was not sufficient to suppress the corregidores and *repartos;* the audiencia and viceroy also had to be abolished, and all dependence on the Spanish monarch broken. (b) The restoration of the Inca empire. Faithful to his reading of the Inca Garcilaso, Túpac Amaru thought that the Inca monarchy could be restored and the descendants of the Cuzco aristocracy placed at its head. (c) The introduction of basic changes in the economic structure: suppression of the mita, elimination of large haciendas, abolition of aduanas and alcabalas, freedom of commerce. The movement claimed the leadership of the curacas and the Inca nobles. This social sector had managed to survive in the colonial regime and was even recognized by the Spaniards. From a position of serving the system they seem to have experienced a change of conscience in the eighteenth century in a process that John Rowe called Inca nationalism. But in order to succeed the movement needed not only peasant support but also the collaboration of other social sectors, especially the creoles. Túpac Amaru thought in terms of a new "body politic" where creoles, mestizos, negroes, and Indians would live in harmony, breaking with distinction of castas and generating solidarity between all those who were not Spaniards. The program had obvious features of what we could call a national movement.

Túpac Amaru, then, did not confine himself to requesting suppression of the mita; he demanded—in spite of the view of Heraclio Bonilla—a whole range of changes and proposed an alternative to the colonial regime. So this was more than a rebellion: it was a popular revolution, not like the bourgeois revolutions of France and England, but similar to those great popular risings such as that of Pugachev in Russia or, in the previous century, those in Naples and Catalonia. This is how independence began in Peru, before other parts of the Spanish empire. In a sense it was a premature event.

To substantiate this, let me suggest that the reader reexamine the texts of Túpac Amaru himself. But if anyone has doubts concerning his self-proclaimed title of Inca-King of Peru or his signature as José I in clear contrast to Charles III of Spain, it would be sufficient carefully to reconstruct the events: formation of a rebel army, appointment of authorities, and raising of taxes in the liberated territories. No one in 1780 had the slightest doubt about the "separatist" purpose of the Cuzco movement. The great fear among members of the consulado was based on real events.

Yet the movement failed. . . . Shortly after it began the peasant masses surged beyond the initial proposals and, at the same time as they were proclaiming Túpac Amaru as Inca, they proceeded with unprecedented violence to destroy Spanish properties and all the symbols of domination. They did not distinguish between peninsulares and creoles, and even confronted wealthy curacas. For these campesinos the content of the revolution ought to be exclusively indigenous: they thought of returning to Tawantinsuyo, but recreating it as an egalitarian society. . . . They sacked the parish churches, destroyed the *obrajes*, attacked the royal treasury. Naturally these actions alienated the creoles and undermined the support of the mestizos. They also explain the ambivalent position of the curacas and nobles of Cuzco. In spite of the role which the Tupamarist program claimed for them, in the end, like Pumacahua, they opted for loyalty to the king of Spain and preservation of a system which, however harmful, provided the security that Túpac Amaru could not guarantee them, once he had been overtaken by his followers. This defection, together with that of the creoles, meant that the movement ended up without a ruling group capable of convincing the participants of the viability of its program. . . .

The unity of the peasant and Indian world in the colonial regime was more apparent than real, and the revolution seemed to release those divisive forces that undermined the popular classes. Against the community Indians, the colonial administration put together an improvised army with the help of corregidores and hacendados, most of it composed of hacienda peasants, a large sector assimilated to the colonial regime and reluctant to engage in any dissidence, in fact more inclined to collaborate in crushing it. Differences between Quechuas and Aymaras also emerged, and clashes between loyal curacas and the mass of the Indians. But these curacas would soon learn that their efforts were not rewarded: from 1782 the crown suppressed the titles of Inca nobility and sought to extinguish all record of the Incas; politically and economically the Cuzco nobles were finished. They were the real losers in 1780. As they disappeared from history as a social force, so Indian and peasant would become synonymous. . . .

The violence experienced from 1780 would never be forgotten by creole intellectuals: from then onwards these had to recognize their minority condition and social isolation. Figures like Hipólito Unanue, Manuel Lorenzo de Vidaurre, José de la Riva Agüero, had the ability and the necessary enlightenment to criticize the colonial regime and the society of estates, but they were also conscious that such criticisms could unleash a force beyond control. Uncertainty, doubt, insecurity, these features came to define the intellectual elite, caught between the aristocracy and the popular classes. Infected by the same fear that filled the ruling class, the intellectuals did not advance beyond a timid reformism. Only at the last minute would they enter the ranks of the patriots.

The Tupamarist revolution was visualized on a scale comprising the whole viceroyalty. Almost by definition, it was not intended to be a regional movement. The new capital of the independent country would be Cuzco and the sierra would prevail over other regions, but the culmination of the revolution would be the taking of Lima. This is why Túpac Amaru sought the support of the slaves, on whose labor depended the export agriculture of the coast. Although there were no more than 40,000 in all Peru, the great majority of slaves lived on the central coast, 10,000 of them in Lima, where they formed 16% of the urban population.

The slaves appeared to possess distinct features of a social class, but in the course of the eighteenth century, as the slave population declined in relative terms as a result of the increase in miscegenation (mulattos and other castas), the blacks integrated into urban culture, forgetting their African languages and cults. Diversity of employment caused the fragmentation of slave society, and in the squares and streets of the city they mingled with the marginal groups, people without jobs or trades who swarmed around Lima. In these conditions a traditional form of social protest, the *palenque,* was forgotten and replaced by banditry. In the previous century the palenque represented a desperate attempt to reproduce, in remote areas of the coastal valleys, African customs and even political hierarchies. But from 1760 the palenques became simply a refuge for runaway slaves who turned to banditry to subsist. This is a common phenomenon, in which violence is situated midway between delinquency and social protest but never implies a real challenge to the system. Sterile violence. There was no "black liberation" equivalent to that of the Indians.

Banditry underlined another fact: the tension between Indians and blacks. While slaves, along with creoles, mestizos, and even poor Spanish were frequently to be found in the bands, Indian peasants were absent and in fact were no less victims of the bandits than were travelers and itinerant merchants. So the *yanaconas* and community Indians of Huacho, Chancay, and Chilca collaborated with the Spanish authorities, reporting on the refuges of the criminals, informing against their operations, and sometimes seizing them. In turn the bandits attacked the Indians with the same cruelty as they used against the Spaniards.

On 5 July 1821, before the entry of the patriot troops into Lima, the city was without a garrison, and panic broke out, spread by the aristocracy and other sectors of society. People were afraid not of outrages by the troops but of a great revolt of the slaves in Lima, a kind of reenactment of the risings in Haiti and Santo Domingo. The British naval officer, Basil Hall, a direct observer of these events, did not share the alarm: "I could not, for one, bring myself to suppose this at all probable; for the slaves had never any leisure to plan such a scheme: their habits were not those of union or enterprise, for they were all domestic servants, and thinly scattered over an immense city, with very rare opportunities of confidential intercourse."

It was precisely in the social fragmentation and the clash of interests that the colonial order found the surest guarantee of its stability. This social disjunction derived from various sources: difference of cultural origins, as between European intellectuals and Andean peasants; race differences, as between blacks and Indians; occupational diversity, and conflicting interests, as between community Indians and hacienda workers, or between curacas and peasants. . . . To attempt to launch a social revolution, as Túpac Amaru wanted, involved struggling with all these divisions which the Spaniards found so useful as mechanisms of social control.

All colonial systems are based on the principle of "divide and rule." Relations between slaves and peasants were constant preoccupations of the Spanish authorities, as related in their correspondence and reports. The census taken in the Peruvian viceroyalty after the Tupamarist revolution was not only intended to establish the size of the population; even more urgently perhaps it was concerned to ascertain the numerical relations between the various ethnic groups, in order to safeguard the social balance. As the viceroy, Gil de Taboada, reported in February 1791: "The proportions of the various castas need not be a cause of anxiety, as they were on other occasions during times of disturbance, out of ignorance of their true ratio. As can be seen in the enclosed table, for every Indian or *originario* there are 5⅛ of the other castas; for every slave there are just over 4⅔ free people. For every colored person, free and slave, there is one white; and in the event of the slaves establishing a common front with the Indians and mestizos, for every one of these there are two whites and free coloreds."

From all the above some conclusions may be suggested. At the end of the eighteenth century the social structure of Peru was in a process of reconstruction. At the top stood a dominant class, protected by the colonial apparatus and commercial expansion. Within the popular sectors social differentiation—some of it spontaneous, some of it deliberately encouraged—prevented the formation of a class structure. The division between slaves and popular sectors in Lima was an extreme example. Only where there was a chance of overcoming this situation, as in Cuzco because of peasant numbers and survival of an Inca aristocracy, was it possible to attempt an alternative to colonialism. But the success of this option depended on the fragile relations between the Indian elite and the mass of the peasantry. In the end the Tupamarist revolution remained open to the possibilities which the peasants had to transform colonial society. Then it was found that the Andean people, apart from their common condition of "colonized," were still divided by significant differences. Paradoxically the defeat of 1780 would not imply the end of native milleniarism: it continued in the independence period and beyond; but the wars of independence caused first the eclipse of the Inca aristocracy and then the irreversible collapse of the colonial dominant class.

The changes experienced by Peruvian society in the fifty years from 1780 to 1830 are obvious enough, but it is also true that even greater expectations were held by the popular sectors. The peasants and the common people of the towns did not imagine that a revolution could be limited to political change or the removal of the aristocracy; for them, consciously or instinctively, revolution meant a fundamental change of structure, a total reversal of the existing order. At the beginning of the nineteenth century several murals in Lima—one of them attributed to the popular artist Poncho Fierro—portrayed the picture of "the world upside down." The criminal waits for the judge, the usurer practices charity, the bulls torment the toreros. If we feel that independence was a failure, it is because it had the possibility of leading to a different outcome, as many of the protagonists imagined. This explains the obsession with the subject in our historiography: to borrow a phrase of Jorge Basadre, it is still seen as a promise unfulfilled.

13

Creoles and Indians, Reluctant Allies

Heraclio Bonilla

The Peruvian whites were always aware of the superior numbers of Indians and mestizos and of the volcano in their midst. Outnumbered as they were, they were reluctant to disavow the colonial state or to put themselves at the head of an Indian movement that they might not be able to control. Their rejection of Indian objectives strengthened their position in relation to Spain. For it was obvious to the colonial authorities that Spanish defenses against Indian rebellion depended on creole cooperation. For these reasons the creoles were conscious of some bargaining power, and when, in the years after 1810, the possibility arose of political reform from the Spanish constitutionalists—reform that would reduce the absolute power of viceregal government and give the creoles a greater share in decision-making—the creoles were ready to move. The colonial state benefited not only from divisions between creoles and Indians but also from disunity within Indian ranks. During the rebellion of Túpac Amaru at least twenty caciques, driven in part by personal, community, and ethnic rivalry, had kept their people loyal to the Crown, and subsequently received rewards and pensions. The most distinguished of these was Mateo Pumacahua, cacique of Chincheros, who still adhered to Spain during the first years of the Spanish American revolution and even served in punitive expeditions to Upper Peru. Pumacahua was rewarded with further titles and offices, though these tended to fall below expectations; he broke with the colonial government and retired disillusioned to his hacienda at Urquillos. Meanwhile the cause of Indian reform had made little progress. In 1811 the Cortes of Cadiz abolished the Indian tribute, and in 1812 it suppressed the mita and personal service. But legislation alone was incapable of effect-

Translated by John Lynch from Heraclio Bonilla, "Clases populares y Estado en el contexto de la crisis colonial," *La Independencia en el Perú* (2nd edn., Instituto de Estudios Peruanos, Lima, 1981), pp. 24–25, 38–56, and printed by permission of the author and publisher.

ing social change, and the reforms were frustrated by vested interests in Peru. Creole alienation, Indian discontent—the situation appeared right for renewed collaboration. Heraclio Bonilla, of the Instituto de Estudios Peruanos and the Pontificia Universidad Católica, Lima, uses the Cuzco rebellion of 1814 to suggest a reinterpretation of creole-Indian relations and their significance in the making of independence.

In Cuzco the election of a governing junta directed by José Angulo in August 1814 was the culmination of a series of moves which had been taking place since the end of 1812 and whose basic aim was to replace the existing authorities of local government. If the structure of this rebellion was of long-term character, the immediate conjuncture that provoked its outbreak was closely linked to the political guarantees contained in the Constitution of 1812, promulgated on 19 March by the Cortes of Cádiz. . . . The objectives of the Constitution were to democratize Spanish government and to suppress all privileges of a feudal kind; with regard to the American colonies, they recognized full political equality between European and American Spaniards . . . cancelled the mita and *repartos*, abolished the mercury monopoly, and suppressed the slave trade. Thus the creoles could now hope to realize their demands within the imperial system itself.

In Peru the news of the Constitution of 1812 was received simultaneously with hope and approval among the creoles, resistance and fear among the colonial authorities. In spite of his misgivings, Viceroy Abascal distributed the copies of the Constitution which arrived in Lima in September 1812, and at the same time he took the measures required of him. Two of these were of particular concern to the creoles: the abolition of the old cabildos and their replacement by elected members, and the nomination of deputies for the Cortes which were due to meet in September 1813. One deputy was to be elected for every 70,000 inhabitants, and elections were to be held every two years. According to this, the viceroyalty of Peru qualified for twenty-two deputies. Following the preliminaries, elections were held in Lima on 13 December 1812 for the new constitutional cabildo; these seemed to confirm the fears of the peninsulares, for only four of the sixteen deputies elected were Europeans.

Copies of the Constitution of 1812 reached Cuzco at the beginning of December, and the mere knowledge of its arrival served to mobilize the creoles. The situation, moreover, was highly propitious. The audiencia of Cuzco, established as a consequence of the Túpac Amaru rebellion, was the political authority of the region in the absence of a permanent president. The executive authority had changed hands five times between 1809 and 1814. And military control was weak owing to the departure of Brigadier José Manuel de Goyeneche and his royalist troops to fight insurgency in the provinces of the Río de la Plata. Four days after the arrival of the Constitution the temporary president of the audiencia, Mateo García Pumacahua, received a communication drawn up by the lawyer Rafael Ramírez de Arellano and endorsed by more than thirty signatures, demanding the immediate publication of the text; "the people will not recognize the authority of the existing *alcaldes* and *regidores* for a day longer than 31 December. Either these demands are met before the end of the month or Cuzco will be leaderless and no one will obey the alcaldes and regidores, for the people have sworn only to the Constitution and they know that it is better to obey the law."

The position of Pumacahua as president of the audiencia was extremely precarious, not only because his appointment was only temporary but for a more serious reason. Pumacahua was the Indian cacique who had given important service to the Crown in actively helping to suppress the rebellion of Túpac Amaru. In recompense he received not only military honors but also appointment to the highest office in the audiencia of Cuzco. This proved to be a far from enviable position because of the deep hostility he met from the creoles. He expressed his resentment when, having imprisoned Arellano for his presumption and ordered the publication of the Constitution, he wrote to the viceroy:

> On 9 December the mail arrived and with it the copies of the Constitution sent by Your Excellency. . . . I ordered a proclamation to be published to the effect that all voters or citizens of the city should attend the publication of the Constitution; no one did so, and only I and the regidores of the old cabildo, together with my assistants, undertook that duty. . . . Many are the people who detest my promotion, ignore my services, and hate my appointment because I am an Indian. . . . Now they seek to repudiate me through the Constitution, which they only wish to observe in those things which suit them and serve their interests, and there is no impartial judge to take cognizance because of the ties between the members of the present municipal council, established with all the defects of which Your Excellency is aware.

The hostility described by Pumacahua contrasted with the enthusiastic reception he received from the common people of the city, who gave him "such firm support that even the ignorant populace carried fragments of his writings with them, because there were few copies."

At last, on 7 February 1813, Pumacahua managed to call an assembly to meet in the plaza of the Convent of La Merced and choose the electors for the new city council. But before they began, a large crowd of the people of Cuzco, before the eyes of Pumacahua himself, set free the lawyers Rafael Arellano and Manuel Borja, and the people themselves offered to stand surety for them. Then, as a result of the voting, the following five electors were chosen: Pedro López de Segovia, deputy legal adviser; Baltazar Villalonga, treasurer; Martín Valer, lieutenant-colonel; Juan José de Olañeta, captain; and Dr. Manuel Borja.

Once the city council was established, the history of this institution until its conclusion was one of permanent conflict with the audiencia, that is with the depositary of viceregal power. In the words of Manuel Pardo, one of its members: "As soon as the constitutional cabildo was installed to its own satisfaction, it began to apply pressure on all the legitimate authorities, principally the royal audiencia and the executive government. The audiencia silently and prudently accepted what it could not prevent; nor did the government take steps to restrain the increasing ambition of the cabildo, reluctant to use force and fearful perhaps of causing greater disorder."

This open conflict between creoles and peninsulares, waged from their respective power bases, the cabildo and the audiencia, intensified when the creoles learnt of the royalist defeat at Salta. Arms took over from words. On 9 October 1813 Vicente Angulo, Gabriel Béjar, and Juan Carbajal tried to capture the barracks, but the attempt failed when Mariano Zubizarreta reported it. The people of Cuzco went ahead nonetheless and sought to occupy the main square, but they were brutally repelled by the royalist forces. The final outcome was the arrest of José Angulo and Manuel Hurtado de Mendoza who were condemned to nine months' imprisonment.

These incidents and the killings in the riot of 5 November drew a strong protest from the cabildo to the audiencia, whose new acting president, Martín Concha, replied that whoever challenged his measures to guarantee public peace and security "had to be counted as seditious and friends of disorder." In the midst of these conflicts the electors of the different provinces of Cuzco proceeded on 14 March 1814 to elect the three deputies, and the reserve, to represent them in the Cortes. These were Francisco de Picoaga, field marshal, Dr. Miguel de Orosco, lawyer and parish priest of Santa Ana, Juan Munive y Mozo, lawyer and parish priest of San Jerónimo, and Gabriel Antolín de Ugarte y Gallegos as reserve.

The creoles kept up their pressure and this secured on 28 June 1814 the release on bail of Vicente Angulo and Juan Carbajal, imprisoned for the events of the previous October and November. The culmination of creole resistance came on the night of 2 August 1814, when José Angulo, Manual Hurtado de Mendoza, and José Gabriel Béjar suborned the troops at the prison, escaped, and started the rebellion. José Angulo, after seizing the regent of the audiencia and the other judges, with the sole exception of Manuel Lorenzo, was recognized the following day by the people as the chief political authority of the city. As Manuel Pardo subsequently recorded, "By daybreak on 3rd almost all officials and Europeans were in the cells of the barracks, and at 8 o'clock in the morning two gallows were erected and confessors were sent to the prison. The plan was to hang them all, but miraculously this was not carried out."

On the next day, 4 August, Angulo faced the three corporations together and, declaring his "most determined adhesion to the Constitution," requested the appointment of a Protective Junta for one year, to be composed of three members and endowed with civil and military jurisdiction. In other words he was seeking to consolidate the revolutionary government politically and militarily. Immediately following the discussion, the judge Manuel de Vidaurre, Colonel Luis Astete, and the lawyer Toribio de la Torre y Salas were elected and appointed. The cabildo, the ecclesiastical cabildo, and the provincial deputation, that is to say the three corporations, gave their backing to the revolt and the demands of José Angulo. The clergy too played a leading role and Bishop José Pérez de Armendáriz actually declared: "If God places a hand on earthly matters, on the revolution of Cuzco he has placed two."

For reasons that are not clear the composition of this Governing Junta was substantially modified in the following weeks, when it was joined by no less a person than the cacique Mateo García Pumacahua. The Indian cacique, as has been seen, headed the audiencia in the early days of the rebellion, but later, in the face of internal tensions and of the combined opposition of creoles and peninsulares, he retired to his village of Urquillos. According to the cabildo's attorneys this was "a shameful dereliction of duty," for he went "without leaving a deputy or anyone with authority to conduct the business of his office." When the first disturbances broke out in October and November Pumacahua was again summoned "without any excuse to present himself at 4 o'clock in the afternoon . . . to fulfil the duties of his office." Again Pumacahua ignored the appeal, and responded with an eloquent silence.

But this silence turned into active commitment when it was José Angulo who gave the call. Unfortunately existing documentation does not allow us fully to explain the political transformation of the Indian cacique from enemy of the rebellion of Túpac Amaru and champion of the colonial order to an effective ally of the creoles in their struggle against viceregal power. It has been argued by Christine Hunefeldt that there was in fact no transformation on the part of the cacique of Chincheros in 1814 and that he simply maintained his undeviating loyalty to the imperial regime, now renewed and represented by the Cortes, as can be seen also in the fact that Pumacahua offered to donate his salary for remittance by viceroy Abascal to Spain, as a contribution to the war against the insurgents. Whatever the motivation, the consequences of Pumacahua's enlistment in the ranks of the rebellion are clear enough. Angulo called on him, as Manuel Pardo explains, "to join the revolution, because he had a decided ascendancy over the Indians, so much so that they called him Inga, and he subsequently adapted himself to the new ideas."

Once Pumacahua was recruited to the command of the rebellion, this was constituted as follows: Marshal Mateo Pumacahua, Colonel Luis Astete, and Lieutenant-Colonel Juan Moscoso, while Vidaurre cautiously withdrew. At the same time Angulo dispatched letters to each of the neighboring provinces explaining the meaning of the rebellion and arguing that it was "made in accordance with the fundamental laws, Article 255 of which allows popular action against magistrates and judges who break the law." As such action would be almost impossible to attempt in legal form, because of the distance from the superior government, the people themselves had the right to apply justice in the early stages of political upheaval. Therefore, "the constitution of the monarchy, loyalty to our beloved monarch, Ferdinand VII, to the sovereign cortes and the serene regency of the kingdom, all are solemnly ratified. Legal, commercial, and political relations with neighboring provinces will be strictly observed by all the corporations of this capital and its districts, in total conformity with the laws and regulations promulgated by the sovereign cortes, whose observance is the sole objective."

However, it was in his Manifesto to the People of Cuzco (16 August 1814) that Angulo spelled out even more clearly the policy of the rebellion. He began by explaining the general causes of discontent in the American colonies, and went on:

> Men have always assembled in society for their security and prosperity: to secure these important objectives they have created laws, and to apply laws they have established governments. As these cannot do everything themselves, it is necessary to make use of subordinate authorities which follow the same policies as the superior government, or the executive power; in the present political situation, this resides in the regency. . . . Unfortunately, the officials actually sent out from the peninsula to govern these distant kingdoms are totally lacking in morality and justice and think only in terms of imposing an atrocious despotism demanding blind obedience. . . . These complaints from America have a long history, three hundred years in fact, and they originated with the Discovery. But as human society everywhere under-

goes progressive and radical change, so America has experienced growth and is ready to leave the infant stage of nations when they are held captive by stronger or cleverer nations. Awareness of our social position has been growing every day, and although we have been systematically retarded in our industry and mechanical skills, Americans have been advancing in political awareness, which everyone derives from the natural law and the impulse to liberty and independence inspired by the very author of our being; and of these only independence is renounced, not liberty, in defense of which people come together in political association.

Angulo then referred to the precise causes of the rebellion in Cuzco and declared:

The provinces and city of Cuzco found themselves at the center of extraordinary events, for in addition to the many infringements of the constitutional law of the monarchy, the events of 5 November, when unarmed people with peaceful intent were fired on and much blood was spilled, remained as a frightful memory; and there was not even the consolation of legal redress or appeal to the courts, which refused to listen or were themselves coerced by fear and expulsions. The contempt and humiliation with which the associates of Salta were treated, because they were not always fortunate in arms; the disregard for the qualifications of Americans in every kind of office; the assignment of the political and military government of this province to the Marqués de Valde-Hoyos, well known in the present troubles for his cruel and ruthless policy in the intendancy of La Paz and then dedicated solely to extracting from this community 15,000 pesos a month, as well as other income for the treasury, availing himself of every means of terror and tyranny for the purpose; so many wrongs, present and threatened, have aggravated the suffering of the community and its armed troops that I was acclaimed their commandant general on the morning of 3 of the present month.

On the economic policy which they planned Angulo wrote:

The merits of many old residents of this city, who in spite of their commitment and services had been long forgotten in deference to incompetent people born in another country, have been rewarded. Measures have been taken for the planting and cultivation of tobacco, a useful but neglected enterprise. . . . Other economic projects suitable for our varied and productive climate will be encouraged. My object is simply to promote the general welfare and to guarantee security and prosperity, reasons for our assembly in society but neglected by our laws and trampled underfoot by the despots and tyrants.

The grievances expressed by Angulo in this extensive document referred to the creoles, to their demands and their particular interests. One looks in vain for the slightest reference to the social condition of the Indians. Nevertheless, beyond these plans, the active enlistment of

Pumacahua and his Indian followers gave the movement in Cuzco a new and violent character. As was recognized by the crown attorney in his legal opinion against the notary José Agustín Chacón y Becerra, charged with collaborating with the enemy:

> This ungrateful wretch, unmindful of the offices he owed to the sovereign, not only conspired to raise this province but even sought to erase all emblems and signs which could call to mind the royal presence. Observing that Pumacahua still used the royal arms on the insignia of his band, he made him remove them and gave him instead a different coat of arms with figures of the Incas, hoping thus to ensure that he would revert to heathenism. This is all the more credible in that the same criminal [Chacón y Becerra] in his confession still claimed that Pumacahua was proud of his noble descent from the ancient Incas, whereas Pumacahua in his declaration stated that this was a false assumption and the only intention was to secure the respect of the Indians towards his person. Yet there is no doubt that the plan common to all of them is to destroy and exterminate every person with a white face, in order to leave only those of their own class.

The strength of the movement begun by Angulo depended directly on the support it could obtain from the creoles and Indians of the neighboring provinces. In this sense, the attempt by the General Junta of Tribunals to increase the tobacco tax aggravated the unrest among hacendados, planters, and consumers; in other words, those with grievances belonged to an important sector of the community. With this in mind, Angulo sent messages to the authorities, pointing out that the Cuzco rebellion "is exceptional in that it has not shed a single drop of blood and has been conducted in accordance with the fundamental laws of the monarchy," and that "in fact there has been no change of government, only of governors who have abused their authority." When these communications were received with silence and hostility, Angulo organized three military expeditions with the intention of spreading the rebellion: the first, commanded by José Gabriel Béjar and Mariano Angulo, to Huamanga; the second, under Pinelo y Muñecas, to Puno and La Paz; and the third, under Vicente Angulo and Pumacahua, to Arequipa.

After some partial successes, such as the occupation of Puno and La Paz, each of these detachments was defeated by royalist troops under the command of General Ramírez, a process culminating in the defeat at Umachiri (11 March 1815), the execution of Pumacahua (17 March), and the relinquishment of the government of Cuzco by Angulo (18 March).

The account of events in Cuzco from December 1812 to March 1815 yields a number of conclusions concerning the significance of the movement and the role played in it by the different social groups of Cuzco. First, and this is an essential difference from the rebellion of Túpac Amaru three decades earlier, the Cuzco rebellion was begun by creoles who were inspired by the Constitution of 1812 and sought to break the monopoly of local power exercised by peninsulares or by native supporters of the viceregal government. In this sense the Cuzco rebellion of 1814 also forms an example, probably the most extreme, of the disturbances in the local structure of power caused by the application of the political reforms.

Once again it is difficult to draw a precise line between tactics and convictions in interpreting expressions of adhesion to the monarch and the metropolis. It is even probable that at the beginning of the rebellion such a distinction did not exist in the minds of the leaders, and that a growing sense of autonomy then emerged as a result of successive clashes between the rebels and the royal armies. In this context the parish priest Mariano José de Arce was the only one openly to express his rejection of the oath of loyalty to Ferdinand VII and to pronounce for independence, to the consternation of Vicente Angulo and Pumacahua. The Constitution of 1812, after all, declared essential equality between Spaniards and Americans, as well as establishing political representation for the creoles; this satisfied the most important demands of the Americans and seemed to encourage the hope that a lasting coexistence within the imperial system was still possible. At this point these are the key problems: How far was the extension and radicalization of the rebellion the result of the leaders' knowledge that Ferdinand VII had been restored and the Constitution of 1812 repealed, and that all hope of reform within the system had vanished? And what effect did events in neighboring Buenos Aires have on the rebellion?

Given the numerical weakness of the creoles, the success of their movement depended closely on their ability to arouse and maintain the active support of the Indian population. This was the explicit aim in recruiting the cacique Pumacahua to the leadership of the rebellion, and it proved to be correct when masses of Indians joined the troops that Pumacahua led to Arequipa, and at the other extreme when no time was lost in the execution of the cacique of Chincheros because of "the powerful influence he has over the extensive Indian communities of this province." But this was not the whole story. The dispersal of the Indian population which followed the ferocious repression of the Túpac Amaru rebellion, as well as the absence of any significant reference to Indian conditions in the objectives of the rebellion of 1814, precluded a similar revolt to that of 1780. On the contrary, it has to be pointed out that the royalist troops of General Ramírez "were composed almost in

their entirety of natives of the same provinces that were in rebellion";
in the same way the presence of the indigenous population was equally
significant in the riots that endorsed the downfall of José Angulo's
government. Two witnesses furnish accurate evidence of the ambiguous and precarious nature of the creole-Indian alliance in the rebellion of 1814. The first consists of the reflections of Ramírez after his
victory over the army of Pumacahua at Umachiri:

> Although the Indian communities tended to favor the rebellion, it is also
> true that the excesses and outrages committed by these evil men from the
> very beginning had caused many individuals to draw back, and had con-
> vinced most that the revolution and war were directed against all those who
> had something to lose. And there was no one, no matter how perverse, who
> did not feel the need to support the legitimate government, and with it their
> lives and properties. An eternal truth which has been amply proved in the
> sad and bitter experience of these six years, and which will always render
> sterile and fruitless all the plans and efforts of rebels incompatible with
> conditions in Peru, and unattainable amidst the diversity of castas it con-
> tains and the opposing interests of each one of them.

The second is a judgement expressed by Manuel Pardo, regent of the
royal audiencia of Cuzco, in his account of these events:

> All those who have lived any length of time in the Americas will have
> noticed the hatred which in general the Spanish creoles nurture in their
> hearts against the Europeans and their government. This antipathy is much
> less pronounced in the Negroes and Indians, for it can be truthfully said that
> these direct their hatred more against the creoles. This is not to deny the
> support that both Negroes and Indians have given to the rebellion, for their
> addiction to robbery, plunder, assassination and every kind of disorder makes
> them amenable to its ideas and readily enlists them in its ranks.

In short, this was a contradictory alliance between whites and Indians, forged through the manipulation of an Indian cacique by the
whites, and the partial employment of scattered Indian forces in military operations and expeditions designed only to further creole objectives. Thus the alliance was extremely precarious. Moreover, in the
same way as 1780 ended any further possibility of an independent mobilization of the Indian population, so 1814 deprived the native population, creoles and Indians alike, of any further initiative towards autonomous mobilization. Until 1824 Cuzco would not only be a bastion of
the colonial order, but would also supply men and resources to defend
the established order at Junín and Ayacucho.

A number of conclusions may be suggested concerning the character
and meaning of the revolts that followed that of Túpac Amaru and
preceded the arrival of the armies of San Martín and Bolívar. In the first

place, they were highly localized, with the exception of the Cuzco rebellion which briefly extended throughout southern Peru. Second, while they broke out in response to long-term colonial oppression, they were also provoked by the upheavals occurring in the metropolis as a result of the fall of the monarchs and the French occupation of the peninsula. Third, their objective was to ensure that old grievances were resolved in a more flexible political structure, as stipulated by the liberal Constitution of 1812. It was only the tough and effective policy of Abascal, the great custodian of the colonial order in the critical years of 1806–1816, that forced the rebels to seek a more radical alternative, as they did in the final stages of the Cuzco rebellion. The composition of all these rebellions revealed a creole leadership obliged to seek the support of the Indian population in order to compensate for the weakness of their own forces. . . . In the event the rebel forces could not reconcile basic differences between whites and Indians, or the rivalries between different groups of Indians. This is a point worth making, for the divisions in colonial society are usually treated only in terms of opposition between conquerors and conquered. Yet events in the southern Andes in 1780, in Huánuco in 1812, and in Cuzco in 1814 show that rebel solidarity was threatened by suspicions and open conflicts within the Indian population, divided as it was into different communities and consisting of different ethnic groups. What was it that maintained and reproduced this division among the Indians? The evidence does not yet exist to explain it adequately, though hypotheses may be suggested. The renewal of fragmentation was closely related to the policy imposed by the colonial state, to the development of extreme differentiation between peasant types, resulting in the emergence of *forastero* Indians, and also to the occupational differences expressed in ethnic terms. These were the means by which the colonial state and its agents, from the very beginning, gained a political victory which force of arms merely confirmed. Finally, in view of the fact that the first reinforcements of the royalist army only reached Peru in 1812 (700 men of the Talavera Regiment), then it is obvious that the repression of these rebellions was basically the work of troops and militias recruited locally, in the case of Cuzco mainly Indian.

14

Poverty and Priesthood in Mexico

Manuel Abad y Queipo

Colonial Mexico was rigid in its social structure, and life at the bottom was hard. Impoverished, brutalized, and divided among themselves, the Indians were a sociocultural group rather than an exclusively racial one. A sign of their status was the tribute, paid by Indians but also by free blacks and mulattos. The revenue was considerable, and it was in the Crown's interest to identify and preserve a tributary class by keeping its members separate from whites—even prohibited from wearing Spanish clothes. The Indians included many mestizos whose cultural and economic position dragged them down. This was the world of the underprivileged, the ultimate victims of inequality, ready to explode at the call of a leader. Such is the assumption underlying the following text. Its author, Manuel Abad y Queipo (1751–1825), was a peninsular Spaniard who arrived in Mexico in 1786 and was appointed judge of chantries and pious works, a position that gave him an expert knowledge of the ecclesiastical economy and its role in colonial Mexico. He became the spokesman for the defense of clerical immunity from royal courts and of Church property against disamortization. In spite of his ecclesiastical career—he became a canon in 1810 and was nominated bishop-elect of Michoacán—Abad y Queipo was essentially secular in his thinking, and, in line with many exponents of Spanish enlightenment, based his arguments on reason and utility rather than revelation and tradition. In his representation of 1799 to the Crown, from which the following extract is taken, he gives a realistic description of social conditions in Mexico, of class conflict, and of measures essential to reform. Some of his proposals, such as the abolition of Indian tribute, were controversial in his own time. Another, such as the proposal to

Translated by John Lynch from Manuel Abad y Queipo, "Representación sobre la inmunidad personal del clero," in José María Luis Mora, *Obras sueltas* (Mexico, 1963), pp. 204–12.

break up Indian community land in favor of individual ownership, has found little favor with modern historians, though it was typical of late colonial reformists and led directly into liberal agrarian ideas in the nineteenth century. Abad y Queipo regarded Mexico as ungovernable without the collaboration of the clergy. This, rather than theological considerations, was one of his basic arguments in resisting Bourbon attacks on the clerical fuero: self interest bound together Crown and clergy, and if the Crown alienated its indispensable ally it would undermine colonial defenses, and open the way to popular insurgency backed by clerical support. In the years after 1810 Abad y Queipo tried unsuccessfully to combine opposition to insurgency with sympathy towards reform. His case is one of many that showed the impossibility of a reformed colonialism and a liberal empire. He was ordered to resign his see and return to Spain, where he was soon subject to the attentions of the Inquisition.

New Spain has close upon four and a half million inhabitants, and these can be divided into three classes, Spaniards, Indians, and castas.[1] The Spaniards form one-tenth of the total, and they alone possess almost all the property and wealth of the kingdom. The other two classes, comprising nine-tenths of the whole, can be divided into two-thirds who are castas and one-third pure Indians. Indians and castas are employed in domestic service, agriculture, and the menial side of trade and industry. That is to say, they are the servants, employees, or laborers of the first class. Consequently between them and the Spanish class there is that conflict of interests and feelings that invariably prevails between those who have nothing and those who have everything, between vassals and lords, leading to envy, thieving, and poor service on the part of some, and to contempt, exploitation, and harshness on the part of others. To some extent these conditions are prevalent all over the world. But in America it is worse, for there are no gradations between classes, no mean; they are all either rich or poor, noble or infamous.

The two classes of Indians and castas live in a state of utter degradation and squalor. The color, ignorance, and poverty of the Indians place them at an infinite distance from a Spaniard, and the laws do not help. Enclosed within a radius of 600 yards which the law assigns to their village, they have no individual property. The community land, which they work under great duress and for no immediate benefit, must be all the more hateful a burden, the more difficult it becomes to make use of its products; for under the new organization imposed by the law of intendancies nothing can be decided concerning community land without recourse to the superior junta of the royal treasury in Mexico City. Prohibited by law from intermixture and union with the other castas, they are deprived of the enlightenment and help that they should receive from communication and dealings with other castas and people. Isolated by their language and their most useless and tyrannical government, they preserve forever their traditions, usages, and gross superstitions, which in each village eight or ten old Indians mysteriously seek to maintain, living idly at the expense and exertions of the others and ruling them with the harshest despotism.

The castas are degraded by law as descendants of negro slaves. They pay tribute, and as the registers are drawn up with great precision the tribute becomes for them an indelible mark of slavery which the passage of time and race mixture in succeeding generations never efface. There are many whose color, physiognomy, and way of life would enable to rise to the class of Spaniards were it not for this stigma which holds them down in their original class. Degraded by law, they are poor and servile, lacking proper education and bearing still some of the stain of their origin; in these circumstances they must feel crushed in spirit, and surrender themselves to their strong passions and fiery temperament. So they break the law to excess. The surprising thing is that they do not break it more, and that in many members of this class good behavior can still be recognized.

The Indians, like the castas, are governed in the first place by the district magistrates, who are not entirely blameless for their present condition. The *alcaldes mayores* are regarded as merchants rather than judges, whose exclusive privilege and the power to enforce it give them authority to conduct a monopoly trade in their province and to extract from it in a five-year period from thirty to two hundred thousand pesos. Their forced and exorbitant sales caused great resentment. Yet in spite of this there were usually two positive features: first, they administered justice impartially and correctly in cases to which they themselves were not a party; second, they promoted industry and agriculture in those products which were important to them. An attempt was made to remedy the abuses of the alcaldes mayores by substituting subdelegates, who were strictly forbidden to engage in trade. But as they were not allocated any income, the remedy proved to be more harmful than the disease. If they rely on income from duties, among impoverished people who only compete in crime, they will perish from hunger. So they are forced to prostitute their jobs, to defraud the poor, and to sell justice. For this reason the intendants have the greatest difficulty in finding suitable candidates for these jobs. The only applicants are the failures of society or those whose conduct and talents do not qualify them for other careers. In such circumstances, what good, what protection can these magistrates provide for the Indians and the castas? How can they earn their good will and respect when extortion and injustice are their essential methods?

The parish priests and their deputies, on the other hand, dedicated solely to the spiritual service and temporal support of these wretched people, win their affection, gratitude, and respect by their ministries and works. They visit and comfort them in sickness and labor. They act as their doctors, prescribe and pay for their medicines, and they themselves sometimes apply the remedies. They also act as their lawyers and mediators with judges and plaintiffs. They defend them against the oppressions of the magistrates and of powerful neighbors. In short, the only ones whom the people can trust are the clergy and the senior magistrates, though recourse to the latter is extremely difficult.

In this state of affairs, what interests can attach these two classes to the first, and all three to the government and the laws? The upper class have the greatest interest in observing the laws, for these guarantee and protect their life, honor, property, and wealth against the envy and assaults of the destitute. But as for the other two classes, who have no property, or honor, or anything to covet or attack, what regard can they have for laws which only serve to mete out punishment for their crimes? What affection and good will can they have for the ministers of the law who only use their authority to send them to prison, the pillory, the penitentiary, and the gallows? What ties can bind these classes to the government, whose beneficent protection they simply cannot understand?

It may be argued that fear of punishment is sufficient to keep the people in subjection to the laws and the government. According to one political authority, there are two classes who invalidate this argument: the powerful, who break the net, and the wretched, who slip through its mesh. If this is true in Europe, it is even more so in America, where the people live without a house or a home, virtual nomads. So let us hear from modern legislators how they propose to keep these classes subject to law and government, by means other than religion, which is preserved in the hearts of the people by the preaching and counsel in pulpit and confessional of the ministers of the Church. These are the true custodians of the laws and guarantors of their observance. It is they who have most influence on the hearts of the people and who strive most to keep them obedient and submissive to the sovereign. They are, therefore, the most powerful force for attaching to the government the two wretched classes, or nine-tenths of the whole population of the kingdom.

The clergy, therefore, have to their credit services of great importance to the government and the entire monarchy, and these easily counterbalance the failings of a few of their members. The need to support their position and to repair the damage we are now suffering has obliged us to draw attention to these facts. The evil which threatens us is great, the moment is critical, and the plea for Your Majesty's indulgence is urgent. If we were more content, we would also be more modest.

We have discussed the pernicious effects of existing land distribution, the lack of property or its equivalent among the people, the degradation of the Indians and castas in practice and in law, the disadvantages of the tribute and of community land, the unsalaried status of judges and consequent ill effects of established laws on the situation of the people, at the same time as the paternal concern of Your Majesty has been exercised on the new legislation so important for the future welfare of these kingdoms. Now it is only right to submit to Your Majesty our proposals for the remedy of these evils, in order to raise the people from their poverty, suppress their vices, and bind them closer to the government in obedience and subjection to the laws.

The first essential is the abolition of the tribute paid by Indians and castas. The second is the abolition of legal discrimination against the castas; they should be declared honest and honorable, eligible for civil offices that do not require noble rank and provided they qualify for them by their good conduct. Third, free distribution of all vacant public lands to Indians and castas. Fourth, free division of Indian community land between the Indians of each village. Fifth, a land law similar to that in Asturias and Galicia, whereby under new tenancy arrangements a village would be allowed to open those lands of the great proprietors left uncultivated for twenty or thirty years, at a just assessment in case of disagreement, on condition that they enclose this land and take any other necessary steps to preserve the rights of property. The provincial intendants would have cognizance of all this in first instance, with appeal to the audiencia of the district, as in all other civil cases. Sixth, free permission for all Spanish classes, castas, and Indians from other villages to reside in Indian villages and to construct houses and buildings, paying a ground rent. Seventh, a decent salary for all district judges, with the exception of the *alcaldes ordinarios*, who ought to discharge this office freely as a council duty. If to all this is added free permission to establish small cotton and woollen workshops, it would increase the impact of the other measures and help the people to take their first steps to improvement. These are already permitted in the case of larger factories through a special licence from the viceroys or governors; but this is hard on the poor and should be re-moved together with all other obstacles, except for the alcabala tax on exports and imports of goods. . . .

Self-interest produces and reinforces the ties binding society to-gether, and these in turn reflect the strength of individual interests. This principle alone, applied to the clergy, would be sufficient to pre-serve intact their immunity from criminal prosecution, though there are also other reasons. The interests of the clergy vary in importance according to the religious order or class they belong to, and within these according to their individual position. They are all solid with the government, but not all in the same way. A *cura* and a senior sacristan both receive their benefices and privileges from Your Majesty. But as these are greater in the case of the cura than in that of the sacristan, then so is the cura's gratitude, support, and respect for the laws which protect him the greater of the two. The different level of benefice pro-duces a different level of support from the beneficiaries, and a different level of solidarity among beneficiaries, such as between one sacristan and another, or between one cura and another. Canons show even more solidarity than do curas and sacristans, because their appointment is higher. And bishops show more than any others, because they receive more appointments from Your Majesty than anyone else. They are your natural counsellors, receive military honors, and often head the high-est tribunals and commissions. They are treated with the greatest honor and respect, defended by the laws, and in short owe to Your Majesty their promotion to bishop and all the privileges, other than those of divine origin, that go with it. This accumulation of offices so unites and identifies them with Your Majesty that they see all your interests as their own and nothing will ever move them from this conviction.

But the rest of the clergy, who do not have an established benefice and live only from the small stipends of their office, receive nothing from the government to distinguish them from the other classes except the privilege of the *fuero*. Of the secular clergy of America eight-tenths are in this category; at least that is the case in this diocese. The regular clergy can be considered the same. Some are assistants to curas, and it is they who perform most of the preaching and hearing of confessions, and who have most to do with the lower two classes of society. So they have great influence over the minds of these classes. Therefore the clerical fuero is the only special tie that attaches them to the govern-ment. Therefore if the fuero is removed, the tie will be broken, and influence over the lower two classes will be weakened. Therefore pru-dence and policy demand that there be no change and no setback.

Sir, we know that all the clergy, by religion and by conscience, are obliged to observe the law and to cooperate in seeing that everyone else does the same. But this is no reason for regarding as superfluous the immunity that they were granted to enable them to observe this duty more effectively. If everyone fulfilled their duty, then judges, laws, punishments, armies and navies would be redundant. The clergy are men, and like everyone else their concern is for self-preservation, honor, and well-being, which is the first principle of their support for the government. Experience confirms this principle. We see from France that the regular clergy, long the victims of neglect and disparagement, and part of the secular clergy whose poverty placed them in the same state, quickly left the sinking ship of monarchy at the first sign of storm; but all the rest of the clergy fought to the death to save it.

15

Pardos in the Colony and in Their Place

City Council of Caracas

The status of the *pardos*, or mulattos, in colonial society was even worse than that of the other mixed group, the mestizos. The pardos were despised for their slave origin and negro-white descent: Discriminatory legislation debarred them from all white status symbols, including education; they were confined to artisan work in the towns and peon-type labor in the country. The creoles were intensely aware of social pressure from below, and fiercely resisted the advance of the "people of color." But Bourbon policy, influenced perhaps by the growth and the demands of the pardo population, introduced an element of social mobility. The pardos were allowed into the militia, which gave them access to fueros, status, and wealth to an extent that many whites did not enjoy. They could also buy legal whiteness through purchase of *cédulas de gracias al sacar.* By law of 10 February 1795 dispensation from the status of pardo was offered for a fee of 1,500 reales de vellón, lowered in 1801 to 700 reales. Successful applicants were authorized to receive an education, marry whites, hold public office, and enter holy orders. The whites reacted sharply to these concessions. In Venezuela, where slaves, blacks, and pardos together formed 61 percent of the population, the creole aristocracy, a relatively small group of white landowners and merchants, protested against the sale of whiteness, resisted popular education, and petitioned against the presence of pardos in the militia. The report of the Caracas city council, an all-white body, of 28 November 1796 was probably the strongest manifestation of these attitudes, revealing an underlying fear on the part of the creoles that the imperial government was wavering in its support for white supremacy in colonial society and that their future would only be safe in their

Translated by John Lynch from "Informe que el ayuntamiento de Caracas hace al rey de España referente a la real cédula de 10 de febrero de 1795," José Félix Blanco and R. Azpurúa, eds., *Documentos para la historia de la vida pública del Libertador* (14 vols., Caracas, 1875–88), I, 267–75.

own hands. The document shows that in Venezuela the creole demand for office was also a bid to control race policy. It was also argued that to govern, indeed to retain, Venezuela, the king needed the loyalty and collaboration of the creoles and should do nothing to risk losing it. The Venezuelan whites, in fact, retained their ascendancy; although the Crown refused to rescind the cédula of 1795 and the policy there expressed, it still maintained the colonial social order and the traditional discrimination against pardos. Very few pardos took up the offer of dispensation, and fewer still successfully bought whiteness. Nevertheless the racism revealed in 1796 was still prevalent in 1810, when the creoles sought to fill the power vacuum before the pardos could do so.

The city council assumes that once a pardo is dispensed from his color he is eligible for all the functions that the laws of the kingdom would otherwise disqualify him and which have previously been reserved for the pure whites of the Indies; so that, leaving the inferior class to which he belongs, a pardo must then be regarded, with Your Majesty's authority, as a member of the white class.

This transition is regarded in the royal cédula as so easy that it is permitted for only a small fee; but it is horrifying to those born and residing in America, for they alone know from whom they are born, and they alone have the years of experience here that enable them to appreciate the immense distance that separates the whites from the pardos, those who are dominant and superior from those who are subordinate and inferior. For the pardos would never dare to believe that the equality with the white residents and natives predicted by the royal cédula would be possible were they not protected and encouraged by those who hold out to them the hope of an absolute equality with access to honors and appointments hitherto reserved exclusively for the whites, now so humiliated and insulted. This calamity stems precisely from ignorance on the part of European officials, who come here already prejudiced against the American-born whites and falsely informed concerning the real situation of the country. One of their errors is the policy of protection for mulattos and other infamous people, who exploit this favor by ingratiating themselves with officials. . . .

The pardos, mulattos, and zambos (all more or less the same in common usage) are descended from negro slaves introduced into this country for labor on the land, a system dictated by necessity, though formerly criticized and now detested as inhuman; these slaves have been treated severely and harshly in order to keep them in subordination, for it is inconceivable that anyone would submit to slavery except from fear of punishment for desertion. In addition to their infamous origin, pardos, mulattos, and zambos are also dishonored by their illegitimacy, for if they are not themselves bastards their parents almost certainly are; and it is also likely that they have fathers, grandfathers, or near relatives who are actually slaves, in some cases with local white families. One can see in the streets a pardo or mulatto illegally dressed as a white, and he has a brother who is still a slave; or another may put on a great show of wealth yet also have nephews and relatives who are slaves.

May it please Your Majesty to consider these questions. Is it acceptable that the white residents and native-born people of this country should admit into their class, to mix with them, a mulatto descended from their own slaves or from those of their parents, a mulatto whose relatives are still slaves, a mulatto whose birth is defaced by illegitimacy and related blemishes? Is it possible to ignore complaints when public order is threatened and Spanish rule itself is placed at risk? . . . For let there be no doubt that the application of this royal cédula is bound to encourage the pretensions of the pardos, and to introduce a new and fatal regime, forming in America a fourth class whose continual agitation, far from maintaining allegiance, will introduce instability and division.

The ignorance of senior European officials and their prejudices against Americans are not the only defects of government. Another problem is the influence and power the pardos have acquired through the establishment of militias led by officers of their own class, a well-intentioned measure but one that experience shows will lead to the ruin of America. Incapable of resisting invasion by a powerful enemy, and as there are sufficient whites for the task of controlling the slaves and maintaining internal order, the militias serve only to increase the arrogance of the pardos, giving them an organization, leaders, and arms, the more easily to prepare a revolution. At the same time they are a means of deceiving people, because an officer dressed up in his uniform, epaulettes, and sword, and with a little color applied to his face, frequently receives mistaken deference which goes to his head and gives him ideas. Moreover, the presence of pardo militias in the cities and villages for purposes of military training and exercises causes them to disdain the cultivation of the land and to abandon the work of agriculture to the whites and the black slaves. Meanwhile, for their own subsistence, the pardos rely on artisan skills, but as they themselves set the price of their products they never bother to improve their work, and so with old age or any other setback they surrender themselves to idleness, begging, and poverty.

The sorry condition of this country is almost beyond belief. The

European Spaniards consider it vital to occupy all the public offices, and they spend their time pressing their claims, regardless of their qualifications. The American Spaniards devote themselves to the cultivation of the land, enduring the toils and tasks of this arduous occupation; or they waste their time and talents in the vain and corrupt life of the cities, which is harmful to their interests and damaging to their reputation. The pardos and free mulattos specialise in the mechanical skills, though now many of them despise such occupations and regard it as unseemly to be both a soldier and a shoemaker, or a barber, while those with more honest ideas never escape from a low job and a life of poverty. The result of all this is that a white never takes an artisan's job for fear of being classed with the pardos; and the pardos will not work on the land so as not to mix with the slaves. In America everyone wants to be a gentleman, to hold public office, to live from government revenue, or at the cost of society, without contributing anything in return.

The city council of Caracas is not claiming that public offices should be confined to Americans and resident Europeans, for that would be another obstacle to good government, another blow to that bond of interests and knowledge needed to preserve the state. But we *are* saying that, according to the principle of alternation, there should be a division of offices between Americans and Europeans, so that they can work together to ensure that laws are adapted to the circumstances of the country, which Americans know best and have the greatest interest in protecting. Otherwise the open conflict that prevails between settlers and officials will continue, the former convinced that their rights are being ignored by prejudiced judges and that their situation is hopeless, the latter believing all the adverse features reported or imagined about Americans. This will be the end of any possibility of order, justice, and tranquillity. From anxiety flows distrust, and from this follow insults and aggression; the body politic then quickly dissolves into conflicting ideas and interests, and it only needs a blow from outside for law and order to collapse.

In these circumstances the basic requisite for retaining this part of Your Majesty's dominions is the loyalty of the resident and American-born Spaniards, who, as they are married and have their property here, seek to live in peace and in the religion and obedience in which they were born. All they ask in return is that Your Majesty maintains them in the honor and traditions of their ancestors, saving them from the outrage of mixing with pardos, seeing them promoted, having them as equals, and experiencing the consequent disorder and corruption of society. In no way can it be right that the pardos, in return for a small payment, and without previous distinguished service to the state, should pass as whites and obtain, or be eligible to obtain, the honors and distinctions proper to those who have undertaken the immense task of preserving their purity of blood by legitimate descent. It is very hard to accept that some can gain, for a negligible sum of money, what it has taken others centuries to preserve through their good character and conduct.

Your Majesty will have been informed that the country is full of mixed families; that there are many pardos who have the wealth of whites; that there are countless lawsuits over purity of blood; and that it is not appropriate to favor discrimination in America. So Your Majesty has looked to the good of your vassals and opened the door to dispensations, in order to reduce lawsuits and avoid other evils. The decision is worthy of so great a king; but in fact the reports are erroneous, superficial, or malicious. . . . The informants, moreover, have not taken account of circumstances in this country; nor have they considered the interests and rights of the metropolis which are closely bound to those of this province. The fact remains that the pardos are now granted access to the education that they have hitherto lacked and ought to continue to lack, and this is accomplished simply by means of dispensation from their inferior status. Soon classes will be swarming with mulatto students; they will try to enter the seminary; they will succeed in obtaining the city council positions; they will gain public offices and treasury posts; and they will be involved in all the public and private business of the province. The result will be resentment and retreat on the part of white and decent people, and while the pardos will be encouraged by their greater numbers, the whites will face disappointment and contempt; those families who conquered and settled this province and paid for it with their lives and labor will be finished, and loyal subjects who have preserved with their loyalty the rule of the kings of Spain will be forever forgotten. The grim day will arrive when Spain will be served by mulattos, zambos, and blacks, whose service will be exacted by force and whose doubtful loyalty will be the cause of violent upheavals; then there will be no one, for the sake of self-interest, honor, purity of blood, and reputation, who will risk his life in calling on sons, friends, relatives, and countrymen to control the lower orders and defend the common cause and their own.

Is it really the intention of Your Majesty to place confidence and security in the hands of men who, far from looking to Spain as the center of their interests, keep their eyes on the dark people of Africa (which is where they come from), to patronize them and raise them against the Spaniards, the authors, so they say, of all their grievances?

Could these new whites be more loyal than the old? Could people of African origin do better for Spain than those of Spanish origin? Who is so mistaken as to believe that the pardos do not favor the blacks, through whom they are flawed, and hate the whites, to whose class they aspire only to insult and slight them? The mulattos look to the blacks with affection, to the whites with disgust.

Those pardos who live in towns and cities usually enlist in the militias, whose fuero exempts them from the surveillance of the *alcaldes ordinarios*, the only judges who could usefully apply themselves to regulating the conduct of the pardos. Their military chiefs are only concerned that they attend zealously for training and are free from interference from the ordinary magistrates, protecting them from ridicule and allowing them license to commit whatever excesses they please. For the military fuero in this province has become a sure asylum for every disorder and crime, as it is thought to consist in allowing the militia commander to protect the soldier at all costs. This is another cause of the insolence and presumption of the mulattos, for no matter how shabby and sordid they look when appearing before the magistrate, they are ready to speak up for themselves and even hurl abuse, simply because they have a red badge in their hat.

These, then, are the pardos, some of them sunk in poverty and consequent idleness, others occupied as blacksmiths, carpenters, silversmiths, tailors, masons, shoemakers, butchers, slaughtermen, and other trades. These can work how and when they please, they can fix their own prices, and they can deceive everyone. It is no use complaining because the civil magistrates and military judges are not interested; they view the province as an inn where they are staying for a time and putting up with the problem, in order to avoid the trouble of resolving it. From this disorder results the decline of industry, and artisans are sure of selling their products, no matter how badly made, and at a price they dictate.

The pardo artisans do not contribute the slightest amount from their earnings to the royal treasury, the city revenue, or any other institution; nor are they assessed for any charge or tax, because the whole weight of taxation falls on agriculture and commerce. In this way the mulattos and pardos of the province (except one or two rare cases who have farm lands and live honestly from agriculture or trade) live in the greatest comfort and freedom in their small houses, working only as long as necessary for that day's bread, and declining other jobs because they consider it beneath themselves to farm the land or to work for landowners; this applies especially to those who are militia officers, sergeants, or corporals. And even those who are not employees but undertake to work for a day wage are so dishonest, crooked, and arrogant, that they abandon work, make off with the advances made to them by the hacendados, and leave the crops to rot and agriculture and commerce to suffer. This is a daily occurrence. They claim they are free men, secure in the knowledge that their officers will not force them to pay up, unless the creditors have some particular influence with the officers.

In addition to this immunity and freedom, the pardos have the military fuero, in which they take great pride at the expense of public order. They hold positions in the militia, enjoy the honors which this confers, and receive the wages appropriate to their service. This allows them to live in idleness and sink into inertia, their only exercise their weekly or monthly training. They receive medals and pensions, a sound enough idea for rewarding merits and services and attracting others. Thus the classes are kept in their due state, and each one is given its proper honor and reward.

The mulattos of this province, then, enjoy the benefits of society without contributing a *maravedí* to its revenues and finances, or to its public and charitable institutions, in spite of the fact that they are twice as numerous as the whites. This has come about because the laws regulating the conduct of mulattos, making them contribute, and ordering them to pay a moderate tax to the treasury, are completely ignored, either because officials are unaware of their existence, or indifferent to their application, or ignorant of their origin.

The remedy for these ills is not to be found in dispensing them from their status, thus encouraging their arrogance and hatred for the whites. Rather they should be obliged to work on the land, to abandon their life of idleness in the cities, to improve their trades and place an official price on their products, and on all occasions to curb their arrogance. . . . The royal cédula dispensing pardos from their color should be suspended, not only for these reasons but also because it can be obtained so easily and cheaply that the high regard that the pardos ought to have of the white condition and its prerogatives is diminished. In this way the state loses one of the principle means of imposing subordination and one of the most powerful ways of rewarding services that would be useful to itself and to the pardos, namely by offering them future promotion to the class of whites in return for some great service to the state or contribution to the work of agriculture or military service.

PART FOUR

POPULAR PROTEST

16

What Is an Indian?

Melchor de Paz

Peru was Spain's richest and most valuable colony after Mexico, yet it was only thinly policed and in the highlands, where Indians formed a majority of the population, the authorities relied upon the tradition of obedience rather than on the power of an army to collect taxes and impose services. An increase in tax demands and the weakness of security forces produced, in 1780, a classic recipe for rebellion—in this case, a great rebellion whose violence shocked the whites and disturbed the authorities. Stability was traditionally maintained by the polarization of Andean society between creoles and Indians; an alliance between the two could spell disaster for Spain. Túpac Amaru was aware of this and appealed for creole support. In the event the creoles held back, and Túpac Amaru had to see his movement isolated by another alliance: one between the creole elite, the Church, and a number of loyal caciques. This is one of the themes of the work by Melchor de Paz, who sought to overcome the news blackout that Spain imposed on the rebellion by preparing his own chronicle of events almost immediately. He was well placed to do so. A creole by birth (Lima, 1740), he was a graduate of the University of San Marcos and secretary of two viceroys, Manuel de Guirior (1777–81) and Agustín de Jáuregui (1781–84). His office gave him access to eyewitness accounts, rebel and official communications, and contemporary reports. These he transcribed into a lengthy chronicle, basically a collection of documents held together by his own commentary, which he wrote in the form of a dialogue. Paz was hostile to the policy of José de Gálvez and highly critical of Antonio de Areche, visitor-general of Peru (1777–82) whom he re-

Translated by John Lynch from Melchor de Paz, "Diálogo sobre los Sucesos varios acaecidos en este Reyno del Perú" [1786], *Guerra separatista. Rebeliones de Indios en Sur América. La sublevación de Tupac Amaru. Crónica de Melchor de Paz.* Ed. Luis Antonio Eguiguren (2 vols., Lima, 1952), I, 85–90, 231–35, 250–51, 340–41, 406–08, II, 420–23.

garded as a creature of the minister and an agent of tax extortion and favoritism towards European Spaniards. According to Paz, the great rebellion was provoked not by repartimientos, which were necessary ingredients of the Indian economy, but by the new taxes introduced by Areche, especially the increased alcabala collected in internal customs houses. His attitude seems to have been that of a creole nationalist and an affronted bureaucrat rather than a defender of his Indian compatriots. One of the documents which he published was an anti-Indian tirade which began, "What is an Indian? An Indian is the lowest form of rational animal." Túpac Amaru's hatred of Europeans, Indian distrust of whites, and creole contempt for Indians can be read in the following passages. The atrocity of the leader's execution, in contrast to the more lenient punishment of creole and black participants, was a Spanish warning to rebel Indians; its inclusion in Paz's chronicle can be read as an ironic criticism of Areche who designed the cruelty and took steps to eradicate the material signs of Inca ideology. All sides learned a lesson from the great rebellion: Spain, that the colony needed an improved military; creoles, that they needed Spain; and Indians, that they could expect nothing from either side. These attitudes help to explain the character of Peruvian independence.

REPORT FROM A LEADING CITIZEN OF AREQUIPA
ON THE REVOLT OF INDIANS AND MALCONTENTS

Once it was known here that Dr. Juan Bautista Pando held a commission to establish a customs house and become its administrator, and that for this purpose he was making inquiries in the coastal valleys of the south to ascertain the products of the haciendas and establish the tax registers, then feelings began to run high and people feared the worst. Eventually they arrived in this city [Arequipa], and from 1 January [1780], when the customs house opened, they immediately abandoned the system employed by the royal treasury officials and began to charge duties without making an exception of foodstuffs or of goods produced by the Indians. Things proceeded in such a way that Pando himself said publicly that the customs duties would increase this year from 80,000 to more than 150,000 pesos; in other words they began the establishment of the customs house where they ought to have ended it.

As a result pasquinades began to appear on the same day threatening the administrator and all his assistants; and in spite of the efforts of the corregidor, [Balthasar de] Semanat, to curb and punish such insolence, it was repeated every day in different places. At the same time parties of masked men on horseback rode through various parts of the city, and they were thought to be the people of the *chacras* [small farms], for they were obviously aroused and angered, saying that they were forced to pay alcabala on wheat, maize, potatoes, and fruits. Meanwhile the muleteers, who are very numerous in the environs of the city, were also outraged at having to unload their cargoes at the customs house and pay alcabalas on aguardiente and other products of the valleys: and on top of this came the order that no one enter the courtyard of the customs house wearing spurs and hats.

The rumors about the common people of the town and those of the chacras were growing. Fearing an upheaval, the corregidor repeatedly warned the administrator that he should proceed with fairness and moderation and should not introduce changes in the practices of the treasury officials until things calmed down. But Pando and his colleague [Pedro de la] Torre ignored this advice and continued on their despotic way, repaying civility and courtesy with impudence and arrogance. Pando declared, among other things, that he had come to increase the royal revenue by virtue of the orders he had received to do so, and that he would sacrifice his life to succeed. He even derided the corregidor, solemnly announcing to the senior town councillors that "The corregidor is terrified and wants me to believe that an upheaval is imminent; he seems to me more like a deluded nun than a soldier."

This was how things were developing when, on the night of Thursday 13 [January], a group of people attacked and threatened the customs house, primarily to reconnoiter the situation. They discovered in fact that the customs officials were careless, overconfident in their security against any hostile move. So on the following night the rioters attacked in greater force, more than two hundred of them, intending to kill Pando and his assistants, though this could not be proved because Pando fled over a wall at the back of his house like a frightened cat, terrified of ending up in a shroud and living up to his own insults against the corregidor. The others, including Torre, paused to open fire, but seeing that people were breaking the doors, Torre put his head out of a window to see who the attackers were and received such a blow that he was lucky not to expire on the spot; he managed to escape, dragged along by his companions.

The mob broke down the doors and rushed in; they burnt some papers, stole 2,032 pesos from the safes, but left everything they considered to be interned for taxation. They left about midnight on 14th and marauded around various houses in the city, frightening a number of the individuals threatened in the pasquinades; these were mainly treasury officials, who escaped from their pursuers as best they could.

The corregidor was in a state of confusion, unable on his own to resolve the causes of the revolt, seeing his life and property at obvious risk, and understandably concerned at the course of events. He gave the orders necessary in this serious situation, and on the morning of 15th went with the senior council officials to the customs house, where he collected all the papers that had not been burnt and delivered them to the treasury officials who were there. They then withdrew, each to his own duty.

A rumor went round all day on 15th that the lives of [Mateo] Cosío, [Juan] Goyeneche, and [Antonio] Alvizuri[1] were also at risk, for they were friends of the corregidor and Pando. The alarm and despondency caused by this news can be imagined; they all shut themselves in their houses expecting the worst at any time. At 10 o'clock at night a great shouting and disturbance was heard from the street of San Francisco and the rioters made a threatening attack on the house of Lastarria. From there they passed by the house of Cosío, then went straight to that of the corregidor, whose death sentence was proclaimed in the latest posters. They found it closed, so they set fire to the windows and doors; but no one was inside, for those in hiding had made their escape. The rioters looted the house and left not a nail in the wall.

They finished their work at 2 o'clock in the morning of 16th, then made their way to Mercaderes street; there they robbed the store of Canderros, leaving not a thing unbroken. . . . From Mercaderes street they went to the jail and freed all the prisoners. They next planned to attack the royal treasury, but ran out of time for it was now 4:30 in the morning.

So the night of 15th and morning of 16th was spent in disturbance and commotion. At daybreak the corregidor withdrew to the cabildo; there too assembled all the residents of rank to offer their lives and resources in defense of the king and the city. They were all promptly enrolled and placed in the best state of defense possible. Don Mateo Cosío, as colonel of cavalry, ordered the assembly of an entire regiment, and in fact the greater part was paraded in the main square at 4 o'clock in the evening. It became known that the people of the countryside were not involved in the riot of the previous night and took no part in the looting. And the fact was established that it was the common people within the city who rose to attack the customs house, though it is not known who prepared the riot launched by the mob. Investigations are proceeding in secret to discover and punish the guilty.

The seven cavalry companies parading at 4 o'clock on the evening of 16th were ordered to cover all the entrances to the city, while the infantry, which only had two companies under arms, remained in the main square ready to go wherever they were needed. The fear was that the people from the chacras, especially those of Tiabaya whose two companies had still not decided to come or to obey, and the people of all that side would strike against the city; consequently all the cavalry troops from the chacras were distrusted. On top of these worries there was real fear of a rising of the Indians of the pampa; and therefore from early morning to 9 o'clock at night Cosío patrolled the outskirts of the city with a company of cavalry accompanied by Pober and two other friends. Everything was quiet, and in the pampa there was nothing to report. But when Cosío returned to the main square, at 9 o'clock, he was immediately informed that the two companies of Tiabaya were on the outskirts of the city. He went there with his own company and persuaded them to come to the main square and serve as loyal subjects of the king.

They readily agreed, and while the captains were reorganizing the two companies, news arrived from the pampa, where Felon was stationed with his company, that more than 800 Indians had attacked him. Cosío hastened to his assistance with the two companies of Tiabaya and a company of the patrician infantry and found him beaten back to the square of Santa Marta. The Indians occupied the entire road of more than 250 meters as far as the pampa. Felon bravely and vigorously resisted the first attack; he killed two Indians, while one of his own men was wounded and a horse killed.

Cosío's reinforcements caused the Indians to retreat, leaving some of their number dead and wounded in the street. Don Martín's company of grenadiers had also arrived in support, with two other companies taken from less threatened places. So the Indians of the pampa were beaten and fled to the hills. That night six dead and four wounded were brought in, and when Cosío patrolled the pampa at daybreak with two companies he found several wounded Indians unable to escape and all their huts deserted. He followed the tracks of the Indians to higher ground beyond the pampa and captured many who were fleeing with their wives and children.

On the morning of 17th those who died in the affray could be seen hanging in the corridors of the cabildo; and in the afternoon two cavalry companies and the infantry company of patricians went out and set fire to all the huts in the pampa. At 2 o'clock in the afternoon of 18th another six Indians who had been captured wounded were hung; and the rest fled with their women and children dying of hunger and deprivation, according to muleteers arriving from the hills, who also reported seeing many wounded and several dead and dying of wounds. The jail is full of Indians, men and women, whose fate will be decided when they have been investigated.

The defeat of the Indians of the pampa seems to have stirred the Indians of all the surrounding areas, for a pasquinade has been removed which announced an assault on the city for tomorrow night, the 20th. In view of this warning (not to be ignored even though it is from the enemy), military precautions continued, with a greater number of cavalry; and all the country people have assembled, though it is harvest time. Up to now, that is 7 o'clock in the morning of 21st, the threat has not been carried out; they know the state of the city's defenses, with cavalry and infantry regiments at full strength.

Today, from 9 to 11 in the morning, there was a meeting of officials, attended by several lawyers, treasury officials, and army captains, to determine the defenses to be mounted from tonight. Two companies of infantry remain under arms, and another two of cavalry occupy all the entrances. It is hoped that this will keep the peace, though it is important to remain on the alert for some time, knowing the character of the Indians and their inclination to treason.

One of the main reasons that turned the rural inhabitants and the common people of the city against the corregidor was the order which he received from the visitor-general to make a tribute register not only of the local and outside Indians but also of the zambos, cholos, and others, who believed this was to make them pay tribute. It will be necessary to suspend this procedure for a long time and to forget about it, for it will always cause the same problems as we are now experiencing.

Arequipa, 21 January 1780.

AN ACCOUNT OF THE OUTRAGE COMMITTED BY JOSEF GABRIEL TÚPAC AMARU, CACIQUE OF PAMPAMARCA, AGAINST THE CORREGIDOR OF TINTA, AND OTHER GRAVE EXCESSES

On Saturday 4 November 1780, the saint's day of our sovereign monarch Charles III (whom God preserve), Colonel Antonio Arriaga, corregidor of the province of Tinta, the parish priest of Pampamarca, and the cacique of the same village, Josef Gabriel Túpac Amaru, dined at the house of Dr. Carlos Rodríguez, parish priest of Yanaoca. After dinner the corregidor had to leave early for Tinta to conclude some unfinished business; the cacique offered to accompany him, as he was his *compadre*, but the corregidor would not hear of it. Josef Gabriel went on ahead to join those whom he had already placed in an ambush at a ravine which the corregidor had to cross. When he arrived there Túpac Amaru and all his men came out to surround him; and although the corregidor recognized the attack and got his hand to his pistol to defend himself, he did not have time to fire, for they immediately threw a lasso round his neck and dragged him from his mule to the ground. They also wounded a clerk who was with him and made prisoners of the rest of his slaves who followed some distance behind. They were all taken to a place well hidden off the road and left there bound and guarded, and they were warned to keep quiet or risk being killed.

The traitor then promptly withdrew to his house in the locality of Tungasuca, and having given his orders returned in the middle of the night to collect the captives and imprison them in the said house. He placed the corregidor in shackles in an underground cell, the clerk in another, and the slaves also. He then ordered the clerk to write a number of letters and summonses, and the corregidor to sign them: one to his chief treasurer, Don Manuel San Roque, others to those who are called Spaniards in these provinces, and others to those whose persons and incomes were useful to him. The letter to the treasurer simply ordered him to come immediately to Tungasuca in the king's service and bring all the wrought and stamped silver, firearms and swords, for which he was sending his compadre and the necessary mules. In the summonses he threatened death to anyone who did not present himself with his arms at Tungasuca. To Don Bernardo de la Madrid and the Galician Don Juan de Figueroas, *obraje* owners, the first of Pomacanchi and the second of Quipococha, he wrote as follows: "Dear Friend, As soon as you receive this you must come to Tungasuca, for we have several matters to discuss tonight; from here I plan to travel to Cuzco to defend my honor. I wish you good health and may God preserve you many years. Tungasuca, 5 November 1780. Your dear friend, Arriaga."

These letters and summonses were sent out after one o'clock at night, and Túpac Amaru himself took the letter to the treasurer, together with two pairs of mules. The cashier recognized the writing and signature of the corregidor, and as he knew that the cacique was the latter's compadre he had no reason to entertain any doubts. The traitor loaded 22,000 pesos in cash, the wrought silver, ninety guns, two boxes of swords, and the arms belonging to the corregidor; and accompanied by retainers of the corregidor whom he said were also summoned, he returned to Tungasuca without stopping and placed them all in prison, including Dn. Bernardo de la Madrid and the Galician Dn. Juan de Figueroa.

Such secrecy was observed in all these proceedings that no one knew the situation of the corregidor. Some were told he had gone to visit highland villages, others that he was working in Tungasuca and could not be distracted. Spies were carefully placed at all the approaches to Cuzco so that no one in the province could carry news of what was happening in Tungasuca.

While armed Indians and mestizos belonging to his faction were arriving in answer to the summonses, Túpac Amaru had a gallows erected in the main square of the village, and he pronounced the death sentence against his compadre the corregidor. When this had been announced, he sent for the parish priest, Dr. Antonio López, who was then in the principal village half a league away, to come and hear the confession of a dying person. He came and discovered that his penitent was the corregidor. He asked him why he was being treated like this, and the corregidor replied that the cacique Túpac Amaru was planning to take his life. To the priest's remonstration Túpac Amaru replied that he had an order from the visitor-general authorized by the royal audiencia of Lima; he had kept it for twenty-six days and feared he would be blamed for any further delay; moreover, he was confident in what he was doing. So the priest ministered to the unhappy corregidor, heard his confession, gave him Viaticum, and supported him in his last six days.

On the morning of Friday 10 November Túpac Amaru ordered that all the people of his province there assembled should form into three columns, two of Spaniards and mestizos armed with guns, swords, and clubs, and one of Indians with slings. In front of everyone he brought out the corregidor in his military dress, removed his uniform in the act of degradation he had witnessed on other occasions, and left him in his shirt. Then he placed on him a white shroud which he had ordered to be made bearing the word "Charity," and commanded him to be taken, accompanied by the parish priest and two other priests, to the place of execution.

When the corregidor had been placed on the scaffold, the tyrant made him declare publicly that he deserved to die in this way. The hangman in this atrocity was the corregidor's own negro slave; but the rope snapped and both fell to the ground. They hung him again, using a lasso for a halter, and so the execution was carried out, witnessed, and accepted by the entire province. Not the slightest voice was raised against the operation; and the most amazing and perfidious thing is that the same collectors and collaborators of the corregidor were those who hurried him on his way to the shameful execution, and on the very scaffold they pulled his feet to finish him off with greater violence.

The cacique then rode on horseback round all the village and its approaches. The crowd were astonished at an action carried out with such extreme cruelty, the execution of a corregidor in the center of his province by one of his own subjects, his client and confidant, in the presence of people who had hitherto respected and feared him. They were so intimidated by this act that no one dared to protest, challenge, or resist what was done. And it was carried out with such caution and secrecy that although the execution was delayed for six days after the arrest, nothing was known in Cuzco until after the death of the corregidor. Two days later the body was buried in the village church with the usual ceremony but without the presence of the cacique who was occupied on other expeditions.

This was the first blow, and with it the tyrant prepared opinion for his boldest plans, showing that he possessed the ability and determination to undertake anything. He had previously been to Lima to register before the royal audiencia his claim to legitimate descent from Dn. Felipe Túpac Amaru, the last of the ruling Incas, executed by order of Viceroy Francisco de Toledo. There all went well for him in his uncontested case for recognition, so that the papers which he got approved gave him an exaggerated idea of his lineage; thus the imprudence of those who handled the documents of his ancestry caused him to overreach himself.

He returned from Lima with more pretensions than he had gone with, but he knew how to hide his intentions behind a veneer of moderation, affability, and generosity alien to his nature, a deception typical of those who seek to gain the affection of others in order subsequently to subjugate the rest. His plans were not discovered until he insolently staged the public execution of the corregidor. More than 6,000 Indians and mestizos were present; he had brought them down from the neighboring districts, and they surrounded the village. Wearing now the royal decorations used by the Incas, he addressed them in their native language, saying: "The time has now come to throw off the heavy yoke which for so many years you have borne at the hands of the Spaniards, while they have burdened you daily with yet more injuries and oppressions. Our plans are to mete out the same punishment to all the corregidores of the kingdom; to exterminate all the Europeans; and to abolish repartimientos, customs duties, and similar exactions which have been ruining the kingdom. Nothing we are doing contradicts our obedience to the king. We will make up for the failings we see in the Catholic religion, for to that we are totally devoted and hold the clergy in great respect; once injustices are removed, our only wish is to win heathen Indians to the faith, and then to retire and enjoy the fruits of our expeditions. Do not lose heart in what has been started; stand out for your freedom. You know that my love for your cause may result in my losing my life in an execution similar to the one you have just seen, but I will gladly accept that for the greater glory of our nation and to see it restored to its former state." He placed a rope round his neck to impress the Indians with the instrument of execution he had just mentioned and put it over his clothes; whereupon they raised a wild cry and offered to follow him and lose their lives rather than desert him.

He then published a proclamation headed "Don Josef Gabriel Túpac Amaru Inca, of the royal blood and principal line." In this he called on his dear creoles of all classes, American Spaniards as well as mestizos and Indians who wished to follow him, protesting that he was a Christian Catholic and that in no way would he violate the privileges of the Church. His only object was to abolish the appointment of corregidores, free the kingdom from customs duties, monopolies, and other tax burdens, and destroy all Europeans as the principal authors of these institutions. Those who opposed and resisted his plans would receive no mercy but experience the full fury of his anger. Several copies of this proclamation and other decrees were dispatched with his associates to be posted in public places in the neighboring cities and provinces such as Cuzco and Arequipa, making it clear that everything was under his command. He wrote circular letters to the priests warning them not to preach against the faithful of their parish joining this movement. He did the same to a number of private individuals, even those whom he had never known and on whom he mistakenly supposed he could rely.

The traitor Túpac Amaru did not attend the burial of the corregidor, for he was occupied on other expeditions, as has been mentioned. These amounted to going personally to Tinta and looting the home of the corregidor of everything he had not been able to take on the first visit when he collected the treasurer. Now he took everything of value that remained, including the mules and foodstuffs, which he appropriated in abundance. He then went to the obrajes of Parupuquio and Pomacanchi. He demolished the first and plundered it of many fine clothes which he used to reward those who supported and assisted the rebellion. In the second he seized an even greater prize, for it appears that he took more than twenty loads of clothes, together with a great supply of foodstuffs, and 13,000 pesos in cash.

He proceeded immediately to the neighboring province of Quispicanchi to bring it under his control and surprise the corregidor Dn. Fernando Cabrera, formerly senior constable of the *visita general* who had arrived from Lima less than a month previously. At the time the corregidor was in the village of Quiquijana, eight leagues distant from Tungasuca; he was lucky to escape under cover of darkness on a mare or mule he was able to procure, and he reached Cuzco safely. He left behind in the village 2,000 pesos of stamped silver and all his jewelry, and these were seized by the rebels. This province declared in Túpac Amaru's favor without opposition, and the Indians kissed his hands and feet as their lord. He distributed among them the clothing which the corregidor had ready for the reparto, and then returned to his village of Tungasuca. There he established his headquarters, with a lot of display and security, and he appointed leaders to organize his followers.

He then intended to hang the Europeans whom he had arrested at the same time as the corregidor Arriaga. But he was prevented by his wife, the cacica Micaela Bastidas (no less cruel a monster than he), who pointed out that these men could be useful in making arms, casting canons and shot, especially the Galician Figueroa, whose skill in these matters was well known. So they were shackled and guarded and put to work on this task.

Tinta, 10 November 1780.

EDICT OF TÚPAC AMARU FOR THE PROVINCE OF CHICHAS

Don José Gabriel Túpac Amaru, Indian of the royal blood and the principal line:

I make known to creole compatriots, inhabitants of the province of Chichas and its environs, that in view of the oppressive yoke of taxation and the tyranny of our callous and merciless oppressors I have reached the end of my patience and have decided to throw off this intolerable burden and to curb the misgovernment we suffer from these officials. This is the reason why the corregidor of this province of Tinta died on a public scaffold; to his defense a group of *chapetones* came from Cuzco, dragging along also my dear creoles, who paid for their courage and boldness with their lives. I am only sorry for our creole compatriots, for it is my intention that they should not suffer any harm but that we should live together as brothers, united in one body, to destroy the Europeans. All this is my considered judgement, with the aim not of opposing in the slightest our holy Catholic religion but only of suppressing this great disorder. The necessary measures have been taken here for the defense, protection, and safeguard of the Spanish creoles, mestizos, zambos, and Indians, and for their tranquillity, because they are all fellow countrymen and compatriots, born as they are in our lands, with the same roots as the native inhabitants, and all equal sufferers from the oppression and tyranny of the Europeans. The said creole compatriots can rest assured that if they follow this advice they will not suffer any harm to their lives or property. But if they ignore my warning and do otherwise, they will accomplish their own ruin, turn my clemency into anger, and reduce their province to ashes. And let me say, I have forces, money, and all the neighboring provinces at my command, united in solidarity between creoles and natives, in addition to the other provinces which are also under my orders. So let them not underestimate my warnings, which derive from my love and mercy and are directed towards the common good of our kingdom, for it is intended to rescue all Spanish compatriots and native inhabitants from the unjust servitude which they have suffered. Remember too that my principal object is to bring an end to offenses against God Our Lord, whose ministers, the priests, will receive the respect due to their state; equally the religious orders and monasteries. By proceeding thus with pious and proper intentions I hope for the mercy of God, who is my guide and light in an enterprise for whose success I need all his assistance.

So that this edict may be known and understood, copies will be posted in suitable places throughout the province. I will know who follows this advice, and will reward the loyal and punish the rebels; then you will appreciate your best interests and not plead ignorance. That is all.

Lampa, 23 December 1780. Don José Gabriel Túpac Amaru, Inca.

ACCOUNT OF EVENTS IN THE VILLAGE OF CHALLAPATA, PROVINCE OF PARIA, 15 JANUARY 1781

As the corregidor of Paria, Dn. Manuel de la Bodega had met with the total refusal of the Indians of the village of Challapata to pay the royal tributes, he decided to change the Indian governor and other leaders in order to curb their defiance, believing that with the punishment of a few who had given him trouble and made themselves head of the opposition, he could avoid the damage spreading to the whole province.

This was his plan, and for it he assembled about eighty men, including some volunteers of higher status from the nearby town of Oruro. With this escort he proceeded to the village of Challapata, where he arrived on 16 January 1781 at 4 o'clock in the morning. He promptly committed to prison five Indians who were held to be the principal accomplices and leaders, and who offered no resistance. With this stratagem the corregidor thought he could initiate proceedings against the offenders and later send them to Chuquisaca. But the tranquillity which he thought he had assured for the operation proved to be illusory, for about 4 o'clock in the afternoon a force of a thousand Indians was observed approaching, divided into two sections under different flags, one red, the other black. They halted in total silence on a nearby hill, and soon afterwards they were joined by a greater horde. At a signal from their mournful bugles, they laid siege to the village; from all sides the corregidor and his men were surrounded, and he managed to take up position in the main square. But by now he was protected by hardly more than twelve men and two negroes, as the rest of his force had taken to flight. Even so, these few held out for more than an hour; but in the end their guns failed to fire, as their powder was damp. Thus they were overcome by the enemy masses and had to take refuge in the church, most of them wounded by stones.

The Indians did not stop at this point. On the contrary, as they never have mercy on the defeated, they became even more enraged, and they attacked the doors of the church with such frenzy that they broke them down together with the surrounding masonry. In this sorry situation the parish priest sought to negotiate with the Indians to avoid a conflagration; in an attempt to pacify them he came out with the Sacred Host held up in his hands, but even the presence of Our Lord and Majesty was not enough to avoid the outrage they now planned. As the corregidor knelt before the King of kings and the Lord of lords, they violently seized him, and with the crowd pressing round they dragged him to the main square, more dead than alive, for while still in the church they struck him on the temple with a heavy stone. They cut off his head, and the vile act was done by the hand of his own slave, who was tied up for the purpose; then they took the head around the village to announce the victory amidst tumultuous cries. After the corregidor was killed so too were a number of individuals, among them a *chapeton* and Dn. Miguel de Figueroa, an *arequipeño,* who were fleeing wounded and dressed as Indians; both of them had bravely accompanied the corregidor. The remainder, who had hidden before the battle, were creoles, mestizos, and cholos; they were rounded up and freed by the rebel leader, who even gave them permission to return to their homes, though on foot. From this it can be inferred that all the violence of this rabble is directed exclusively against European Spaniards, or Spaniards who appear Europeans.

So horrible a deed has placed this town [Oruro] in a state of great anxiety, as it is virtually surrounded by the province of Paria and also adjoins that of Sicasica, which although it has not reached such extremes is only waiting for a chance to take the same step. The province of Carangas is similarly inclined, for having captured their corregidor Dn. Matias Ibañez on the early morning of 26th of this month, not only did they kill him with equal cruelty but they also killed more than thirty Spaniards who accompanied him. The heads of the corregidores have been immediately dispatched under heavy escort to the rebel Josef Gabriel Túpac Amaru, whom they now recognize as their king and lord since the death of Tomás Catari. God have mercy on us and save this town from the ruin that threatens it.

Oruro, 30 January 1781.

ACCOUNT OF THE FINAL PROCEEDINGS AGAINST JOSEF GABRIEL TÚPAC
AMARU AND OTHER ACCUSED, AND THEIR DEATH SENTENCE

Josef Gabriel Túpac Amaru was taken from his wife and children, and
they were all placed in different prisons, these miserable and ridiculous
fanatics. The case against them was prepared by the visitor-general and
all the details were in the hands of the judge Dn. Benito de la Mata
Linares, who also initiated the preparation of confessions. Túpac Amaru maintained a stubborn refusal to confess, in spite of being subjected to severe torture and to the pains of the *garrucha*. He had an
arm dislocated and other bones broken. But none of this sufficed to
make him confess the truth in answer to the questioning: he only
declared in agony and despair that the visitor-general and he were the
cause of all the kingdom's suffering, statements which were not included in the court records as they were considered to lack judgement
and reason.

The trial took over a month and then the execution was prepared.
The visitor-general requested the bishop to allow absolution of the
guilty from the censures they had incurred. This was granted and the
appropriate powers were delegated to the canon confessor, Dr. Josef
Pérez, who processed from the cathedral robed in a choir cope accompanied by a cathedral priest and six clerics in surplices, preceded by a
crucifix held aloft. The ceremony was performed according to the prescribed rites, and the offenders received the grace they had requested
and submitted respectfully to the church. They were then placed in
chapel to await execution; they were fortunate criminals, for they
could have died like many of their faction without the aid of the
Church and excommunicated for their enormous crimes. They were
allocated priests of approved conduct, sound doctrine and education,
among them four canons, and the visitor-general asked the bishop to
agree to visit and comfort them on the eve of the execution. This
prince of the Church, escorted by three senior officials, saw them all in
their respective jails: he spoke to them words of great feeling and
charity, urging them to repentance and exhorting them not to leave this
world without admitting their complicity in the rebellion, otherwise
they would leave behind turmoil and misery, for which they would be
responsible to God and deserving of eternal punishment. He directed
these sentiments particularly to Josef Gabriel Túpac Amaru as the
principal author of the rebellion, and spoke so effectively that he
caused tears to flow. They all replied that on this and other points they
had cleared their consciences. . . .

On 18 May 1781 soldiers cordoned off the main square [of Cuzco], and the delinquents were brought out one after the other to the foot of the scaffold, dragged in bags by horses. When they were all assembled the first of those who had been so sentenced were hanged; these comprised Francisco Túpac Amaru, uncle of the rebel, Ypolito Túpac Amaru, Antonio Bastidas, Andrés Castelo, Antonio Oblitas, the zambo who had been the executioner of the corregidor Arriaga, and Diego Berdejo. The first three had their tongues cut out and then they were hanged. The cacica of Acos, Tomasa Tito Condemaita, and Micaela Bastidas, wife of the rebel, were garrotted in deference to their sex. The first had her tongue cut out before dying; the second refused to have her tongue cut out and the executioner did it after her death, and they were both hung on the scaffold. That left Josef Gabriel Túpac Amaru, who had been assigned the severest and most complex execution. From the foot of the scaffold where he had been a wretched spectator of the death of his son and wife, he was dragged away an appropriate distance at the back of a horse, as he had been brought out; there they cut out his tongue. They then tied him firmly by hands and feet to four mounted horses; as these galloped away they dislocated his body but could not dismember it as demanded by the sentence, for the horses were not strong or fast enough for the purpose. So the visitor-general ordered the executioner to decapitate him in order to finish him off; and he arrested the corregidor of the city and another official for the faulty arrangements. Thus did the wretched Túpac Amaru end his days after considering himself monarch of Peru for more than five months. His head was hung on the scaffold, where the other eight corpses were also hanging; in due course the executioners took them down and quartered the bodies, as they also did to that of Túpac Amaru. The body of Túpac Amaru and his wife were taken in pieces to Piccho, where he had established his headquarters for the invasion of the city. There they were burnt and the heads have been sent to hang in the village of Tinta, the arms and legs to other places. The youngest son of the rebel called Fernando and aged ten years six months was saved from capital punishment by his imbecility and was sentenced to life imprisonment in Africa and to witness the bloody spectacle of his parents and the others, which he saw at the foot of the scaffold guarded by four grenadiers and chained by the feet.

On the same day as this most necessary act of justice the visitor-general gave proof of his heartfelt charity, for he went very early to the cathedral, and having confessed and received communion he requested many masses for those who were going to be executed; he heard all the masses on his knees, dispensing with the ceremonial due to his rank.

17

Andean Insurrection:
Time and Space

Steve J. Stern

Andean insurrection was not confined to southern Peru. The rebellion of Túpac Amaru had repercussions outside the southern highlands, above all in the center-north, where Indian rebellion had its own history and its own character. Steve Stern, Professor of History in the University of Wisconsin-Madison, argues that insurrectionary threats, actions, and utopias emerged in central-northern Peru as early as the 1740s and 1750s; behind these movements lay new Indian strategies to protect perceived rights by collective violence against an encroaching colonial state. In the course of the eighteenth century Indian protest gathered momentum across a wide territory and in diverse highland regions, not only as an expression of traditional grievance but in the expectation of an Inca revival and a passage to a new age. Why did this movement culminate in one particular area, southern Peru, at a particular moment in time, 1780? The present study addresses the longer term as well as the immediate conjuncture.

Tarma, too, was wracked by disturbances in 1781, but in this case the details remain frustratingly obscure. What we do know is that Indians invaded and destroyed two obraje-hacienda complexes, and a smallish textile workshop (*chorrillo*). The targets of the invaders included San Juan de Colpas, "Tarma's most celebrated obraje." Before the takeover, San Juan de Colpas yielded an annual rent and interest income of 8,800 pesos—a scale implying a huge complex exploiting several hundred laborers at a time. Not surprisingly, Tarma's corregidores had traditionally focused considerable mercantile attentions on San Juan de

Reprinted from Steve J. Stern, "The Age of Andean Insurrection, 1742–1782: A Reappraisal," in Steve J. Stern, ed., *Resistance, Rebellion and Consciousness in the Andean Peasant World, 18th to 20th Centuries* (Madison, Wisconsin: University of Wisconsin Press, 1987), pp. 67–77, by permission of the author and publisher.

Colpas, which served as a labor center to which Indians were sent to work off the debts owed on the district's extremely high reparto de mercancías accounts. In December 1780, however, the Túpac Amaru revolution suddenly changed the traditional rules. Viceroy Jáuregui, hoping to speed the pacification of the insurrectionary south, abolished the repartimiento de mercancías. In Tarma, the abolition decree backfired. Once Indians learned of the measure, "excited by the desire for liberty, they destroyed the installations [of San Juan de Colpas], and began to take measures to establish themselves [on its lands], constituting a formal pueblo . . . and distributing the lands amongst themselves." Similar land invasions destroyed the obraje of Michivilca, and the smaller workshop "Exaltación de Roco." On all three sites the Indians built "pueblos with churches, municipal buildings, and jails."

Our first major point, in evaluating the center-north during the era of Túpac Amaru II, is by now clear. Violent and sometimes ambitious revolts struck Tarma-Jauja, the strategic provinces of the central sierra, precisely as insurrectionary war unfolded in the south. Even after the suppression of the southern insurrection, colonial authority in the central sierra stood on rather shaky ground. Viceroy Jáuregui (1780–1784) reported a riot in Chupaca (southern Jauja region), and ongoing land conflicts simmered in the Yanamarca Valley (just north of the town of Jauja) during 1784–1791. In 1791, the tension forced landowners and colonial land judges to retire to Jauja for safety.

To this point we should immediately add a second: the military balance of forces in Tarma-Jauja during 1780–1782 made it especially difficult for rebels to become insurrectionaries.[1] By this time, we should recall, Tarma-Jauja had become a center of security whose seasoned veterans of repression helped suppress revolts outside and inside their own districts. The speedy availability of regular officers and troops from Tarma, Jauja, and if necessary, Lima, made it relatively easy for authorities to either suppress or isolate quickly rebellions in the central sierra. In general, it was in the center-north sierra and along the Pacific coast that security was beefed up, in the 1750s and after, to counter the dangers of Indian revolt and British attack. Military governors and troops ruled over Tarma-Jauja; the coastal defenses were reformed; and the sprawling Cajamarca corregimiento district was divided into three corregimientos (Huambos, Huamachuco, and Cajamarca), whose smaller size and Indian militias would make the north more manageable.

The balance of forces in the southern highlands contrasts sharply. In the south, authorities ruled over a vast, sprawling territory more isolated from centers of colonial military strength on the coast, and more reliant on rather unreliable provincial militias. Under these circumstances, authorities would find it more difficult to prevent the organization of insurrectionary armies, or the spread of rebellion from one locale to the next.

Finally, we should place the Tarma-Jauja experience in the wider context of the center-north. We need not engage here in a detailed analysis of political life and popular unrest in other center-north provinces. Suffice it to say that recent research now casts doubt on earlier assumptions that center-north provinces remained largely uninvolved in or unaffected by the explosion of Andean unrest, violence, and utopias in 1780–1782. The new research is recasting our understanding of two major regions: Cajamarca-Huamachuco, northern sierra provinces overlooking coastal Lambayeque and Trujillo, and Huamanga, the highland region just south of Jauja.

Cajamarca-Huamachuco experienced repeated local rebellions in the eighteenth century, but its history of revolt once seemed rather disconnected from unrest in the south. This was the case especially because Cajamarca-Huamachuco appeared quiescent for three years following a local riot in Otusco in September 1780. We now know, however, that the Otusco rebellion, unlike the classic village riots studied by Taylor in Mexico, did not quite burn itself out in several days or weeks; that in January 1781, rumors circulated that an emissary of Túpac Amaru II had arrived on the Lambayeque coast and contacted Otusco's rebels; that to ward off danger, colonial authorities mounted a security campaign to control Indians and castas in and near Lambayeque; and that by April, the volatile mix of rumor and security patrols, provoked, in the coastal pueblo of Moche, mass panic and flight. Moche's inhabitants fled to escape soldiers believed to be marching from Lima and Trujillo to quarter the bodies of the locals. We know, too, that Lorenzo Suárez, a chief from Huamachuco, was implicated in the abortive tupamarista revolt in Huarochiri in 1783.

Similarly, Huamanga's apparent calm has proved rather deceptive under closer scrutiny. Lorenzo Huertas has demonstrated a complex ferment of disturbances, rumors, and repression. Despite several precautions taken, in the closing months of 1780 and in early 1781, to organize small military cuartels and to disarm Indians, riots broke out or nearly broke out in the northern Huamanga district of Huanta during 1781. The disturbances were partly provoked by the reparto de mercancías, and partly by attempts to draft Indians and castas into the army that Huamanga would send to fight Túpac Amaru in Cuzco. In Chungui, where eastern Huanta descended toward the jungle, the colonials faced a more ambitious challenge. Pablo Challco, a "notorious idolater," publicly proclaimed the coronation of Túpac Amaru II as king in December 1780, and led a movement whose followers—until their final defeat in October 1781—rejected the authority of corregidores and priests. Earlier that year, in August, a company of Spanish merchants passing through Vischongo (in the Río Pampas zone, considerably south of Huanta) were shocked to stumble upon a large Indian festival celebrating Túpac Amaru II (who was by then dead). The merchants—either armed or accompanied by soldiers—attacked to break up the celebration, but the Indians "rioted" and "took possession of the hills because they were rebels." Even after the final defeat of the southern insurrections, the memory of Túpac Amaru II continued to evoke sympathy and repression. Before his recapture in 1784, Diego Jaquica, an escaped prisoner, native *curandero* (healer), and self-proclaimed relative of Túpac Amaru, wandered through the region and attended public celebrations such as marriages and religious festivals. During his wanderings, Jaquica received respectful treatment as he recounted the epic history of the Túpac Amaru revolution.

The failure of the great southern insurrections to expand into the center-north is a more complex historical issue than previously acknowledged, and is not reducible to trends in socioeconomic structure that made the peoples of the central or northern sierras either less likely to revolt, or less receptive to messianic and insurrectionary ideas. Not only have we seriously underestimated the repercussions of Juan Santos Atahualpa's movement in the central sierra at midcentury. We have also relied on a data base, when interpreting the regional bases of Andean mobilization in the 1780s, that is profoundly incomplete and misleading. Even in the south, the data base is flawed. The failure of the insurrection in the center-north probably had as much to do with organizational, military, and political matters—some of them outgrowths, ironically, of the very gravity of the crisis in the central sierra at midcentury—as with differences in well-being or rebelliousness rooted in "structural" trends in population, economy, mercantile exploitation, and the like.

Set in the context of recent research on Cajamarca, Huamanga, and Tarma-Jauja, we can no longer dismiss other examples of revolt, insurrectionary ambition, or tupamarista sympathy in the center-north as mere aberrations. Consciousness of the tupamarista project embraced north, center, and south, as did violent revolt itself. As a lampoon in Huaraz (northern sierra) warned on Christmas 1781, shortly before a local rebellion broke out, "if in the lands above [i.e., to the south] there have been two Túpac Amarus [José Gabriel, and his cousin and successor Diego Cristóbal], here there are two hundred." In the final analysis, the well known Huarochirí revolt of 1783, far from an aberration, fits in well with the larger picture of the center-north during the era of Túpac Amaru II. This was a revolt at once ambitious and visionary in ideological terms, but severely constrained in practical and organizational terms. For high officials hardened by the great southern wars, Huarochirí's was a revolt rather easily isolated and repressed.

Deeply rooted in the political culture of the eighteenth century, the idea of a neo-Inca liberator could resurface even after its time had passed. More than a full generation after Túpac Amaru's defeat, neo-Inca messianic ideas still struck a responsive chord in the central highlands. In 1812, during the independence crisis, thousands of Indians invaded Huánuco, the small capital "city" of the province just north of Tarma. The Huánuco revolt led the interim intendant of Tarma (an intendancy that included the old corregimiento districts of Huánuco, Tarma, and Jauja in its jurisdiction), Don Ygnacio Valdivieso, to launch a secret investigation to stop possible spillover effects in Tarma and Jauja. To Valdivieso's dismay, he discovered a preexisting undercurrent of messianic rumor and threats of violence, and had to take decisive action, including a round-up of ringleaders, to head off possible revolt. In widely scattered parts of Tarma and Jauja, Inca "emissaries" had spread word, as early as May 1811, that an impending change of eras would liberate Indians and do away with Europeans (*chapetones*). That same month, the Buenos Aires patriot lawyer Juan José Castelli, who had led a patriot expedition into Bolivia, declared at the ancient Tihuanaco ruins that the patriot forces would abolish Indian tribute, redistribute land, establish a school system for all, and decree legal equality for Indians. Castelli's efforts to win a reliable Indian following in Bolivia proved fruitless. From the distance of Tarma-Jauja, however, Indians saw him as a neo-Inca liberator: "they said that the son of the Inca was about to arrive, and that Casteli [sic] was right." During the violence in Huánuco in 1812, Indians spoke of the arrival of "King Castelli" or "Castell Inga."

If the thesis of this essay is correct, we must embark on a major reappraisal of the chronology, geography, and explanation of Andean insurrection. We have long recognized, of course, that repeated violence in explicit defiance of colonial authority, and the myth of an imminent Inca-led liberation, constituted powerful eighteenth-century forces. Most Andeanist scholars would agree that the rise of revolt and insurrectionary utopias in dynamic relation to one another created, at least in the south in the 1780s, a major crisis of colonial rule.

What has been lost, however, in recent efforts to discern with greater rigor the social and economic bases of insurrection, is an appreciation of the breadth of the crisis and its underlying causes. We have overly narrowed our focus. . . . The breakdown of Spanish colonial authority over poor Indians and castas—as manifested by explicit and violent defiance of once accepted authority, and by the rise of new ideologies envisioning a transformed social order—was even graver than we have conceded. Its territorial reach encompassed the northern sierras of Peru, as well as the southern territory that became an insurrectionary battleground. The crisis of authority included the strategic central sierra districts—Huarochirí, Tarma, and Jauja—that overlooked Lima, the capital city, and that constituted a major gateway between north and south. And the rise of an urgent insurrectionary threat dates back *at least* to the 1740s, and spanned forty years or more before its definitive suppression. To be sure, details of timing, intensity, organizational capacity, and the like varied by region, and this regional variation influenced the outcome of the insurrectionary crisis. But this was a crisis of rule whose proportions approached those which destroyed French colonial rule in Haiti. The gravity and scale of the crisis are all the more striking if one considers the differences in geography and physical environment, repertoire of social control devices (cooption and patronage, repression, counterintelligence, etc.), population density and racial-ethnic composition, colonial experience, and metropolitan politics that gave Spanish colonial rulers great advantage over their French counterparts.

As we search for a more satisfactory explanation of the Age of Andean Insurrection, we will need to revise not only our chronology and geography, but also our methodological tools. We will need to move away from mechanistic approaches to causation that explain the "why," "when," and "where" of insurrectionary mobilization largely in terms reducible to categories of social structure, or to rates of economic pillage. Methodologically, we need to move in two directions. First, we must pay greater respect to the interplay of structural, conjunctural, and episodic levels of analysis. It is this multiplicity of time scales and causation levels which may help us to understand the erosion of colonial authority, in the long term, over a very wide Andean area encompassing most of Peru-Bolivia; the variations of timing and locale that created "miniconjunctures" within the larger insurrectionary conjuncture of 1742–1782; and the transformation of serious insurrectionary threats, at given moments, into insurrectionary events, aborted revolts or conspiracies, or prevented "nonevents." A second methodological corrective would devote closer attention to the interplay of material exploitation or hardship on the one hand, and consciousness or moral outrage on the other. It is the moral memory—or myth—of an alternative, Andean-based social order, a cultural memory nurtured and sustained by Andean peoples during an earlier period of "resistant adaption" to colonial rule that in part explains why economic pillage led not merely to local revolt, nor even to insurrectionary conspiracies under a Hispanic-Christian millennial banner, but rather to dreams of a great transformation under nativist or neo-Inca auspices.

Our revised methodology need not imply that regional variation is unworthy of investigation, or that the spatial method pioneered by Cornblit and Golte has little to offer. Comparative spatial analysis, if harnessed to a more well-developed data base and a less mechanistic methodology, could yield truly exciting results. Close microanalysis of local districts *within* insurrectionary provinces, for example, might clarify aspects of leadership, social composition, economic interest, and the like that swung a district to support the insurrectionaries or royalists once an insurrection was under way. Similarly, if we move back to a macrolevel, the particularities of various regions will, in all likelihood, inject important nuances into the larger history of Andean insurrection. In the case of Tarma-Jauja, for example, I suspect that land pressure, a growing population of "Indianized mestizos," and the fluidity of racial boundaries in the plebeian culture of Tarma's mining camps and in Jauja's Indian-mestizo villages, would all loom larger in discussion of the causes and political culture of rebellion than in Cuzco-Puno. Recognition of such variations would undoubtedly illuminate important aspects of the insurrectionary crisis, even if we believe—as I do—that underlying common trends undermined colonial authority in both regions, and created an insurrectionary conjuncture long before the 1770s.

My own hypothesis, subject of course to verification and revision as scholarly research unfolds, is that the changing political economy of mercantile exploitation undermined preexisting strategies and relations of colonial rule and Andean resistance, by the 1730s, across virtually all of highland Peru-Bolivia. The changing relations of mercantile exploitation directly threatened the continuity of colonial political authority, and its rather fragile and partial legitimacy among Andean peasants. During the earlier period of commercial expansion and prosperity in the late sixteenth and early seventeenth centuries, corregidores, judges, and priests could more readily accede to Indian pressure to transform them into "mediating," partly "co-optable" figures of authority. The diverse paths to commercial prosperity open to colonial aristocrat-entrepreneurs and officials, who were divided by their own internal rivalries, allowed Indians a measure of "institutional space" by which to manipulate, bend, or bribe colonial officials and intermediaries to the Indians' own partial advantage. In the long run, this pattern facilitated the rise of paternal quid pro quos that simultaneously allowed for significant Indian resistance and self-protection from some of the worst depredations, but left intact the structure of exploitation and formal colonial authority. As a practical matter, such quid pro quos between colonial patrons or intermediaries and Indian clients probably afforded greater space for Andean self-protection as time went on, and the earlier success and efficiency of the colonial system unravelled. By the middle decades of the seventeenth century, the Hapsburg model of Andean colonial rule and prosperity perfected by Viceroy Francisco de Toledo (1569–1581) had entered serious decay and revision. The very ability of Indians to "co-opt" partially figures of paternal authority, and to develop such "co-options" into a major strategy of resistance and self-protection, may also help account for the tendency of peasants to look upon the King of Spain as the ultimate "protector" standing above or outside the local American system.

By the early eighteenth century, however, the determined efforts of the Crown and of Lima's commercial bourgeoisie to increase the efficacy of mercantile exploitation, in the face of stagnant markets in Andean America and Spain's weakness as an imperial competitor, had effectively destroyed the earlier pattern. Corregidores, after the 1678 "reform" that transformed their posts into speculative ventures auctioned to high bidders in Spain, now found themselves saddled by huge debts as they entered their five-year terms of office. In addition, they now faced a rather stagnant commercial economy whose internal markets expanded mainly through force. The combined pressures of debt and commercial stagnation transformed the corregidores into ruthlessly one-dimensional exploiters of Indian lands and labor through the reparto de mercancías system, i.e., the forced distribution of unwanted goods at inflated prices. The Spanish colonial state—allied to Lima's commercial bourgeoisie, committed to a more efficient imperial system, vitally interested in revenues from the sale of corregidor posts to high bidders, and from taxation of a commercial economy expanding by force—would not seriously contemplate reforming the new structure of mercantile exploitation until the political crises of the 1750s and 1770s. In fact, the colonial state had made the political standing of corregidores even more volatile through its considerable efforts, especially under Viceroys Palata (1686–1689) and Castelfuerte (1724–1736), to expand tribute collection, update census counts, and revitalize the mita, the institution whereby peasant communities sent rotating drafts of laborers to the mines and other colonial enterprises, or paid monies to hire substitute laborers.

Given these circumstances, and a growing Indian population in need of more lands and productive resources, earlier quid pro quos, strategies of native resistance, and fragile colonial legitimacies all broke down. Corregidores became particularly pointed targets of popular wrath. But the new economic pressures on corregidores subjected *all* the collaborators in local power groups to new strains that restricted the possibilities of their partial "co-option" by Indians, and raised the political stakes of such accommodations. Although research on the social and political activities of priests is still in its infancy, the new circumstances of the eighteenth century probably sharpened latent rivalries between priests and corregidores, forced some priests to resort to provocative new fees and land claims to secure their own revenues, and generally eroded the priests' ability to play meaningful mediating roles without directly challenging the authority of corregidores. In most instances, priests probably sought to avoid extreme and dangerous outcomes, but the political pressure-cooker sometimes boiled over, converting some priests into sympathetic allies, even instigators, of peasant revolts against corregidores, and others, as in Jauja in 1781, into targets of rebellion. The political crisis sharply affected, too, the ability of Andean chiefs to defend their own legitimacy as "brokers" between peasants and the colonial regime.

Future research may find this hypothesis wanting, and would in any event need to supplement it with an explanation of the rise of neo-Inca "insurrectionary utopias" as colonial authority and legitimacy entered into crisis. But however we explain the Age of Andean Insurrection, the severity, breadth, and ideological components of the insurrectionary crisis will raise important issues across time and space. Placed in a comparative Spanish American framework, the contrasts with Ecuador and Mexico are striking. Despite notable revolts in Ecuador, a benign Inca myth failed to develop into a powerful political force. What explains the contrasting character of revolt and political culture in Ecuador and Peru-Bolivia? The research of William B. Taylor on peasant rebellion in Mexico again underscores the particularity of Peru-Bolivia. Villagers rioted repeatedly in the Indian heartland of Mexico in the eighteenth century, but in most cases the rebellions proved eminently containable. The riots, although significant in redressing local grievances, posed little threat to the wider social order. Neo-Aztec ideological motifs, such as they were, blended into the protonational creole ideology emerging in the eighteenth century. In Andean Peru-Bolivia, by contrast, local violence and tension repeatedly seemed to threaten possible insurrection waving the banner of a lost—and soon to be restored—native Andean glory. Protonational creole ideology, far from subsuming neo-Inca motifs, found itself in dangerous competition with more "nativist" protonational ideologies. Again, what explains the contrasting character of revolt and political culture in Mexico and Peru-Bolivia?

Once we recognize the particularity of the political culture of eighteenth-century Andean peasants, we encounter further implications across time. In Peru-Bolivia, in the late colonial period, peasants did not live, struggle, or think in terms that isolated them from an emerging "national question." On the contrary, protonational symbols had great importance in the life of peasants and small-holders. Yet these protonational symbols were tied not to an emerging creole nationalism, but to notions of an Andean- or Inca-led social order. Andean peasants saw themselves as part of a wider protonational culture, and sought their liberation on terms that, far from isolating them from an overarching state, would link them to a new and just state. The myth of Castelli as Inca liberator, in the same highland region that also appeared to support more "creole" patriot guerrilla bands during the Wars of Independence, should force us to view skeptically the application of assumptions about peasant "parochialism" and "antinational" localism to Andean peoples. The fact that most all native Andean peoples were peasants did not necessarily prevent them from viewing their nineteenth-century destinies in terms linked to a national identity and project. The real issues are how, and to what extent, Andean notions of nationhood gave way to more creole versions of nationhood in the nineteenth century; and to what extent the eventual rise of creole nationality so excluded Andean peoples from meaningful (i.e., partly self-interested) "citizenship" that it forced them into an "antinational" posture.

But we have leaped ahead of our story. The last words belong to an anonymous eighteenth-century songwriter from Cajamarca. Tied to a regional rhythm of life and rebellion so apparently disconnected from the insurrectionary wars raging in the south, our songwriter was nonetheless drawn—upon news of Túpac Amaru's death in 1781—to the nearby warm-water springs that once provided relaxation to visiting Incas, and that serve today as a tourist attraction. There, our songwriter could contemplate the profound sense of loss:

> At the waters where I awaited
> I had come heeding your call,
> Feeling within your imminent arrival,
> Wondering when you would come.

18

The Sources of
Popular Protest

Anthony McFarlane

The advance of the Bourbon state, the curbing of local participation, new pressures on the Indians, and the general increase of taxation did not go unchallenged. Resistance to government innovation and abuse of power found expression in protest and rebellion, culminating in the revolts of 1780–1781 in Peru, New Granada,and Venezuela. These often began as temporary coalitions of social groups, which the creoles first led and then, alarmed by the pressure from below, abandoned, leaving the popular base to find its own level of resistance. Were these movements "antecedents" of independence? Or did the rebels appeal rather to a past utopia when bureaucratic centralization and tax oppression were unknown? Anthony McFarlane, Senior Lecturer in Latin American History in the University of Warwick, explores civil disturbances in New Granada during the eighteenth century, focusing particularly on the political behavior of the popular classes as expressions of their attitudes towards colonial government and its agents. Anti-tax riots in Vélez (1740) and Ocaña (1760) were followed by a series of civil disorders in the southern regions of the viceroyalty, culminating in a major rebellion in Quito (1765), and recurring in other regions until the end of the colonial regime. These movements took place in both town and country; they involved Indians, mestizos, mulattos, and whites in various combinations; they ranged from Indian protests against white oppression, to attacks on Spanish officials by mestizos and creoles, and risings of blacks and slaves; and they were expressions not simply of anger and despair but of political beliefs and community interests. They showed that tax demands could not be made with impunity, that official corruption would not be ignored, and that innovation would nor-

From Anthony McFarlane, "Civil Disorders and Popular Protests in Late Colonial New Granada," *Hispanic American Historical Review*, 64:1, pp. 37–54. Copyright Duke University Press, 1984. Reprinted with permission of the publisher.

mally be resisted. Behind them lay a popular conception of freedom and a tradition of collective action, not directly related to independence but significant for all government.

As protests against official incursions into local economic life, these disturbances reflect unstated assumptions about the legitimate claims of government and its agents. These assumptions were basically conservative: they did not challenge the right of government to levy taxation or to organize the administration of the colony, but protested against specific taxes and the behaviour of particular officials. Indeed, in several of the cases examined, tumults were only part of more prolonged actions, in which members of communities expressed their ultimate confidence in government by carrying their protests beyond the local level by appeals to higher authorities. In this sense, these protests were ultimately respectful of royal authority: they were directed against changes in taxation, not taxation itself; against the representatives of government, not government itself. While respect for governmental authority was encouraged by habits and traditions of deference, combined with the threat of punishment, it also depended on official observance of existing customs and practices. If these were ignored or broken by fiscal innovations or new economic incursions by local officials, defiance of authority could be regarded as a justifiable means of defending local interests. Implicitly, then, these disturbances carried a claim to "rights," if only in the vague sense that they embodied a readiness to defend the status quo against the fiscal and economic pressures of government and its agents. Such implicit claims to unspecified "rights" were also reflected in disturbances that arose from conflicts over office-holding and the administration of the law. In both these matters, respect for authority was neither automatic nor uncritical. By taking direct action to hinder the holding of office by unpopular individuals, and to pressure local magistrates to enforce the law in particular ways, members of communities in New Granada again showed pretensions to rights of intervention and participation to which the Bourbon state allowed them no explicit or formal claim.

One manifestation of such pretensions is found in disturbances that produced demonstrations of hostility toward local officials, aimed at preventing them from taking office or at expelling them from office. The choice of a local official appears to have been a matter in which members of communities felt that they should have some say. This attitude is reflected in disturbances that occurred when an official was not to local taste. On Sunday, January 9, 1724, a large crowd of citizens of the small mestizo town of Monguí near Tunja turned out to express a vocal vote against the newly appointed *juez ordinario* by giving him a tumultuous reception when he arrived to take up residence. On arriving in Monguí the magistrate found a mob of about a hundred men, armed with swords, waiting in the town square to greet him with threatening gestures and shouts of "We will not receive don Juan de Vargas," "We don't want him," "Any other alcalde is better." The crowd then pursued him, forcing him to retire to his house outside the town. A similar incident occurred in the hamlet of El Plato, near Mompós, in 1803. When don Joseph Vicente Gómez, a relatively wealthy man from the nearby town of Tenerife and the collector of tithes in El Plato, was designated interim magistrate by the cabildo of Tenerife, the vecinos of El Plato banded together "in tumultuous uproar" to reject him. Even when he was replaced, collective action against him did not cease. On two occasions in July 1803, crowds gathered to demand his expulsion from the village on the grounds that he had insulted the local people by calling them thieves, and refused to contribute to community works. When an alcalde of Tenerife was sent to investigate, and refused to expel Gómez, the locals rioted against the alcalde, filling his courtroom with dirt, posting a crude and insulting pasquinade, and abusing him with threats and insults until he retreated to Tenerife.

In other incidents, also reported as "tumultos" or "motines," intimidation of unpopular officials was staged by small groups operating in a semiclandestine manner, rather than crowds engaged in public demonstrations. These incidents usually arose from rivalries within small communities, in which groups of vecinos related by ties of kinship or friendship attacked officials of whom for some reason they disapproved. While the motives behind such attacks are often obscure, the manner in which they were carried out shows that they were more than merely criminal assaults by lawless thugs. Thus, when don Joachim de Lis, *alcalde provincial* of the town of Purificación, was attacked on the night of December 31, 1776, his assailants were not simply indulging in a spree of mindless violence, but were making a calculated show of force for political ends. The gang of eight men and two women, "all armed and disguised in different costumes," who burst into Lis's house and manhandled him did so in order to force him to sign a document formally renouncing his post as *alcalde provincial*. As the men were all members of the town council and their attack took place on New Year's Eve—the day before the new alcaldes were chosen—the timing and nature of the assault were clearly related to political goals. Similar tactics of intimidation were employed in Moniquirá, a mestizo parish in the Province of Tunja, on December 28, 1802. In this incident, a group of about a dozen people, including some women disguised as men, made a nocturnal attack on don Rafael Conde, who was about to become the alcalde in the coming year. They assaulted Conde, warned him that "many alcaldes in the world had been killed," and told him that he would suffer the same fate if he took up his post. . . .

An interesting aspect of these incidents is the element of ritual apparent in the behaviour of the assailants. In both cases, reference is made to the use of costumes or disguise, although these did nothing to camouflage the identities of their wearers. This feature is more clearly described in an incident of assault on an official that occurred in Cheva, Tunja Province, in 1809. On the night of November 13 of that year, the corregidor of Gameza was attacked in his home in Cheva by a group of some twenty-five people who, he alleged, were led by the local parish priest. He reported that this group, "their hands and faces stained in black, dressed in petticoats worn back to front, and headscarves . . . and armed with daggers and cudgels, led by the said priest, in similar disguise" had broken into his house, yelling curses and insults. They had dragged the corregidor, still dressed in his underclothes, from his bed and, showering him with blows to his buttocks, mounted him on a mule and galloped him violently around. They then brought out his wife in a similar manner, tied them together on the same steed, and rode them far from the village before abandoning them, with a warning never to return to Cheva, on pain of death. The subsequent investigation into this affair shows that it arose from a clash between the corregidor and prominent vecinos of Cheva, including the *juez pedáneo* and the collector of tithes, over access to Indian labor.

These affrays involving local factions are another indication of a popular readiness to participate and intervene in colonial political life. Although they were the work of small groups behaving in a more-or-less covert manner, they were not simply the violent acts of criminal gangs in pursuit of personal vendettas. They were rather an aspect of local politics in which, by engaging in disputes over office or bringing pressure to bear on officials to conform to private needs, the participants displayed an underlying assumption that authority should be exercised in collusion with local interests. Because they were marked by attacks on officers of government, these affrays were treated as acts of rebellion. But if they were illegal, they were not anti-institutional. They did not attack the machinery of the state, but sought to control and manipulate its agents.

The employment of force by groups seeking to exert pressure on officials is also found in incidents of riot that occurred in the city of Tunja in 1727 and in the town of Çali in 1743. . . . The Tunja riot of January 23, 1727, took place when a crowd sought to pressure magistrates to enforce the law in an equitable manner, following a street brawl in which a peninsular Spaniard had wounded a mestizo shepherd. Both men were apprehended by prominent local citizens who were in the vicinity at the time of the fight, and a curious crowd soon gathered. The alcalde ordinario, don José Calvo, quickly made his way to the scene, having been informed that a crowd had gathered in the main square and that the city would be lost if he failed to arrest the Spaniard, Pedro Sertuche. Calvo was persuaded, however, that the two men should be held separately. He ordered that Sertuche be placed under house arrest, in a house that was the home and property of a fellow peninsular. On the other hand, the injured mestizo, Vicente Barbosa, was sent to the city jail.

This unequal treatment provoked a strong reaction from local peasants and small tradesmen. A vociferous crowd of some twenty-five men and women, including relatives of Barbosa, gathered outside the house where Sertuche was held and staged a threatening demonstration. Members of the crowd complained loudly that there was no justice in the city, and that it was becoming like the Sierra Morena. This disparaging reference to Spain was accompanied by shouts of "Death to Sertuche and all Spaniards," and "From here to the Sierra Morena, death to all Spaniards." It was also said that people had shouted acclaim for the *maestre de campo* as their king, referring to a prominent creole, don Martín Camacho, present at the time. This crowd became so aggressive that it was decided that Sertuche should be imprisoned in the city jail, if only for his own safety. In the meantime, his erstwhile opponent, Barbosa, had been released from the jail by another crowd before Sertuche was placed there, bound with manacles at the behest of the mob. Later that night, there was another disturbance caused by people trying to break into the jail to attack Sertuche.

The immediate causes of this riot are plain enough. After a violent brawl between a Spaniard and a mestizo, in which the Spaniard used a firearm to wound his opponent, the local magistrate's unequal treatment of the two offenders stirred angry feelings among local people. More interesting is the manner in which the action developed and the attitudes that it reveals. It is clear that this was far from the frenzied outburst of a mob hungry for revenge; on the contrary, it was a structured show of force carried out by a threatening, but basically orderly, crowd. Although some witnesses drew attention to the fact that members of the crowd carried swords, stones, and cudgels, there were no attacks on either persons or property. Indeed, most witnesses stressed that the crowd behaved in a restrained and respectful manner. It is also apparent that an element of class antagonism was present and contributed to the development of events. The incident brought a confrontation between individuals who came from distinct social groups. On one side stood the friends and partisans of the peninsular Spaniard, all of them prominent citizens and office-holders in the city. On the other were the relatives and allies of Barbosa, the active nucleus of the protesting crowd, including peasants, artisans, and small traders. Thus the incident was colored by the opposition of rich and poor, of powerful and humble. The antagonism of plebians to patricians, however, was not indiscriminate. The threatening shouts against Spaniards were accompanied by cries of acclaim for a prominent local creole, don Martín Camacho, whom members of the crowd evidently regarded as a possible champion for their cause. In the subsequent investigation, there was never any direct accusation that Camacho had instigated or played a leading role in the riot. But he took part in a subsequent incident which shows that tensions between Spaniards and colonials were aroused. He admitted that the day after the riot he had posted a handbill in the town square, challenging those Spaniards who had been heard to make insulting remarks about himself and fellow creoles during the events of the preceding day. His prompt and public reaction to this alleged slander suggests that antagonism between colonials and Spaniards was not far below the surface of social life in the city, and that it affected both rich and poor.

The disturbance in Tunja, then, is of interest for several reasons. First, it suggests the existence of a popular sense of justice, by showing that the poorer members of the community could be moved to concerted action when they felt that basic norms of justice were being flouted. Second, it indicates that although the crowd was ready to use threatening behavior to force municipal officials to meet its demands, it nevertheless recognized the authority implicit in their offices. Third, it reveals an animosity toward peninsular immigrants, a sensitivity toward their arrogant behavior, and a vague sense that local men were the rightful leaders of the community.

In the Tunja incident, popular action was directed toward forcing a magistrate to discharge his duties in an equitable manner. In a riot that occurred in Cali in 1743, a crowd took direct action to prevent a magistrate from perpetrating a perceived violation of the rights of a citizen. The riot took place on February 20, 1743, when a large crowd made a nocturnal attack on the town jail to release a prisoner, and destroyed a gibbet that had recently been erected in the main square. This incident, however, also involved enmities between colonials and Spaniards, reflected in an assault on the house of one of the alcaldes of Cali, who was a peninsular merchant.

Underlying this event was a long history of factional strife in eigh-teenth-century Cali, stemming from a struggle for control of the ca-bildo between newly arrived peninsular merchants and members of the established creole families. In the disturbances of 1743, the clergy ap-pear to have played a leading part in both instigating and leading the riot, and the evidence collected suggests that it was part of a campaign of resistance against the incumbent alcaldes. The riot of February 20, however, was more than simply a clash of patrician factions. It in-volved the mobilization of a crowd for the purpose of forestalling a threatened violation of the normal methods of the law. Rumors had circulated in the city to the effect that a prisoner was about to be tortured—to extract information about a pasquinade—and subsequently hanged. To prevent this, the jail was attacked, and a large crowd mus-tered in the main square where, despite the parade of the Holy Sacra-ment by priests seeking to restore calm and despite being fired upon by an embattled alcalde, it refused to disperse until the gibbet had been cut to pieces. Although some witnesses state that most of the rioting crowd was drunk, this was evidently not simply a disorderly melee, but the work of a crowd acting with a definite purpose and a degree of discipline.

Although the direction of a riot undoubtedly owed something to organization by leaders of a faction active in town politics, the rioting crowd should not necessarily be regarded as the blind and unwitting instrument of elite groups competing for control of urban government. The prior circulation of rumors about the alleged mistreatment of a prisoner suggests that the populace had to have some justification for action. In spreading the word that the alcaldes were abusing their power, the populace made an appeal to principles of justice both to promote and to legitimize crowd action of an unlawful kind. By attack-ing the jail, however, and destroying the gibbet, the crowd did not aim to overthrow the law; it sought rather to prevent a perceived abuse of the law by local magistrates by briefly taking the law into its own hands. Thus beneath the surface of this rowdy incident in urban poli-tics, we once again may dimly discern a popular conception of justice and of the law that did not tolerate the unrestrained exercise of power by representatives of the state. . . .

At a general level, these incidents indicate that, while the inarticu-late mass of the colonial populace had no opportunity to participate in the formal organizations and institutions of government, they were able to express their grievances and voice their beliefs by informal means. Although of sporadic timing and scattered incidence, the events described strengthen the impression given by some contemporary ob-servers that the mass of the colonial population could be a restive and potentially turbulent force. For the emissaries of the Bourbon state in New Granada, this was a measure of the lamentable lawlessness of the lower orders, who were insufficiently exposed to the disciplinary guidance of church and state. In a vivid formulation of this view, Archbishop-Viceroy Caballero y Góngora condemned the insubordination of the lower classes in unequivocal terms. The mestizos, he stated, were without "the two principal sentiments which Nature inspires in rational man—belief in one God, whom he should love, and in one king, whom it is just to obey." As for Indians and Blacks, according to the archbishop, they were governed by even baser feelings. In all, the common people formed an "indomitable monster," whose criminal proclivities were at the root of the colony's ills.

Made soon after the Comunero revolt, Caballero y Góngora's remarks reflect the instinctive horror of popular rebellion natural to a high official of church and state; hence, they may exaggerate the extent of popular insubordination. Nevertheless, the Archbishop-Viceroy's comments reflected a basic reality of colonial life. Governmental control over the extensive territory and diverse society of New Granada was undoubtedly weak and uneven. The largely mestizo population, most of which was thinly spread over large rural areas, was accustomed to little direct interference from government; indeed, in some areas in late eighteenth-century New Granada, Bourbon officials were still trying to build a basic infrastructure of royal administration. Furthermore, though the population was divided by considerable inequalities of wealth and social status, lower-class habits of deference do not seem to have been as well developed as those of their counterparts in Europe: the uncouth and insolent manners of the lower orders occasionally drew scandalized comment from peninsular observers during the eighteenth century, while the familiarity of the lower classes with their social superiors was to be a source of surprise for foreign visitors during the early years of independence. When colonial government sought to impose its will without regard for these conditions and the conventions they had fostered, it risked defiance, sometimes on a widespread scale. This was the lesson of the aguardiente riots of 1765, a lesson that, ignored by the reformist visitor-general in 1781, was to be repeated by the comuneros in a still more obvious way. Thereafter, viceregal government became more sensitive to the threat of colonial insubordination. Thus, in 1803, Viceroy Pedro de Mendinueta commented upon the low level of wages paid to agricultural workers at a time when prices were rising, and observed that a time might come when the poor would force the landowners to yield a large share of their wealth. He also testified to the continuing existence of that strong undercurrent of popular animosity toward the tax collector, and warned the crown against imposing additional fiscal burdens on the colony, for fear that this might provoke a rebellious response.

When the refractory disposition of the New Granadan population was openly expressed, it did not take the simple form of unbridled vandalism. Among the features shared by the disturbances described above were those elements of structured and discriminating behavior that historians have frequently found in the actions of rioters and rebels in other parts of colonial America and in contemporary Europe. From the incidents described above it seems, first, that defiance of authority was rarely a simple spontaneous outburst of collective anger. Tumults often took place during hours of darkness, perhaps because this made it easier for the participants to conceal their identities. At times, crowds were brought together by some signal, such as the tolling of church bells or the beating of a drum, both of which were commonly used to gather people together for normal social functions. The use of signals and the cover of darkness suggest that there was an element of preparation behind some incidents of civil disorder, though others—like that which occurred in Tunja in 1727—arose as a spontaneous response to the actions of the authorities. There were, in addition, occasions on which disturbances merged with, or developed from, public gatherings, particularly public festivities. . . .

The extent of community participation is difficult to measure and compare. At times, it might be large, as in the Vélez, Ocaña, and Quito riots, where a substantial proportion of the townspeople joined in action. At other times, it was relatively small, measured in tens rather than in hundreds. In many cases, the documentation is vague on numbers, referring only to "many people," to "a multitude," or to some such ill-defined quantity. Generally, however, we may assume that crowds were small, reflecting the small size of the communities from which they were drawn.

The kinds of people who participated in civil disorders also varied with the local setting, depending on the size of the community and its ethnic composition. In most of the disturbances discussed, participants included people of different social rank, though the documentation is invariably uninformative about the occupations or economic positions of those involved. The documentation does convey, though, the impression that disturbances engaged a cross-section of the community, or in incidents in villages such as El Plato or Chinú, virtually the entire community acting in concert. In the disturbances in Vélez, Ocaña, Zaragoza, and El Plato, as well as in the incidents of nocturnal attacks on officials, municipal officers, local clerics, and leading citizens played prominent roles in promoting action against government officials, with the support of undifferentiated crowds and gangs loosely described by some general term like the *plebe,* or "people of inferior quality." It seems, then, that participants in such collective actions mirrored the structure of local society, with leading parts played by prominent veci-nos backed by their social inferiors. At times, such men may have been coopted as leaders without their full consent. Some years after the riot in Chinú in 1798, a witness confessed on his deathbed that a Catalan vecino who had been imprisoned for leading the disturbances in the village had been forced to accept a position of leadership by threats to his land and property. Such cooptation—on pain of death or damage to property—was also used by Comunero rebels to coerce men of local standing to take positions of command in the movement. By this means, the rebels showed their concern to present their protest as that of the community as a whole, represented through the traditional me-dium of its leading citizens, and thereby to help legitimate their ac-tions. Apart from the case of Chinú, there are traces of this behavior in tumults that took place in Tunja, where the *maestre de campo* was called upon to champion lower-class rioters, and in Vélez, where the *alférez real* was acclaimed the "King of Vélez."

Evidently the civil disorders of late colonial New Granada were nei-ther inspired nor guided by any specific or explicitly elaborated politi-cal ideas, they rarely had repercussions outside their immediate lo-calities, and they left no permanent forms of political organization. Nevertheless, they were not entirely innocent of political ideas or sig-nificance. In the structured forms of collective protest and acts of defiance against government and its agents, we may dimly detect atti-tudes and beliefs that were normally unstated, and rarely expressed in written or explicit form. In their reactions to the fiscal and economic impositions of government, to the appointment of officials opposed by members of a local community, or to perceived abuses of authority by incumbent officials, the small and highly localized disturbances de-scribed herein throw back some reflections of popular attitudes and values, especially with respect to the relations of government to its subjects. These attitudes are similar to those encountered in other precapitalist agrarian societies: a belief in a right to land and the use of its products; a belief in the right to produce and consume essential items of consumption (foodstuffs, tobacco, and aguardiente) without arbitrary taxation; the idea that local customs should be respected and justice fairly administered. These attitudes implicitly defined a basic notion of freedom: the right to resist arbitrary intrusions by govern-ment and its agents. This minimal and residual notion of freedom was nurtured by the colonial experience of government. Despite its imposing structure of law and bureaucracy, Spanish government in New Granada, as in other colonies, held only loose control over the mass of the population. In this sense, the society of New Granada shared in that freedom which Mario Góngora has described as "peculiar to the Americas—a form of liberty existing outside the framework of the state . . . not based on any well-defined notion or any new concept of the state . . . [but] . . . rooted in laxity."

This popular outlook, expressed in the minor civil disorders discussed, also played an important part in the emergence and development of the Comunero rebellion. In his analysis of the rhetoric and ideas of the Comuneros, Phelan argued that the movement was informed by beliefs about the common good of the community, the right of the community to express its interests to government and to resist unjust laws, by force if necessary. Phelan observed that these ideas were remarkably similar to those of sixteenth- and seventeenth-century Spanish political thinkers, and he suggested that they had been conveyed to the colonial context through the practices of Hapsburg government. Comunero leaders were not conversant with Spanish political theory; their acquaintance with such ideas came from experience of Hapsburg political practices that had established and observed an "unwritten constitution" in New Granada, a set of conventions and customary procedures that symbolized a pact between the monarch and his subjects.[1] While Phelan's emphasis on the influence of Hapsburg paternalism is well-placed, it must be stressed, however, that these ideas were not confined to the creole patriciate or derived solely from its conception of government. Just as the ideas of sixteenth-century Spanish political thinkers were in part a distillation of popular beliefs and attitudes, so the ideas of the Comuneros in eighteenth-century New Granada reflected popular attitudes that arose from local experience. In an isolated and backward agrarian society, where the writ of metropolitan government ran thin outside the main cities, local experience nurtured a belief in the community outside the state, with its own customs and conventions, and the right to defy governmental authority and to oppose the exercise of power when it collided with local interests. It is this outlook that is periodically reflected in civil disorders and that also informed the Comunero rebellion. The distinctive feature of the Comunero rebellion was that it brought popular agitation under creole leadership, molding the diffuse actions and attitudes of lower-class rioters into an explicit and coherent program of demands. But at the heart of the movement was that same defiance of arbitrary government and taxation that lay behind other, lesser civil disorders.

So, despite the special characteristics of the Comunero rebellion, it may be seen as another expression of a tradition of popular actions undertaken in defense of the customary arrangements and practices of local community life. Expressed in sporadic, multifarious actions rather than in precise arguments, revealed in criminal proceedings rather than political treatises, this tradition is inarticulate and elusive; but the ability of the populace to act collectively, in pursuit of common goals and against prescribed targets, suggests that, even in this backward and isolated colonial society, there existed a popular conception of the proper functions and limits of government that constituted a significant, if neglected, dimension of social life.

19

Riots and Rebellions

Brian R. Hamnett

The eighteenth century saw great competition for land and renewed growth of large estates in central Mexico and Oaxaca; these trends were exacerbated by population increase—which stimulated growth but also increased the pressure on land, and by the new economic opportunities in the regional, viceregal, and world markets during a time of mining boom and freer trade. Such pressures were not necessarily felt in every Indian village, but there were regions where oppression prevailed, where social crisis could simmer and mass outrage erupt, waiting only for mobilization by a strong leader. The Bajío in particular, where haciendas were expanding at the expense of small rancheros and a growing number of families were reduced to living as poor tenants and squatters, became a breeding ground for bandits and insurgents. Rural and peasant grievances were not always expressed in violence or outlawry; encroaching haciendas, landless villages, dearth and recession did not necessarily constitute causes that would arouse rebels and attract leadership. The permanent structures of rural Mexico were more or less accepted; it was the extraordinary grievances or exceptional maladies that produced dissent and banditry. Brian Hamnett, Reader in Latin American History in the University of Essex, has identified the regional sources of popular discontent and placed these in a wider context of revolution. He points out that poverty, harvest failures, and subsistence crises do not in themselves explain the outbreak of revolution. Further factors always need to be present: the existence of a political crisis at the center with consequent loss of control over large regions; local grievances and their exploitation by effective leadership; the power and distribution of the armed forces.

But rather than describe local unrest as a "cause" of revolution, he sees a continuity of grievance and rebellion extending from the colony, through the revolution, and into the independent republic.

During the colonial and early national period four types of conflict appear most frequently. The first type resulted from administrative abuses or fiscal pressures. It involved confrontation between subjects and state employees or their merchant-investors. The second type derived from conditions on the land, and involved day laborers, resident workers, tenants, estate-managers and landlords. In the third category changes in customary rights or mining practices provided the source of discord. Fourthly, pressure on the food supply, following harvest failure, dislocated many peasant communities and generated varying degrees of unrest in town and country. . . . None of [these conflicts] posed any serious challenge either to the viceregal government or to the dominant groups in the locality. Their causes varied and the districts in which they took place differed widely. In consequence, though certain common features are distinguishable, conditions did not exist for their development into broadly-based regional rebellions capable of challenging the colonial régime. Such a political vision, in any case, would have advanced well beyond the limited context of the village or district protest movement.

Conflict resulting from administrative abuses or fiscal pressures were the most common types of conflict in the colonial period; often little more than demonstrations or protests. While such rebellions cannot under any circumstances be regarded as precursors for the rising of 1810, they, nevertheless, drew attention to persistent, unresolved problems, and to areas in which grievances had become pronounced. The existence of such problems and the failure to secure redress may explain the deep-rooted nature of the insurgency in such localities during the 1810s. The insurrection subsumed many of these pre-existing tensions and gave them wider range on a broader scale of conflict. Even so, few, if any, such conflicts ceased to exist either after a locally successful counter-insurgency policy or after the achievement of Mexican Independence in 1821. On the contrary, the origins of many nineteenth-century rebellions lay precisely in these colonial roots.

Administrative abuses provoked opposition: where redress failed through legitimate channels, recourse to violence followed. Such often proved to be the rule. A well-documented source of conflict was the *repartimiento.* In contravention of the law local administrators (*alcaldes mayores*) enforced trade monopolies on behalf of their merchant backers (*habilitadores*) in the districts entrusted to them by a metropolitan government that could not afford to pay their salaries. The abuses that frequently arose at the hands of the *alcaldes mayores* or their lieutenants provided the mainspring of grievances. In its sporadic struggle for reform, the viceregal government often found itself reduced to impotence or simply outpaced by events. . . . It is worth examining the case of Papantla, since the experience of insurgency in the 1810s should be set within the context of a series of earlier and subsequent rebellions. Previous revolts had taken place in Papantla in 1743 and 1768. In the latter year, the issue had been the *alcalde mayor's* proposal to cut down trees. When the rebellion of 1787 broke out, the 100 or so men of the Mixed Company of Militia, in theory stationed there, were nowhere to be seen. They lived in remote *ranchos* in the Tuxpan district. It took a whole month to put together one company. Papantla was a district in which considerable mercantile capital was invested in the vanilla trade, an important Mexican export to Europe. In 1804, its population came to 26,028. Like so many other districts in the gulf coastal zone and in the warm uplands, clandestine tobacco plantings were detected in Papantla by the authorities, which in the mid-1790s embarked upon sporadic campaigns to uproot them, in face of local opposition. During the nineteenth century, the district continued to be a scene of conflict. In the 1810s, it remained for long an insurgent stronghold in the Huasteca of Veracruz, in close association with the rebel base areas of Misantla and Nautla. . . . A similar history of turbulence could be seen in the case of Acayucan. This cotton-producing district had, like the dye or textile-producing districts of Oaxaca, experience of the *repartimiento*. The men worked on the plantations, while the women spun and wove at home. There and in the districts of Tlalixcoyán, Medellín and Tuxtla (Cotaxtla) merchants of Puebla with interests in textile production traditionally capitalised the process of cotton production through the agency of the local *alcaldes mayores*. During the 1780s and the 1790s the latter had on occasions sought to preserve trade monopolies and keep out interlopers. The districts of Acayucan, Tlalixcoyán and Cosamaloapan became centers of insurgent activity after 1812. One of the causes may have been the general economic decline and social dislocation of the Gulf coast hinterland zones . . . and the impoverishment of the *colono* and *ranchero* element of the rural population in the two decades before 1810, as a result [of which] the dispossessed farming population had resorted to crime as a means of earning a livelihood. . . .

The regions to the north-east and south-east of the Valley of Mexico contained some of the most turbulent communities in the viceroyalty, a situation not mitigated by the presence of the silver-mining zone of

Real del Monte in the immediate vicinity of Pachuca. These areas would become centers of deeply rooted insurgency for much of the 1810s. Taylor refers to the Actopan revolt of 1756 in opposition to a labor draft for the drainage of mines precisely at the time of the crop harvest. In response to a projected draft of 2,000 individuals, an alliance of villagers with lower-class townspeople led to a three day riot and eight deaths or injuries among the Spanish element of the population. In the Tulancingo district in 1769 several thousand villagers from places as distant as Mextitlán and Tenango took part in a millenarian upsurge fired by the cult of Guadalupe.

These were the zones of maguey cultivation, lands yielding poor cereal crops, hard pressed through their ecological vulnerability. Here the huge estates of the Condes de Jala and Regla were concentrated. Regla, of course, had risen to prosperity as a result of timely investments in the Real del Monte mines. . . . The districts of Zempoala and Otumba had become centers of unrest from at least 1780. Several villages claimed exemption from *pulque* tax on alcohol used for their own consumption. In consequence, the Royal Customs Administrator in Apan complained in February 1802 that the Indians of Zempoala district had always been unruly and disobedient when it came to *pulque* tax payment. They had not even shrunk from violence in their resistance to it. In Tulancingo the subdelegate put the Indian governor and officials in prison in 1807 after refusal to pay an extra tax for the repair of the parish church. Almost from the first these regions became areas of entrenched insurgent support. Late in 1813 the Royalist commander in Pachuca, Lieutenant Colonel Francisco de Villaldea, felt that he could not count upon the loyalty of the urban militia forces that garrisoned the town and Real de Monte. Furthermore certain citizens of Pachuca maintained close contact with the insurgents in the countryside. By April 1814 Villaldea concluded that the situation throughout the entire region was "critical." Until Zempoala which he identified as the focus of rebellion in 1814–15 had been reduced, he saw no hope for the pacification of the Llanos de Apan, without which the silver supply, the *pulque* estates and the transit routes to Mexico City would continue to be endangered. Pressure from hacienda owners continued to provide causes of rebellion in Otumba and Pachuca in 1847–8.

In all the above categories of unrest a striking feature is their prevalence throughout the eighteenth century and their recurrence during the nineteenth century. Many districts, then, remained trouble spots of long duration, in which outstanding tensions became for a time subsumed in the broader insurrection of 1810–21, conveniently described as the War of Independence. In this sense the latter represented merely another stage—albeit a more consciousness-raising affair—in a protracted series of conflicts, that appeared to have neither a beginning nor an end. . . .

Local rebellion and village unrest could not and did not of themselves challenge either the colonial élites or the republican state that emerged after 1823. Such regions as those mentioned above, moreover, were quite distinct from those from which, for very different reasons, the insurrection of September 1810 arose. Nevertheless, they help to account for the long duration of the local insurgency which resulted from it. Taylor has argued for the absence of any general insurrections against colonial rule, or in the form of class war: "nearly all were spontaneous, short-lived armed outbursts by members of a single community in reaction to threats from outside; they were 'popular' uprisings in which virtually the entire community acted collectively and usually with identifiable leadership."[1] Those we have examined so far certainly correspond to this model. Mexican revolts tended to focus upon hated symbols of outside authority or upon agents of alien power— the official royal residences in towns, the district administrators, the *repartidores.* . . . Such instinctive reactions did not presuppose political objectives on a wider scale. Dispute rarely focused around the role of the crown or the person of the king: rebellion occurred in default of redress and in protest at the actions of the king's servants, or, indeed, those of the Church, or the *seigneurie.* Most times the Spanish colonial system was capable of absorbing the shocks thus meted out to it. Limited rebellion did not presage collapse.

Labour or land disputes rarely give rise to outright rebellions. Similarly their easy appearance in the archival documentation should not lead us to assume a frequent breakdown of social relations among rural communities. We should not conclude from the evidence of disputes that a constant tension between employers or administrators and day laborers or resident workers characterised rural life. On the contrary, evidence also exists—more by the lack of it than by its abundance—of harmonious relationships among the multifarious groups living and working together in the locality. It is certainly true that isolated rebellions, themselves little more than incidents, occurred on the land, but the countryside was not seething with discontent. They originated from working conditions, physical or verbal abuse of the labor force, from changes in recognised practices, disputes over land or water rights, from peasant incursion into hacienda lands, or from invasions of peasant cereal lands by landlords' livestock. . . .

A series of disputes resulting from abuse of labor occurred throughout the province of Puebla from the 1770s involving in particular the districts of Atlixco, Huejotzingo and San Juan de los Llanos. The resident labor force (*gañanes*) secured the support of the viceroy and audiencia for a series of official statements to the effect that *gañanes* were free men possessed of the right to take their labor where they chose. Option to exercise this right occasioned a series of appeals by landowners based upon the arguments that workers were naturally "idle" and "drunken." Evidence exists of their failure to retain resident laborers on their lands in some cases. *Gañanes*, moreover, would not tolerate verbal abuse or physical ill-treatment without protest. They frequently successfully resisted it or collectively demonstrated their indignation when it occurred. Between 1776 and 1778 the *alcalde mayor* of Tepeaca registered nine cases of ill-treatment of workers by proprietors, administrators or their dependents. One frequent cause of worker complaint was employer indebtedness to the labor force. Failure to pay wages, often through economic difficulties of proprietorship, encouraged *gañanes* to assert their right to take their labor elsewhere. . . . *Gañanes* on the Hacienda de San Sebastián Puchingo in San Juan de los Llanos appealed in 1782 for the finalising of accounts. Their spokesman, Melchor Nicolás, described as their "*capitán*," complained to the *alcalde mayor* of their discontent and impoverishment, as a result of failure to pay them whether in cash or kind anything more than a derisory amount of maize with which to feed their families. . . . Although instructed by the district administrator to pay up, the owners dragged their feet, and, instead, threatened to burn down the laborers' homes and prevent further maize sowings, if they did not quit hacienda land. It seems, however, that a settlement of obligations was actually made in the long run.

On the other hand, counter-charges of Indian "drunkenness and idleness" came from the district administrators of Atlixco and Huejotzingo. They blamed Viceroy Bucareli's *bando* of 14 July 1773, which regulated conditions of labor on hacienda lands. The resident laborers of Tepeaca appealed to the viceroy to confirm their status as free workmen; this he did in the *bando* of 21 August 1779, which the viceregal decree of 28 March 1784 confirmed. In a further *bando* of 23 March 1785 the viceregal government upheld the rights of workers as free men and reiterated the prohibition set in 1687 that no more than $5 was to be lent to individual laborers. The crown sought to prevent the reduction of the hacienda labor force to serfdom through indebtedness. The principle of a cash wage and the prohibition of corporal punishment were also repeated. At the same time, however, the viceregal government instructed district administrators, in consort with the parish clergy, to curb "idleness."

Government legislation did not, of course, prevent the recurrence of abuses. In 1779 resident laborers in the district of San Juan de los Llanos took matters into their own hands. An employee on the Hacienda de Virreyes, the property of Juan García, had beaten a workman. A body of laborers thereupon marched in protest to the owners's residence. The *alcalde mayor* responded by hastily forming a body of men and arresting twenty-five of the demonstrators, whom he escorted to the district jail. No severe punishments, however, followed. On the contrary, the owner expressed his willingness to take the workers back after a mild chastisement for their lack of "due subordination." Since at that time he was not short of labor, he offered them the opportunity to liquidate their accounts with him and leave his employment. In these dealings the Indian governor and *alcaldes* (village officials) acted as intermediaries between García and his recalcitrant laborers. The latter chose to go their own way. . . .

The viceregal government referred the entire question of abuse and free status to the Council of the Indies, which in April 1788 upheld the spirit of the *bandos*, but warned that Indians should not be permitted to relapse into idleness. In reaching its decision, the metropolitan government sought to balance the interests of the parties involved—"this matter is among the gravest that could arise in New Spain. To favour hacienda owners would diminish the liberty of the Indians, which the law sustains. To favour the Indians, however, would damage the agricultural sector by encouraging idleness. Therefore, it is necessary to proceed in such a way as to reconcile the one with the other. They are both equally important." The crown upheld the principle of voluntary labor, paid in cash.

The gradual recovery of village population levels in the course of the eighteenth century added a further dimension to the sources of local conflict. Many villages engaged in law suits with one another, or with adjacent haciendas and *ranchos*, concerning possession of disputed borderlands. Sometimes, lack of past incentives had left such lands uncultivated. On the other occasions, Indian communities had rented land not utilised by their own farmers to the owners of private estates. They had often in this way lost them as the decades passed. In general, the norm in New Spain continued to be an appeal to the law, rather than to force. Village authorities would produce their land titles, which dated back to the sixteenth century or beyond: landowners would take their stand on rival documented claims. To the audiencia fell the task of deliberation. During the latter part of the eighteenth century many land disputes involved requests by hacienda laborers for formal incorporation as a legally recognised *república de indios*, with the official endowment of the minimum land circumference, the 600 *varas* of the *fundo legal*. Many such petitions argued that existing land resources could no longer sustain the increased number to feed. The response of the viceregal government to such Indian petitions proved in many instances to be favourable. . . .

Indian villagers in the Puebla district of Cholula took matters into their own hands in 1809. When years of litigation failed, the Indians of Chalchoapan invaded lands possessed at that time by the Hacienda del Portezuelo. Two neighboring subdelegates had been attempting to determine the issue. Litigation and arbitration were the traditional methods of resolving disputes, rather than violent action. Indeed, the contentious instinct of the Indian villages aroused the hostile criticism of the Intendant of Puebla, Manuel de Flon, who during the 1780s and 1790s had championed their position on such issues as the *repartimiento*. Flon, a man whose patience was easily lost, scathingly commented on the villagers' aptitude for litigation—"it is well known and a constant occurrence that the Indians with a blind passion and tenacity pursue in the law courts of this realm their claims to the land." According to Flon, Chalchoapan, frustrated by failure of redress, had already resorted to "several noisy demonstrations," designed to further its claims by direct methods. The Intendant in 1809, aware of the weakness of the district subdelegates in their localities, feared an escalation of violence. The source of obstruction was the Provincial Junta of Consolidation in Puebla, which had taken control of the estate under the Consolidation procedure of 1805. Portezuela owed 20,000 pesos to Pious Foundations and a further 24,000 pesos of unpaid interest. For this reason the Junta was anxious to find a buyer as quickly as possible. The villagers' claims threatened not only to deter any prospective purchaser, but also to reduce the extent of the estate by one-half. A motivation for the Indians' land invasion in September–October 1809 may well have been the urgency of access to further maize lands, in view of the mounting food shortages of those months. The Viceroy, however, pledged his support for methods the Intendant chose to adopt to contain the villagers' "insubordination". . . .

The long-lasting conflicts in the central zone of Guadalajara arose from hacienda pressures on peasant subsistence lands. The recovery of the Indian population by the latter half of the eighteenth century made the problem of village land shortage an urgent one. The end result was peasant direct action during the 1780s and again during the insurgency of the 1810s, periods, moreover, in which the impact of severe food shortages in 1784–6 and 1808–10 may well have contributed to the desperate search for further subsistence lands. In this sense, it is likely that peasant militancy during the early 1810s would have occurred, irrespective of whether P. Miguel Hidalgo had appeared in the central district of Guadalajara or not. These land disputes involved a chain of villages situated beyond the western shore of Lake Chapala as far south as Lake Zacoalco: they included Zacoalco itself and the villages of Santa Ana Acatlán, Tizapán, Tizapanito and Atotonilco. Population recovery within these peasant communities had placed renewed demands on diminishing subsistence lands, often of poor quality, at a time of significant growth in the urban market and consequent hacienda response to its cereal requirements. The villages struggled to preserve their identity and protect their lands from encroachment by the private estates that surrounded their communities. The territorial expansion of the haciendas owned by the Porres Baranda, the Vizcarra and the Echaurri had made it impossible for the Indian villages to break out of their confinement. Initially, Indian resistance to hacienda encroachment did not signify either opposition to the private estate as such or to the Spanish colonial authorities. On the contrary, villagers in Guadalajara as elsewhere appealed to Spanish colonial law and sought redress through the legitimate channels. It is difficult to discover, however, whether Indian perceptions altered and their aims radicalised under the impact of insurgency. Rebel control of the countryside would have presented villagers with the opportunity to take back what they believed to be their own properties and to cultivate their lands as they saw fit. . . .

[As villages resorted to direct action and land occupation, haciendas organised their counter-offensive.] The formation of virtual hacienda self-defense forces suggests an early anticipation of the type of forces created both spontaneously and under official military supervision during the counter-insurgency of the 1810s. It points significantly to the implicit connection between the land disputes of the pre-insurgency and rebel affiliation during the 1810s. Not only do we see how the hacienda was capable of creating its own defense mechanism, virtually independent of the colonial state, but also we can catch a glimpse of how the aggrieved peasant might have become transformed into the insurgent participant of the 1810s. Furthermore, the hacienda's capacity for self-protection through reliance upon its internal structure of wealth and power divided the rural working population into those who derived security and position from their membership of the patron-client network and those who remained outside it, the dispossessed but dissident villagers.

The above instances do not necessarily indicate a general trend. They are discussed as local incidents in their own right, and their relevance is primarily to their own localities. It is, however, precisely in such localised conflicts that the roots of insurgency lay. Wider issues capable of linking one theatre of conflict to another remained absent until the coalescence of factors in 1808–10. Conflicts such as the above did not foreshadow a general insurrection. Nevertheless, their frequently long duration, the frustration of redress through litigation, and the resort to unilateral action by either of the contending parties helped to keep alive bitter memories in the locality. Such conflicts helped to explain why individuals or whole communities became susceptible to recruitment into insurgency movements after September 1810. . . .

None of the above cases led to revolutions, still less to a revolution of independence. Even so, they provided in many cases long-lasting conflicts, especially where frustration had led to the use of force by either or each of the contending parties. These examples of lasting bitterness may have contributed to insurgent sympathies during the 1810s. Many of the late colonial trouble spots became theatres of persistent insurgency, sometimes into the 1820s, and even into the 1840s and beyond. These conflicts similarly did not in themselves involve the attainment of political goals at the national level. The outbreak of generalised insurrection in New Spain required a broad coincidence of factors. In ordinary circumstances the relatively highly paid mineworkers could scarcely find an identity of interest with the hacienda workers. Nevertheless, the question of the survival of the *partido* (mineworker's share of the ore) continued to result in unsettled conditions throughout the mining zones. Tense labor relations during the decades before 1810 probably contributed to the expansion of insurgent support from the cereal and textile zones of the Bajío to the mining communities of the sierra.

It would take the impact of the subsistence crisis of 1808–10 to provide common conditions of hunger and unemployment. Even so, unemployment and hunger were regular occurrences in New Spain; but they did not contribute to revolutionary uprisings in the centuries prior to 1810. None of the other subsistence crises coincided with a national insurrection. Given its uniqueness, the insurrection of 1810 requires a broader explanation than the impact of subsistence crisis alone. Many problems remain, not the least of which is the precise significance of the type of isolated conflict and localised rebellion we have examined. To what extent should we view them as part of a pattern? It will not be possible at this stage to argue unequivocally for the existence of subtle connections between them, though, of course, such may well have been the case. While it is correct to argue, that incoherent, individual cases demonstrated no underlying progression or direction in the tensions evident from time to time during the colonial period, we can, nevertheless, also point to certain identifiable roots of conflict that recur. But do they recur with sufficient frequency—if not predictability—for us to regard them as parts of a pattern or process? Perhaps, our guide should be the evidence of local continuities of long duration. It would be risky indeed to regard the ample evidence of late colonial tensions as evidence of a deepening crisis of Spanish rule. Many of the conflicts of the 1770s, 1780s or 1790s reappeared in the 1820s, 1830s or 1840s and for a long time after. Instead of regarding late colonial disputes as preludes to general insurrection—or to a "War of Independence"—we should place the struggles of the Independence period within the context of the on-going local disputes that linked the late colonial and early national periods in unbroken continuity.

PART FIVE

IDEAS AND INTERESTS

20

The Hispanic Tradition

O. Carlos Stoetzer

The intellectual sources of the Spanish American revolutions have been much debated by historians. Some have found them in the Spanish political heritage and in the so-called *doctrinas populistas* of Francisco Suárez and the Spanish neo-scholastics. According to this approach, Spanish "constitutionalism," formerly expressed in regional rights and the power of the cabildos, was a living tradition that could still be invoked, while the theories of popular sovereignty held by sixteenth- and seventeenth-century Spanish theologians were preserved in the colonial universities and subsequently used to justify revolution. This interpretation has been developed particularly by historians in Spain, Colombia, and Argentina. But it has been placed in a more general theoretical and political framework by Carlos Stoetzer, formerly Professor of History at Fordham University, who argues that the Spanish American revolutions had little to do with either the Enlightenment or the North American or French revolutions, but were deeply rooted in Spanish and medieval tradition, and that the political thought that produced them was that of Francisco Suárez and Spanish neo-scholasticism. These ideas invite a number of questions. Were the political ideas of the neo-scholastics preserved as a continuous tradition in Spanish America, or were they rediscovered in 1810 and used as a convenient justification for revolution? What is the precise link, beyond the formula "in line with," between the contractual theories used by the revolutionaries and the political thought of Suárez? And did the revolutionaries perceive themselves as *suarecistas*?

Suárez took over from the earlier Scholastics the concept that the principle of authority is derived from God because of the social nature of man, whose will originates the social compact and in turn decides who is to exercise civil authority. He pointed out that to establish a civil authority which has full legality, the free consent of the governed must be obtained. In order for the inorganic, individual wills to constitute a political *civitas* which gives them an organic character, there must be free consent of the components. It is the *pactum* which establishes this unity. This social contract, whether tacit or expressed precedes the political *pactum*. Hence, for Suárez, no civil authority can come into existence without the consent of the people, expressed in the social contract. According to Suárez, the state is set up with the social contract; it is not simply a plurality of individuals and families, in an amorphous, atomistic, individualistic, and mechanical way, but an organic union brought about free upon mutual consent for the realization of the *bonum commune*. The result is a united *corpus politicum mysticum*.

Great confusion has resulted from Suárez' theory of the social contract and his assertion that the natural form of government is pure democracy. However, this assertion referred only to the abstract, since through the principle of *translatio*—not *designatio*—the social contract gave him the means of constructing a theory of government which could successfully oppose absolutism and a political doctrine which allowed civil authority to rest in the hands of one, a few, or many under the following principles: (a) the fundamental equality of all men vis-à-vis the holder or holders of power in the state, (b) the lack of any special divine intervention at the transfer of authority to the person upon whom it is conferred, and (c) the necessity of popular consent for such transfer through the social contract. He based the establishment of the state on the equality and liberty of man to prove that it was the whole nation, the people only, from whom the state could be derived.

It was clear to Suárez that, once a society has been established and an authority designated to govern it, the people who comprise that society abandoned a state of shapelessness to become what really deserved to be called a society. When such a society invested authority in a ruler, it expressed a collective will. The fact that some individual possessed certain qualities to rule did not mean that he had a right to this position; only the people can confer that right upon an individual. According to Suárez and other Late Scholastic thinkers, however, once civil authority is established it is no longer based on the people but located and represented in the person or persons designated to exercise power. In sum, the ruler is invested with the power given by God with the consent of the people through a true compact, and the people cannot throw off this power so long as this pact is not broken or dissolved.

While the people cannot act as it wishes once authority has been transferred to the ruler, they can do so when there is sufficient reason for such action—in the case of the *tyrannus a regimine* [rulers who abuse authority legally obtained], for example—and they must act when the ruler disappears without any legitimate successor. When the ruler through the *translatio* theory receives the *potestas*, there actually exist two authorities, one in the king and another in the state . . . though the latter does not function while the king asserts the rights given by the people. But should royal power be abolished or left vacant, the nation can make free use of its rights and can resist the ruler if he governs contrary to the medieval concept of the *bonum commune.* The powers of *translatio* are not absolute; they are valid only as long as the ruler governs rightly. Passive and even active resistance is lawful if the ruler turns toward tyranny; but under no circumstances are the people exempt from obedience to the ruler, once he has been invested with authority through *translatio* and so long as he adheres to the common ideal: the *summum bonum.* This theory was taught in Spanish America from the sixteenth century, and became the lever with which the Spanish American Revolution began. . . .

To sum up the political thought in the Spanish world prior to the eighteenth century: it was essentially Scholastic and based on St. Thomas' *De regno ad regem Cypri* and *Summa theologica,* and Francisco Suárez' *De legibus* and *Defensio fidei,* as well as on such sixteenth- and seventeenth-century writers as Domingo de Soto, Diego de Covarrubias, Domingo Báñez, Friar Juan Márquez, Francisco de Quevedo y Villegas, Diego Saavedra Fajardo, Juan de Mariana, Luis de Molina, and Francisco de Vitoria. . . . These doctrines were a vivid reality of Spanish government in the Indies, and can be summarized as follows:

1. Any political authority is of human law, not divine law, and therefore can legitimately be chosen by the people.

2. By natural law, sovereign authority originating in God belongs to the people, who cannot totally reject this authority; if the governors cannot create an order for the common good, then the people can take steps to remedy the situation.

3. Civil authority is legally acquired only with the consent of the people (whether express or tacit, prior or posterior), since the people are the only subject of sovereignty.

4. Authority thus conferred on the king cannot be despotic; otherwise the right of resistance and tyrannicide is legal. It thus includes personal rights based on natural law, the norms of prudence and justice, and positive law, for the enforcement of which power is invested in the king.

5. And last but not least, if the king dies or abdicates, or is deposed without a legitimate successor, sovereignty reverts to the political community.

These were the official theories of government prevailing in Spain and in the Indies; they were practised by government officials, preached and taught in churches, universities, and colleges, and governed the mind of the kings and the opinion of the people in both Spain and the Spanish lands overseas. . . .

To understand the actual picture of the Spanish American reality in the eighteenth century and on the eve of independence, it should be borne in mind that Enlightened despotism waged a relentless campaign against the "subversive" theories of Suárez. At the time of the expulsion of the Jesuits, the bishopric of Santiago alone accounted for fourteen Jesuit educational centers serving more than a thousand students. When after the expulsion the Jesuit boarding school of San Francisco Javier was reopened by Governor Guill y Gonzaga under the direction of two secular priests, it was expressly stated that the philosophy of Suárez would not be taught. Also, a *real cédula* of October 18, 1768, repeated a few days later, forbade in all Spanish American centers of higher learning the teachings of the Jesuit school, particularly Suárez, Mariana, and Molina. An illustration of this policy was the cancellation in 1795 by Viceroy José de Espeleta in New Granada of the chair of natural law (which dealt with such Late Scholastics as Covarrubias and Vázquez de Menchaca). Moreover, the banning of Late Scholastic theories, which Campomanes called subversive and heretical, was followed by the spreading of such absolutist theories as those proclaimed in New Granada by the Capuchin Finestrad, in Peru by Viceroy Taboada y Lemus, and in the different areas of the River Plate by the Carmelite Bishop San Alberto, Governor Ribera, Fernández de Agüero, and Maciel. . . .

In spite of all the efforts to combat the Jesuit teachings concerning the right to rebel and the right of tyrannicide, Scholasticism continued to be taught in the philosophy courses in the universities and colleges. After the Jesuits were expelled, they were replaced not by adherents of the modern philosophies but by their own students who, in most cases, were even more strongly imbued with traditional thought. Examples of this occur in the universities of Charcas and in the Carolinian College in Upper Peru where the theories of Suárez were taught by such former Jesuit pupils as Salinas, Segovia, Montoya, and Herrera. The same was also true of Chile and of other learning centers in Spanish America.

Scholasticism was still so strong at the end of the eighteenth century and prior to independence that it was responsible for the educational background of most of the leading men of the Spanish American Revolution. John Tate Lanning has pointed out that

> Anyone examining the record of the South American wars of independence will be amazed at the critical acumen and philosophical audacity of Sánchez Carrión, Antonio Nariño, Bernardo Monteagudo, Andrés Bello, José Joaquín Olmedo, and Hipólito Unanúe. They were not leaders who sprang fully educated from the brow of Zeus. They were the fruits of an educational discipline which was thoroughly scholastic, although it was in a free society that their mature intellects unfolded.

Lanning goes on to observe that a student of the theoretical foundation of the Spanish American Revolution would come to the conclusion that the Enlightened thought of "Rousseau, Voltaire, Montesquieu, or even Raynal" would not be so significant, and that

> the names which would seem of transcendent importance . . . would be, instead, St. Thomas Aquinas, Descartes, Newton, Condillac, Pierre Gassendi, and Malebranche. Without them Raynal, Condorcet, Diderot, Benjamin Franklin, and Thomas Paine would scarcely have been heard and certainly not understood.

[The vitality of Scholastic theory can be demonstrated in the revolution of May 1810 in Buenos Aires. The social contract which was applied in Buenos Aires in the May Revolution was that of Suárez.] This was not Rousseau's contract. In the first place, the contract which the revolutionaries used during and after the May Revolution is one which links the subjects to the ruler and not one which unites the citizens among themselves. This is a fundamental difference, since the first is the Suarezian formula which Rousseau not only denies but refutes. Rousseau considered as social contract only that by which a people really becomes a people, and attains this through public deliberation or convention. This is not the pact which the revolutionaries of the Argentine May Revolution or those in other Spanish American territories dreamed about; their political theories of popular sovereignty had to do with the link between the people on one side and the monarch on the other, between the kings of Spain and the peoples of Spanish America. . . .

From the debates of the *cabildo abierto* of May 22, 1810, in Buenos Aires it is clear that only Suárez' contract-theory was meant; there is no evidence of any Rousseauan influence at this period. Besides Saavedra and all the other members who spoke at the meeting, Juan José Castelli's exposition was in line with Scholastic thought when he explained the existence of a pact between the Spanish kings and the peoples of Spanish America, and it was on this basis that his entire argument for the establishment of a junta in Buenos Aires was put forward. With the dissolution of the *Suprema Junta Central* the sovereign Spanish government had ended, and Castelli derived from this historical fact the resumption by the people of Buenos Aires of the rights of sovereignty, and their free exercise in the establishment of a new government, mainly because King Ferdinand VII had lost his authority over Spain. Castelli made a similar statement in Upper Peru on April 3, 1811, when he said that he did not recognize the authority of the viceroys and their subordinate authorities to negotiate for and on behalf of the peoples and for their welfare, since their destiny depended only on the people's free consent, "because the people is the origin of all authority and the magistrates are but a curator of its interests, and dependent on contingencies."

Castelli, like many of his contemporaries, studied at the University of Córdoba and played a leading role in the *cabildo* of 1810. Like Mariano Moreno, he also has been associated with the ideas of the French Revolution because of his radical opinions and his fervent, enthusiastic revolutionary temperament. . . . [The Manifesto of the junta, written by Moreno] clearly demonstrated the Late Scholastic impact made upon Moreno in the University of Charcas where, despite the expulsion of the Jesuits and the prohibition of their teachings after 1767, Jesuit thinking was still a vivid reality. In many . . . writings of Moreno, composed while he was the Secretary of the Provisional Junta of Buenos Aires (until December 1810), similar Suarezian formulas are to be found, such as on the Congress convoked and on the State's Constitution of November 2 and November 28 1810: "The authority of the peoples in the present cause is derived from the resumption of supreme authority which through the captivity of the King has returned to the origin from which the Monarch derived it, and the exercise of said power is subject to new forms which freely may be given to it."

21

Enlightenment
and Independence

Charles C. Griffin

The influence of the Enlightenment in Latin America remains an elusive subject, whose study has not kept pace with that of institutional, social, and economic history. In particular, what was the political impact of the Enlightenment? How deeply did it penetrate? Is it to be regarded as a "cause" of independence, or is this too simple an approach? The Enlightenment did not necessarily justify colonial liberation, and not all the "men of the Enlightenment" were revolutionaries. It is perhaps more useful to explore the variety of ways in which the Enlightenment made itself felt in Latin America, the responses it evoked, and its influence in the post-revolutionary world, as Professor Charles Griffin (1902–1976), who taught at Vassar College, does in the following extract, first published in 1961.

In the course of the Latin American independence movement, country after country, at various times and in different words, based its declaration of independence on claims to natural rights of which each complained it had been unjustly deprived by the mother country. Though far from being unanimously held when the first Spanish American revolts occurred in the wake of Napoleon's invasion of the Peninsula in 1808, this view was already clearly manifest in the propaganda of the Hidalgo revolt of 1810 in New Spain and the contemporaneous uprisings in northern South America. Many rebel leaders justified their revolt on much less sweeping grounds, and subsequently they were echoed by conservative historians like the Mexican Lucas Alamán. Nevertheless, the political success of the rebel governments tended to win acceptance of the "natural rights" view of the antecedents of revo-

Reprinted from "The Enlightenment and Latin American Independence," in A. P. Whitaker (ed.), *Latin America and the Enlightenment* (2nd ed., Cornell University Press, Ithaca, N.Y., 1961), pp. 119–41, by permission of the publisher.

lution. It was natural, therefore, that it should have been adopted and perpetuated by the early historians of the independence movement.

This emphasis on the assertion of natural rights against tyranny involved assigning a major role to the political ideas of the Enlightenment as a cause of revolution. The writings of Montesquieu, Voltaire, and Rousseau were held to be at the root of the revolutionary movement, for from what other source could the notion have reached Latin America that man was born free, that he had natural rights, that governments not based on popular consent and not respectful of these rights were tyrannies?

With this in mind, diligent search was made for evidence of the transmission of these subversive principles during the last colonial generations—a search which met with considerable success. It was found that throughout Spanish and Portuguese America in the latter eighteenth century there were numbers of men who were familiar with notorious and officially prohibited books of the *philosophes*, including the highly inflammatory work of the Abbé Raynal. The dangers to such readers owing to Spanish regulation of the book trade and the activities of the Inquisition were emphasized.

Once the importance of the ideas of the Enlightenment as a cause of revolution was accepted, it followed that the popularization of these ideas in the previous revolutionary movements in the United States of America and in France was a significant means by which the fundamental ideas came to be transmitted to Latin America. The French Declaration of the Rights of Man and of the Citizen, it could be shown, had been published in Spanish and circulated in Spanish America. North American revolutionary documents had also served as models for South America. To top it all, there were the precursors: the Chilean friar Camilo Henríquez, the Peruvian Jesuit Viscardo y Guzmán, the New Granadan publicist Antonio Nariño, and most important of all, the eminent Venezuelan Francisco de Miranda. All these men could be shown to have exhibited in their writings in one way or another a debt to the enlightened thought of their time. The propaganda activities of these men and others like them reinforced the direct influence of foreign writers and provided a channel through which their ideas could be directed to literate Creoles.

In recent decades the pendulum of historical interpretation has swung away from the earlier emphasis on the Enlightenment as the cause of the Latin American independence movement. This tendency is the result of two major changes of historical outlook. First, thanks to the studies of Ernst Cassirer, Carl Becker, and others, the stress has been shifted from the political to the philosophical and scientific aspects of the Enlightenment, from Montesquieu, Voltaire, and Rousseau to Descartes, Locke, and Newton. And it has been shown that insofar as the Enlightenment had a political influence, this was by no means always favorable to revolution but quite as often to reform within the established order, and even at times to enlightened despotism. While findings of this kind have not yet been thoroughly applied to the impact of the Enlightenment in Latin America, they have shaken the faith of many present-day historians in the simplistic version of its impact there that prevailed up to a generation ago.

The other major change has been the growing preoccupation of the twentieth century with economic and social history. The study of economic conditions in the immediately pre-revolutionary period has made it possible to show the conflicting interests of groups of merchants, plantation-owners, and stockmen in various colonial regions and how these were affected by colonial laws and administrative practices. Marxian interpretations of Latin American independence have also appeared. Other authors have stressed the importance of cleavages among colonial social and racial groups and the effects of tensions of this nature in some parts of Latin America, while still others have traced the activities of the new learned societies of the *amigos del país* type in promoting useful knowledge.

Another reason for the recent downgrading of the importance of the political teachings of the *philosophes* has been a new emphasis on the limited objectives of the revolts in Spanish America in their early stages. One school of historians explains the beginning of the revolutions, in southern South America at least, as the result of a constitutional crisis in the empire in which the idea of independence had no place at all. Spaniards in America claimed, in view of the captivity of the monarch, Ferdinand VII, the right to the autonomous pursuit of the cause of resistance to Napoleon, just as the nationalists in Spain itself did. It was only later, it is claimed, as a result of the bitterness engendered by war, that the idea of independence appeared. In some regions it was dominant for many years.

Still another point of view which minimizes the Enlightenment as a direct cause of independence in Spanish America has recently been put forward by certain Hispanizing authors. . . . There has been a new emphasis on the essentially liberal and anti-autocratic character of the medieval Spanish tradition. Royal authority was limited and contractual; the liberties of the municipalities of Castile did not end until the final defeat of the *comuneros* at Villalar in the reign of Charles I. Under the façade of absolutism created by the Habsburg and Bourbon monarchs, it is claimed, the spirit of the medieval *fueros* lived on and

manifested itself anew both in Spanish liberalism and constitutionalism after the Napoleonic invasion and in the revolution in the American colonies.

This view, though strongly asserted and not lacking in plausibility, is
difficult to prove by direct evidence. The same can be said about the
attempt of certain authors to magnify the importance of the political
theories of the seventeenth-century Jesuit writer Francisco Suárez for
the thought of the revolutionary generation in Spanish America. There
can be no doubt that Suárez, like other Jesuit theologians, stressed the
duties of the monarch to his subjects and denied the principle of the
divine right of kings. Royal power came from God but was exercised
through popular consent. This version of Catholic political thought,
however, had not been generally accepted in the Spanish universities
and even less by writers on Spanish or colonial law. Since the expulsion
of the Jesuits in the reign of Charles III there had even been a requirement enforced by royal order on all university professors in the Indies
to deny under oath that they were teaching the objectionable political
principles of the Jesuits. In these circumstances the importance of
Suarecismo may be seriously questioned.

What can be said in the light of our present knowledge, and of the
various revisionist interpretations which have been mentioned, about
the relation between the Enlightenment and the independence of Latin
America? In the first place, it might be well to eschew any attempt to
carry forward the debate as to the relative importance of ideas and of
other factors as "causes" of the independence movement. Modern social science and modern historiography alike frown on the somewhat
oversimple concept of causation which appeared in much of the earlier
historical literature devoted to Latin American independence. As Crane
Brinton has noted: "Ideas are always a part of the pre-revolutionary
situation, and we are quite content to let it go at that. No ideas, no
revolution. This does not mean that ideas cause revolution. . . . It
merely means that ideas form part of the mutually dependent variables
we are studying." If we accept this view we shall avoid the attempt to
determine causal relationships. The task before us, then, becomes one
of bringing out the ways in which the ideas of the Enlightenment
manifested themselves in Spanish and Portuguese America in the era
of independence.

What recent historical research has brought out very clearly is that the
Enlightenment influenced Latin American political behaviour in a wide
variety of ways, among which innovation in political theories and principles was only one. Far more important than these in its effects on the
revolutionary age may have been a faith in reason as the guide for the

human spirit in its search for truth, without regard for the principle of authority, whether it was invoked on behalf of the philosophy of Aristotle, the theology of the Roman Catholic Church, or royal absolutism.

Faith in reason lay at the roots of a general intellectual revolution in the universities of Spanish America which was far more important than has generally been realized until recently. In every country *letrados* trained in institutions as far apart as San Carlos of Guatemala and San Francisco Xavier of Chuquisaca in Upper Peru were being accustomed to the questioning of the accepted and to solving problems by rational and empirical methods. As Lanning has pointed out in his study of the Enlightenment in Guatemala, university graduates played a significant role in the independence movement. He states: "The modernization of the colonial mind through perfectly normal and unpolitical channels was more basic to this role than any verbal Bastille-storming. We have already seen that American youth was not in darkness about any essential advance in the world. A student who knew everything leading up to and from Newton and embraced popular sovereignty could deny a Corsican usurper 'spontaneous consent' and make casual use of encyclopedists and *philosophes* when they became available."

A generation whose world view was changed by the study of science and modern philosophy in the eighteenth-century universities in Spanish America did not have to read Rousseau or Voltaire in order to be able to cope with the political crisis of its time. The list of men trained in such ways of thinking and who were influential in the revolutionary period is a long one, for almost all the civilian leaders of the revolution in Spanish America were products of the colonial universities. José Bonifacio de Andrada, the chief collaborator of Pedro I in the establishment of the Brazilian empire, was a graduate and one-time teacher at the Portuguese university of Coimbra, for there were no colonial universities in Brazil, but his intellectual formation in modern science and philosophy was essentially similar to that of the leaders in Spanish America.

Also prominent among the characteristics of the Enlightenment was a zest for the acquisition and dissemination of practical and useful knowledge. This is widely exemplified among the statesmen of the revolutionary period. Closely related to the general interest in the spread of knowledge was the effort to promote public primary education. In the midst of the struggle for independence decrees founding new schools and reorganizing old ones were frequent in all parts of Spanish America. Many of these were established in Mexico and South America on the system promoted by the English Quaker, Joseph Lancaster, which involved the teaching, step by step, of older children as monitors who would in turn teach other children what they learned. They were promising projects, and if they often came to naught it was not because of any lack of interest among the Latin American leaders, but rather because of the almost constant state of bankruptcy of national treasuries.

Equally representative of the thought of the Enlightenment is the philanthropic sentiment which brought about, at least in theory, a recognition of the rights of Indians by the revolutionary leaders. In part this was a mere reflection of the romantic cult of the noble savage in Europe, but it had practical consequences. Hidalgo abolished the tribute which weighed so heavily on Indians and *castas* in Mexico. In Colombia new republican legislation attempted to create freer conditions for Indian citizens. San Martín exhibited his interest by seeing that Quechua translations of his proclamations were issued in the attempt to win the good will of native populations in Peru.

Progress in the emancipation of Negro slaves was an even more important example of the philanthropy encouraged by the Enlightenment than any changes in the status of Indians. Slavery was ended during the revolutionary period in Mexico, Río de la Plata, and Chile.[1] Steps were begun toward gradual emancipation in Colombia. The institution survived only in regions where it was strongly entrenched, as in Peru and Brazil. The slave trade was almost entirely eliminated, persisting on any large scale only in Brazil.

Finally, the Enlightenment bequeathed to the era of revolution in Latin America the belief in progress that was all but universal in the latter period. In earlier ages men had been the victims of ignorance and error; in the future they would inherit an earthly millennium toward which the progress of the human mind would lead them. This belief had animated some of the enlightened bureaucrats of the last days of colonial rule like the second Count of Revillagigedo in New Spain or Ambrosio O'Higgins in Chile and Peru. Many royalists of the early period of revolution were also devotees of progress, especially some of the men who, in America and Europe, worked with the *cortes* of Cadiz. Abad y Queipo, the bishop-elect of Michoacán, Antonio Larrazábal, the Guatemalan representative to the *cortes*, and even some Spanish generals like Canterac and La Serna belonged to this type. Lastly, almost all the patriot leaders were believers in progress. It is true that San Martín weighed down at last by illness and the harassment of administrative work, became a pessimist; Bolívar too, at the end, wondered whether he and his associates had done anything more than plow the sea, but these views were exceptional. By and large it was necessary for revolutionary leaders to believe in the bright future in the midst of suffering and poverty, and they did so. The patriot governments of Spanish America in the era of the wars of independence were usually too busy with military operations against the royalists, too much concerned with challenges from domestic factions, too greatly handicapped by empty treasuries and exhausted credit to do much more than maintain themselves precariously. A few regimes, however, during the decade and a half of war and revolution, were briefly in a position to illustrate the continuing vitality of the ideas of the Enlightenment. These were paralleled by the enlightened rule set up by the regency of Dom João in Brazil.

In the first place, we see the continuation of the idea that the state should assume responsibility for developing economic resources. Rivadavia, as minister of the province of Buenos Aires (1821), attempted to establish new towns on the southern Indian frontier, improved the facilities of the port, studied the betterment of the city's water supply, and made plans for bringing immigrants from Europe in order to improve agriculture and industry. O'Higgins, as supreme director of Chile, showed a similar interest in bringing in skilled workmen from Europe and in improving the sanitation, paving, and lighting of Santiago. In Colombia, Vice-President Santander, while charged with the administrative duties of the presidency, studied the possibility of canals and railways for his country and established in Bogotá a school of mathematics and of mines in order to stimulate that industry. He too sought to encourage the immigration of skilled and industrious foreigners. Similar policies were followed by the government of the regent João after his arrival in the New World. The production of coffee was stimulated by royal protection; the iron and textile industries were also encouraged. The effort of O'Higgins to do away with the system of entail in Chile was characteristic of this aim to free and to stimulate economic activity. Of course, the general adoption of liberal commercial policies opening ports to the ships of all nations by all Latin American governments was in harmony with the development policies mentioned above.

Equally similar to the policies of enlightened despots of the preceding century were steps taken in all of the regimes referred to above to improve education and culture. Rivadavia founded the University of Buenos Aires in 1821; O'Higgins re-established the Instituto Nacional in Santiago in 1819; Santander was responsible in 1826 for the adoption of a general plan of education for Colombia that provided for new universities in Bogotá, Caracas, and Quito. Soon after the Portuguese court arrived in Brazil new military and naval academies were founded;

instruction in medicine was established both in Rio de Janeiro and in Bahia, to say nothing of a number of other special technical chairs and courses. Parallel to these educational institutions were the new museums and libraries which appeared on the scene. Santander established a museum in Bogotá. National libraries were founded in Brazil, Buenos Aires, and Santiago.

There is also a similarity between the secular viewpoint of the European Enlightenment and the attitudes of some of these regimes of the revolutionary period toward the Church. Perhaps the most extreme in this respect was the Buenos Aires regime under the leadership of Rivadavia which launched itself upon an anti-clerical program involving the abolition of the *fueros* of the clergy, the abolition of some monastic establishments, and the setting up of charity on a secular basis in the *Sociedad de Beneficencia*. O'Higgins also clashed with the clergy. Santander, though he was cautious, was *persona non grata* to the clergy because of his masonic affiliations and his regalist position on the question of ecclesiastical patronage. In Brazil it cannot be said that there was anti-clericalism in this period, but the government did strongly support the supremacy of the crown over the Church. This was also a period of extreme political radicalism among the clergy and one in which the clergy itself was somewhat secular in its interests.

The mere recitation of these manifold civic activities recalls the programs of European states in the era of the Enlightenment and indicates how in the midst of war and revolution efforts were continued to encourage economic and cultural progress.

Although it is proper to stress the pervasive influence of a whole gamut of ideas, it must be admitted that the revolutions for independence had a particularly close relation to political ideas and theories because they were political movements. There is a real difficulty in analysing these relationships because, as already noted, there were divergent elements in the political ideas of the Enlightenment. On the one hand, insistence on rationality as a justification for political institutions called into question traditional authority in church and state, but was not democratic. It could manifest itself in the idea of enlightened absolutism as well as in admiration for the oligarchical constitutionalism of England. On the other hand, a current stemming from Rousseau and carried forward by such authors as Thomas Paine stressed the social contract, the sovereignty of the people, and theoretical democracy.

Before 1808 the chief influence of the political ideas of the Enlightenment on Latin America was to encourage rational and efficient administration. This was primarily apparent in the activities of the Spanish and Portuguese imperial authorities and in such conspicuous figures among them as the Marqués de Pombal and José de Gálvez. These men and their subordinate associates in colonial administration attempted to rationalize government. In these efforts they won some conspicuous successes, but their total accomplishments have lately been judged to have been limited. But it was not the colonial administrators alone who were influenced by this current of ideas. Many Creoles in this period took a public-spirited interest in the improvement of government in their respective countries and distinguished themselves in civic activities. Among them were Manuel Salas (Chile), Antonio Alzate (Mexico), Francisco Espejo (Quito), Hipólito Unanue (Peru), and Manuel Belgrano (Buenos Aires). Some of these men whose political experience began in colonial days were also leaders in the early stages of revolution.

The revolutionary influence of the thought of the Enlightenment in this period was a minor current. We cannot disregard the long and notorious career of Francisco de Miranda, but it is necessary to realize that subversive propaganda had surprisingly little effect in Latin America before 1808. There can be little doubt that the general reaction to the French Revolution and its ideas was strongly negative. One must remember, too, that Miranda's ideas were not particularly democratic, as his draft scheme for Spanish American government clearly indicates.

Without meaning to do so, it is possible that the political principles of the Bourbon monarchs of Spain may have helped to promote revolution in America. The expulsion of the Jesuits has been held by some to have alienated many subjects of the crown, though the political activities in this field of the exiled Jesuits themselves seem to have been very minor. It has also been maintained that the colonial *cabildos*, previously in decay, were strengthened by the reforming zeal of royal intendants and were thus enabled to assume a more effective revolutionary role in 1810.

We come next to the early years of revolution following the Napoleonic invasion of the Iberian peninsula. In this period there seems to have been a very sharp difference in the character and inspiration of revolts in the different parts of the Spanish empire. Although there were all sorts of other factors involved, it would seem that in Mexico during the Hidalgo revolt and in northern South America about the same time there was a tendency to accept the principles of 1789 with little or no reservation. This was, at least, the style of language, if not of actual behavior. On the other hand, the influence of such ideas was smaller in the southern part of the continent. Brazil remained quiet under the rule of Prince Regent João. In Buenos Aires and in Chile the influence of a Creole aristocracy with reformist, autonomist, but not necessarily democratic ideas was dominant. There were some powerful voices raised in support of independence, republicanism, and liberal democracy, but the general acceptance of the need for independence was slow to develop, in spite of the speeches and newspaper articles of such men as Mariano Moreno (who translated Rousseau), Bernardo Monteagudo, and Camilo Henríquez. The leader of the Uruguayan *orientales*, José Gervasio Artigas, was a steadfast supporter of democratic republicanism, but he had little power during most of these years. However, if the voice of revolutionary democracy was largely stifled by the more powerful forces of oligarchy and by the rivalries and conflicts of ambitious generals and politicians, it must be remembered that the articles of Moreno in the *Gaceta de Buenos Aires* and of Camilo Henríquez in the *Aurora de Chile* expressed a democratic idealism to which the revolution would return for inspiration in later years.

In the years following 1815 there was a general retreat from radical democracy throughout the whole of Latin America. The quasi-constitutional dictatorship in Buenos Aires under Juan Martín de Pueyrredón, the dictatorship of O'Higgins in Chile, the protectorate of San Martín in Peru, and the power exercised by Simón Bolívar in Venezuela and Colombia until 1821 in no case denied the principle of popular sovereignty, but they did not operate under it. In practice they did not differ from frankly authoritarian governments and their behavior stems more closely from the earlier enlightened despotism than from revolutionary ideology. The shift in thought is well illustrated by the changes in the political ideas of Simón Bolívar. The enthusiastic Jacobin of 1810 and 1811 gave way rapidly to the more cautious and hard-headed author of the Cartagena manifesto and to his still liberal but less democratic principles communicated to the Congress of Angostura in 1819. Republics were unstable and weak. The executive of a republic must be strengthened to avoid the danger of anarchy. Especially in view of the lack of racial, social, or geographical homogeneity, it was important to hold tendencies towards disorder in check by creating strong centralized power.

In Brazil one can see the same moderating and centralizing tendency at work. Though radical republican ideas flared briefly in the northeast in 1817, independence was won only when Pedro I declared himself emperor in 1822 by the will of his people. He rejected the constitutional draft evolved by the constitutional assembly and handed down from the throne the Constitution of 1824 which kept the imperial power predominant over the legislature and weakened the popular principle.

In Mexico there was not only a chastening moderation in the assertion of the ideas of popular government, there was even a negation of it.

The chief supporters of Iturbide's revolution of 1821 were conservatives who rejected the ideas of 1789 and reasserted the values of a hierarchical order for an independent Mexico. Throughout the remaining years of the revolutions for independence the flickers of democratic radicalism were fitful and short-lived.

Any attempt to analyze the political ideas of the final years of revolution merges with the study of post-independence conflict between liberals and conservatives and between centralism and federalism. It becomes more and more difficult to trace clearly the relation between the ideas of the Enlightenment and those of the new era. There was a steady evolution which transformed what had been "enlightened" or what had been "Jacobin" into "liberal." Further, there was often a merging of principles which had earlier been opposed. One example of this kind of change is that represented by the regime of Bernardino Rivadavia in the United provinces in the mid-twenties. It was highly enlightened in a number of ways, promoting education, economic progress, and good administration. It even had some of the anti-clerical prejudices of the *philosophes*. At the same time, it represented an oligarchical faction in the city of Buenos Aires which was very far from popular or democratic. At the same time, the federal party, which opposed Rivadavia's regime, was at once theoretically democratic and in practice barbarous and tyrannical in the character of its leadership. In dealing with this period it is no longer very profitable to make connections between political groups and the sources of their inspiration, for all these groups had been in one way or another influenced by the Enlightenment.

The foregoing consideration of the Enlightenment and the movement for Latin American independence differs from the usual treatment of this subject in that it is not concerned primarily with the evaluation of the Enlightenment as a "cause" of the later revolutionary movement. It attempts, rather, to show the continued presence of various characteristics of the Enlightenment in the latter era. A rational approach to learning and to the solution of human problems, a concern for economic development and progress, interest in education and useful knowledge, and a tendency to clash with the principle of authority in church and state—these were all manifest at different times and places in Latin America between 1808 and 1826. The variant forms of enlightened political theory were also manifested in different ways, as we have noted, in the pre-revolutionary, early, and later years of the struggle for independence.

22

The Making of an Insurgent

Manuel Belgrano

The career of Manuel Belgrano (1770–1820) exemplifies many of the stages of enlightenment suggested in the previous text: new ideas, reformism within the colonial structure, and finally revolution. Belgrano was born in Buenos Aires, educated at the Universities of Salamanca and Valladolid in Spain, and made a name for himself in the last years of colonial rule as secretary of the consulado, which was set up in Buenos Aires in 1794, and as an economist. He edited the *Correo de Comercio* in 1809, played a prominent part in the revolution of May 1810, was a member of the governing junta which was then established in Buenos Aires, and finally became a general leading the armies of the revolution to distant provinces. The following passage from his autobiography describes the disillusionment of a young creole intellectual first in Spain and then in Spanish America as the trust he had placed in a reforming crown and the hopes he had entertained of promoting economic growth gradually faded away.

I was born in Buenos Aires; my parents were Don Domingo Belgrano y Peri, known as Pérez, a native of Onella [Spain], and Doña María Josefa González Casero, a native of Buenos Aires. My father was a merchant, and since he lived in the days of monopoly he became sufficiently wealthy to live comfortably and to give his children the best education to be had in those days.

I learned my first letters, Latin grammar, philosophy, and a smattering of theology in Buenos Aires. I was then sent to Spain to become a lawyer, and there I studied at Salamanca, graduated at Valladolid, continued my studies in Madrid, and was admitted to the bar in Valladolid.

Translated by John Lynch from Manuel Belgrano, *Autobiografía*, in *Biblioteca de Mayo*, Tomo II (Senado de la Nación, Buenos Aires, 1960), pp. 953–68.

I must confess that I was less interested in a legal career than in the study of modern languages, political economy, and public law, and when I was fortunate enough to meet men dedicated to the common good who introduced me to their useful ideas, I was seized with the desire to promote public welfare and to enhance my reputation in working for such an important object, to the advantage especially of my own country.

Since I was in Spain in 1789 at a time when the French Revolution was causing a change in ideas, particularly among the men of letters with whom I associated, the ideas of liberty, equality, security, and property, took a firm hold on me, and I saw only tyrants in those who would prevent a man, whatever his origin, from enjoying the rights with which God and Nature had endowed him, and which even human societies had agreed, directly or indirectly, to establish. At the time when I completed my training in 1793 political economy enjoyed great popularity in Spain, and I think that this was the reason why I was appointed secretary of the consulado of Buenos Aires, established when Gardoquí was minister, though I had not made the slightest attempt to obtain the post, and the official of the department concerned with these matters even asked me to nominate well-qualified persons who could be appointed to similar bodies to be established in the chief commercial centers in America.

When I understood that these bodies would be, in effect, societies concerning themselves with agriculture, industry, and commerce, a vast field of activity unfolded itself to my imagination, for I was ignorant of Spain's administration of its colonies. I had heard muffled rumors of complaint and discontent among Americans, but I attributed these to their failure to secure their claims, and not at all to a perverted policy of the Spaniards which had been systematically pursued since the conquest.

Such were my illusions when I was appointed, and such the brilliant prospects which seemed to me to be opening up for America, that I imagined myself compiling reports on the provinces which would provide the information to enable the authorities to take measures for their welfare; and perhaps this would have been the intention of an enlightened minister like Gardoquí, who had lived in the United States. And although even then I was denied the resources that I requested to enable me to fulfil my office, I held my peace in the belief that, once the funds of the consulado were available, the problem would be resolved.

Finally I left Spain for Buenos Aires. I cannot sufficiently express the surprise I felt when I met the men appointed by the king to be members of the junta that was to deal with agriculture, industry, and commerce and promote the welfare of the provinces composing the viceroyalty of Buenos Aires. All were Spanish merchants. With the exception of one or two they knew nothing but their monopolistic business, namely, to buy at four and sell for eight. An idea of their knowledge and of their "liberal" attitude towards the country, as well as of their determination to preserve the monopoly from which they drew their wealth, can be gained from one incident, without need of further proof.

The Court of Spain, as I have since appreciated, vacillated in the methods by which it exploited its colonies: and thus we have seen liberal and illiberal measures applied simultaneously, proof of the Spanish fear of losing the colonies. On one occasion it decided to encourage agriculture; to provide labor it adopted the cruel slave trade, and gave its operators certain privileges, including permission to export agricultural produce to foreign countries. This gave rise to a great dispute as to whether hides, the principal element in the commerce of Buenos Aires, were or were not "agricultural produce." The dispute had already been taken to the Crown before the establishment of the consulado, and had generated a great quantity of papers, when the king finally asked the consulado to report. It would be tedious to go into the details of the extraordinary debate which followed; suffice it to say that these men who were supposed to promote the welfare of the country decided that hides were not agricultural produce and therefore ought not to be included in the privilege of export in exchange for trading in Negroes.

I became discouraged, and realized that the country could expect nothing from men who placed their private interests above the common good. But since my position gave me an opportunity to write and speak about some useful topics, I decided at least to plant a few seeds that some day might bear fruit, either through the efforts of others or through the passage of time.

I wrote various reports about the establishment of schools. The scarcity of pilots, and the direct interest of the merchants in the project, presented favorable circumstances for the establishment of a school of mathematics, and I obtained agreement to this on condition of getting the approval of the Crown. But this it never gave. On the contrary, it did not rest until the school was abolished, because although the Spaniards recognized the justice and utility of such establishments in America, they were openly opposed to them because of a mistaken view, in my opinion, of how the colonies might best be retained.

I was no more successful with a drawing school which I also managed to establish without it costing even half a *real* for the master. The fact is that neither these nor other proposals to the Crown for the development of the three important branches of agriculture, industry, and commerce, with which the consulado was concerned, met with official approval. The sole concern of the Crown was with the revenue that it derived from each. It was said that all these establishments were luxuries, and that Buenos Aires was not yet in a condition to support them.

I promoted various other useful and necessary projects, with more or less the same results. It will be for the future historian of the consulado to describe them. For myself I shall only say that from the beginning of 1794 to July 1806 I passed my time in futile efforts to promote the public good. All foundered on the opposition of the government of Buenos Aires, of Madrid, or of the merchants who composed the consulado, for whom there was no other reason, justice, utility, or necessity than their commercial interest. Anything that came into conflict with that interest was vetoed and that was that.

It is well known how General Beresford entered Buenos Aires with about 1,400 men in 1806. At that time I had been a captain in the militia for ten years, more from caprice than from any particular liking for military matters. My first experience of war came at that time. The marquis of Sobremonte, then viceroy of the Río de la Plata, sent for me several days before Beresford's unfortunate entrance and asked me to form a company of cavalry from among the young men engaged in commerce; he said that he would give me professional officers to train them. I sought recruits but could not find any, because of the great hostility felt for the militia in Buenos Aires, at once a blow to the authorities and a sign of their weakness.

The general alarm was sounded, and, moved by a sense of honor, I flew to the fort, the point of assembly. There all was disorder and discord, the inevitable result with groups of men unaccustomed to discipline or authority. Companies were formed and I was attached to one of them. I was ashamed of my ignorance of the most trivial details of military affairs, and I had to rely on the instructions of a veteran officer, who also joined voluntarily, for he was given no assignment.

This was the first company which marched to occupy the *Casa de las Filipinas*. Meanwhile the others argued with the viceroy himself that they were obliged only to defend the city and not to go out into the country; consequently they would agree only to defend the Barrancas. The result was that the enemy, meeting with no opposition from veteran troops or disciplined militia, forced all the entrances with the greatest ease. There was some feeble firing on the part of my company and some others in an effort to stop the enemy, but in vain, and when the order came to retreat and we were falling back I myself heard someone say: "They did well to order us to retreat, for we were not made for this sort of thing."

I must confess that I grew angry, and that I never regretted more deeply my ignorance, as I have already said, of even the rudiments of military affairs. My distress was all the greater when I saw the entrance of the enemy troops, and realized how few of them there were in comparison with a city the size of Buenos Aires. I was obsessed by this idea, and almost went out of my mind, for it was painful to me to see my country under foreign domination, and above all in such a state of degradation that it could be conquered by the daring action of the brave and honorable Beresford, whose valor, in so perilous an undertaking, I admired and always shall admire.

On the other hand let me recall the record of the consulado in these events, protesting as it did its loyalty to the king of Spain. It proved again the well-established truth that the only country, king, or religion that the merchant knows is his self-interest; he works only for that end; and his present opposition to the liberty and independence of America has no other motive. . . .

[Buenos Aires was captured on 27 June 1806. The viceroy fled. But, under the leadership of Santiago Liniers, a Frenchman long in the service of the Spanish Crown, the British were expelled on 12 August. A second British invasion, under Lieutenant General Whitelocke, and with the support of Brigadier General Craufurd, began in June 1807 and was a disastrous failure. On 7 July Whitelocke capitulated. A conversation between Belgrano and General Craufurd, after the capitulation, follows.]

Thus, having convinced himself that I had no French sympathies or connections, he [General Craufurd] told me of his ideas about our independence, perhaps in the hope of forming new links with this country, since that of conquest had failed. I described our condition to him, and made it plain that we wanted our old master or none; that we were far from possessing the means required for the achievement of independence; that even if it were won under the protection of England, she would abandon us if she saw some advantage in Europe, and then we would fall under the Spanish sword; that every nation sought its own interest and did not care about the misfortunes of others. He agreed with me, and when I had shown how we lacked the means for winning independence, he was of the opinion that it would take a century to achieve.

Such are the calculations of men! A year passed, and behold, without any effort on our part to become independent, God himself gave us our opportunity with the events of 1808 in Spain and Bayonne. Then it was that the ideals of liberty and independence came to life in America, and the Americans for the first time began to speak openly of their rights.

23

Atlantic Network

Peggy Liss

Latin America felt the impact of the outside world not only in the realm of ideas but also through trade and international relations. The rival empires of the Atlantic world did not live in total isolation from each other, and the interests of the metropolitan powers in Europe were not confined to their own dominions. Peggy Liss, historian of early modern Spain and Latin America, studies the comparative history of the Atlantic empires of the eighteenth century within a framework of international trade, the Enlightenment, and the age of revolution. What were the precise relations between the various revolutions of the time—the industrial, North American, French, and Latin American? "How similar, or different were the perceptions and outlooks of people directing nations and societies throughout the Atlantic world?" She concludes that there was indeed a multinational network linking trade and revolution, and binding empires, revolutionary movements, and new republics in a single, if divided, world. In reaching these conclusions she provides, among other things, a modern interpretation of the influence of the American and French revolutions on Latin America.

i

When the thirteen Anglo-American colonies declared independence in 1776, the most pressing and immediate effects on Spanish America came through Spanish reaction and the impact of new Spanish measures. Spain, although it joined France against Britain only in 1779, in December 1776 began secretly to aid the British American rebels, and freer intercourse was customary between the Anglo-American insur-

Reprinted from Peggy K. Liss, *Atlantic Empires: The Network of Trade and Revolution, 1713–1826* (The Johns Hopkins University Press, Baltimore/London, 1983), pp. 127–32, 142–46, 155–58, 170–76, 180–81, by permission of the author and publisher.

gents and Spanish American regions. From 1776 some Latin American ports were open for varying periods to United States ships, and individual Spanish viceroys and governors in America from time to time licensed vessels from North America to bring in badly needed provisions and war supplies. . . .

Although some prominent liberal Spaniards publicly praised the rebels, Spanish statesmen realized that the Revolution of 1776 might eventually loosen Spain's grip on the New World. Floridablanca, chief minister from 1777, foresaw Spanish America vulnerable to both England and Anglo-America, and George Rogers Clark's expedition into the Illinois country in 1778 heightened his awareness of the ambitions of the emerging republic. . . . Even though Bernardo de Gálvez [governor of Louisiana] was patently sympathetic to the English colonists, and the captain general in Havana, Navarro, counted on Anglo-American provisions and military cooperation and, in profusely thanking Miralles for sending portraits of Washington, gratuitously added that "his great talent ensures that his memory will pass down to future centuries," these same high authorities and others were edgy about Anglo-American expansion and commercial competition and about British rebels influencing Spanish Americans to revolt. . . .

In 1781 Navarro, then intendant of Louisiana, warned the court of "the turbulent, ambitious Americans" and opposed granting free navigation of the Mississippi and so opening the West to them. That year, too, José de Abalos, intendant, governor, and captain general of Venezuela, saw as connected the recent rebellions in South America and "the sad and lamentable rising in the United States of North America," and he asked, rhetorically, of Charles III: if Great Britain could not subdue its relatively close colonies, "What prudent human would not fear greatly an equal tragedy in the astonishingly extended dominions of Spain in these Indies?" He both predicted United States independence and strongly suggested that Spanish princes be sent to govern and hold the Spanish colonies for the monarchy. Meanwhile, José de Gálvez's envoy, Francisco de Saavedra, corroborated finding in Mexico unrest and resentment due to official corruption and to new and higher wartime taxes, and declared Mexicans understandably aggrieved. He predicted, in view of British American independence, catastrophe if Spanish Americans were not better treated and more closely tied to the metropolis:

> The creoles today are in a very different state than that of some years ago. They have been enlightened greatly in a short time. The new philosophy is making much more rapid progress there than in Spain (the zeal for religion

which was the most powerful brake to contain them weakens by the minute). The treatment of the Anglo-Americans and foreigners has infused them with new ideas concerning the rights of men and of sovereigns; and the introduction of French books, of which there are an immense amount there, is making a species of revolution in their mode of thinking.

The "French" books he described as "thousands of copies of works by Voltaire, Rousseau, Raynal, and Robertson." The war he thought impolitic and inopportune, serving only to arouse Spanish Americans and to create a formidable enemy on Spanish borders. . . .

Many Spanish Americans, as well as officials, received news of events in the thirteen British colonies. The Lima *Gazeta* in 1776 discussed the course of the war—General Washington had forced General Howe to evacuate Boston—and its high cost to Britain, where there was opposition to a parliamentary bill to defray war costs, on the basis that such imposts weighed on commerce and caused artisans to emigrate; the writer referred to "the American party". . . . In Buenos Aires, rapidly growing as a commercial center from 1776, the course of Anglo-American events was followed too through European periodicals and, there and elsewhere, known through books on American history published in Europe. When in 1780 Gálvez informed its viceroy, Vértiz, that he had heard that the English were secretly preparing an expedition against La Plata and Chile, Vértiz answered that military forces were weak there, a spirit of rebellion was widespread, and "a general alteration and discontent" was being spread rapidly by the "bad example of the day." A prominent Chilean, José Antonio Rojas, sent information to William Robertson, whose *History of America,* published in London in 1777, was immediately translated into Spanish. Robertson, whose writings Saavedra had listed among those flooding Mexico (although the government had forbidden them to be sent to Spanish America), and, erroneously, as French, had much to say not only about Anglo-America but also about the decadence of the Spanish colonies—all with a point of view quite similar to that of Adam Smith. Rojas, in Spain from 1772, secured a license to read prohibited works and shipped to America crates of books, including new anonymous works on America, as well as sets of Raynal, "this divine man," Rojas wrote, whose books were prohibited for being so clear and truthful. . . . Abalos too reported an influx of such works in Venezuela during 1780 and 1781, particularly copies of Raynal. (The edition of 1781 summarized the Declaration of Independence and *Common Sense.*) By 1783, the Mexican Holy Office was finding seditious materials more and more prevalent, and was dolefully inveighing against what is discerned as a growing "enchantment with novelty."

Some Latin Americans are known to have had direct contact in those years with leaders of the American Revolution, as well as with their ideas and ideologies. There was, of course, much intermingling of people and projects in New Orleans, Havana, and other areas of unified war effort. Rojas, later a proponent of independence, and probably author in 1776 of a list of complaints drawn up on behalf of native born Chileans, is known to have met Franklin in France. By 1777 at least one creole, José Ignacio Moreno, in Caracas, cherished copies of the proclamations made in 1774 and 1775 by the Continental Congress in Philadelphia. Recently discovered has been his commonplace book containing handwritten transcripts of the proclamations. . . . Moreno was a priest and held a chair of philosophy and theology at the University of Caracas. A man of means, he owned haciendas, slaves, scientific instruments, a journeyman press, and a library—in his interests, another creole counterpart to Jefferson. And, in 1797, he would be implicated in a republican conspiracy. By 1777, then, he, and undoubtedly other creoles as well, were familiar with and regarded highly some of the concepts characterizing the early stages of the movement for independence in British North America. Moreno had copied Anglo-American complaints: of slavery to Britain and of impending ruin, of arbitrary laws, of new exactions without consent, of garrisoning of troops and poor government, of the threat to commerce and the American need for markets. He preserved phrases alluding to and endorsing the blessing of liberty, individual and property rights, constitutional principles of self-preservation based upon compacts with sovereign rulers, and the cause of America.

During the American Revolution, numerous creole merchants and planters, with productivity up and change in the air, thirsted for unrestricted trade. Landowners and newer merchants then perceived a need to get directly into the world market and came into conflict with consulados and their associates in advocating liberty of commerce. The so-called free trade reglamento of 1778 opened more Spanish ports to trade with Spanish America and briefly benefited its residents in sales abroad and cheaper imports; with Spain's entry into the war of 1779, Britain blocked the sea routes and North Americans tended to replace Spanish carriers. The net result was to diminish exchange between Spain and its Americas during the war and to allow Spanish Americans even more, and more direct, access to outside buyers and sellers. Competition in exporting then grew, often cutting across designations of peninsulars and creoles, and almost everywhere the number of merchants in both external and domestic trade rose rapidly. In addition, wartime conditions, including the British blockade and climbing demand, in some Latin American regions acted as further stimulants to internal production. . . .

At the war's end many creoles, especially those in Mexico under the new viceroy, the war hero Bernardo de Gálvez, expressed a new respect for the victorious British Americans—just as, some of them explained, Spain had done during peace negotiations at Paris. The epic contest in America and its outcome had heightened their pride and self-awareness. As Alexander von Humboldt later remarked, after the Peace of Versailles creoles preferred to say, "I am not a Spaniard; I am an American."

Thus, Spanish involvement in the British American struggle, although half-hearted and primarily meant to weaken England, had reverberations in and for Spanish America. Wartime measures intensified a reform program sparked by earlier competition with Britain and emphasized the aspects of that program calculated for defense and to raise funds for Spain. Antigovernment feeling heightened, and led in South America to widespread disaffection and rebellion. And in this tense colonial situation, Spain's North American quasi allies competed with it for trade and provided an ideological and actual example subversive of Spain's own interests. Moreover, the American Revolution was indirectly responsible for Spain's double bind: the confluence of the costs and dislocations of both war and reform. These, in combination with the triumph of the new nation, then intensified among many creoles, whether of more liberal or conservative bent, and whether prospering or harder pressed, a desire for greater self-government and self-determination and an awareness of America as a unique and esteemed entity. . . .

Unquestionably, the new nation appeared to Spaniards in Europe and America to be a going concern in the 1780s. While wartime attitudes of mixed wariness and admiration endured, as did respect for Franklin, Washington, Jefferson, and other leaders, joined to them was admiration for the nation's prosperity. The latter was seen as due largely to a sizable carrying trade and the export of farm produce and of some manufactures, all of which was made possible by access to world markets, including those of Latin America and Iberia. Authorities worried about this well-being; creoles hoped to emulate it. Spain after 1783 did reestablish control over its colonies, unlike Britain after 1763, and even took Britain's failure as a lesson, but the ongoing example and activities of the British North American republic helped to make that control tenuous. . . .

A crucial nexus in contacts between the Americans in the 1780s was the Caribbean, the hub of direct and indirect trade and, during the war, a major staging area for military and naval campaigns. It was in Cuba that a creole very important to subsequent Spanish American history came into contact with Anglo-American patriots and entrepreneurs, and it was from Havana that he sailed to the United States in 1783— from there, Francisco de Miranda proceeded to England and into the history books. Miranda's career, still imperfectly known, says much about the interplay of the example of the United States, late eighteenth-century ideas and international relations, and creole aspirations. It also sheds some light on the international nature of trade arrangements in the Caribbean.

Miranda later said he first entertained ideas of Spanish American independence in 1781 when, as captain in the Spanish forces allied with those of the British American rebels, he took part in Gálvez's campaigns—when Spanish troops transported in North American ships sailed from Havana against the English in Pensacola and, again, against New Providence Island in the Bahamas. He also engaged in smuggling in association with North Americans and played an as yet unquantified part in the complex multi-national trading ventures of the period. He later wrote:

> When I realized on receiving the *capitulaciones de Zipaquirá* how simple and inexperienced the Americans were and on the other hand how astute and perfidious the Spanish agents had proved, I thought it best to suffer for a time in patience until the Anglo-American colonies achieved their independence, which was bound to be . . . the infallible preliminary to our own.

While in Cuba, too, he exchanged letters with creole dissidents in Venezuela—among them Juan Vicente Bolívar, Simón's brother—who addressed him as their leader. . . .

In the course of his seventeenth-month visit to the United States, Miranda reported meeting not only Livingston and Robert Morris but also a number of revolutionary leaders, including signers of the Declaration of Independence, and he at least saw George Washington and, although not mentioned in his diary, had a number of conversations with Alexander Hamilton. John Adams later recalled that Hamilton had been "one of [Miranda's] most intimate friends and advisers." Miranda greatly admired these connections; his with such men, and theirs with world-changing events. Clearly the young, attractive, intelligent, tremendously intense and energetic creole, after a life on the fringe of society in Caracas and in the Spanish army, liked being entertained and lionized as a distinguished visitor by affluent and important republicans. The abundant evidence of material prosperity, industriousness, and thriving commerce and agriculture also impressed him. He was, however, both amused and put off by displays of social equality, and very unhappy at finding his servant at table with him in a Connecticut inn. The positive aspects of life in the United States he attributed to what he termed the perseverance of the British constitution. "Good God," he commented in his diary, "What a contrast to the Spanish system!" It was in New York in 1784 that he probably conferred with Hamilton and it was there, Miranda said later, that he committed himself to work for the independence of Spanish America, in imitation of the United States and in cooperation with England. . . .

To the more liberal and enlightened creoles the new American republic stood as a model of ideals in action. It stood for material well-being and for innovation itself. It made all things look possible through talent and human effort, through inhabitants of a region unifying and vigorously applying useful knowledge and the tenets of political economy to regional problems and social ills. While the use of the United States as an exemplar was then largely limited to one of economic advance and of some supporting social institutions, yet it did represent to Latin Americans liberty—political, economic, and social; a liberal liberty.

The revolutionary war itself, and Spain's involvement, had other sorts of impacts on Latin America. It had deflected reform goals in the face of an increased Spanish need for American funds, so that the first of many forced loans, in 1779, was a harbinger of a shift in Spanish relations with its America, henceforth characterized by erratic alternation in the easing and tightening up of government and of trade. That loan, too, and the curtailment of funds to maintain soldiers in Peru, contributed to the onset of Túpac Amaru's rebellion, which had its own reverberations, and that call for money exacerbated discontent and sparked conspiracies throughout Spanish America.

ii

By 1788, the end of the reign of Charles III, Latin Americans were caught up, directly or indirectly, in several revolutions. The American Revolution and its aftermath, together with the Enlightenment and the onset of the industrial revolution, all had great impact on Spanish policies and on Spanish Americans. . . .

The first stages of the French Revolution, coalescing with the amended royal program, served as a catalyst, radicalizing broadening desires for improvement in Spanish America and intensifying the stepped up rhetoric of reform, including that of political change—raising hope, as in Spain, of the possibility of instituting that form of republicanism, constitutional monarchy. Moreover, the outbreak of revolution in France, while only one factor within the spectrum of international relations and the complex ideological climate, coincided, and its impact intermeshed, with the increasing interest Britain and the United States displayed in Latin America and in penetrating the Pacific. This confluence caused Spanish authorities in America to tighten security and to question American loyalties and led some creoles to resent a sensed alteration in official attitudes, including a diminishing of trust. . . .

In 1785, the Holy Office in Mexico had attested to the popularity of French books in banning some of them, notably the writings of the radical philosophe, Helvetius, and Raynal's history of the Indies . . . even after 1789, French fashions remained much in vogue throughout Latin America among the more liberal, the educated, and the upward aspiring, although the French Revolution had become too radical for creole tastes, with some exceptions. . . . In 1794 Antonio Nariño [a wealthy creole official in New Granada] was tried for translating and secretly publishing the French *Declaration of the Rights of Man*, of 1789. He was accused, too, of plotting to put into effect "the Constitution of Philadelphia." In defending himself before the Bogotá audiencia, he argued that the declaration of the rights of man was first made by the United States of America and only afterwards by the National Assembly of France. He was correct in that the Bill of Rights was the immediate antecedent to the French declaration. The French document, he went on, with a good deal of truth, was in fact composed of eternal and universal principles within the patrimony of Western culture and very well-known to Spanish authors. While Nariño probably sought to present his radical views in their most acceptable form, and while another dissident, the Mexican friar Servando Teresa de Mier, later cited his argument when there was again need for such circumspection, both were aware that much of Spanish American revolutionary theory was indeed extremely eclectic. Nariño, in defending the doctrine of popular sovereignty, went on to say that the most important aspects of the rights of man reflected Thomistic concepts and the ideas of Heneccius and Seneca, and were to be found in *Las Siete Partidas* and other Spanish legal compilations. A creole tendency, basically scholastic, to cite eminent authorities right and left (here literally) in support of one's arguments is, incidentally, a principal reason why disagreement persists among scholars on the relative influence on Latin American independence projects of Spanish, French, English, and United States sources. Nariño argued to little avail. He was sentenced to 10 years' labor in Africa and escaped en route, making his way to Paris, London, and then back to New Granada. . . .

From the 1780s on, creole dissidents who would later spur revolts had made London a center of their activities. After Britain lost its American colonies, some of its high officials and prominent merchants, alert to the strategic and commercial advantages of an independent Spanish America, helped creoles to ready plans for divesting Spain of its Indies. Among the first to listen sympathetically to Miranda was Thomas Pownall, the former governor of Massachusetts, who during the Nootka crisis introduced him to William Pitt. Although the British government was the most cordial, these creoles also found friends in high places in France and the United States—but wherever they sought aid, it was the United States republican model they most often cited. Most of them, especially after 1793, came to dread the excesses of the French Revolution. Many of them admired the British system and considered a constitutional monarchy best (as did liberal Spaniards in that decade), yet to most the United States offered a functioning, American, revolutionary analogy. All of them recognized the continuing affinities in the English and United States systems. By the late eighteenth century, then, a broad and supraregional network existed of Spanish American revolutionaries active at home and overseas.

By 1796, when Spain declared war on England, London had become the hub of those creoles working for Spanish American independence. From the 1780s, during an earlier war, men sympathetic to or involved in the revolts of Túpac Amaru and the comuneros had received British pensions. . . . Juan Pablo Viscardo [a former Jesuit], a native of Guayaquil, who lived in London from 1794 until his death in 1798, also on government pension, left his papers to Rufus King, the American ambassador. King turned them over to Miranda, who extracted from them the document he subsequently published as *Carta dirigida a los Españoles Americanos*. . . . Viscardo's tract owed a good deal to Thomas Paine's *Common Sense*, which later became widely known in Spanish America. The *Carta* was soon circulating in Venezuela, and it was banned by the Inquisition in Mexico. Its author scoffed at the Spanish claim to have spread Union and Equality, saying that instead the government had slighted its obligations and that Americans were a different people who—in the oft-repeated phrase borrowed from Paine—nature had separated from Spain by immense seas. He pressed for independence: "The valor with which the English colonies of America have fought for liberty, which now they enjoy gloriously, covers with shame our indolence. . . . They have ceded us the palm," he went on; may their valor awaken our honor. His vision of a new free era ended on an economic crescendo: prosperity would come. The tyranny of Spanish kings and pensinsulars in America would be extinguished, and then: "What an agreeable spectacle the coasts of America will present, covered with men of all nations exchanging their products for ours. They will come too to settle and enrich us with their hard work. . . . America will be a great family of brothers."

Viscardo declared that Spanish rulers had honored neither Spanish nor American natural rights. They defamed Spain's constitution and broke contracts with the conquerors of America. Americans, who were descended from brave conquistadors and Indian women, had been badly treated by kings and their European-born officials, when by natural right American dominion was theirs. He cited Garcilaso de la Vega, el Inca, and Antonio de Ulloa on the escalation of prices in the Indies and on abuses by corregidores. "The augment of troops and of the navy costs us a lot and defends us not at all," he complained, and he wanted all ports open. Americans should go everywhere and buy and sell directly: "Then our riches will circulate among us and enlarge our industry." By "we" he appeared to refer to creoles, including mestizos. . . .

The radicalization of Vargas, Nariño, Espejo, and *afrancesados* in Mexico between 1790 and 1794 occurred in large part through a combination of the French Revolution and Spain's war with France. Throughout Latin America, two concepts reinforced by the French uprising and bearing out both conclusions gained currency from 1789 on, building up their own heads of antipensinular steam. One was the idea that the duty and dignity of the citizen lay in political activity. The other, related notion was that if the citizens of a state no longer approved of political arrangements, they could alter or replace them. In all this, the French Revolution intensified and spread the same discontents fanned by the revolt of 1776, although some were exacerbated too by contact with theories and advocates of political economy, and it radicalized and disseminated the concepts of natural rights and popular sovereignty emanating earlier from North America—indeed, it romanticized them, and even heightened creole pride in being American. To many creoles, as to Jefferson, the French upheaval initially had seemed to broaden the promise of the American Revolution, and as the French example became less acceptable to propertied creoles and Brazilians, it was the Anglo-American that emerged with even greater luster, as related but preferable.

It is probable that numerous Latin Americans, as did Europeans, during the 1790s favored a constitutional monarchy, if for varying reasons. Both Iberian and Latin American reformers usually tended to view Spain or Portugal, and their own regions of empire, as ailing, but they felt the sick body could be cured through their own ministrations and—still a majority view—in connection with the monarch. There was, though, growing social unrest, racial and ethnic tension, and the broadening of a radical network dedicated to achieving absolute independence; and in Spanish America, governmental and leading creole attitudes and actions from 1793 did little to allay any of them. . . . By late 1796 and the war with Britain [most creoles] saw earlier dreams of an American progress to be achieved hand in hand with the government dimming, that the policy of unity and equality was a sham. They saw a political situation lacking direction, in Spain a corrupt court, new wars and huge expenses, less effective and, even when better liked, often less respected officials, a restless and potentially threatening multiracial populace, and their own entry to domestic authority and to outside markets clogged. From the late 1790s such people, putting new value on their own self-interest and on that of their home regions and repeatedly voicing frustration and the sense of being shackled or at least burdened by a decrepit imperial system, more often employed language used by discontented Anglo-Americans in the decade preceding 1776, and they sought similar goals for themselves and their countries.

iii

When war with Britain brought a closing of sea lanes, particularly from 1797 when Nelson blockaded Cádiz and Russian ships appeared on the Pacific coast, Spain became more kindly disposed to the United States as a counterweight to Britain. [A decree of 1797 allowed a legal trade with Spanish America in neutral vessels.] With the ordinance of 1797, not only did North American trade with Latin America swell and massive shipments of United States flour go to Havana, where before large, legitimate, regular shipments had come only through Spain, but there was even more United States investment in Cuban sugar. Ships from the United States supplied most Caribbean food imports and did business with Venezuelan ports, Cartagena, La Plata, and the Pacific coast. By 1798, the Mexican press reported most ships into Vera Cruz North American. Among creoles, the attendant upsurge of commerce, in which they saw United States carriers predominate, whetted appetites for more, and more direct, trade. Creoles actively solicited trade and United States merchants responded, until market gluts of imports once again soon dampened rosy expectations. . . .

In Caracas, disagreements rent the consulado. They were part of wider quarrels, which would intensify in the following years, between planters and established wholesalers, and by extension between hinterland and port. Planters, with exports halved, and prices down, strapped by a scarcity of labor and worried by the Coro revolt and general unrest, while socially conservative were economically liberal. In accord with the intendant, they welcomed ports opened to direct commerce with friends and neutrals, particularly with North Americans, in order to market their products and because there too United States flour had come before legally by way of Spain and had arrived stale and often spoiled. Wholesalers too wanted to use neutral carriers. They urged naval protection and suggested an agent be sent to the United States to get its ships to carry out cacao and bring in flour, other provisions, and naval stores, but complained on patriotic but not unselfish grounds that Anglo-Americans must stop bringing in British textiles. It was here that they parted company with the hacendados, who argued for importing dry goods without restrictions.

In Mexico, too, trade with Spain had nearly ceased, and in Vera Cruz wheat, sugar, and indigo awaiting export had perished on the docks. Riots ensued and prices of European goods rose steeply until the authorities approved neutral carriers. Then, although the consulado objected to Anglo-Americans putting into port, some Vera Cruz firms began dealing with them, and some merchants acted as agents for North Americans. Even after the revocation in 1799 of the 1797 reglamento, [Viceroy] Azanza permitted neutral trade and favored Tomás Murphy, a merchant married to the viceroy's cousin. Murphy had advised Revillagigedo, was friendly with Godoy, and had connections to United States houses and to dealers in Jamaica. While Azanza wrote home that Anglo-Americans would profit most from current arrangements, there were Mexican merchants too who prospered as never before. Although Mexican grains could not compete with United States wheat and flour in Havana, or in Santo Domingo, Puerto Rico, Louisiana, or Venezuela, growers saw that neutral trade enabled some export; without it there would be none. Vera Cruz then supplanted the capital as the commercial center of New Spain, yet merchants of the Mexican consulado did well too. Unable to ship funds to Spain, they once again invested them internally, especially profiting the textile industry, which during the war grew extraordinarily. Smuggling too continued to flourish; Humboldt estimated a quarter of New Spain's imports then arrived as contraband.

Porteños experienced general mercantile upsurge. More of them turned to more speculative trade. Exchange rose with the United States and with the Portuguese as well, and more of them invested their own capital and began acquiring their own vessels. Local shipyards were busy, and in 1798 the entrepreneur [Tomás Antonio] Romero ordered ships from New England, as did other merchants. He continued to buy blacks from dealers in Newport and Boston, and he and others established an important commercial network in both permitted exchange and in contraband with North Americans. Medium quality textiles then appeared, mostly German and imitating luxury fabrics. Among their carriers were Shaler and Cleveland, who introduced cargoes from Hamburg. Even so, interior textiles revived during the war. La Plata did lose markets for hides, but more wheat went out to Cuba and Brazil, and the preponderant export remained silver.

The war, inflation, and reliance on neutral trade both irritated antagonisms between Spanish Americans and the metropolis and intensified numerous frictions among Latin American regions and within Latin American society. First of all, although more interregional trade was sanctioned (and was often carried on in Anglo-American vessels), yet ultimately regional competition for markets sharpened. Within Mexico, Puebla wheat and textiles competed with those of the Bajío. In La Plata, a struggle went on between rural Buenos Aires, Entre Ríos, and the Banda Oriental in exporting hides. Moreover, as soon as Buenos Aires was cut off by blockade, Tampico sent salt beef to Havana. And in Mexico Havana's thriving trade with the United States was resented, especially since it undercut Mexican exports of wheat and sugar.

Secondly, although cooperation grew in some areas, in general rivalry heightened within consulados. The clash intensified between the old mercantile aristocracy and newer interests—those usually younger, smaller, more adventurous traders allied with producers. They favored more open, speculative trade and smaller profit margins, and their goals often dovetailed with those of regional officials. It was new men and hacendados who profited most when the viceroy in Buenos Aires, and in Caracas the intendant, authorized trade with neutrals even before receiving the order of 1797. They were spurred by a need for provisions and carriers to export commodities, and for revenues resulting from legitimate trade. It was not only Azanza who got around the revocation decree. The intendant in Caracas initially refused to publish it, explaining he wanted "to avoid forwarding the attempts being made by the king's enemies to revolutionize these provinces." He also wanted to sell and ship out the government-owned tobacco.

Thirdly, competition between consulados stiffened. While in Cuba an equilibrium obtained within the consulado and generally among planters, merchants, and producers of finished products, all profiting from Havana's favored position in sugar exports and as an entrepôt for neutral trade, that consulado was often at odds with the merchant guild of Vera Cruz. In Lima and the Mexican capital, where older consulados and other entrenched corporations existed, those guilds not only clashed with newer ones but also they and high clergy often quarrelled with viceroys and other public officials. In Guatemala, with indigo exports dwindling due to increasing competition from Caracas and the East Indies, Jacobo de Villaurrutia, as president of the audiencia, continued to side with planters in repeatedly pleading for freer commerce and specifically for opening legitimate trade with the United States, thereby arousing the ire of the consulado and other officials. . . .

More open trade and the effects of royal policy after 1800 contributed to depressing further much of the interregional trade of Spanish American products. The cheaper manufactured cotton goods from England and Germany, often imported in United States ships, competed more successfully in South America with trade in interior textiles. Thus, the Ecuadorian and general Andean highland exchange with Lima now suffered keenly, as did analogous interior trades with Chile and Buenos Aires. Rivalry mounted between ports or administration centers and hinterlands. And a decree of 1801 forbade Mexican exchange with other parts of Spanish America. Regional isolation and sense of particularism were rising, undoubtedly sped by Latin Americans finding their regional economies more often in competition with one another and ever more geared to foreign exchange. The rage to export aggravated these conditions. So did United States exports and re-exports, carriers, and republican influence.

In these circumstances, creoles saw their own well-being as more closely tied to that of their provinces and regional productivity and its protection as more urgent, often as *the* key to progress. They saw their local economies expanding or having the potential to expand, yet their economic problems only multiplying. . . . Accordingly, from 1800 to 1808, many more creoles slid from the heights of optimism, even over-optimism, concerning the immediate prospects of their regions to an anguished seeking to discover why in fact conditions were getting worse. New gazettes were revealing and disseminating the descent from great expectations to disappointment and soul-searching. The creole goal was still to find the way to progress, certain that it existed. In this endeavor, not only the North American example of the efficacy of combining economic with greater political liberty was at hand. There were also available numerous sources corroborating the advantages of public control of economic and political affairs. From Madrid in 1801, for example, the consulado of Vera Cruz received from its resident agent a list of books for a proposed library. Mentioned were works by Spanish economists, periodicals, the 1784 Spanish edition of *The Wealth of Nations*, a French book on the constitutions of Europe and the United States, and much on North American trade; and one volume concerned the influence of republican government on Anglo-American prosperity. . . .

Porteños saw the revocation of neutral commerce loosely imposed, and competition for contraband trade between mercantile groups winked at by viceroys, especially with renewal of war with England, from 1802. Yet complaints, voiced by Belgrano and others in the 1790s, echoed in the new *Telégrafo Mercantil*, which noted the mutual dependence of producers and merchants, then urged exporting in porteño-owned vessels and promoting finishing industries—in this discussion suggesting importing master tanners from the United States and also emulating that country in exporting wheat and flour. Yet more trenchant were essays in the *Semanario de agricultura, industria, y comercio*. The interests of its editor, Juan Hipólito Vieytes, aligned with those of more liberal consulado members and Belgrano; they were solely economic, with little pretence of literary content. Vieytes reprinted articles by Franklin, and he admired British power and prosperity and cited reputable authorities on political economy, including Jovellanos, Campillo, Ward, Foronda, and Hume. And in 1804, in a long exposition of Adam Smith's ideas, he concluded that capital should be invested in America in order to develop, in consecutive stages, cultivation, manufactures, and foreign trade, and he viewed economic freedom as a step to greater political liberty.

24

Confessions of a Radical

Antonio Nariño

Resentment of Spain, awareness of nationality, liberal ideas, admiration for France, expectations of Britain—these were the traits of the enlightened creole. It was a profile almost exactly reproduced by Antonio Nariño and illustrated in the following document, a classic understatement at once ironic, taunting, and naive. Unlike the majority of creoles, Nariño possessed both wealth and office, and in Bogotá he kept a foot in both camps, being a friend of the viceroy as well as a leader of intellectual dissidents. In 1794, however, he was arrested and tried for translating and printing the French *Declaration of the Rights of Man*. In his defense before the audiencia of Bogotá he presented his ideas as Catholic and traditional, and derived from various sources, though in fact some of them echoed Rousseau. He was found guilty of treason and sentenced to ten years' hard labor in an African penitentiary. He escaped in Cádiz and traveled to Paris and London before returning to New Granada, where he tested popular opinion on revolution, surrendered to the authorities, and like many creole intellectuals in Spanish America argued without success for reformism within the colonial state, until that state collapsed in 1810.

Confident in His Majesty's mercy, I hereby declare everything I have done from the time I left Madrid to my arrival in this city [Bogotá], in order that knowledge of my errors may serve to preserve the public order and security of these provinces.

After I arrived in Madrid I sought a further hearing of the case found against me by the royal audiencia [of Bogotá] in order to present my defense. As time passed and I could not obtain any ruling which might

Translated by John Lynch from "Confesión de Nariño al Virrey," 30 July 1797, in Eduardo Posada and Pedro M. Ibáñez, eds., *El Precursor. Documentos sobre la vida pública del General Antonio Nariño* (Biblioteca de Historia Nacional, 2, Bogotá, 1903), pp. 223–33.

even safeguard me from the sentence I had received in Bogotá, I began to fear the worst. I did not know what action to take: to abandon the country without establishing my innocence would be imprudent, while to risk the possibility of further unforeseen adversities, and the confirmation of a sentence worse than death itself, would be an act of folly. I saw my honor impugned, my family disgraced, and myself doomed to spend the rest of my days abandoned in prison. Such were my problems and anxieties, when war with England threatened. I was struck by the overwhelming idea that this could be a desperate remedy for my situation; so I decided to go to France and there await the outcome of my case without risk to myself. In the event of the sentence being confirmed, I would proceed to England and by joining an enemy nation open by force a door which in my opinion injustice had closed on me. The idea was too rash to put into operation immediately and of a kind which prevented me from discussing it with any living soul; but observing that time was passing, and as I had reason to fear even more for my safety, I decided to make a hasty escape to France. I had previously requested a remittance of 2000 pesos, and with a few *reales* that I still had left from the money I had brought with me I set out.

From France I wrote to Madrid asking them to urge my attorney to keep a constant watch on the progress of the case, for I hoped that my absence would not be noticed by the government and I would be able to return at the first favorable sign. I spent about two months in France without receiving any news, and always doubtful about the fate of my family and about my desperate plan. I spent this time attending the courts, studying the new laws, the Constitution, and the history of the revolution; and I sought to inform myself as well as I could on all these matters. As war was about to be declared, and I heard that a royal bodyguard who was in France with permission had been arrested for using a false name, I decided to bring forward my departure for London in case I suffered a similar fate and was stranded in France by the war and unable to travel to England. Before leaving I wrote to Madrid saying that I was going to England out of curiosity, as I was so close and had nothing else to do.

In London I passed myself off as a Spanish merchant, and was accepted as such by the Spaniards there. On my arrival I wrote to our ambassador, visited the consul, and lodged with an American, and no one suspected me or my movements. I began as I had done in France: I learned as much as I could of the English constitution, the land and sea forces of England, its revenue, national debt, and so on. The Treaty of Alliance between France and Spain was published, to be followed immediately by formal declaration of war against Great Britain, the only exception to Spain's neutrality. I understood that preparations were being made to attack the Philippines, and I pass on this information in case there is still time to make use of it.

In these circumstances, I felt I ought to make some moves, and so I sent a note to Minister Pitt, informing him in effect that I was a Spanish American and needed to discuss important matters with the ministry, for which purpose I requested a private audience with him. I did not receive a reply. I tried again, with no more success. Meanwhile, I had secured the friendship of two Englishmen, one called Campbell, the other Short, well-known London merchants. I disclosed myself to them in order through their means to obtain the audience I was seeking from the prime minister, and we agreed to make a trip together into the country in order to discuss the matter calmly and freely. After many discussions we decided that it would be better to deal not with Pitt but with Lord Liverpool, minister of state, with whom they had some friendship. We also decided that at first they would simply speak to the minister in these terms: there was in London a Spanish American who was thoroughly resentful of his own nation [Spain], as he had informed them; they had sounded out his attitude and they believed that in the present circumstances it would not be out of place for the minister to speak to him. This they did, and the minister received the news and the idea well; but he told them that no move could be made until the actual declaration of war, because the Spanish American was possibly a spy who was testing the intentions of the ministry. I remained content with this reply, but not so the two Englishmen, who continued to see me daily and to lose no opportunity of discussing the matter with me. It would be tedious to describe all the details of my dealings with them. Suffice it to say that I was aware of their intentions, which were to get as much advantage as possible from me, even when my application was unsuccessful. In spite of everything, I could not refrain from giving them an account of the resources of our Kingdom [New Granada], its population and products, first to show that I knew what I was talking about and my plan was not reckless, and second to motivate them with the prospect of the great advantage that would accrue to their commerce if my application were successful. I explained, too, that as we were accustomed to European products and did not have manufactures of our own, it was indispensable that a European nation should supply us with everything. That being the case, even if I was acting in bad faith, necessity itself would oblige us to buy from them all our manufactures and sell them the raw materials which we ourselves were unable to manufacture. But at the same time I described to them the great problems any European nation would have if it tried to take us by force, both because of the rough and difficult roads and the rigor of the climate, and because the combination of regular troops, militia forces and the people of the country, together with denial of provisions, would make it impossible for any European forces to invade us successfully.

The news of the declaration of war arrived at last, and it was proposed to me openly in the name of the minister that if I reduced my request to one that simply involved handing over the Kingdom [of New Granada] to Great Britain, I would have all the assistance that was needed; that I should put in writing everything I planned for this project, either to have the arms and equipment prepared in Europe, or in the colonies, in which case orders would be sent to the authorities, and a 40-gun frigate would be immediately fitted out to transport me safely; that in case of failure, I would have asylum in England, and if things went well I could count on a brilliant future. I refused this proposal outright, for it was never my intention to seek foreign domination. Instead I limited my request to one which simply asked to know whether, in the event of a break with the metropolis, England would assist us with arms, munitions, and a squadron to patrol our seas and intercept reinforcements from Spain, in return for a number of commercial advantages. Some further details came up, and I pressed for an answer. They replied that if a break with Spain was definitely undertaken, then during the war we could count on all the assistance we needed, arms, munitions, and a naval squadron; this would not only patrol our seas, but also bombard Cartagena, if this were necessary, in conjunction with an attack from within, to force its surrender and bring it into use as a supply base for the interior. With this in mind they gave me the following addresses: Dr. Herman Goverts, Hamburg; Juppon and Broch, Guernsey; Richard Budo, Jersey; Mr. Campbell, Anderson, and Warnfort, 4 Throgmorton St., London; Mr. Bartholomew Short, same address. In the whole time I was in London I received not a single letter, for the mail was lost.

I promptly left for France, anxious to know how my case was proceeding and intending to remain only a short time in Paris before continuing to Bordeaux. But I took ill on the journey and was forced to remain some time in Paris; from there I wrote to Spain, asking them to reply to me in Bordeaux, for I was detained longer than I had planned. In Paris I became acquainted with someone who told me he was going to London with the idea of seeking the assistance of England for Peru, and that he was in contact with some of the principal citizens of Lima; he mentioned some, but I have no recollection of their names. He also said that he was a native of Havana; he was of average height, colored, and about fifty years old. I persuaded him to join me, because too many applications at one time could frustrate the undertaking; I pointed out that my plan was well advanced, and once I had obtained my request then he could secure his. I suspected, correctly, that this man, who was probably better documented than I and who spoke for a country, Peru, which is better known and more highly regarded than ours, would gain preference and spoil my chances. He was interested in my information and advice, and I do not know whether he agreed with me simply to take advantage of them, for up to now I have no further news of him. I gave him letters of recommendation, and he arranged to leave the day after my departure for Bordeaux and to write to me, using the address D. Francisco Simón Alvarez de Ortú, the same that I have given to all the others. That has never been my name, and I have simply used it as an address to avoid any possibility of disclosing my identity.

Before leaving Paris I left a letter, to be delivered to the Directory at the proper time, making clear that the English would not invade our country except in support of the Americans, and that in accordance with a chapter of the Directory's own Constitution France could not in that case give assistance to Spain against them. I had no further business in Paris, and no other persons knew of my plans.

I proceeded to Bordeaux, and in spite of my existing plans I was still anxious to know the outcome of my case. The most easy, honest, normal, and secure way should always be preferred to one full of risks and danger; therefore, as I found no letters on my arrival, I wrote [to Madrid] from there, always with the same object, and I received a reply. It was known in November from the actual prisoners in Cádiz that they had been placed at liberty, though prohibited from returning to America; the lampoonists were sent to Africa; as for my treatment, nothing was known, because although my attorney had seen the official of the ministry he had been told nothing. It may be that there was some mistake in this information, from what I have subsequently learned, but there is no doubt that this is what was communicated to me. At the time there was a neutral vessel about to sail, called *La Sicilia de Bastón*, bound for St. Bartholomew. This ship took passengers, something difficult to find among the other neutral ships, for it was feared that if the English intercepted them they would be detained on the pretext that one of the passengers was owner of the cargo, a frequent occurrence. I do not mention all my ideas of that time. I will say only that it is to this impetuous and imprudent decision that I owe my present happiness, because if I had remained in Bordeaux, as I should have done, awaiting the conclusion of my case, and it had not been favorable, I would have embarked with a definite intention and, without waiting to reach this city [Bogotá], would perhaps have activated my detestable plan. Before leaving Bordeaux I wrote to people in this city, though the letters have not arrived. I said not a word of my plan or of my return, and neither before nor since my arrival have I written to anyone in this city or the Kingdom on these matters. I also wrote to Madrid, saying that I was going to Brittany and they should direct my mail to Mr. Seironaburcher, care of Mr. Gramont, with whom I also left instructions to forward my letters.

On the voyage I became friendly with Mr. Coulon, a businessman of Philadelphia, and I arranged that he and his brother should take the necessary steps to lay in stocks of arms, a good transaction there, but that they should not proceed to purchase them until they received word from me. His address is P. Coulon, 64 North Front Street, Philadelphia. I also left correspondence with Mr. du Peyron, merchant of Basseterre in Guadaloupe.

From St. Bartholomew I went to St. Thomas with a recommendation to Mr. Toulousan, among others; he greeted me warmly and took me one day to dine in the house of Mr. Petiton. The conversation turned to this Kingdom [New Granada], and as the said Petiton referred to some details of its fertility, its products, and so on, I asked him if he had ever been here. He said no, but a certain D. Fermín had stayed in his house, and he was from New Granada and had given him information. It immediately occurred to me that this D. Fermín could be Vargas. I questioned him more closely and I had no doubts. I knew that Vargas was in Jamaica, for the English had taken him prisoner, that previously he had engaged in business on a small scale, and that he now lived by practicing as a doctor or surgeon. I knew nothing of any other plans he might have. In spite of the fact that Mr. Petiton was urging him to return to St. Thomas, I wrote to him from there saying that if he wished to return to his own country he should stay where he was until I got in touch with him from New Granada and that if he wished to write to me he should use the address that I indicated. In St. Thomas I left instructions with the leading commercial house, whose address is: for Trinidad, Mr. Cipriani, and for Mr. Isaac López, merchant of St. Thomas; Mr. Toulousan, care of Mr. Levy and Gómez. From there I wrote to London, where I had also written from Bordeaux.

I proceeded from St. Thomas to Curaçao, with an introduction to, among others, a certain D. Pedro, known as Pedrote, who has served in Cartagena de Indias; he was subsequently commissioned as an enemy privateer and has taken many prizes from us. I advised him to come to this Kingdom and perhaps we could do business together, in either contraband goods or agricultural products; and if he was interested I would write to him from here. He readily agreed that I write to him, and we arranged to do this through a certain Palé, in whose house I stayed. I told Pedrote nothing of my ideas; but as he was ill-disposed and resentful towards Spain I did not doubt that he would collaborate once action against her had begun. I then moved on to Coro in a Spanish vessel with my corresponding passport from Curaçao and so, as a Spaniard, from Coro to the ports of Maracaibo; without stopping in that city I sailed on the lake as far as Santa Rosa, and from there I continued to Chiriguaná. In this village, which is near the hacienda of *Estanques*, the parish priest told me that there had been a man in the hacienda carrying a large traveling bag on his back with a beard like a Capuchin friar but without a habit; he was very well educated and spoke of foreign countries. But the priest had not been able to discover who he was or why he was traveling in that way, because he cleverly evaded all questions on these subjects. The news of this strange person caused me to question the priest closely, and although the description coincided in many aspects with the appearance of Vargas, the length of the beard indicated otherwise, for it was only a year since he had left St. Thomas. I continued on my way to Bailadores, La Grita, Cúcuta, Pamplona, Tequia, Cerinza, Tunja, Chocontá, until I reached this city; during the whole of this journey I made a point of sounding out the feelings of the people, without putting forward any ideas of my own. When I arrived here I realised that there was no news of my case as the mail had not arrived, and so after only six days rest I resumed my travels with the idea of further discovering the roads and the feelings of the people in the districts of Tunja, Vélez, and Girón. I spent two months on this expedition during the harshest winter, without arms or escort, or any company apart from a servant, who was usually the owner of the mules. My first thought was to see D. N. Bol and to get as much out of him as I could, depending on how I found him, either by declaring myself openly, or by disguising the reason for my coming, in order to obtain from him information which would lead me to the people whom I could trust. But as I did not make contact with this person, I sought to find out what opinion was held of him in the village where he lived; inquiries among people near here convince me that he was generally hated, among other things because he was thought to have saved his own person after the revolution of 1782 by sacrificing the poor. I realised that I was on the point of taking a step that was not only useless but dangerous, and so I resolved to count only on the people and not to take any chance with my life or destiny beyond what they decided. With this firm resolution I continued my journey through all the villages between here and Pamplona by the Socorro road, and from

Pamplona to here by the Girón road, having first travelled the Tunja road; these are the main roads which correspond to the three *corregimientos* and where the most numerous and largest villages are to be found. The result of this journey has been to discover that the people are everywhere discontented, and that along with this discontent they fortunately have a great ignorance as to what government is; that is to say, even when they might wish to change things, their ignorance prevents them from knowing how to proceed.

[I returned to this capital, determined to wait quietly for the mail. But as this was delayed I decided to place myself at the mercy of His Majesty through the mediation of Your Excellency, the viceroy, to acknowledge my past errors, to beg forgiveness for my crimes, and to expiate them by service to the king.]

Santa Fe, 30 July 1797   Antonio Nariño

PART SIX

INCIPIENT NATIONALISM

25

The New Americans

Alexander von Humboldt

Alexander von Humboldt (1769–1859), scientist and traveler, spent nearly five years in Spanish America, from 1799–1804, exploring, collecting, and observing. As he journeyed through South America, the Caribbean, and finally Mexico, he met and conversed with leading officials, residents, mineowners and landowners; he had access to government papers; he researched in official archives; and he recorded the great natural resources of America, the products of estates, plantations, and mines. But Humboldt's visit, while it was backed by the colonial state, coincided with the declining phase of Bourbon reformism and a rising curve of creole frustration. He concluded that the imperial authorities were not equal to the vital tasks of economic growth, social change, and political innovation. He warned that the flaws and prejudices of colonial government, the example of the United States of America, and the influence of the opinions of the age were undermining the loyalty of the creoles towards Spain. Oppressive, though weak, government combined with creole dissent was a fatal mixture, one which helped to strengthen the growing sense of American identity that he observed. His own researches helped to promote that identity; by demonstrating the range of institutions, educational facilities, and wealth of resources contained in the regions of Spanish America, especially in Mexico, Humboldt showed Americans, and the world, that these countries possessed many of the qualifications of independent states. But Humboldt was also aware of the racial divisions in American society, and in Venezuela he saw that national identity, of which even the whites had different perceptions, did not include the slaves

Reprinted from Alexander von Humboldt, *Political Essay on the Kingdom of New Spain.* Translated and edited by John Black (4 vols., London, 1811), I, 204–06, 209–11; and from *Personal Narrative of Travels to the Equinoctial Regions of the New Continent during the Years 1799–1804.* Translated by Helen Maria Williams (6 vols., London, 1814–29), III, 414–15, 428–41, 472–76.

and blacks, who were bound rather in a Caribbean network of resentment and rebellion.

MEXICO

Amongst the inhabitants of pure origin the whites would occupy the second place, considering them only in the relation of number. They are divided into whites born in Europe, and descendants of Europeans born in the Spanish colonies of America or in the Asiatic islands. The former bear the name of *chapetones* or *gachupines,* and the second that of *criollos.* The natives of the Canary Islands, who go under the general denomination of *isleños* (islanders), and who are the *gérans* of the plantations, are considered as Europeans. The Spanish laws allow the same rights to all whites; but those who have the execution of the laws endeavor to destroy an equality which shocks the European pride. The government, suspicious of the Creoles, bestows the great places exclusively on the natives of Old Spain. For some years back they have disposed at Madrid even of the most trifling employments in the administration of the customs and the tobacco revenue. At an epoch when everything tended to a uniform relaxation in the springs of the state, the system of venality made an alarming progress. For the most part it was by no means a suspicious and distrustful policy, it was pecuniary interest alone which bestowed all employments on Europeans. The result has been a jealousy and perpetual hatred between the *chapetons* and the Creoles. The most miserable European, without education, and without intellectual cultivation, thinks himself superior to the whites born in the new continent. He knows that, protected by his countrymen, and favored by chances common enough in a country where fortunes are as rapidly acquired as they are lost, he may one day reach places to which the access is almost interdicted to the natives, even to those of them distinguished for their talents, knowledge, and moral qualities. The natives prefer the denomination of *Americans* to that of Creoles. Since the peace of Versailles, and, in particular, since the year 1789, we frequently hear proudly declared: "I am not a *Spaniard*, I am an *American*!", words which betray the workings of a long resentment. In the eye of law every white Creole is a Spaniard; but the abuse of the laws, the false measures of the colonial government, the example of the United States of America, and the influence of the opinions of the age, have relaxed the ties which formerly united more closely the Spanish Creoles to the European Spaniards. A wise administration may reestablish harmony, calm their passions and resentments, and yet preserve for a long time the union among the members of one and the same great family scattered over Europe and America, from the Patagonian coast to the north of California. . . .

It would be difficult to estimate exactly how many Europeans there are among the 1,200,000 whites who inhabit New Spain. As in the capital of Mexico itself, where the government brings together the greatest number of Spaniards, in a population of more than 135,000 souls, not more than 2,500 individuals are born in Europe, it is more than probable that the whole kingdom does not contain more than 70 or 80,000.[1] They constitute, therefore, only the 70th part of the whole population, and the proportion of Europeans to white Creoles is as one to fourteen.

The Spanish laws prohibit all entry into the American possessions to every European not born in the peninsula. The words European and Spaniard have become synonymous in Mexico and Peru. The inhabitants of the remote provinces have, therefore, a difficulty in conceiving that there can be Europeans who do not speak their language; and they consider this ignorance as a mark of low extraction, because, everywhere around them, all, except the very lowest class of the people, speak Spanish. Better acquainted with the history of the sixteenth century than with that of our own times, they imagine that Spain continues to possess a decided preponderance over the rest of Europe. To them the peninsula appears the very center of European civilization. It is otherwise with the Americans of the capital. Those of them who are acquainted with the French or English literature fall easily into a contrary extreme; and have still a more unfavorable opinion of the mother country than the French had at a time when communication was less frequent between Spain and the rest of Europe. They prefer strangers from other countries to the Spaniards; and they flatter themselves with the idea that intellectual cultivation has made more rapid progress in the colonies than in the peninsula.

This progress is indeed very remarkable at Mexico, the Havanah, Lima, Santa Fe, Quito, Popayan, and Caracas. Of all these great cities the Havanah bears the greatest resemblance to those of Europe in customs, refinements of luxury, and the tone of society. At Havanah the state of politics, and their influence on commerce, is best understood. However, notwithstanding the efforts of the *Patriotic Society of the Island of Cuba*, which encourages the sciences with the most generous zeal, they prosper very slowly in a country where cultivation and the price of colonial produce engross the whole attention of the inhabitants. The study of the mathematics, chemistry, mineralogy, and botany, is more general at Mexico, Santa Fe, and Lima. We everywhere observe a great intellectual activity, and among the youth a wonderful facility of seizing the principles of science. It is said that this facility is still more remarkable among the inhabitants of Quito and Lima than at Mexico and Santa Fe. The former appear to possess more versatility of mind and a more lively imagination; while the Mexicans and the natives of Santa Fe have the reputation of greater perseverance in the studies to which they have once addicted themselves.

No city of the new continent, without even excepting those of the United States, can display such great and solid scientific establishments as the capital of Mexico. I shall content myself here with naming the School of Mines, directed by the learned Elhuyar . . . ; the Botanic Garden; and the Academy of Painting and Sculpture. This academy bears the title of *Academia de los Nobles Artes de Mexico.* It owes its existence to the patriotism of several Mexican individuals, and to the protection of the minister Galvez. The government assigned it a spacious building, in which there is a much finer and more complete collection of casts than is to be found in any part of Germany. We are astonished on seeing that the Apollo Belvedere, the group of Laocoön, and still more colossal statues, have been conveyed through mountainous roads at least as narrow as those of St. Gothard; and we are surprised at finding these masterpieces of antiquity collected together under the torrid zone, in a tableland higher than the convent of the great St. Bernard. The collection of casts brought to Mexico cost the king 200,000 francs. The remains of the Mexican sculpture, those colossal statues of basalt and porphyry, which are covered with Aztec hieroglyphics, and bear some relation to the Egyptian and Hindu style, ought to be collected together in the edifice of the academy, or rather in one of the courts which belong to it. It would be curious to see these monuments of the first cultivation of our species, the works of a semi-barbarous people inhabiting the Mexican Andes, placed beside the beautiful forms produced under the sky of Greece and Italy.

The revenues of the Academy of Fine Arts at Mexico amount to 123,000 francs, of which the government gives 60,000, the body of Mexican miners nearly 25,000, the *consulado,* or association of merchants of the capital, more than 15,000. It is impossible not to perceive the influence of this establishment on the taste of the nation. This influence is particularly visible in the symmetry of the buildings, in the perfection with which the hewing of stone is conducted, and in the ornaments of the capitals and stucco relievos. What a number of beautiful edifices are to be seen at Mexico! nay, even in provincial towns like Guanaxuato and Queretaro! These monuments, which frequently cost a million or a million-and-a-half of francs, would appear to advantage in the finest streets of Paris, Berlin, and Petersburg. M. Tolsa, professor of sculpture at Mexico, was even able to cast an equestrian statue of King Charles the Fourth; a work which, with the exception of the Marcus Aurelius at Rome, surpasses in beauty and purity of style everything which remains in this way in Europe. Instruction is communicated *gratis* at the Academy of Fine Arts. It is not confined alone to the drawing of landscapes and figures; they have had the good sense to employ other means for exciting the national industry. The academy labors successfully to introduce among the artisans a taste for elegance and beautiful forms. Large rooms, well lighted by Argand's lamps, contain every evening some hundreds of young people, of whom some draw from *relievo* or living models, while others copy drawings of furniture, chandeliers, or other ornaments in bronze. In this assemblage (and this is very remarkable in the midst of a country where the prejudices of the nobility against the castes are so inveterate) rank, color, and race is confounded: we see the Indian and the *mestizo* sitting beside the white, and the son of a poor artisan in emulation with the children of the great lords of the country. It is a consolation to observe, that under every zone the cultivation of science and art establishes a certain equality among men, and obliterates for a time, at least, all those petty passions of which the effects are so prejudicial to social happiness.

Since the close of the reign of Charles the Third, and under that of Charles the Fourth, the study of the physical sciences has made great progress, not only in Mexico, but in general in all the Spanish colonies. No European government has sacrificed greater sums to advance the knowledge of the vegetable kingdom than the Spanish government. Three *botanical expeditions*, in Peru, New Granada, and New Spain, under the direction of MM. Ruiz and Pavon, Don José Celestino Mutis, and MM. Sesse and Mociño, have cost the state nearly two millions of francs. Moreover, botanical gardens have been established at Manilla and the Canary Islands. The commission destined to draw plans of the canal of *los Guines* was also appointed to examine the vegetable productions of the island of Cuba. All these researches, conducted during twenty years in the most fertile regions of the new continent, have not only enriched science with more than four thousand new species of plants, but also contributed much to diffuse a taste for natural history among the inhabitants of the country. The city of Mexico exhibits a very interesting botanical garden within the very precincts of the viceroy's palace. Professor Cervantes gives annual courses there, which are very well attended. This *savant* possesses, besides his herbals, a rich collection of Mexican minerals. M. Mociño, whom we just now mentioned as one of the coadjutors of M. Sesse, and who has pushed his laborious excursions from the kingdom of Guatemala to the northwest coast or island of Vancouver and Quadra; and M. Echeveria, a painter of plants and animals, whose works will bear a comparison with the most perfect productions of the kind in Europe, are both of them natives of New Spain. They had both attained a distinguished rank among *savants* and artists before quitting their country.[2]

VENEZUELA

When I passed for the first time that tableland [the route from the coast upward and inland to Caracas], on my way to the capital of Venezuela, I found several travelers assembled round the little inn of Guayavo, to rest their mules. They were inhabitants of Caraccas, and were disputing on the efforts toward independence, which had been made a short time before. Joseph España had perished on the scaffold; and his wife groaned in a prison, because she had given an asylum to her husband when a fugitive, and had not denounced him to the government. I was struck with the agitation which prevailed in every mind, and the bitterness with which questions were debated, on which men of the same country ought not to have differed in opinion. While they descanted on the hatred of the Mulattoes against the free Negroes and Whites, on the wealth of the monks, and the difficulty of holding slaves in obedience, a cold wind, that seemed to descend from the lofty summit of the Silla of Caraccas, enveloped us in a thick fog, and put an end to the animated conversation. We sought for shelter, in the Venta del Guayavo. When we entered the inn, an old man, who had spoken with the most calmness, reminded the others how imprudent it was, in a time of denunciation, on the mountain as well as in the city, to engage in political discussion. These words, uttered in a spot of so wild an aspect, made a lively impression on my mind; which was often renewed during our journies in the Andes of New Grenada and Peru. In Europe, where nations decided their quarrels in the plains, we climb the mountains in search of solitude and liberty. In the New World, the Cordilleras are inhabited to the height of twelve thousand feet; and thither men carry with them their political dissentions, and their little and hateful passions. . . .

The coasts of Venezuela, from their extent, their stretching toward the east, the number of their ports, and the safety of their anchorage at different seasons, possess all the advantages of the interior Caribbean Sea. The communications with the greater islands, and even with those that are to windward, can no where be more frequent than from the ports of Cumana, Barcelona, La Guayra, Porto Cabello, Coro, and Maracaybo; and no where has it been found more difficult to restrain an illicit commerce with strangers. Can we wonder, that this facility of commercial intercourse with the inhabitants of free America, and the agitated nations of Europe, should have augmented in conjunction, in the provinces united under the Capitania-General of Venezuela, opulence, knowledge, and that restless desire of a local government, which is blended with the love of liberty and republican forms?

In the Capitania-General of Caraccas, the Indian population is inconsiderable, at least beyond the Missions, and in the cultivated zone. At the moménts of great political dissension, the natives excite no fear in the whites, or the mingled casts. Computing, in 1800, the total population of the seven united provinces at nine hundred thousand souls, it appeared to me, that the Indians made only one ninth; while at Mexico they form nearly one half of the inhabitants.[3]

Among the casts that compose the population of Venezuela, that of the Blacks, which awakens at once the interest due to misfortune, and the dread of a violent reaction, is not important from its number; but it is so from its accumulation on a small space of territory. We shall soon see, that in all the Capitania-General the slaves do not exceed a fifteenth of the whole population. In the island of Cuba, of all those in the West Indies where the Negroes bear the smallest proportion to the Whites, they were, in 1811, as one in three. The seven united provinces of Venezuela have sixty thousand slaves; Cuba, the extent of which is eight times less, has two hundred and twelve thousand. Considering the sea of the West India islands, of which the Gulf of Mexico makes a part, as an interior sea with several mouths, it is important to fix our attention on the political relations, that result from this singular configuration of the New Continent, between countries placed around the same basin. Notwithstanding the isolated state, in which the greater part of the mother countries endeavour to hold their colonies, the agitations that take place are not the less communicated from one to the other. The elements of discord are every where the same; and, as if by instinct, a concert is established between men of the same colour, although separated by difference of language and inhabiting opposite coasts. That American Mediterranean, formed by the shores of Venezuela, New Grenada, Mexico, the United States, and the West India islands, may count upon its borders near a million and a half of free and enslaved Blacks; but so unequally distributed, that there are very few to the south, and scarcely any in the region of the west. Their great accumulation is on the northern and eastern coasts. This may be said to be the African part of the interior basin. It is natural, that the commotions, which since 1792 have manifested themselves in St. Domingo, should have been propagated to the coast of Venezuela. So long as Spain possessed those fine colonies in tranquility, the little resistance of the slaves was entirely repressed: but when a struggle of another kind, that for independence, began, the Blacks by their menacing position excited alternately the apprehensions of the opposite parties; and the gradual or instantaneous abolition of slavery has been proclaimed in different regions of Spanish America, less from motives of justice and humanity, than to secure the aid of an intrepid race of men, habituated to privation, and fighting for their own cause. . . .

The sixty thousand slaves, which the seven united provinces of Venezuela contain, are so unequally divided, that in the province of Caraccas alone there are nearly forty thousand, one fifth of which are Mulattoes; in that of Maracaybo, ten or twelve thousand; in those of Cumana and Barcelona, scarcely six thousand. To judge of the influence which the slaves and the men of colour exert in general on the public tranquility, it is not enough to know their number, we must consider their accumulation at certain points, and their manner of life, as cultivators or inhabitants of towns. In the province of Venezuela, the slaves are assembled together on a space of no great extent, between the coast, and a line that passes (at twelve leagues from the coast) through Panaquire, Yare, Sabana de Ocumare, Villa de Cura, and Nirgua. The Llanos or vast plains of Calaboso, San Carlos, Guanare, and Barquecimeto, contain only four or five thousand, who are scattered among the farms, and employed in the care of cattle. The number of freed men is very considerable; the Spanish laws and customs are favourable to affranchisement. A master cannot refuse liberty to a slave who offers him the sum of three hundred piastres, even thought he may have cost him double that price, on account of his industry, or a particular aptitude for the trade he practises. Instances of persons, who by their will bestow liberty on a certain number of slaves, is more common in the province of Venezuela, than in any other place. A short time before we visited the fertile valleys of Aragua, and the lake of Valencia, a lady, who inhabited the great village of Victoria, ordered her children, on her deathbed, to give liberty to all her slaves, to the number of thirty. I love to record facts that do honour to the character of a people, from whom Mr. Bonpland and myself received so many marks of kindness and affection.

What is most interesting in the colonies next to the state of the Blacks, is to know the number of white Creoles, whom I call Hispano-Americans, and that of the Whites born in Europe. It is difficult to acquire notions sufficiently exact on so delicate a point. The people in the New, as well as in the Old World, abhor numberings, suspecting them to be made in order to augment the weight of taxes. . . . In the

Capitania-General of Caraccas [there are a maximum of] two hundred, or two hundred and ten thousand Hispano-Americans, in a total population of nine hundred thousand souls. The number of Europeans included in the white race (not comprehending the troops sent from the mother country) does not exceed twelve or fifteen thousand. . . .

[In Peru the rebellion of Túpac Amaru in 1781 caused the whites to become even more conscious than before of their number and that of the Indians.] It was reserved for our times, to see the whites direct this attention towards themselves; and examine from motives of distrust, the elements of which their cast is composed. Every enterprise in favour of independence and liberty puts the national or American party in opposition with the men of the mother country. When I arrived in Caraccas, the latter had just escaped from the danger, with which they thought they were menaced by the insurrection projected by España. The consequences of that bold attempt were the more serious, because, instead of investigating the real causes of the popular discontent, it was thought, that the mother country would be saved by employing vigorous measures. At present the commotions, which have arisen from the banks of the Rio de la Plata to New Mexico, an extent of fourteen hundred leagues, have divided men of common origin.

It seems to excite surprise in Europe, that the Spaniards of the mother country, of whom we have remarked the small number, have made during ages so long and so firm a resistance. Men forget, that the European party in all the colonies is necessarily augmented by a great mass of the natives [Hispano-Americans.] Family interests, the desire of uninterrupted tranquility, the fear of engaging in an enterprise that might fail, prevent these latter from embracing the cause of independence, or aspiring to establish a local and representative government, though dependent on the mother country. Some shrink from violent measures, and flatter themselves, that a gradual reform may render the colonial system less oppressive. They see in revolutions only the loss of their slaves, the spoliation of the clergy, and the introduction of religious toleration, which they believe to be incompatible with the purity of the established worship. Others belong to the small number of families, which, either from hereditary opulence, or having been long settled in the colonies, exercise a real municipal aristocracy. They would rather be deprived of certain rights, than share them with all; they would prefer even a foreign yoke to the exercise of authority by the Americans of an inferior cast; they abhor every constitution founded on equality of rights; and above all, they dread the loss of those decorations and titles, which they have with so much difficulty acquired, and which, as we have observed above, compose so essential a part of their domestic happiness. Others again, and their number is very considerable, live in the country on the produce of their lands; and enjoy that liberty, which, in a country where there is only a scattered population, is obtained even under the most oppressive governments. Aspiring to no places themselves, they see them with indifference filled by men, whose power can never reach them, and whose names are to them almost unknown. They would no doubt prefer a national government, and complete liberty of commerce, to the ancient state of the colonies; but this desire does not sufficiently subdue the love of ease, and the habits of an indolent life, to impel them to long and painful sacrifices.

In characterizing these different tendencies of political opinion in the colonies, from the various intercourse I have had with all classes of the inhabitants, I have developed the causes of the long and peaceful dominion of the mother country over America. The calm has been the result of habit, of the preponderance of a few leading families, and above all of the equilibrium established between the hostile forces. But security founded on disunion must be shaken, whenever a large body of men, forgetting their individual animosities, shall be united by a sentiment of common interest; when that sentiment, once awakened, is strengthened by resistance; and when the progress of knowledge, and change of manners, shall diminish the influence of habit and ancient ideas. . . .

[The study of science prevails in Mexico and Bogotá; literature in Quito and Lima; and] more accurate notions of the political relations of countries, and more enlarged views of the state of colonies and their mother countries, at the Havannah and Caraccas. The numerous communications with commercial Europe, with that sea of the West Indies, which we have described as a mediterranean with many outlets, have had a powerful influence on the progress of society in the island of Cuba, and in the five provinces of Venezuela. Civilization has in no other part of Spanish America assumed a more European physiognomy. The great number of Indian cultivators, who inhabit Mexico and the interior of New Granada, have impressed a peculiar, I might almost say an exotic character, on those vast countries. Notwithstanding the increase of the black population, we seem to be nearer Cadiz and the United States at Caraccas and the Havannah, than in any other part of the New World.

Caraccas being situate on the continent, and its population less mutable than that of the islands, the national manners have been better preserved than at the Havannah. Society does not present very animated and varied pleasures; but that feeling of comfort is experienced in domestic life, which leads to uniform cheerfulness and cordiality united with politeness of manners. There exists at Caraccas, as in every place where a great change in the ideas is preparing, two races of men, we might say two distinct generations; one, of which but a small number remains, preserves a strong attachment for ancient customs, simplicity of manners, and moderation in their desires. They live only in the images of the past. America appears to them a property conquered by their ancestors. Abhorring what is called the enlightened state of the age, they carefully preserve hereditary prejudices as a part of their patrimony. The other class, less occupied even by the present than by the future, have a propensity, often ill-judged, for new habits and ideas. When this tendency is allied to the love of solid instruction, restrained and guided by a strong and enlightened reason, its effects become beneficial to society. I knew at Caraccas, among the second generation, several men equally distinguished by their taste for study, the mildness of their manners, and the elevation of their sentiments. I have also known men, who, disdaining all that is excellent in the character, the literature, and the arts of the Spaniards, have lost their national individuality, without having acquired from their connexions with foreigners any just ideas of the real bases of happiness and social order. . . .

Men take a pleasure at Cumana, and in other commercial towns of Terra Firme, in exaggerating the pretensions to nobility of the most illustrious families of Caraccas, known by the name of *los Mantuanos.* I am ignorant in what manner these pretensions were formerly manifested; but it appeared to me, that the progress of knowledge, and the changes effected in manners, have gradually and pretty generally destroyed whatever is offensive in those distinctions among the Whites. . . .

But it is not only the progress of ideas, and the conflict between two classes of different origin [descendants of the conquerors and more recent immigrants] which have induced the privileged castes to abandon their pretensions, or at least to conceal them carefully. Aristocracy in the Spanish colonies has a counterpoise of another kind, and of which the action becomes every day more powerful. A sentiment of equality among the Whites has penetrated every bosom. Wherever men of colour are either considered as slaves or as having been enfranchised, what constitutes nobility is hereditary liberty, is the proud boast of having never reckoned among ancestors any but freemen. In the colonies, the colour of the skin is the real badge of nobility. In Mexico, as well as in Peru, at Caraccas as in the island of Cuba, a barefooted fellow is often heard exclaiming: "Does that rich white man think himself whiter than I am?"

26

Creole Patriotism

D. A. Brading

The revolutions for independence in Spanish America are not normally described as national liberation movements. This is partly because political rhetoric and the historian's idiom are subject to fashion and change, partly because Spanish American nationalism itself has not been recognized in its early manifestations. Had the kind of colonial self-consciousness that made North Americans in the eighteenth century begin to think of themselves as a separate people also been growing in Spanish America? Were the demands of the creoles for political and economic power part of an awareness of their own identity as Americans, distinct from that of Spaniards? Were the revolutions genuinely nationalist movements, which, although stimulated by external forces, had roots in their own American past? If so, what were the sources of American nationalism? One of the historians who have explored this question is David Brading, who places ideology high in the motivation of the insurgent leadership, and here introduces examples of Mexican patriots and the ideas that inspired them.

That the course of Mexican Independence should have been influenced by so archaic a set of ideas as Creole patriotism is something of a puzzle. Certainly readers of Alexander von Humboldt's *Political Essay on the Kingdom of New Spain*, which emphasised both the extraordinary wealth and recent scientific advance of the country, might well have expected as smooth a transition to home rule as occurred in Brazil, where the Crown Prince simply proclaimed himself Emperor. Of all the viceregal cities, Mexico had most claim to be a true capital, with its principal streets lined with the palaces of an aristocracy with estates

Reprinted from D. A. Brading, *Prophecy and Myth in Mexican History* (Centre of Latin American Studies, University of Cambridge, 1984), pp. 37–44, by permission of the author.

distributed throughout the provinces. The great merchant houses of Mexico City controlled the commercial life of the entire colony. Then again, the Bourbon reforms of the late eighteenth century, had endowed New Spain with all administrative machinery of an absolutist state, including a regular army, 10,000 strong, recruited locally, with officers both European and American Spaniards. Moreover, if Humboldt also drew attention to the endemic rivalry of the Creoles and gachupines, as the Peninsular Spaniards were called, well, this was an ancient dispute. More important perhaps was his comment on the gross disparities in wealth between the elite and the populace, since here were ample grounds for riot or insurrection.

Nevertheless, when in 1808 news first arrived of the Napoleonic invasion of Spain, the chance existed of a peaceful attainment of home rule. The City Council of Mexico, a bastion of the Creole interest, urged the Viceroy to summon a junta representative of the kingdom, in order, so they argued, "to fill immediately the immense gap which now separates the sovereign power from the authorities which govern." With an argument based on the medieval laws of Partida and on natural law texts used in Spanish universities, they declared that with the abdication of the legitimate monarch, Ferdinand VII, sovereignty returned to its original source, the people, with the corollary that the existing bureaucracy had lost its mandate. The key premise here was that New Spain constituted a true kingdom united to Spain by common loyalty to the monarch. In consequence, the City Council further advised the Viceroy to take no cognizance of the self-elected juntas of Seville and Asturias which at this point had sent agents demanding Mexican recognition of their sovereignty. In the event, the colonial bureaucracy took fright and conspired with the merchant guild, then dominated by Peninsular Spaniards, to force the Viceroy to resign, so as to install an officer less open to Creole persuasion. With this single act of violence, any hope of a peaceful solution of the constitutional crisis was lost.

Unlike South America where revolution centred on the capitals, in New Spain the challenge came from the provinces. In 1810 in the intendancy of Guanajuato, a group of country gentry who had planned to mobilize the militia found their movement engulfed by a mass insurrection of the populace led by Miguel Hidalgo, a country vicar of progressive views. In the same way that in Southern Italy and in Spain the Catholic clergy called out the peasantry in campaign against the French and their liberal collaborators, so equally in Mexico a sector of the clergy aroused the populace, Indian and mestizo, across a wide area encompassing the modern states of Jalisco, Michoacán, Guanajuato and Guerrero, in a war to defend religion, asserting that the viceregal authorities planned to betray the country to the French. The religious character of the insurgency was confirmed by the celebration of high mass and *te deums* in the cathedrals of Valladolid and Guadalajara. Nor did the clerical domination of the movement dwindle after the defeat and execution of Hidalgo, since the leader of its second, southern phase, José María Morelos, was also a priest who recruited several other clergymen as his generals. When the Viceroy abolished the immunity from royal courts hitherto enjoyed by the clergy, no matter how criminal or rebellious, one insurgent general, so it is reported, "gave his troops for their banner a great flag with a red cross . . . with the arms of the Church and a motto which said: 'Die for ecclesiastical immunity'." More potent and persuasive as a symbol, however, was the image of Our Lady of Guadalupe which Hidalgo gave his followers, who thereafter marched to the cries of "Long live our Lady of Guadalupe! Long live Ferdinand VII! Death to the Gachupines!"

To grasp the meaning of these slogans, we must turn to Creole patriotism, that complex of themes and emotions which expressed the American Spaniards' quest for a social identity. Already in the late sixteenth century, the sons and grandsons of the first Conquerors and settlers recalled with nostalgia the heroic days of the Conquest and besieged the Crown with demands for appointment to public office. The more intellectual among them, usually clergymen, came to fix upon the Aztec empire as the chief glory of their Mexican *patria*. Behind this return to history lay the bitter grievance that the Creole had been deprived of his rightful inheritance—the government of a kingdom conquered by his ancestors. The Crown's preference for Pensinsular Spaniards in public office was matched by the success of gachupín immigrants who dominated commerce and overtook the Creoles in the pursuit of wealth and position. By the eighteenth century, the rivalry between two halves of the Spanish nation resident in America found expression in wounding stereotypes, the gachupín depicted as an ignorant, avaricious tradesman and the Creole as a well-born wastrel. Resentment in New Spain deepened after 1763 when the ministers of Charles III greatly expanded the colonial bureaucracy while taking explicit measures to reduce Creole participation. The campaign against Church privilege and wealth mainly affected the native-born clergy. At much the same time, the stereotypes of Aztec barbarism and Creole incapacity, objects of controversy for almost two centuries between chroniclers in Spain and Mexico, were now repeated and exaggerated in Europe by Buffon, the Abbé Raynal and the Scottish historian Robertson. It was left to an exiled Mexican Jesuit, Francisco Javier

Clavijero, to defend the Indian from the more gross of these attacks from the Enlightenment, restating in his *Ancient History of Mexico* the traditional Creole insistence on the Aztec empire as an advanced civilisation.

Whereas this emphasis on the Indian past can be encountered in other provinces of the Spanish Empire, in Mexico patriotic sentiment found further focus in the cult of Our Lady of Guadalupe. For the story of the apparition of the Virgin Mary in 1531 to the Indian Juan Diego and the miraculous imprinting of her image on his cape, a painting of the Virgin as an Indian or mestiza, was seized upon by the Creole clergy as the spiritual glory of their patria. Pilgrimage to the sanctuary at Tepeyac, situated on a hill outside Mexico City, grew steadily. In 1747 the dioceses of New Spain acclaimed Our Lady of Guadalupe as their patron and all the provincial capitals built special shrines, often located on their outskirts, in replication of Tepeyac. The story of the apparition came to constitute what students of religion call a foundation myth, since it was now argued that the Mexican Church owed its start, not to the human efforts of the Spanish missionaries, but rather to the intervention of the Virgin Mary. Moreover, the veneration of the image, together with the miracles associated with its cult, entailed a doctrine of election, to the effect that the Mother of God had chosen the people of New Spain for her especial protection. *Non fecit taliter a omni natione* ran the message inscribed on eighteenth century copies of the image. All the ethnic groups of Mexico—Creoles, Indians, mulattoes and mestizos—were united as a single nation subject to the "Our Holy Mother of Guadalupe." When the Insurgency marched under her banner it drew sap from the very taproot of Mexican nationality.

From the very start of his rebellion, Hidalgo claimed to derive his authority from the nation, writing to the local intendant that his movement sought to liberate the Mexicans from the tyranny they had suffered for the three centuries since the Conquest and hence recover the God-given rights of "the Mexican nation." His immediate aim was the expulsion of all gachupines from Mexico. For if the insurgency was inspired by an almost instinctive nationalism, it was fired by a bitter resentment of the Peninsular Spaniards.

The Indians and castas hated the gachupines as grasping tradesmen and hard-handed managers of estates and mines. So deep ran this feeling in Mexico that the historian Justo Sierra later compared it to the popular anti-semitism of Eastern Europe. At the same time, the insurgent attack on the gachupines can be compared to the proscription of the nobility in the French Revolution. For if in France one section of the propertied classes, the bourgeoisie, purchased sans-culotte support by the execution of aristocrats, so similarly in New Spain the Creole clergy and their gentry associates won mestizo and Indian support by encouraging a general assault on the property as well as the persons of the Peninsular Spaniards. Moreover, whereas the traditional Creole plaint had always centred on the question of public office, Hidalgo framed his denunciation in terms carefully attuned to popular grievance, describing the gachupines as "unnatural men, who have broken the closest bonds of blood, abandoning their fathers, brothers, wives and their own children . . . to cross immense oceans. The force behind all their toil is sordid avarice . . . they are Catholics through policy, their true god is Mammon."

The emphasis on the nation was confirmed by an insistence on ethnic equality. From the start Hidalgo abolished the capitation tax paid only by Indians and mulattoes. More positively, Morelos publicly declared: "with the exception of the Europeans, all the population henceforth shall not be named according to their *calidad* (that is to say, by their ethnic quality) as Indians, mulattoes or other castes, but all generally as Americans." At one stroke, he sought to end the entire invidious system whereby the civic rights and fiscal obligations of an individual were immutably defined at birth by inscription in the baptismal registers which were kept for each ethnic group. Characteristically, this demand for ethnic equality took the form of an affirmation of common identity as Mexicans rather than being derived from any declaration of the rights of man. At the same time, Morelos sharply condemned any attempt to convert the insurgency into an attack on the rich or against all whites, insisting that the Creoles had been the first to take up arms in defence of the Indians and the castas. All Americans were brothers in Christ. He concluded: "this equality in *calidad* and liberty is the natural and the divine problem and it is only virtue which should distinguish a man and make him useful to Church and State."

At the Congress of Chilpancingo, held in 1813 to frame a Declaration of Independence, Morelos presented a document called "Sentiments of the Nation" in which after once more insisting on the abolition of ethnic distinctions, he adjured Congress to devise laws "to moderate opulence and poverty" so as to raise the wages of the poor. Needless to say, "Most Holy Mary of Guadalupe" was to be acclaimed as "Patron of our liberty." Equally significant, he proposed that all foreigners, other than a few useful artisans, should be banned from Mexico, with overseas merchants restricted to the ports. In an earlier declaration, he had proffered the archaic image of a republic governed by soldiers and priests, each with their taxes and jurisdiction. This image returned in the clause where Morelos advised that Mexican troops should be forbidden to leave national territory other than to defend the preaching of the gospel to the natives of the north. This emphasis on a confessional republic, insulated from foreign influence, was further reinforced in the Constitutional Decree of Apatzingán, where in addition to the standard declaration of Roman Catholicism as the only true religion, it was laid down that the rights of citizenship would be forfeit by the crimes of heresy and apostasy. Appointed Generalissimo by the Congress, Morelos took the title, "Servant of the Nation," one more reminder of his unique contribution to the Spanish American Revolution.

Unlike the contemporary peasant uprisings in Europe, the Mexican Insurgency possessed its own, highly idiosyncratic ideology, based on Creole patriotism. In 1813 the exiled Dominican, Fray Servando Teresa de Mier, published in London a *History of the Revolution in New Spain anciently known as Anáhuac*, in which after a bitter denunciation of royalist cruelties against the insurgency he formulated arguments for Independence. The old Creole plaint that they were excluded from public office, a denial of their ancestral rights as heirs of the Conquerors, was audaciously reinterpreted as the failure of the Spanish Crown to observe the basic social pact binding the Creoles to the King. This pact, Mier hastened to add, did not refer to the "anti-social contract" of Rousseau, that "web of sophistries" which had led to the French Revolution, but rather denoted "the solemn and explicit pact which the Americans celebrated with the Kings of Spain and is authenticated in the very code of its laws. That is our Magna Carta." At the same time, Mier shifted the claim of ancestral rights, skilfully defining the Creoles as heirs of the mendicant orders which had joined with Bartolomé de Las Casas in his defence of the Indians. The famous New Laws of 1542, which freed the Indian from slavery and labour obligations were presented as New Spain's "fundamental laws or its true constitution. The foundations of the Laws of the Indies were then laid, laws which at best were little more than conclusions taken from the writings of Las Casas." The object of this line of argument was to demonstrate that in no sense could Mexico be described as a colony of Spain. Instead, as the City Council had argued in 1808, it formed a true kingdom, with its own magistrates, courts, universities and laws. At the same time, its constitution had not been respected by the Crown so that New Spain had suffered from an abominable tyranny exercised both by the royal bureaucracy and the mercantile oligarchy.

Coupled with this doctrine of an historic, if unobserved constitution, Mier deployed a bitter line of rhetoric in which he compared the ruthless royalist campaign against Hidalgo and Morelos to the massacres perpetrated by the Spanish Conquerors. Where once Cortés at

Cholula or Alvarado at Tenochtitlan had slaughtered the Indians, so now in Guanajuato and Jalisco Generals Calleja and Cruz executed their insurgent captives. The subsequent promotion of Calleja to viceroy evoked a comparison with the government of the Duke of Alba in the Low Countries. In short, so Mier asserted, the scenes of contemporary cruelty offered sufficient material for a continuation to be written of Las Casas' *Most Brief Account of the Destruction of the Indies*. As part of his polemic against the Spaniards, Mier promoted the publication in London, Philadelphia and Mexico, of no less than three separate editions of this famous tract.

In this use of history as an arsenal of argument for Independence, Mier was joined by Carlos María Bustamante, a lawyer and journalist, who enlisted in the Insurgency under Morelos. Already as editor of the *Diario de México*, he had published materials on Indian history and in the decades after Independence he was to become the chief celebrant of both the Insurgency and the Indian past. In 1813 he wrote the opening speech delivered by Morelos at the Congress of Chilpancingo. It was an extraordinary composition. For after a cursory, almost disdainful mention of the doctrine of the sovereignty of the people, brandished by the Spaniards against the French yet denied to the Americans, the text compared the Mexicans to the people of Israel in Egypt suffering under Pharoah. But now, so it was claimed, God himself had heard their pleas and had decreed their liberation, sending his Spirit to move their hearts and lead them into battle. In an audacious metaphor, the Almighty was compared to the Mexican eagle, protecting his people with both wings and talons. At the same time, independence was presented as an act of restoration: "We are about to re-establish the Mexican empire, improving its government." The continuity between Aztec past and Mexican present was emphasised in the following invocation.

"Spirits of Moctehuzoma, Cacamatzin, Cuauhtimotzin, Xicotencalt and of Catzonzi, as once you celebrated the feast in which you were slaughtered by the treacherous sword of Alvarado, now celebrate this happy moment in which your sons have united to avenge the crimes and outrages committed against you, and to free themselves from the claws of tyranny and fanaticism that were going to grasp them for ever. To the 12th of August of 1521 there succeeds the 14th of September 1813. In that day the chains of our serfdom were fastened in Mexico-Tenochtitlan, in this day in the happy village of Chilpancingo they were broken for ever."

In this speech, written by Bustamante and read by Morelos, we encounter a clear affirmation of a Mexican nation, already in existence before the Conquest, now about to recover its Independence. That its author was himself the son of a Spaniard only serves to highlight the drama of the occasion. Creole patriotism, which began as the articulation of the social identity of American Spaniards, was here transmuted into the insurgent ideology of Mexican nationalism. Hidalgo and Cuauthémoc were thus united in common struggle against the Spanish foe. At the same time, this type of argument allowed the clerical leadership of the insurgency to avoid any emphasis on such doctrines as popular sovereignty and universal human rights. Indeed, the Act of Independence, drafted at Chilpancingo, was an obscurely-worded document, which, after an invocation of Providence and events in Europe as its chief cause, hastened to guarantee the property and privileges of the clergy.

Despite widespread popular support, the Mexican Insurgency was crushed and both Hidalgo and Morelos suffered execution. Confronted by a rebellion which threatened to ravage all landed property, the upper classes rallied to the Crown and a generation of young Creoles hastened to enlist in the royalist army, adopting the ethos and career of the professional soldier. It was these men who in 1821 turned on their royal master, at a time when the Peninsula was caught up in liberal revolution, and achieved Independence with the Plan of Iguala which guaranteed constitutional monarchy, union of American and European Spaniards, and Church privilege. Despite the conservative nature of this revolt, the Act of Independence drew on insurgent ideology, since it proclaimed: "The Mexican nation, which for three hundred years has had neither its own will nor free use of its voice, today leaves the oppression in which it has lived." Moreover, when the leader of the coup, Agustín de Iturbide, proclaimed himself Emperor, former insurgents joined with dissident royalists to overthrow his short-lived regime. At the constituent congress which was summoned to frame a constitution, both Padre Mier and Carlos María de Bustamante played an influential role, obtaining the recognition of Hidalgo and Morelos as the Founding Fathers—*Padres de la Patria*—of Mexico, even if their hopes of re-naming the country Anáhuac were disappointed. But their proposals for a unitary republic with a strong central executive were defeated by a party of liberals who brought in a federal system copied from the Constitution of the United States. In the decades which followed former insurgents, new liberals and professional soldiers disputed for command. The nationalism of the independence era gave way to the clash of liberals and conservatives and was not to be revived, albeit in secular form, until the Revolution.

27

An American's Convictions

Simón Bolívar

Simón Bolívar's celebrated "Answer of a South American to a Gentleman of this Island," usually known as "The Jamaica Letter," was dated from Kingston on 6 September 1815 and addressed to a Mr. Henry Cullen of Falmouth, Jamaica. Bolívar was writing in exile, defeated by the Spaniards, repudiated by his own people, and living in circumstances of personal and public poverty. The Jamaica Letter is important for three reasons. First, it is a guide to Bolívar's political thought and to its sources in classical and Enlightenment literature. Second, it is a realistic appraisal of the state of the Spanish American revolution and its future prospects. Third, it is a statement of republican identity and national aspirations from a revolutionary who had already defined his campaign as a war to the death between Americans and Spaniards. Bolívar discusses the great questions of nationality, its components, its origins, and its expression in forms of government; and he poses the dilemma between indigenous and creole traditions.

Success will crown our efforts, because the destiny of America has been irrevocably decided. The tie that bound her to Spain has been severed; only the force of opinion maintained that tie and kept the parts of that immense monarchy together. But that which formerly bound them now divides them. The hatred that the Peninsula has inspired in us is greater than the ocean which separates us. It would be less difficult to unite the two continents than to reconcile the spirits of the two countries. The habit of obedience; a community of interest, knowledge, and religion; mutual good will; affection for the birthplace and glory of our forefathers; in short, everything that in-

Translated by John Lynch from Simón Bolívar, "Contestación de un americano meridional a un caballero de esta isla," Kingston, setiembre 6 de 1815, Sociedad Bolivariana de Venezuela, *Escritos del Libertador*, VIII (Caracas, 1972), 222–48.

spired our hopes came to us from Spain. As a result there was born a
principle of loyalty that seemed eternal, in spite of the conduct of our
rulers which weakened that sympathy or, rather, that bond imposed
by their domination. At present the opposite is true. Death, dishonor,
and every harm threaten us and cause us to live in fear; there is
nothing we have not suffered at the hands of that unnatural step-
mother. The veil has been torn aside. We have now seen the light, yet
they want to return us to darkness. Our chains have been broken and
we have been freed; yet our enemies seek to enslave us again. For this
reason America fights desperately, and seldom has desperation failed
to achieve victory.

Because successes have been partial and spasmodic, we must not lose
faith. In some places the fighters for independence triumph, while in
others the tyrants have the advantage. What is the final result? Is not
the entire New World in motion, armed for defense? We have only to
look around to witness a simultaneous struggle all over this immense
hemisphere.

The fighting in the River Plate provinces has freed that territory and
led their victorious armies to Upper Peru, arousing Arequipa and
alarming the royalists in Lima. Nearly one million inhabitants there
now enjoy liberty.

The kingdom of Chile, populated by 800,000 souls, is fighting the
enemy who seeks to subdue her; but seeks in vain, because those who
long ago put an end to their conquests, the free and indomitable Arau-
canians, are neighbors and compatriots of those fighting in Chile, and
their sublime example is proof enough that a people who love independence will eventually achieve it.

The viceroyalty of Peru, whose population reaches a million and a
half inhabitants, is without doubt the most submissive and is forced to
make the most sacrifices for the royal cause; and, although the possibility of cooperating with that part of America may be remote, the fact
remains that it is not tranquil, nor is it capable of resisting the torrent
that threatens most of its provinces.

New Granada, which may be considered the heart of America, obeys
a general government, save for the territory of Quito which is held only
with the greatest difficulty by its enemies, as it is strongly devoted to
the country's cause; and the provinces of Panama and Santa Marta
suffer, not without pain, the tyranny of their masters. Two and a half
million people inhabit New Granada, and they are actually defending
that territory against the Spanish army under General Morillo, who
will probably suffer defeat at the impregnable fortress of Cartagena.
But should he take that city, it will be at the price of heavy losses, and

he will then lack sufficient forces to subdue the long-suffering and brave inhabitants of the interior.

As for the heroic and unhappy Venezuela, events there have moved so rapidly and the devastation has been so great that it has been reduced virtually to utter destitution and terrible desolation, although it was once among the finest countries that were the pride of America. Its tyrants govern a desert, and all they have left to oppress are the unfortunate survivors who, having escaped death, maintain a precarious existence. A few women, children, and old people are all that remain. Most of the men have perished rather than be slaves; those who survive fight on furiously in the countryside and towns of the interior, determined either to die or drive into the sea the insatiable agents of blood and crimes, rivals of those first monsters who wiped out America's primitive race. Nearly a million people were reckoned to live in Venezuela, and it is no exaggeration to say that a quarter of these have succumbed either to the earthquake, sword, hunger, plague, or flight, all except the earthquake consequences of the war.

New Spain, including Guatemala, had 7,800,000 inhabitants in 1808, according to Baron von Humboldt. Since that time, the insurrection, which has disturbed virtually all of her provinces, has appreciably reduced that apparently correct figure, for over a million men have perished, as you can seen in the report of Mr. Walton, who faithfully describes the bloody crimes committed in that rich empire. There the struggle continues by dint of human and every other type of sacrifice, for the Spaniards spare nothing that might enable them to subjugate those who have had the misfortune of being born on that soil, which appears destined to be steeped in the blood of its offspring. In spite of everything, the Mexicans will be free, for they have embraced their country's cause, resolved to avenge their forefathers or follow them to the grave. Already they say with Raynal: The time has come at last to repay the Spaniards torture for torture and to drown that race of exterminators in its own blood or in the sea.

The islands of Puerto Rico and Cuba, with a combined population of some 700,000 to 800,000 souls, are the most tranquil possessions of the Spaniards, because they are beyond range of contact with the fighters for independence. But are not the people of those islands Americans? Are they not oppressed? Do they not desire their own happiness?

This picture represents an area of military operations of 2,000 longitudinal and 900 latitudinal leagues at its greatest point, in which 16,000,000 Americans defend their rights or suffer oppression at the hands of Spain, once the world's greatest empire but now too weak to rule the new hemisphere or even to maintain herself in the old. And shall Europe, the civilized, the merchant, the lover of liberty, allow an aged serpent to devour the fairest part of our globe, simply to satisfy its venomous rage? Is Europe deaf to the clamor of her own interests? Has she no eyes to see justice? Has she grown so hardened as to become insensible? The more I consider these questions, the more they confuse me. I am led to think that they want America to disappear; but that is impossible because all Europe is not Spain. What madness for our enemy to hope to reconquer America without a navy, without funds, and almost without troops! Those which she has are barely adequate to enforce obedience on her own people and maintain defense against her neighbors. Moreover, can that nation monopolize the commerce of half the world when it lacks manufactures, agricultural products, crafts and sciences, and even a policy? Assume that this mad venture were successful, and further assume that pacification followed, would not the sons of present-day Americans, together with the sons of the European reconquerors, develop in twenty years time the same patriotic objectives that are now being fought for?

Europe would do Spain a service by dissuading her from her obstinate folly, thereby at least saving her the costs she is incurring and the blood she is shedding. And if Spain will confine her attention to her own country she can build her prosperity and power upon more solid foundations than doubtful conquests, precarious commerce, and forced exactions on distant, hostile, and powerful peoples. Europe itself, as a matter of sound policy, should have prepared and accomplished the project of American independence, not only because the world balance of power demands it, but also because this is the legitimate and certain means of acquiring overseas commercial establishments. A Europe that is not moved by the violent passions of vengeance, ambition, and greed, as is Spain, would seem to be entitled by all the rules of equity to teach Spain where her best interests lie.

All those writers who have treated the subject agree on this point. Consequently, we have had reason to hope that the civilized nations would hasten to our aid to enable us to gain that good which would be advantageous to both hemispheres. How vain have been these hopes! Not only the Europeans but even our brothers of the North have been passive spectators of this struggle which, by its very essence, is the most just, and in its results the most noble and significant of any that have been sustained in ancient or modern times. Indeed, can the far-reaching effects of freedom for the hemisphere of Columbus ever be calculated? . . .

It is even more difficult to foresee the future fate of the New World, to determine its political principles, or to prophesy the nature of the government it will adopt. Every idea concerning the future of this country seems to me to be risky speculation. When mankind was in its infancy, sunk in uncertainty, ignorance, and error, was it possible to foresee what system it would adopt for its preservation? Who would dare to say that one nation would be a republic, another a monarchy, one nation great, another small? As I see it, this is our own situation. We are a young people. We inhabit a world apart, encircled by vast seas. We are novices in almost all the arts and sciences, although in a sense we are old in the ways of civil society. I look upon the present state of America as similar to that of Rome after its fall, when each part adopted a political system conforming to its interest and situation or was led by the individual ambitions of particular chiefs, families, or groups. With this important difference: those separate parts later reestablished their ancient nations, subject to the changes imposed by conditions or events. But we hardly retain a vestige of our former state; moreover, we are neither Indians nor Europeans, but a species midway between the legitimate proprietors of the country and the Spanish usurpers. In short, Americans by birth, we derive our rights from Europe, and we have to assert these rights against the rights of the natives, and at the same time defend ourselves against the hostility of the invaders. This places us in a most extraordinary and complicated position. Despite the element of guesswork in attempting to predict the political course of America, I shall hazard some conjectures which, of course, represent personal opinions, and are dictated by rational desires rather than reasoned calculations.

The role of the inhabitants of the American hemisphere has been for centuries purely passive. Politically they were nonexistent. We were in a position even lower than slavery, and therefore it was more difficult for us to rise to the enjoyment of freedom. Allow me these observations in order to establish the question. States are slaves either through the nature of their constitution or through its abuse. A people is therefore enslaved when the government, by its nature or its vices, encroaches on and usurps the rights of the citizen or subject. Applying these principles, we find that America was denied not only its freedom but even an active and dominant tyranny. Let me explain. In absolutist regimes there are no recognized limits to the exercise of the powers of government. The will of the great sultan, khan, bey, and other despotic rulers is the supreme law, applied more or less arbitrarily by the minor pashas, khans, and satraps of Turkey and Persia, who have an organized system of oppression in which subjects participate according to the authority vested in them. To them is entrusted the administration of civil, military, political, fiscal, and religious matters. But, in the final analysis, the rulers of Ispahan are Persians; the viziers of the Grand Turk are Turks; and the sultans of Tartary are Tartars. China does not seek its military and civilian leaders from the land of Genghis Khan, her conqueror, in spite of the fact that the Chinese of today are the direct descendants of those who were subjugated by the ancestors of the present-day Tartars.

How different is our situation! We have been oppressed by a system that has not only deprived us of our rights but has kept us in a state of permanent infancy with regard to public affairs. If we could at least have managed our domestic concerns and our internal administration, we could have learned the process and mechanics of government; we would also have enjoyed a personal standing, thereby commanding a certain automatic respect from the people, which is so necessary to preserve amidst revolutions. That is why I say we were even deprived of an active tyranny, as we were not permitted to exercise its functions.

Americans, under the existing Spanish system and perhaps to a greater extent than ever before, occupy a position in society no better than that of serfs suitable for labor, or at best that of mere consumers. Yet even this status is subject to irksome restrictions, such as the prohibition against the cultivation of European crops, the existence of royal monopolies, the ban on factories that the Peninsula itself does not possess, the exclusive trading privileges even in articles of prime necessity, and the barriers between American provinces designed to prevent mutual trade, enterprise, and understanding. In short, do you wish to know what our future was?—to cultivate fields of indigo, grain, coffee, sugar cane, cacao, and cotton; to raise cattle on the empty plains; to hunt wild beasts in the wilderness; to mine the earth for gold to satisfy the insatiable greed of Spain.

So negative was our condition that I can find nothing comparable in any other civilized society, examine as I may the history and politics of all nations. Is it not an outrage and a violation of human rights to expect a land so happily endowed, so vast, rich, and populous, to remain merely passive?

As I have just explained, we were cut off and virtually removed from the world as far as knowledge of government and administration of the state were concerned. We were never viceroys or governors, save in exceptional circumstances; seldom archbishops and bishops; diplomats never; as soldiers, only subordinates; nobles, without real privileges. In brief, we were neither magistrates nor financiers and seldom merchants—all in direct contravention of our institutions.

The Emperor Charles V made a pact with the discoverers, conquerors, and settlers of America, and this, as Guerra puts it, is our social contract.[1] The monarchs of Spain made a solemn agreement with them, that they were to act on their own account and at their own risk, and they were prohibited from making any charge on the royal treasury. In return, they were granted the right to be lords of the land, to organize the administration and to exercise appellate jurisdiction, together with many other immunities and privileges too extensive to list. The King undertook never to alienate the American provinces, for he had no jurisdiction over them other than that of ultimate sovereignty, while the conquerors possessed what amounted to feudal holdings for themselves and their descendants. At the same time there are explicit laws favoring almost exclusively the natives of the country who are of Spanish extraction in appointments to civil, ecclesiastical, and financial offices. Thus, in open violation of the laws and the existing agreements, those born in America have been despoiled of the constitutional rights embodied in their code.

From what I have said it is easy to deduce that America was not prepared for secession from the metropolis; secession was suddenly brought about by the effect of the unlawful concessions of Bayonne and the unjust war that the Regency declared on us, lacking as it did any legal right or legitimacy to do so. . . .

The Americans have risen rapidly without previous knowledge and, what is worse, without previous experience of public affairs, to enact upon the world stage the eminent roles of legislators, magistrates, administrators of the treasury, diplomats, generals, and every position of authority, supreme and subordinate, that comprises the hierarchy of a fully established state.

When the French eagles, stopped only by the walls of Cádiz, routed the fragile governments of the Peninsula, we were left orphans. Before that we had been left to the mercy of a foreign usurper. Now we were deceived with promises of our due rights and flattered with false hopes. Finally, uncertain of our future destiny, and facing anarchy for want of a legitimate, just, and liberal government, we cast ourselves into the chaos of revolution. Our first thought was to establish internal security against the enemies within, and then we sought our external security. Authorities were set up to replace those we had deposed, and these were empowered to direct the course of our revolution and to take advantage of the favorable opportunity which would enable us to establish a constitutional government worthy of our century and adequate to our situation.

The first step taken by all the new governments was to establish popular juntas. These promptly made rules for summoning congresses, which in turn produced great changes. Venezuela set up a democratic and federal government, after declaring the rights of man, providing for a balance of powers, and passing general laws in favor of the liberty of the subject, of the press, and other liberties. Finally, an independent government was constituted. New Granada followed the same political institutions and reforms introduced by Venezuela, taking as the fundamental basis of its constitution the most exaggerated federal system the world has ever seen; recently the central executive power has been strengthened and has received the authority it requires. I understand that Buenos Aires and Chile have followed the same course; but in view of the great distance, scarcity of information, and lack of reliable news, I shall not even attempt to sketch their progress. Events in Mexico, too, have been so varied, complex, rapid, and unhappy that it is impossible to follow clearly the course of that revolution. . . .

Events in Tierra Firme have proved that wholly representative institutions are not suited to our character, customs, and present knowledge. In Caracas the spirit of party arose in the societies, assemblies, and popular elections; and parties led us back into slavery. Thus, while Venezuela has been the American republic with the most advanced political institutions, it has also been the clearest example of the unsuitability of the democratic and federal system for our newborn states. In New Granada, the excessive powers of the provincial governments and the lack of centralization in the federal government have reduced that fair country to its present state. For this reason its enemies, though weak, have been able to hold out against all expectations. As long as our countrymen do not acquire the political talents and virtues that distinguish our brothers of the north, wholly popular systems, far from working to our advantage, will, I greatly fear, come to be our ruin. Unfortunately, these qualities seem to be beyond our reach in the degree to which they are required. On the contrary, we are dominated by the vices contracted under the rule of Spain, a nation which has only distinguished itself in ferocity, ambition, vengeance, and greed.

It is harder, Montesquieu has written, to free a nation from slavery than to enslave a free nation. This truth is confirmed by the annals of all times, which show that most free nations have been put under the yoke, but very few enslaved nations have recovered their liberty. In spite of this lesson, South Americans have endeavored to obtain liberal, even perfect institutions, doubtless out of that universal human instinct to seek the greatest possible happiness; and this is bound to follow in civil societies founded on the principles of justice, liberty, and equality. But are we capable of maintaining in proper balance the difficult management of a republic? Is it conceivable that a people just released from its chains can soar to the heights of liberty without, like

Icarus, melting its wings and falling into the abyss? Such a marvel is inconceivable and without precedent, and lies beyond all reasonable hopes.

More than anyone, I desire to see the greatest nation in the world created in America, greatest not so much by its size and wealth as by its freedom and glory. Although I seek perfection for the government of my country, I cannot persuade myself that the New World can, at the moment, be organized as one great republic. Because it is impossible, I dare not desire it; much less do I desire to have a universal monarchy in America, because this plan is not only inappropriate but also impossible. Present wrongs would not be righted, and our emancipation would be fruitless. The American states need the care of paternal governments to heal the sores and wounds of despotism and war. The metropolis, for example, might be Mexico, the only country qualified for the position by her intrinsic power, without which there can be no metropolis. Let us assume the isthmus of Panama were the central point of this vast continent. Would not all the parts continue in their lethargy and even in their present disorder? For a single government to infuse life into the New World, to mobilize all the means to public prosperity, to improve, educate, and perfect the New World, that government would need the powers of a god, or at least the knowledge and virtues of all mankind.

The spirit of party which now afflicts our states would then burn with greater fury, for want of a sufficient power to restrain it. Moreover, the lords of the chief cities would not allow the preponderance of those of the metropolis, whom they would regard as so many tyrants, and their jealousy would be such as to compare them even with the hated Spaniards. In short, such a monarchy would be like a monstrous colossus, which would collapse under its own weight at the slightest convulsion.

Mr. de Pradt has wisely divided America into fifteen or seventeen independent states, governed by as many monarchs. I agree with the first suggestion, as America can well tolerate seventeen nations; on the second, though it could easily be achieved, it would not be appropriate, and so I am not in favor of American monarchies. My reasons are these: the accepted interest of a republic is limited to its preservation, prosperity, and glory. As they are opposed to imperial rule, republicans have no cause to expand the boundaries of their nation to the detriment of their own resources, simply to force their neighbors to share a liberal constitution. They would acquire no rights or advantages by conquering their neighbors, unless they were to make them colonies, conquests, or allies, after the example of Rome. Such ideas and examples are directly opposed to the principles of justice common to republican systems; and, what is more, they are directly opposed to the interests of their citizens, because a state that is too large in itself or in conjunction with its dependencies, finally falls into decay. Its free government is transformed into tyranny; it neglects the principles that should preserve it and ultimately becomes a despotism. The distinctive feature of small republics is permanence: that of large republics is change, but always with a tendency towards empire. Almost all small republics have had long lives. Among the larger republics, only Rome lasted for several centuries, for its capital was a republic, unlike the rest of its dominions which were governed by various laws and institutions.

The policy of a king is very different. His constant desire is to increase his possessions, wealth, and powers; understandably, for his authority grows with these acquisitions, both over his neighbors and over his own vassals, who fear him because his power is as formidable as his empire, and this is maintained by war and conquest. For these reasons I think that Americans, being anxious for peace, science, art, commerce, and agriculture, would prefer republics to kingdoms. And these desires, I think, conform with the aims of Europe.

Among the popular and representative systems, I do not favor the federal system, for it is too perfect and demands political virtues and talents far superior to our own. For the same reason I reject a monarchy that is a mixture of aristocracy and democracy, although such a government has brought great fortune and splendor to England. Because, between republics and monarchies, it is not possible for us to chose the most perfect and complete form of government, let us at least avoid falling into demagogic anarchy or monocratic tyranny. Let us seek a mean between these extremes, which would only wreck us on the reefs of misfortune and dishonor. As I consider the future destiny of America, I venture to say, let us not adopt the best system of government, but the one that is most viable. . . .

The American provinces are fighting for their emancipation, and they will ultimately succeed; this much we can conclude. Some provinces will duly form federal and some centralist republics; the larger areas will almost inevitably establish monarchies, some of which will fail so badly that they will disintegrate in either immediate or future revolutions. To consolidate a great monarchy will not be easy, but to consolidate a great republic will be impossible.

It is a grandiose idea to think of making the New World into a single nation, with a single bond to unite the parts with the whole. It is argued that as it has a common origin, language, customs, and religion, it ought therefore to have a single government which would bring its different component states into confederation. But this is not possible, for America is divided by climate, geography, interests, and character. How sublime it would be if the Isthmus of Panama could be for us what the Isthmus of Corinth was for the Greeks! I hope that one day we may be fortunate enough to assemble there an august congress of representatives of the republics, kingdoms, and empires, to deliberate upon the high issues of peace and war with the nations of the other three parts of the world. This type of organization may come to pass in some happier period of our emancipation. But any other project, comparable to that of Abbé St. Pierre who dreamed of a European congress to decide the fate and interests of those nations, would be ill-founded.

"Great and salutary changes," you say, "can frequently be brought about through the efforts of individuals." The South Americans have a tradition that when Quetzalcoatl, the Hermes or Buddha of South America, gave up his rule and left his people, he promised them he would return at a chosen time to reestablish his government and restore their prosperity. Does not this tradition encourage a conviction that he may shortly return? Can you imagine the effect if an individual were to appear among these people, revealing the features of Quetzalcoatl, their Buddha of the forest, or those of Mercury, of whom other nations have spoken? Do you suppose that this would attract all regions of America? Is not unity the greatest prerequisite to enable them to expel the Spaniards, their troops, and the supporters of corrupt Spain, and to establish a powerful empire with a free government and benevolent laws?

Like you, I believe that individual actions can produce general results, especially in revolutions. But is that hero, that great prophet or God of Anáhuac, Quetzalcoatl, capable of producing the prodigious advantages that you suggest? This figure is hardly known to the Mexican people, least of all as a benefactor: such is the fate of the defeated, even if they are gods. It is only the historians and writers who have undertaken a careful investigation of his origin, the truth or falsity of his teaching, his prophecies, and the account of his departure from Mexico. Whether he was an apostle of Christ or a pagan is openly debated. Some associate his name with St. Thomas; others with the Feathered Serpent; while still others say he is the famous prophet of Yucatán, Chilan-Cambal. In a word, most Mexican authors, polemicists, and secular historians have discussed, at greater or lesser length, the question of the true character of Quetzalcoatl. The fact is, according to Acosta, that he established a religion that, in its rites, dogmas, and mysteries, bore a remarkable similarity to the religion of Jesus, which it probably most resembles. Nevertheless, many Catholic writers have sought to dismiss the idea that he was a true prophet, and they refuse to associate him with St. Thomas, as other celebrated authors have done. The general opinion is that Quetzalcoatl was a divine lawmaker among the pagan peoples of Anáhuac; that their great Montezuma was his lieutenant, deriving his authority from that source. Hence it may be inferred that our Mexicans would not follow the pagan Quetzalcoatl, however familiar and favorable an identity he might have, for they profess the most intolerant and exclusive of all religions.

Happily the leaders of Mexican independence have made use of this fanaticism to good effect, by proclaiming the famous Virgin of Guadalupe the queen of the patriots, invoking her name in all difficult circumstances, and placing her image on their banners. In this way political enthusiasm has fused with religion to produce an immense fervor for the sacred cause of liberty. The veneration of this image in Mexico is far greater than the passion that the wisest prophet could inspire.

Unity is surely what we need to complete the work of our emancipation. The division among us, however, is not surprising, for it is characteristic of civil wars to form two parties, conservatives and reformers. The former are usually the more numerous, because the force of habit induces obedience to the established order; the latter are always fewer in number although more vocal and enlightened. Thus, weight of numbers is counterbalanced by moral force; the conflict is prolonged, and the results are uncertain. Fortunately, in our case, numbers have followed intelligence.

I shall tell you what we need in order to expel the Spaniards and to found a free government. It is unity, certainly; but such unity will only come about through sensible planning and effective actions, not through divine intervention. America stands together because it is abandoned by all other nations. It is isolated in the world, bereft of diplomatic relations and military support, and exposed to attack by Spain, which has more military resources than we can possibly acquire clandestinely.

When the outcome is not assured, when the state is weak and success remote, all men hesitate and opinion is divided; passions rage, stirred up by the enemy for an easy victory. As soon as we are strong, under the patronage of a liberal nation that will lend us its protection, we will reach agreement in cultivating the virtues and talents that lead to glory. Then will we nobly march towards that great prosperity for which South America is destined. Then will the sciences and the arts, which originated in the East and have enlightened Europe, take wing towards a free Colombia and a welcoming home. These, Sir, are the thoughts and observations that I have the honor to submit to you, so that you may accept or reject them according to their merit. I beg you to understand that I have ventured to explain them because I do not wish to appear discourteous rather than because I consider myself competent to enlighten you on these matters.

I am, etc.   Bolívar

28

The Cause of the Revolutions

Lucas Alamán

As can be seen from the previous texts, tension between creoles and peninsulares underlay many of the problems of colonial government. The antipathy between the two groups was fed from numerous sources and took various forms. Some historians have emphasized the resentment of creoles at their exclusion from the highest offices and have seen independence as the struggle of the creoles to gain political power commensurate with their economic position. Others have drawn attention to the practical exclusion of creoles from the transatlantic, as distinct from regional, trade. Yet others have underlined the basic difference in character and interests between creoles and Spaniards, and the awareness among creoles of a distinct identity and a sense of nationality. Recent historians, or some of them, have argued that the function of colonial elites as economic entrepreneurs investing in agriculture, mining, and trade tended to fuse the peninsular and creole sectors; linked groups of landed, merchant, and bureaucratic oligarchies brought peninsulares and creoles together as a white ruling class confronting the popular masses below them. Yet the fact of division remains: Creoles were aware of status, resented discrimination, and retained ambitions. The following evidence is persuasive, as it comes from a source by no means unsympathetic to Spain. Lucas Alamán (1792–1853) was the son of an immigrant merchant who describes the Spaniards and creoles of that time as he remembered them. He respected Spanish values and admired the colonial legacy left by Spain; although he eventually accepted independence, he deplored the violence and liberalism that accompanied it. Historian as well as statesman, Alamán presented the conservative version of the revolution and the republic in his *Historia de Méjico*, a brilliant exercise in the writ-

Translated by John Lynch from Lucas Alamán, *Historia de Méjico* (5 vols., Mexico, 1849–52), I, 8–20.

ing of contemporary history which he published in 1849–1852. There are two questions to ask of Alamán's interpretation. (1) Were there not exceptions to his picture of the feckless creole? (2) Are alleged character defects an adequate explanation of creole inferiority, rather than political discrimination and economic adversity? Alamán is aware of these problems: He admits the possibility of exceptions, and further suggests that creoles were better educated than peninsulares, which made them all the more dangerous. Above all, he recognizes the existence of discrimination and consequent grievance: In fact, it is the "cause" of independence.

The number of European-born Spaniards residing in New Spain in 1808 was calculated at 70,000.[1] They occupied all the principal appointments in the administration, the Church, the judiciary, and the army; they virtually monopolized trade, and they possessed great wealth consisting of capital placed in various investments, and of estates and properties of all kinds. Those who did not come to take up offices generally left home very young, the sons of poor but honest families, especially from the Basque provinces and the mountains of Santander, and they were usually of good habits. As their ambition was to make a fortune, they were ready to go out and look for it and to take any kind of productive work, undaunted by distance, danger, or climate. Some came here to enter service in the house of a relative or friend of the family; others found a job with their countrymen. All became dependants, subject to severe discipline, and from the very beginning they learned to regard work and thrift as the only road to wealth. Life was more relaxed in Mexico City and Veracruz, but in all the cities of the interior, no matter how rich and populous, the dependants of each household were held to a very strict system and an almost monastic regime. This type of Spartan upbringing made of the Spaniards residing in America a breed of men unknown in Spain itself and not seen since in America.

As they advanced in fortune or gained in merit, they usually married a daughter of the house, especially if they were relatives, or they set up on their own account and married creole women, for there were very few Spanish women, and these were usually wives of officials. With wealth and relatives among the respectable families of each place came social esteem, municipal offices, and influence, which sometimes degenerated into absolute preponderance. Once they were established in this way, the Spaniards never thought of returning to their country, for they were convinced that their only career lay in advancing their interests, improving their place of residence, and securing the comfort and honor of their family. This meant that for every Spaniard who became rich there was some advantage to the country, a wealthy family took root, or alternatively pious and charitable foundations were established to shelter orphans and help the needy and destitute, of whom there are numerous cases in Mexico City. These fortunes were founded on strenuous efforts in agriculture, long involvement in trade, or the more risky work of mining; and although such occupations did not normally open the way to instant wealth, they helped to create a culture of thrift, and families learned to live carefully, without luxury in furniture or dress. In this way a number of medium-sized fortunes were created, which were to be found in all the towns, even in smaller places; yet carefulness with money did not prevent acts of generosity on occasions of public disasters or when the needs of the state required it, which as is well known they frequently did.

The creoles rarely kept to the thrifty ways of their parents or followed the profession that had made their fathers rich; as for the fathers, amidst the comforts that their incomes guaranteed, they did not subject their own sons to the severe discipline in which they themselves had been reared. Anxious to give them a more distinguished education and one suitable to their place in society, they entered them for studies leading to the Church or the law, or else they allowed them to waste their lives in idleness and dissipation . . . an upbringing that had perverse results. While the European dependants married to the master's daughter carried on the business of the house and came to be the support of the family, increasing the portion of the inheritance that had come to the wife, the creole sons squandered their inheritance in a few years and were left ruined and destitute, trying to find an easy job in an office and a mere subsistence, instead of securing an independent existence through an active and hardworking life. The literary education that they were sometimes given and the appearance of gentlemen that they acquired in living like the idle rich caused them to despise the Europeans as mean and greedy when they were simply thrifty and hardworking; and they regarded the Europeans as inferior to themselves because they engaged in trade and professions that they regarded as unworthy of the class to which, by the same means, their fathers had raised them.

Whether from the effects of this depraved education, or from the influence of a climate that leads to profligacy and soft living, the creoles were usually lazy and negligent. They were clever and talented but rarely given to sound and considered judgement, quick to learn but ill-prepared to execute, living for today and never thinking of tomorrow, extravagant in good times and resigned in adversity. The result of these baneful tendencies was that wealth was short-lived, and the efforts of

the Europeans in working to make their fortunes and leave them to
their children could be compared to the bottomless pit of the Danaides,
which was never filled no matter how much was cast into it. To continue in wealth and prosperity, therefore, the Spanish race in America
needed constantly to renew itself with further European families, as
those formed by their predecessors fell into obscurity and poverty.

By law there was no difference between these two classes of Spaniards, including even mestizos born to each of Indian mothers, but
there was a difference in fact, and from this stemmed an open rivalry
between the two; although this was long dormant, there was a danger
that it would erupt, with fatal consequences, when the occasion presented itself. As has been seen, the Europeans held all the senior appointments, partly because this was Spanish policy, partly because
they were better placed to seek and obtain them, as they lived near the
source of all favors.[2] The creoles rarely obtained appointments, and
then only in exceptional circumstances, or when they went to court to
apply for them; and although they held all the minor offices, which
were the more numerous, this simply aroused their real ambition,
which was to occupy all the senior posts. In the first two centuries after
the conquest an ecclesiastical career had offered greater advancement
to Americans, and many of them obtained bishoprics, canonries, university chairs, and rich benefices.[3] But these favors were reduced, and
in spite of a royal order that they should occupy half of all cathedral
canonries, following the representation made by the city council of
Mexico on 2 May 1792, the suggestion of archbishop Alonso Núñez de
Haro prevailed and they were confined to inferior appointments, to
keep them a state of subordination. In 1808 all but one of the bishoprics
of New Spain, most of the canonries, and many of the richest parishes
were in the hands of Europeans. They also prevailed in the religious
orders, though to avoid disturbances arising from rivalry between Europeans and creoles some orders had established a rule of *alternativa*,
whereby a European was elected in one election and a creole in the
next. . . . This preference shown to Europeans in administrative appointments and ecclesiastical benefices has been the principal reason
for rivalry between the two classes. Add to this the fact that Europeans,
as we have seen, possessed great wealth, the just reward of their work
and application but one that aroused the envy of Americans who regarded it as yet further evidence of encroachment; that Europeans with
their power and wealth were sometimes more favored by the fair sex
and secured more advantageous marriages; and that for all these reasons together they had obtained a decided preponderance over those
born in the country, then it will not be difficult to account for the

increasing jealousy and rivalry between Europeans and creoles, which ended in mortal hatred and hostility.

All these generalizations I have made on the character of European and American Spaniards obviously admit exceptions. There were many Americans whose application and prudence exempted them from the defects of their class. In the discharge of such offices as they obtained, there were numerous American prelates distinguished for their zeal and virtues; in the judiciary many magistrates of integrity and knowledge; and in public appointments many reputable officials. At the same time there were many Europeans, especially those from the southern provinces of Spain, whose conduct was out of character with the industry and frugality of their countrymen, and the expression "an incorrigible gachupin" came to mean the epitome of all the vices, which at times drove them into the most dreadful crimes.

In the years immediately following the conquest, many Spanish women came to America; some were wives of the conquerors, others sought more favorable marriages than they could hope for in Spain, considering their modest incomes. Many of these were from very distinguished families, including the daughters of Leonel de Cervantes, *comendador* of the Order of Santiago, from whom descended some of the leading families of Mexico, and including too those brought to Guatemala by Doña Beatriz de la Cueva, of the family of the dukes of Alburquerque, when she came as wife of D. Pedro de Alvarado. But in the course of time Spanish women stopped coming to America, except as wives of officials and there were very few of these. Thus all the white women in New Spain were of the creole class. These did not share the defects of their brothers, and it came to be a well-known fact that in America the women were worth more than the men. Allowing for exceptions to all generalizations, and especially for life in the capital and some other large cities where lax behavior was quite common, it must be acknowledged that middle-income families in the provinces were models of respectability; their creole women were loving wives, good mothers, modest, hardworking and kind, and the only defect they could be charged with was that their very kindness served to encourage the ruinous ways of their sons.

The few descendants of the conquerors who still remained and others who derived a distinguished origin from families who were distinguished in Spain, together with senior officials and wealthy people who had obtained a title or order, or acquired a municipal office in perpetuity, these formed a nobility, indistinguishable from the rest of the Spanish class except for their wealth, and when this was exhausted they fell once more into the common class. Even in their decline, however, they preserved certain privileges, because it was essential to belong to this class to be admitted to the clergy, to the status of the *fuero*, and to the militia. All those who acquired wealth belonged to this class, for everyone wanted to pass for Spaniards and nobles. They were distinguished from the rest of the population by their dress, all of them being more or less well dressed, while the people in general were not so. Thus they became known by the name of *gente decente*, and this rather than birth was the distinctive character attributed to them. The main ambition of those who made a fortune from trade or found a bonanza in mining was to obtain a title of count or marquis, with membership of the Order of Santiago or Calatrava, or later the Order of Charles III. These titles carried with them the creation of an entail, though the condition was not always fulfilled, and in any case there were many entails without titles, designed simply to perpetuate fortunes. This object was frustrated by the encumbrances imposed on entailed properties, with the permission of the audiencia. The result was that these, and indeed all the rural and urban real estate of the country, were mortgaged in favor of the clergy and pious foundations. . . .

It cannot be said that the Spanish class, meaning by that all those born both in Spain and in America, was an educated class; but what there was of education in the country was confined to them. Among the Europeans, those who came with appointments in the judiciary and the clergy had an education proper to their professions, but only rarely anything more than this; the same can be said of officials. Those who came to seek a fortune had no education, and they acquired by experience what was needed for trade, mining, and agriculture. Americans, on the other hand, were increasing and deepening their knowledge, and their superior education was one of the reasons that caused them to regard Europeans with contempt, and was responsible for encouraging their opposition towards their rivals. Nevertheless, this education was virtually confined to legal and clerical circles and limited to Mexico City and capitals of dioceses where there were colleges. For many years the only institution of higher education was the University of Mexico, which was endowed by the king of Spain with the same privileges as those of the University of Salamanca and was highly favored by the viceroys. The Jesuits, who arrived in Mexico in 1572, established their own colleges in several principal cities where they settled, and later they opened diocesan seminaries, as prescribed by the Council of Trent. But it was in the Society's own colleges that education underwent greatest expansion, because in addition to philosophy and theology, literature was also taught, and many compositions in Latin prose and verse left by their pupils testify to the good taste inspired by the lessons they received. The expulsion of the Jesuit order in 1767 was a severe blow to education, for their colleges were closed, and although some continued under government administration they failed to preserve their former prestige. By virtue of their religious and political principles the Jesuits would have helped to prolong dependence on the metropolis, but equally an independence achieved by a better educated upper and middle class of society would have been more successful. The Franciscans also had colleges, but they only taught ecclesiastical subjects and were never renowned.

Education in New Spain, therefore, was confined to the study of philosophy, as a preparatory subject, and to theology, law, and medicine, the latter not highly regarded. These subjects were taken as a means to a lucrative career, but those who were already well-off saw no reason to educate themselves and left the study of letters to clerics and lawyers, who alone were called "*letrados*." Instead of trying to improve their minds or at least to seek a respectable amusement and recreation, they abandoned themselves to gambling and pleasure, or passed their time in idleness and ignorance. Only a few dedicated individuals acquired an education in history and other subjects, by virtue of reading and private study, although this was made difficult by the scarcity and high price of books. In the faculties where teaching took place there would have been men of high distinction, especially among the clerics, for whom canonries by competitive examination were a strong incentive to study. But in general there was great ignorance on the subject of politics and even in geography and other elementary subjects. . . . The exact sciences useful for mining were studied in the college of that name, a recent foundation, strongly supported and producing a few distinguished men; but its usefulness was never commensurate with its costs. This was also true in the case of the academy of fine arts established in the reign of Charles III, of which it suffices to say that there were good painters before this school was founded and none afterwards.

The Spanish class, therefore, was dominant in New Spain, not for its numbers but for its influence and power; and as a minority cannot prevail politically over a majority, except through the effect of the privileges which it enjoys, the laws had aimed primarily at securing this preponderance. This class possessed all the wealth of the country; in it resided whatever education existed; it alone obtained public offices and could carry arms; and it alone enjoyed political and civil rights. Its division between Europeans and creoles was the cause of the revolutions I am going to describe: the creoles destroyed the Europeans, but the means they unleashed to achieve this end also threatened their own share of power.

PART SEVEN

BRAZIL: FROM COLONY TO EMPIRE

29

Colonial Roots of Independence

A. J. R. Russell-Wood

The Napoleonic invasion of the Iberian peninsula in 1807–1808 pre-cipitated great movements of political emancipation in Latin Amer-ica. The Portuguese royal family sought safety in Brazil. There it found a society marked by deep lines of social, racial, and regional divisions, and uneasily poised between loyalism and resistance. In the event the transition from colony to kingdom, to independent empire was a gradual process. There was no abrupt break with the colonial past, no destructive civil war. When the royal family re-turned to Portugal in 1821, the heir to the Crown became emperor of Brazil, imposed a constitution, sought international recognition, and, with the support of a national elite, set the independent empire on its long history. But these events were not fortuitous; independence was not simply a product of external shock. Its roots lay deep in the colonial past. The discovery of gold in Minas Gerais heralded adver-sity as well as wealth; in its wake came political change, economic disruption, ethnic tensions, and international interest. From 1700 the Portuguese Crown intervened more directly in Brazil, to control min-ing, monopolize trade, extract revenue, and impose centralizing and absolutist policies. These culminated in the regime of the marquis of Pombal, whose "nationalizing" policies favored the metropolis rather than the colony and sowed the seeds of future independence. The second half of the eighteenth century was a time of crisis for the Portuguese empire in America, as A. J. R. Russell-Wood, Professor of History, The Johns Hopkins University, explains.

Reprinted from A. J. R. Russell-Wood, "Preconditions and Precipitants of the Independence Move-ment in Portuguese America," A. J. R. Russell-Wood, ed., *From Colony to Nation: Essays on the Independence of Brazil* (The Johns Hopkins University Press, Baltimore/London, 1975), pp. 18–36, by permission of the author and publisher.

Throughout the colonial period the viceroy of Brazil was less important than his counterparts in Mexico and Peru, but it was only in the
eighteenth century that his jurisdiction came under serious challenge.
Although repeated complaints by viceroys had led the king to order all
governors of captaincies to inform the viceroy of developments in their
areas, the admonition was largely ignored. Petulance and rancor characterized the relations between the viceroy and governors throughout
the eighteenth century. The effective authority of the viceroy was diminished, in part because of increased regalism but even more because
of the enhanced authority granted to governors of the newly created
captaincies. From being *primus inter pares*, the viceroy was now placed
on almost equal footing with the governors of the captaincies. This
shift was accelerated by the change in the economic epicenter from the
northeast to the central-southern area, coupled with the need to have a
seat of authority to oversee diplomatic negotiations and military supplies for the Luso-Spanish war in the Platine area. In fact, since 1748 the
jurisdiction of the brilliant Gomes Freire de Andrada (governor of Rio
de Janeiro from 1733 to 1763) had embraced the entire central and southern regions of the colony, giving him greater importance than the viceroy in Salvador. The transfer of the capital from Salvador to Rio de
Janeiro in 1763 was indicative of this change of emphasis and was to be
decisive in the future fortunes of Brazil.

At the local level of government, there was increased intervention in
municipal affairs by viceroys, governors, and officers of the fisc and
judiciary. The king sought to curb the excesses of self-opinionated and
dynamic town councilors by appointing a trained lawyer (*juiz de fora*)
to preside over the meetings of Câmaras municipais in regions of critical economic or political importance. Local crown judges (*ouvidores*)
exercised increasing vigilance over municipal elections and caused frequent complaints of infringement of municipal autonomy. On more
than one occasion the governor of Minas Gerais declared elections null
and void because of dishonesty, influence-peddling, and conflicts of
interest on the part of councilors. Although the town councils of Portuguese America were more representative of local interests and had
more "muscle" than their counterparts in Spanish America, in the
eighteenth century there was a concerted attempt by the crown to
whittle away at their jealously guarded autonomy and a growing tendency to reject the plethora of petitions for the granting of prerogatives
and privileges to municipal councils in Brazil.

The composition of society and the evolution of culture in colonial
Brazil did not escape the attention of the crown, although here royal
policies had less far-reaching consequences and aroused less open hos-

tility on the part of the populace. The crown-sponsored migrations of married couples from the Atlantic islands contributed to the settlement and colonization of the southern captaincies in the late seventeenth and eighteenth centuries. In contrast, the racial composition of the north of Brazil, previously associated with an Amerindian and mameluke population was dramatically altered by the importation of large numbers of slaves from West Africa under the auspices of the Maranhão-Pará company. Legislation promulgated during the reign of Dom José I (1750–77) was to have a profound influence on human relationships. The marquis of Pombal decreed not only that Amerindians who had become Catholics should be on an equal footing with white settlers in the eyes of the law and be eligible for administrative posts but also that special benefits should be granted to white settlers marrying Amerindians. The pejorative term *caboclo* was outlawed. Pombal's measure abolishing the distinction between "Old Christians" and "New Christians" and his harsh laws against anti-semitism represented liberation from a value system which had divided Portuguese society since 1497. It is worth noting, however, that if "purity of blood" (a changing concept susceptible to regional variations) was no longer demanded of crypto-Jews and Amerindians, it continued to apply to blacks and mulattos; Pombaline measures abolishing slavery in Portugal (1761–73) were not extended to the slavocratic society and economy of Brazil.

The most serious casualty of the Pombaline brand of regalism was the Society of Jesus. The expulsion of the Society from Portugal and her dominions in 1759 resulted in the secularization of the missionary *aldeias* and destroyed overnight the educational programs of the Jesuit colleges throughout Brazil, which had become centers of intellectual and cultural activity. The intellectual life of the colony was further stultified throughout the colonial period by repeated royal rejections of petitions for the establishment of an university on Brazilian soil. An increasing number of Brazilian families sent their sons to the universities of Montpelier, Coimbra, Edinburgh, and Paris, and it was this generation of graduates who imported into the colony the ideas of the Enlightenment in eighteenth-century Europe and publications prohibited by crown censorship. These found fertile soil in the academies and groups of scholars which flourished in Brazil during the eighteenth century. There can be little doubt that the philosophy of the Enlightenment, disseminated by the printed word and by word of mouth, played a vital role in the *inconfidências* of the second half of the eighteenth century and contributed to that intellectual ambience in which ideas of independence fermented and finally crystallized in the early nineteenth century. . . .

The Brazilian reaction to increased crown control over colonial affairs ranged from grumblings and mutterings by disaffected groups to passive resistance and actual dissent. Frequently, it is difficult to ascertain whether insurrections were really worthy of the designation "revolts" or were no more than urban *jacqueries*. Nevertheless, they were symptomatic of an increased tendency to question the relevance of crown authority to the colony. Orders emanating from Lisbon were scrutinized; their applicability to the Brazilian situation was assessed; outrage was expressed within and outside the government. In short, there was greater demand for more colonial consultation and even participation in the determining of policies dealing specifically with the oceanic commerce of Brazil as well as with domestic issues.

Discussion of the origins, content, and nature of the colonists' resistance to the increasing imposition of metropolitan authority during the eighteenth century must be prefaced by brief consideration of two important factors. The first is regionalism, which prevailed (and still prevails, in large part) throughout the colonial period. The second is the very nature of the infrastructure of Brazilian society. Neither was a direct precipitant of the independence movement, but both were constant factors in the historical background against which individual incidents were enacted. The two were interrelated and together bore on the economic progress of the colony. As such they were to be affected by crown attitudes and policies.

[Settlement was concentrated on the coastal strip, and there were no roads along the coast or to the interior.] These geographic factors alone produced a chronic demographic imbalance not only between the littoral and the hinterland but even among different areas of the coastal region itself. Furthermore, crown policy failed to encourage the opening of roads and actively discouraged commerce between the different regions. It is small wonder that for many a Brazilian student attendance at Coimbra University not only introduced him to Europe but enabled him for the first time, through contact with students from other parts of Brazil, to appreciate the vastness and diversity of his own country. It was this understanding which contributed so decisively to the ideology behind the movement toward independence in Brazil.

Regionalism was only one of the profound structural weaknesses pervading the society of colonial Brazil. Homogeneity and commonality of purpose were totally absent in a highly stratified and privilege-oriented society. Status was all-important. But there were inconsistencies in the ascribed positions of certain groups, and factors determining the standing of an individual within society could change. Slavocratic societies are frequently depicted either in terms of a master-slave dichotomy or in terms of a pyramid, with a white landowning aristocracy at the top and back dispossessed slaves at the bottom. Neither model is applicable to colonial Brazil, where status was determined by a variety of factors, each of importance in its own right and in its interaction with others. For a white person these were: color of skin, place of birth, religion, financial position, parentage, professional training, and social position of spouse. These factors also applied to coloreds, with the addition of civil status, *viz.*, slave or free. The importance of any one factor varied depending on regional and chronological differences, and their relationship to each other also varied accordingly. The particular strength of one, e.g., financial position, in an individual could offset a weakness, e.g., "defect of blood," but no single positive factor could eradicate a combination of negative attributes. In the eighteenth century greater social mobility resulted in the reassessment of many traditional criteria for determining social standing, and this provoked resentment and even animosity among different social groups.

If the sugar planters and cattle ranchers were considered (and considered themselves) as comprising a landed aristocracy, by the early eighteenth century the emergence of an urban mercantile class was making itself felt precisely in those areas which had been dominated by the rural aristocracy. The transition was not effected without strife, as demonstrated by the co-called War of the Peddlers (*Guerra dos Mascates*) in Pernambuco in 1711, which found echoes elsewhere. This episode also casts light on another stress point in Brazilian colonial society: the animosity felt by Brazilian-born Portuguese subjects (white or black) for those other "loyal subjects of the king of Portugal" born in Portugal or coming from West Africa. This aversion was critical in the course taken in the evolution of Brazilian society and, in a more refined form, was to contribute decisively to the current of opinion which spurred Brazil toward independence. Also, it should not be forgotten that for much of the colonial period Brazilian society was divided between "Old Christians" and "New Christians." If the Pombaline decrees effectively outlawed this distinction, they failed to eradicate from the popular mind the requirement of "purity of blood" demanded of their appointees for two and half centuries by church and state.

It cannot be overemphasized that internal dissent and division was not limited to the white community. Among coloreds antagonism and tensions existed between freemen and slaves, between mulattos and blacks, and between Brazilian-born free blacks and mulattos and African-born slaves who had earned their freedom; cultural and tribal distinctions and language barriers also carried over in the New World and effectively destroyed any cohesion among coloreds in Brazil.

Regionalism and the stresses and strains in Brazilian society were exacerbated in the course of the eighteenth century as the result of unforeseen (and unforeseeable) developments in the economy and the indifference shown by the Portuguese crown toward their social repercussions. The discoveries in Minas Gerais threw into sharp focus tensions and differences which might otherwise have smouldered below the surface for decades had it not been for the violent dislocation of the economic epicenter of Brazil from the northeast and the no less dramatic relocation of people. The economy of the northeast had been based on agriculture. The financial return was good but not spectacular. The fortunes of men, be they plantation owners, overseers, or slaves, were tied to the land. A large initial capital investment guaranteed a stable, patriarchal society based on black labor. Salvador and Recife were governed from country estates, whose owners rode into the city to attend council meetings and functions of the more prestigious brotherhoods. This security was destroyed by the discovery of gold. Sugar plantations were deserted; slaves were beyond the means of debt-crippled planters; the pool of free and slave labor moved inland; currency was in short supply. Salvador ceased to be the capital of Brazil. The society of Minas Gerais, radically different from that of the coast, was characterized by mobility, by insecurity both physical and financial, by opportunism, and by the almost complete absence of patriarchalism. In some respects its great wealth enabled it to be cosmopolitan as Salvador or Recife had never been, but its inhabitants could never shake off the psychological barrier of being beyond the mountains.

The avowedly mercantilist policy of the Portuguese crown was to view with apparent equanimity the decline of agriculture in the northeast; it did not hesitate to throw its support behind the mining industries because of the quicker returns to be derived from gold and diamonds. Repeated petitions of an admittedly hysterical nature from the city councils of Recife and Salvador that the king stop the exodus of slaves from the littoral or even close down the mines altogether were largely ignored by Lisbon. Moreover, the influx of "outsiders" in search of fortune was resented by those who had come to Brazil as colonists and felt with some justification that the fruits of the sudden windfall should be theirs. The Portuguese crown showed little interest in attempting to effect a reconciliation between the *reinóis* and the Brazilians so long as the antagonism between the two did not erupt into open hostility which could affect production adversely. Nor did it formulate a policy to correct the chronic economic and demographic imbalance between the agricultural littoral and the mining highlands.

Regional tensions were to become increasingly apparent in the years immediately preceding independence. It was no coincidence that it was in the northeast that Dom Pedro found it difficult to establish a constituency. This opposition was not directed against the prince personally, nor did it represent disapproval of the perpetuation of a monarchical form of government rather than the establishment of outright republicanism. Rather, it expressed the *nordestinos'* resentment of the attitudes of the court in Rio de Janeiro toward the region.

The crown contributed to the tensions within Brazilian society because of two aspects of royal policy: the king's attitude toward native-born Brazilians, and the concession of privileges. The king's correspondence with viceroys and governors alike is liberally peppered with pejorative epithets about native-born Brazilians, who are portrayed as lazy, immoral, and spendthrift. These characterizations are frequently coupled with an insistence on the "purity of blood" of crown appointees. To be Brazilian-born was to be suspect. Thus the crown persistently preferred Portuguese-born subjects over native applicants for posts in Brazil, causing intense rivalry between the *reinóis* and the Brazilians. The crown policy of bestowing benefices and granting privileges to individuals and corporate groups further divided Brazilian colonial society. Briefly these special favors may be categorized as follows: those granted to individuals in return for particular services, e.g., mining discoveries; those granted to the members of a guild, society, or brotherhood, e.g, goldsmiths or the Santa Casa de Misericórdia; those granted to people in certain professions or occupations, e.g., soldiers of the garrison, students, or employees of the royal mints; corporate privileges, e.g., those given to a town or city. At the individual level such concessions effectively restricted interpersonal relations, imposing further artificial divisions on an already highly stratified society. Corporate privileges inspired rivalries and competition in a nation whose development demanded collective efforts and cooperation. Whether or not the intention was to unify the population of Brazil or whether this was another instance of regalism by the assertion of royal control through privileges is debatable, but the result was the division and not the coalescence of Brazilian society.

A casual reader of Brazilian history might gain the impression that the eighteenth century was characterized by wars and revolts. Nationalist fervor on the part of Brazilian writers and loose translations by English-speaking scholars have furthered this erroneous impression: we hear of the "war" of the *emboabas*, the "war" of the *mascates*, the "revolt" of Vila Rica (1720), the Minas "conspiracy" (1789), the "social revolution" in Salvador (1798), to name but a few. Three points must be made to place such events in perspective. First, in no case did such a cause gain overall support from all sectors of society; second, in all cases the impact of the struggle remained localized, and there were no repercussions beyond the immediate region; third, despite loose talk of separatism in Pernambuco in 1710 and 1711, in no case did there exist any planned strategy to cast off royal control and establish a republic. Antipathy towards metropolitan authority, and more particularly towards crown appointees, was strong, but in no instance was it directed against the sovereign personally or against the institution of monarchy. In fact, invariably the cause of such "revolts" or disturbances is to be found in a change or a challenge to the accepted social and economic status quo. . . .

The strongest reaction by the colonists was against the Pombaline policy of nationalizing the Luso-Brazilian trade. All too often it was the Brazilian merchant who felt that his interests were being sacrificed to those of the crown and the metropolitan merchant as was the case with Pombal's policy of establishing monopolistic chartered companies for Brazil. That the English merchants of Lisbon should be dismayed at this development was understandable but foreseeable. However, insufficient thought had been given to the impact of this policy on small traders in Portugal and Brazil, who saw their livelihood threatened by such companies and were vociferous in denouncing them. They formed common cause with the Jesuits in the Mesa do Bem Comum, whose deputies harangued the crown and Pombal from street corner and pulpit. The authorities took a strong stand, viewing such resistance as subversion of royal authority. The Mesa was suppressed in 1755. Furthermore, some policies intended for the good of Brazil engendered resistance rather than cooperation. This was the reaction by the colonials of Salvador, Recife, Rio de Janeiro, and São Luís to the Pombal-inspired Boards of Inspection intended to protect, stimulate, and fiscalize the production of major export crops, especially sugar and tobacco. In reality, Brazilian producers saw the boards as threatening their commercial interests while furthering state intervention in their enterprises. . . .

In an age of regalism, increased metropolitan domination of the colonial pact, and greater nationalization of the economy, a curious paradox was born in Portuguese America. On the one hand, there developed a very real consciousness of and pride in being Brazilian-born and an American. On the other hand, Brazilians became more aware of the changes taking place in eighteenth-century Europe and more cosmopolitan in their social mores and ideological development. Whether or not such heightened consciousness and awareness may justifiably be seen as symptomatic of nationalism is debatable and, in my view, doubtful. . . . An indication of the depth of the pride in being Brazilian is afforded by the group of Brazilian students at Coimbra University in the 1690s. From the correspondence of one student to his father in Salvador emerges the picture of a true esprit de corps among the Brazilian students, who saw the success of one of their number as a feather in the cap for Brazil. The student wrote defiantly that "if in matters of intellect the sons of Brazil do not exceed those of Portugal, at least they are their equals." These students and their successors in European universities played a vital role in thwarting the efforts of the Portuguese crown to curb the introduction into Brazil and dissemination of the ideas and writings of the Enlightenment taking place in France and England. English ideas and "abominable French principles" found fertile soil in Brazil. Their direct impact was frequently limited to the upper classes and intellectuals, and they stimulated a flurry of revolutionary activities among the upper classes of Brazilian society in the late eighteenth and early nineteenth centuries, either openly or under the protective shield of the Masonic lodges which flourished as centers of debate and discussion.

One may fairly ask to what degree the true nature of liberalism and the implications of constitutionalist principles were understood in Brazil. The prism through which the Brazilian viewed such currents of opinion differed markedly from that of his European counterpart. The infrastructure, the needs, and the aspirations of Brazilian society had little in common with English and French society of the period. Appreciation of the very nature and aims of the Enlightenment was difficult for a Brazilian. The transfer of its implications to the Brazilian milieu was all but impossible. Despite these caveats, however, there can be no doubt that such ideological innovations and nationalist spirit were factors in the abortive Inconfidência Mineira of 1789 and the Inconfidência Bahiana of 1798. For those not versed in the literature of the Enlightenment the dramatic precedents of the American war of independence and the French Revolution carried an unambiguous message. Both *inconfidências* saw the active involvement of intellectuals, soldiers, royal appointees, servants of the crown, and coloreds. For each group the significance and implications of the *inconfidências* were different, satisfying the hopes and aspirations of an individual or one sector of the community. A great deal of ink has been expended on these two insurrections, and the participants in the outbreak in Minas Gerais have been glorified as martyrs in the national pantheon of heroes (ironically enough, the colored leaders of the Bahian conspiracy were not so honored). But it is well to bear in mind that in both cases the immediate precipitants were of an economic and social nature. The increasing

cost of food stuffs and a decline in mining production caused hardship
in Minas Gerais. The imposition of the *derrama* by the count of Bar-
bacena was the proverbial final straw. In Bahia there was dissatisfaction
with inequality in pay and privileges between colored and white soldiers of the garrison and with the closing of certain ranks to coloreds.
In both cases there was an intellectual undercurrent, slogans of liberty
and equality were flaunted, and rumors of the establishment of a republic and self-rule were common. But in reality the cause was espoused by
certain classes only, its repercussions were local, the outbreaks were
badly organized, and the revolts were easily suppressed. In fact, the
only revolt in colonial Brazil worthy of the name occurred in Pernambuco in 1817. With openly republican intentions from the outset, the
dissidents in Recife found supporters among clerics, laymen, administrators, planters, and soldiers in the surrounding region. The revolt
gained rapid momentum, faltered, and was finally suppressed after two
months. The severity of the reprisals failed to quench the republican
spirit and merely succeeded in fueling the animosity between Brazilians
and the Portuguese soldiers of the garrison. It was not surprising that
this region was to be at best lukewarm in its support of Dom Pedro and
was the stage for further disturbances later in the century. . . .

The arrival in Brazil of the future Dom João VI and the establishment of a royal court in Rio de Janeiro in 1808 signified to the Brazilian
people that there would be a change in emphasis and balance of power
in the colonial relationship. The psychological and economic benefits
accruing to the colony from the presence of the court cannot be overemphasized. From the time of his first landfall Dom João went out of
his way to grant privileges and favors to individuals and groups and to
encourage trading interests. But the mere arrival of a monarch with his
court could not dispel the problems confronting the colony. Colonial
society was still in a state of evolution rather than consolidation. Regional tensions and antagonisms between different groups were as
strong as ever. There was chronic maldistribution of wealth, and rates
of economic growth varied enormously from region to region. The only
constant was the presence of slavery as a basic ingredient of colonial
life, and attitudes toward the role of the slave remained immutable and
impervious to outside influences.

By a decree of January 28, 1808, Dom João opened the ports of Brazil
to foreign trade. This was an event of momentous importance, transcending the arrival of the royal court and even the declaration of
independence. At one stroke of the pen Dom João reversed the Pombaline policies for the nationalization of the Luso-Brazilian trade; swept
away three centuries of crown suspicion, distrust, and paranoia toward

foreign merchants and traders in Brazilian waters; and permitted Brazilians to trade legally beyond the narrow commercial network of the Portuguese empire. It was ironic that the transfer of the court and the resulting euphoria which swept Brazil would not have been possible without British naval dominance of the South Atlantic. The opening of the ports freed Brazilian commerce from the fetters of Portugal only for it to fall victim to the economic imperialism of the United Kingdom.

As had been the case so often before, the destiny of Brazil was determined by events beyond its shores as much as by internal developments. In fact it is doubtful whether, had it not been for such external pressures, there would have been any factor in Brazil of sufficient force and overall appeal to bring about a unilateral declaration of independence. Obviously, the French invasion of Portugal in 1807 directly motivated the flight of the court to Brazil, and the new range of possibilities and options which this presence on Brazilian soil afforded brought to a head many of the tensions within the country. Some historians point to the constitutionalist liberal revolution in Oporto in 1820 as a precipitant of Brazilian independence. But this uprising was an expression of internal dissent in Portugal and did not radically affect the chain of events already set in motion in Brazil. Although more distant in space, events in North America and northern Europe were what provided the ambience for and made possible the declaration of independence in Brazil. The declaration of independence by the English colonies in North America had a profound psychological effect throughout the continent and served as an example for Latin neighbors. The maturing of industrial capitalism in England and the advocacy of mercantilist policies and economic liberalism had far-reaching effects on trading patterns and customs in the nineteenth century. Furthermore, the discord prevailing in Europe in the early nineteenth century lessened the likelihood of European military intervention in the Americas, a situation well appreciated in the United States, which was encouraged to recognize new revolutionary governments in certain areas of Latin America.

The return of Dom João VI to Portugal in 1821, leaving Dom Pedro in Rio de Janeiro, did nothing to calm the tensions existing between colony and mother country. The decision to transfer the court to Brazil had been ill-received in Lisbon, although it was an inevitable expedient. Once the immediate threat of French occupation of Portugal had diminished, the continued presence of the king in Brazil merely fueled the resentment already felt towards the colony by members of the Côrtes in Lisbon. Recognition that the roles of colony and metropolis had been neatly reversed was bitter but unavoidable. The decree of

December 16, 1815, whereby Brazil was raised to the status of a kingdom on a level with Portugal, did nothing to smooth the already ruffled feathers of the deputies in the Côrtes. Thus the reception accorded to the Brazilian deputies to the constituent Côrtes was not calculated to be friendly, nor was their brief likely to inspire any rapprochement with their Portuguese counterparts: political and economic equality between the two countries, the establishment of parallel organs of government in Portugal and Brazil, and alternation of the seat of government between Lisbon and Rio de Janeiro. The rejection of these proposals out of hand by the Portuguese deputies demonstrated their political myopia. Their ridicule, contempt, scorn, and open antagonism were widely reported in the colony and contributed to a common feeling of insult and outrage which brought together otherwise disassociated factions.

In Brazil it is doubtful whether at any time there had been any intention of definitive separation from Portugal or any large support for a republican cause. Although in the eighteenth and early nineteenth centuries factions in Minas Gerais and in the northeast espoused republicanism, their influence and following were limited. For the most part Brazilians were content to accept the continuation of a monarchical form of government. The struggles between republicans and royalists which took place in Spanish America were absent in Brazil. In fact the social tensions, regionalisms, economic disparities, and presence of a hard-core colonial administration prevented the independence movement in Brazil from being truly nationalist in spirit or revolutionary in execution. But there was a general determination to be Brazilians and to be recognized as such, coupled with the demand for recognition of the very quintessence of Brazilian civilization, as something sui generis, imbued with Brésilianité. Finally, the Brazilians wanted recognition of the special nature of Brazilian society and the particular interests of the Brazilian economy, but few saw it as a prelude to independence, or failure to gain it as a prerequisite for a separatist movement. In fact, Brazilian deputies constantly emphasized Brazilian loyalty to the crown of Portugal, union of the kingdoms of Portugal and Brazil, and a willingness to negotiate and to reach an accommodation.

Any hopes of such an accommodation were dimmed by the attitude of the Portuguese Côrtes towards Brazil in 1821 and 1822. Brazilian fears that Portugal intended to reduce Brazil to its former colonial status were obviously well founded. Any doubts as to the intention of the Côrtes to re-establish unilateral control, by force if necessary, were dispelled. Fear of "enslavement" to Portuguese interests brought together sectors of society previously divided or undecided. Many of the most influential figures in Brazilian society publicly supported union with Portugal; others of no less prominence and distinction favored the total independence of Brazil; still others remained undecided and, in some cases, resigned to the outcome. In the end, the more extreme groups were willing to compromise, and polarization was replaced by accommodation. There can be little doubt that, had it not been for the intransigent and highhanded attitude adopted by the Côrtes, compromise and negotiation would have been possible even on the eve of independence.

Three factors contributed to Brazilian acceptance, albeit reluctant, of the fact that no viable alternative to independence from Portugal existed: first the inability of Dom João to provide decisive leadership, coupled with the accession issue; second, British pressure; third, the administrative and militaristic policy of the Côrtes. Rather than firmly supporting either free trade or mercantilism, Dom João attempted to free the Brazilian economy while continuing to protect Portuguese interests. The result was a series of conflicting and contradictory measures which failed to win the approval of either Portuguese or Brazilian merchants. British pressure on the king to loosen economic restrictions was strong. In the wake of the establishment of a representative government in Portugal, England was particularly insistent on the return of Dom João to Portugal. Finally, the changing administrative and economic policies of the Côrtes after 1821 made reconciliation impossible. Measures intended to harass foreign merchants were passed; an attempt was made to make the provincial governors in Brazil subordinate to the Côrtes in Lisbon and not to Rio de Janeiro; other administrative reforms were aimed at enhancing the authority of the metropolis. The final blow was the ill-advised decision to dispatch Portuguese troops to Rio de Janeiro and Pernambuco. The question of the nature of independence had been reduced to one of direct confrontation, with the Côrtes on the one hand and Brazil, striving to preserve its few existing concessions and liberties, on the other. For political, economic, social, and emotional reasons, independence had become a necessity for Portuguese America.

30

Economic Imperative

Caio Prado Júnior

Economic forces played their part in the disintegration of imperial rule in Brazil no less than in Spanish America, for economic injustice is a potent stimulant to revolution; and where injustice yields to reform, that too can lead to demands for further change. The Marxist interpretation, however, of which we have a classic example below, goes further than this. It argues that the independence of a colony always results from the fact that its economic evolution becomes incompatible with its colonial status. In the case of Brazil, independence flowed inevitably from "contradictions" in the colonial regime, whose political framework was bound to crack under the twin pressures of outside economic forces and the colony's own development. Independence was thus an opportunity for the Brazilian ruling class to assert its interests, with only a marginal element of popular participation. Caio Prado Júnior (1907–1989) was one of Brazil's leading Marxist intellectuals, and his *Economic History of Brazil* occupies an important place in Brazilian historiography.

The social structure of Brazil, relatively simple in the first century and a half after discovery, became more complex in the second half of the seventeenth century, when the increase in the wealth and economic development of the country created new economic and social forms. An economy characterized by mobility of exchange, by trade and credit, grew up alongside the agricultural economy which had been hitherto predominant. Thus a bourgeoisie of rich merchants emerged which, by means of its rapidly amassed wealth, began to neutralize the power of the landed aristocracy, hitherto the only affluent class and conse-

Translated by John Lynch from Caio Prado Júnior, *Evolução Política do Brasil e outros estudos* (Editôra Brasiliense, São Paulo, 2nd ed., 1957), pp. 35–54, and printed by permission of the author.

quently the only one to enjoy prestige in the colony. The new economy transformed the cities of the coast, on which it was based, into centers of population and wealth. Recife, which before the Dutch occupation was no more than a collection of huts occupied almost entirely by humble fishermen, came to outshine Olinda, the capital of Pernambuco, which was the city of the nobility. Recife was remodeled by Nassau, who established the seat of government there, so that by the time the Dutch were expelled it already contained 1,600 households and 15,000 inhabitants. Fifty years later the population had doubled, "nearly all of them merchants," according to a contemporary witness.

This bourgeoisie consisted almost entirely of natives of Portugal. In fact, it was the recent immigrants from Portugal who gave vigor to the trade of the colony. After the Dutch war, and as a result of the economic depression of the mother country, the flow of emigrants to Brazil mounted considerably, to a point at which the Portuguese government became alarmed at the prospect of the depopulation of the kingdom. And these new elements preferred to devote themselves to trade. Later, they would rush in large numbers to the mines. In the beginning, however, they did not engage in farming, a fact that did not escape the attention of contemporaries; this can be explained in several ways. By then agriculture no longer enjoyed the appeal it had possessed in the early years of settlement. Brazilian agricultural prices were falling, especially sugar prices. Previously sugar had been produced almost exclusively in Brazil, but now Brazilian sugar began to face competition from the Spanish and English possessions in the Caribbean. Furthermore, the great majority of the new settlers did not have the resources to engage in a relatively large-scale industry such as Brazilian agriculture. Consequently, if they were neither employed as ordinary wage earners—which was difficult in existing conditions when slave labor predominated—nor went into the mines, they were induced to enter commerce, at that time scorned by the propertied classes in the colony. They came, indeed, to create for the Portuguese what amounted to a monopoly of commercial positions; and, from these, Brazilians were completely excluded by the ruthless competition of the established merchants.

This situation lasted for a long time. Until independence, and even well into the imperial period, as we shall see, Brazilian commerce was run entirely by foreigners, and native Brazilians were systematically excluded from it. In his report of 1779, the viceroy of Rio de Janeiro, the marquis of Lavradio, pointed out this fact, remarking that "as soon as they [the Portuguese] arrive here, they think of nothing but making themselves masters of all the trade there is, and refuse to employ anybody born in Brazil, even as a cashier, for fear he might one day become a businessman himself."

The interests of this commercial class naturally tied it closely to the colonial government of Brazil. Legislation by the imperial government kept out competitors from other nations, who could not establish themselves in the country. Furthermore, the Portuguese merchants in the colony held direct or indirect interests in the chartered companies, either as share-holders, which very many of them were, or as their representatives in Brazil. In addition they were often holders of royal contracts—patents, monopolies, tax-farming in the colony. Thus they grew wealthy in the shadow of the oppressive commercial policy of the mother country, and as such came to constitute born adversaries of the other classes in the colony.

Hostility to Portuguese businessmen, who might be described as the representatives of Portuguese oppression in Brazil, was aggravated by the steadily worsening conditions of the rural landowners. In contrast to the ever-increasing prosperity of the merchants, the farmers were heading for ruin. In the north the Dutch wars, which for more than twenty years devastated the whole territory from Ceará to Bahia, causing sugar mills to be destroyed and cane fields to be burnt, had dealt them a shattering blow. They were also weakened in the course of the eighteenth century by the boom in mining, which on the one hand drew away slave labor and so produced a scarcity, and on the other resulted in a rise in the price of all products consumed in the colony. On top of all this they were also hampered by the royal monopolies, at the same time that their products were falling in value owing to competition from other countries. . . . This was the position of farming at the end of the seventeenth century and the beginning of the eighteenth. For all these reasons, there were few landowners who were not falling into debt, to such a degree indeed that few remained whose estates were not entirely mortgaged. And the creditors, of course, were the merchants, the commission agents and bankers. Consequently a fresh source of rivalry was added to the others. . . .

In this way opposing interests, divided by the economic and social development of the colony, aligned against each other. On the one side were the interests of the Brazilians, especially the rural proprietors, the landowning aristocracy of the country who suffered most directly from the burden of colonial oppression; on the other were the interests of the mother country and its allies, the Portuguese merchants who formed the commercial bourgeoisie.

This divergence of interests was accompanied by the political transformation of the colony, though not without bitter struggles. Political authority gradually slipped out of the hands of the landowners. In the first place, the merchant bourgeoisie competed for posts in municipal administration with the landowners, who had hitherto held a monopoly in this field. . . . More important, and more enduring in its effects, was the decline in the actual authority of the *câmaras*. Governors and other royal officials began to move up from the second rank, to which their offices had previously been relegated. At the same time, as royal authority increased so the powers of the hitherto sovereign *câmaras* diminished. Municipal power was giving way to imperial power. . . . The privileges hitherto enjoyed by municipal administrations were inexorably reduced. *Câmaras* were forbidden to set up committees, to cite governors before the council, to refuse summonses to the palace, to make public appearances as a corporation, or to disobey any royal order. Pereira da Silva wrote: "With the passage of time, and owing to the many and various imperial decrees, the *câmaras* lost the greater part of the functions they had assumed and were reduced, like those of Portugal itself, to the simple form of local corporations restricted to the limits set by the legislation in force."

It was the political authority of the mother country that was being strengthened. The attitude of the governors had changed: it is enough to compare the eighteenth-century governors with their predecessors. These were no longer humble officials deferring to the *câmaras*, attending carefully to their wishes, and using the utmost tact to avoid annoying the all-powerful colonists. They were more like the brutal Rodrigo César de Meneses, who had hardly reached his captaincy before he ordered the building of a fort and the execution inside it of some condemned men, as an example to the colonists. . . . Even São Paulo, which until the end of the seventeenth century enjoyed a degree of autonomy that almost completely overshadowed the presence of the Portuguese government and gave its inhabitants the reputation of being "a race of almost savage energy, taking pleasure in adventures, and both independent and republican in their customs, so that for a long time they remained completely separated from Portugal," even São Paulo at the beginning of the eighteenth century was absorbed into the new administrative system and became strictly dependent on the central government.

Brazil's political evolution, however, followed step by step upon the economic transformation taking place from the mid-seventeenth century onwards. This transformation, consisting of greater economic penetration by Portugal, had repercussions in the political field with the gradual disappearance of the local self-government Brazil had enjoyed during the first century and a half of colonization. Authority was transferred from the hands of the landed proprietors, the old ruling class, into those of the Portuguese crown, and there it remained and was consolidated. The *câmaras* were successively deprived of all their powers and privileges, and were forced to yield to the power of the governors. During the eighteenth century only one authority existed in the colony—that of the metropolis, Portugal.

But the political equilibrium of the colonial regime was destined to be destroyed. Opposing forces were at work, relentlessly undermining its foundations, and on occasion revealing themselves above the surface in violent conflicts and dissensions, so that the stability of the regime was increasingly threatened. In the economic field national interests clashed with those of Portugal; in the political field local autonomy as exercised in self-administration by the colonists collided with rule by officialdom representing the sovereign power of the Portuguese crown. The collision of these opposing forces underlies the fundamental conflict of interests between the country's growth and the restrictive framework of the colonial regime. It was from this conflict that Brazilian emancipation stemmed.

The transfer of the Portuguese court to Brazil in 1808 gave Brazilian political emancipation a unique character among the independence movements in the American colonies. All of these colonies, at more or less the same time, broke the bonds which subjected them to the nations of the Old World. But whereas elsewhere the separation was violent and was settled on the battlefield, in Brazil it was the government of the mother country itself that, under the pressure of circumstances, fortuitous though they were, made the colony the seat of the monarchy. And it was the imperial government, paradoxically, that laid the foundations of Brazilian autonomy.

The coming of the court resulted from a combination of circumstances originating in the European conflicts of the period. But in the final analysis it was really a skilful manoeuvre of British diplomacy. The abnormal state of the Old World, in the grip of the convulsions unleashed by the French Revolution of 1789, was turned to account by England in order to complete her traditional policy, the economic absorption of the little kingdom of Portugal.

The question then at issue was that of freedom of trade with the Portuguese colonies, especially Brazil. England had a great interest in these markets, until then practically closed to her trade. It is true that by the treaty of 1654 she had secured from Portugal the right to send her ships to Brazil. But this was a partial concession and very limited in its advantages. Not only had the trade to be carried on indirectly, via Portugal, since Portuguese ports had to be visited before departure from Europe and on return to it, but more to the point, the ships had to sail in convoy with the Portuguese fleets, and consequently were subject to the burdens that resulted from this provision. It is also true that direct trade was in fact quite usual and, as the English consul in Lisbon himself admitted, the departure of ships for Brazil was even announced publicly in London. But all this was a precarious business, for such trade infringed the letter of the treaties, and was therefore constantly subject to protests and retaliation from the Portuguese government. For this reason it hardly satisfied British aspirations.

The problem appeared to have been resolved by the transfer of the court. At least, this was the expectation in England. By leaving Portugal the government increased its dependence on England, since the move had the express effect of recognizing her tutelage. Moreover, as Portugal had now fallen into French hands, it was no longer possible to carry on the trade of Brazil through Portuguese ports.

As soon as he had landed in Brazil the first act of the prince regent was precisely to order that its ports be opened to trade with "friendly nations," in other words with England. As for Brazil, the English manoeuvre profoundly changed its political and social conditions. The transfer of the court amounted in effect to the attainment of Brazilian independence. Certainly independence would have come sooner or later, even without the presence of the prince regent, who was later to be king of Portugal. But it is also certain that Brazil's role as the temporary seat of the crown was the final and immediate cause of independence replacing, advantageously or not, the armed struggle which occurred in the other American colonies.

If the chronological divisions with which historians mark the social and political evolution of peoples are not merely to register external and formal features, but are rather to reflect their deeper significance, the date of Brazilian independence would certainly be put forward fourteen years and be counted from the arrival of the court in 1808. By establishing the seat of the sovereign in Brazil, the regent *ipso facto* abolished the colonial regime under which the country had hitherto lived. The characteristics of such a regime vanished, except perhaps the circumstance that the country was still ruled by a government composed of foreigners. Piece by piece the old machinery of the colonial administration was dismantled and replaced by another more suited to a sovereign state. Economic restrictions lapsed and the interests of Brazil began to take first place in political debates within the government. These were the direct and immediate effects of the arrival of the court. Practically all the measures were taken within the same year, 1808, measures that even a government drawn wholly from the country itself could hardly have bettered.

These events were without doubt directly related to the coming of the regent. As Portugal was evacuated and occupied first by the French and then by the British, she no longer had the power to fulfil her functions as mother country; thus the simple fact of having to carry on his government in Brazil naturally called for a political and administrative order that could no longer be that of a simple colony. The regent of Portugal was favorable to the national interests of Brazil. His attitude was conditioned partly by the Brazilian environment, which he could not avoid, and partly perhaps by the private though undeclared desire to take up permanent residence in Brazil. But, whatever the inspiration of Dom João's policy, the fact is that the fourteen years between his arrival and the formal proclamation of independence cannot be counted as part of the colonial period of Brazilian history.

One can imagine the repercussions among those whose interests were bound up with the colonial regime, when this curious reversal of roles made the Portuguese sovereign and his policy almost unconscious instruments of Brazilian national autonomy. One of the principal effects of this was the constitutional revolution of Oporto. This revolution, it is true, had domestic causes in Portugal. It was directed essentially against the established order there, that is against absolute monarchy and the economic, social, political, and administrative regime bound up with absolute monarchy. But it is also true that the serious damage suffered by Portuguese interests because of the new policy adopted by the sovereign towards Brazil led important groups in Portugal to embrace the cause of the revolution for that reason alone. For this policy meant nothing less than the abolition of centuries-old system of living parasitically on her colony to which Portugal had become accustomed and on which, it may be affirmed, her economy was based. Trade with Brazil, which the opening of the ports in 1808 and the treaty of 1810 transferred to England, represented not less than nine-tenths of all Portuguese foreign trade. Brazil was the only customer—by force of circumstances, of course—for the mediocre products of Portuguese industry; now, in free conditions, these were incapable of competing with those from England. The loss of their principal, and almost their only, market was a death blow to Portuguese manufacturers. Furthermore, the various other sources of revenue that Portugal drew from Brazil suddenly dried up, forcing the country into a desperate economic situation. It was against these developments that the constitutional revolt of Oporto was directed, as the attitude of the *côrtes* called by the revolutionaries was to prove: one of its chief concerns was to restore Brazil to its old colonial status.

In Brazil too the policy of Dom João met with an unfavorable reception in some circles, namely among the class which flourished under the protection of the colonial system, with which directly or indirectly its interests were bound up. These were the Portuguese merchants. They too were hit by the suppression of the innumerable restrictions weighing down the Brazilian economy. With the decline of the colonial regime they could feel the old privileges and favors crumbling. Until then they had been sole lords of the trade of the colony; now they were excluded from it by competitors from other countries. After the arrival of Dom João these not only found the ports of Brazil open but also came to be favored by numerous advantages, such as the right to have magistrates of their own, religious liberty, and so on. Consequently those who had previously monopolized Brazilian trade naturally became opponents of the new system and allied themselves with the revolution in Portugal by means of which they hoped for a return to the past. And it was they who were among the principal agents of this revolution in Brazil.

However, in order to understand the constitutional revolution and the reaction it caused in Brazil, it is necessary to consider also another aspect that it revealed. The upheaval brought into sharp focus the different economic and social contradictions embedded in colonial society. . . . They could no longer be contained within the established order by the forces of tradition and inertia. Examples of these were the deep social distinctions dividing classes and social groups one from another and relegating the mass of the population to a miserable standard of living and a state of moral squalor. There were also contradictions of an ethnic nature, resulting from the depressed position of the Negro slave and, to a lesser degree, of the Indian, and entailing prejudice against all individuals, even free men, who were dark-skinned. In this category fell the great majority of the population, and they rose against a form of social organization that, in addition to its disastrous moral effects, signified for them exclusion from almost all the benefits life in the colony could offer. The condition of the slaves was another source of disturbance. The usual apparent tranquillity of the slaves (despite the existence of fugitive slaves, fugitive slave settlements, and even slave insurrections) should not be regarded as evidence of their complete submission. They were in a constant state of silent revolt, hardly noticed because it was smothered by the entire weight and organized strength of the established order.

All these contradictions and tensions were brought to the surface when the colony was swept by the constitutional revolution. The country was thrown into turmoil, in which great mass movements brought about or accompanied the overthrow of the local governments of the various captaincies, their replacement by elected *juntas*, and the establishment of a constitutional regime in Brazil. Even the sovereign was affected by the agitation and, as a consequence of the rising of February 26, 1821 in Rio de Janeiro, where the court resided, was obliged to accept the new regime, by reorganizing his government to include elements enjoying the confidence of the people and by swearing to uphold the constitution which was being prepared by the *côrtes* assembled in Lisbon.

The Portuguese revolution produced a convulsion in Brazil which spread from the north to the south of the country, and assumed complex and even at times contradictory features by reason of the extremely heterogeneous interests and demands that found expression in it. As we saw, it contained reactionary forces, whose only purpose was to restore the country to its colonial past and thus to its economic and social isolation. Alongside these forces, paradoxically, others lined up, particularly the upper classes in the colony, who hoped that the revolution and the establishment of a constitutional regime would restore to them the privileges, liberties, and autonomy that Brazil had acquired in the early years of almost private self-government, and that had been highly favorable to their position. Finally, there were the popular forces we have mentioned—the oppressed strata of the Brazilian population who, in the constitution that was being offered to them caught glimpses of economic and social liberation.

The conflict of these forces, each manoeuvring to secure victory for its own demands, produced the different events that make up the uneasy period from 1821 onwards. Without entering into details, their general result can be outlined. In the development of the constitutional revolution in Brazil it was the second group of forces—that is, the "Brazilian party," as it was now called, representing the upper classes in the colony, the great landed proprietors and their allies—that was to win supremacy. The reaction in favor of a restoration of the colonial system was doomed to defeat, despite the support of the mother country and the Portuguese *côrtes*, because it was no longer possible to hold up the course of events and make Brazil take a step backward in the march of history. Such a movement was halted by the nature of the country, whose very existence, as we have seen, was incompatible with the strait jacket of the old and already outdated colonial regime.

As for the mass of the people, they were not politically mature enough to assert their demands with success; nor were material conditions in Brazil favorable to their economic and social liberation. These reasons also account for the lack of continuity and the absence of sure direction in popular movements. Such movements, despite the impressive size they occasionally attained, never managed to propose reforms and solutions compatible with existing conditions. Moreover, the relations then existing between classes, against which they protested, were solidly embedded in the fundamental economic structure of Brazil. . . . Not only did this structure not change; it grew stronger. And for this reason the class relations stemming from it could not be significantly modified. Thus the popular struggle was ineffective and the revolution went no further than Brazil was prepared for, that is liberation from the colonial yoke, political emancipation. More far-reaching reforms had to await other times and another opportunity, more favorable and further advanced in the historical evolution of the country. In this way popular agitation was overcome and gradually assuaged; and the existing organization of society remained more or less intact.

It was only in the direction of political independence that the constitutional revolution developed. The control of this process fell into the hands of the "Brazilian party," which was naturally fitted for the task, for its interests and objects at that moment coincided with the march of events. The party saw a convenient instrument for its purpose in the crown prince Dom Pedro, who acted as regent after the departure of his father, the king. They knew how to use him, by drawing him, perhaps without his at first even realizing it, into the struggle against the Portuguese *côrtes* and the plans to recolonize Brazil. This manoeuvre was crowned with complete success, and led to full independence; and this was the great achievement of José Bonifacio and of the others who followed him in this policy.

31

Politics and Society in Brazilian Independence

Emilia Viotti da Costa

The economic factor on its own is too exclusive a historical category to explain the background and process of Brazil's transition from colony to empire. Emilia Viotti da Costa, Professor of History at Yale University, restores politics to its place in the pattern of causation, focuses more closely on social groups, and reveals too the role of ideas. The elites who took power in Brazil in 1822—the owners of plantations, the merchants, and the bureaucrats—had strong roots in the colony. From the colony they inherited an agrarian structure based on slave labor and a primary export system that survived from the eighteenth century. Ideas, too, they took from the century of Enlightenment, reducing them to a form of liberalism compatible with Brazilian society, providing a rationale for independence and an ideology for their subsequent rule. This made an exception of liberty for slaves and of equality for blacks and mulattos, and served to preserve colonial forms and values in independent Brazil.

That the traditional colonial system had become obsolete was something neither the Crown nor the colonists perceived immediately. The Crown was conscious only of gold smuggling, fiscal evasions, losses to the royal treasury, contraband, and the colonists' continual transgression of the law. The colonists, on the other hand, rebelled against particular institutions or measures taken by the Crown—increases in taxes, restrictions on free communication between the provinces, the exploitative nature of certain monopolies, the inefficiency of the courts, the corruption and arbitrariness of the Crown's officials, and discrimination against subjects born in the colony.

Gradually, however, colonial uprisings and the violent repression that followed them revealed the fundamental antagonism between the interests of the colony and those of the mother country. The colonists, who at the beginning had considered themselves the Portuguese of Brazil, perceived more and more clearly that their interests were linked to Brazil rather than Portugal. And their struggles, which at first had seemed to be conflicts between subjects of the same king, began to be perceived as struggles between colonists and the mother country. Since the colonists identified the interests of the Crown with those of the mother country, their anticolonialism led them to criticize the indiscriminate power of the king and to stress the sovereignty of the people. It was for these reasons and within this context that colonists became receptive to liberal ideas.

In eighteenth-century Brazil, Rousseau, Montesquieu, Raynal, and even more radical authors like Mably were eagerly read by the intellectual elite in spite of censorship. But even more important than these books to the spread of revolutionary ideas were the American and French revolutions.

Resenting colonial domination and royal absolutism, the colonists found in the two revolutions a model to be followed. In the last two decades of the eighteenth century the tensions undermining the colonial system were expressed in a series of conspiracies inspired by the new revolutionary ideology.

Among the books confiscated from Luis Vieira, a priest involved in the conspiracy of 1789 in Minas (Inconfidencia Mineira), were copies of Montesquieu, D'Alembert, Turgot, Raynal, and Mably. Tiradentes, one of the leaders of the same conspiracy, was charged by Portuguese authorities with an attempt to translate a French edition of the United States' Constitution. Others who were arrested and tried in 1789 were accused of having praised the American Revolution or of following the "French party." Some years later, in 1792, when a conspiracy was discovered in Rio, the men arrested were accused of plotting a rebellion to establish a "democratic, free, and independent government." They were clearly influenced by what were known at the time as "the abominable French principles." When a group was arrested for conspiracy in Bahía in 1798, one of the leaders was charged with inciting others to "become French" so they could live in equality and abundance. "To become French" meant to adopt the revolutionary ideas that France exported to the world.

The inquiry set up by the count of Rezende, then viceroy, to investigate the conspiracy of 1792 revealed some of the "sinful thoughts" circulating in public places as well as private houses where some individuals were inveighing against religion and the divine power of kings in "scandalous and impious speeches." According to the inquiry these men denied the existence of miracles and declared that kings had received power from men rather than God. They openly asserted that if the Bible had given kings power to punish their vassals, it had also given vassals the power to punish their kings. The suspects said that men were born free and could claim their freedom at any time. And they argued as well that the laws in France were fair and should be adopted in Brazil. Some had gone so far as to hope that the French would conquer Rio de Janeiro. In the opinion of the authorities in charge of the investigation, the revolutionaries should be severely punished since they had tried "to seduce the rustic and ignorant people and to alienate them from their legitimate and natural sovereign."

But neither arrests nor threats of exile or death could stop the revolutionary process. Censorship proved a vain attempt to limit the dissemination of ideas that challenged the existing order. Equally useless were the harsh punishments that came down upon the rebels. Books continued to arrive in the country and students who traveled abroad to study in Portugal or France brought home new ideas. They gathered in private houses or on street corners, in literary and scientific academies or in secret societies to discuss the books they had read, to comment on the things they had seen, and to talk about their dreams. Revolutionary ideas passed from person to person and, in spite of violent repression, the "abominable French principles" continued to inspire new uprisings. As late as 1817, a group of rebels in Pernambuco still perceived the French constitutions of 1791, 1793, and 1795 as models to be followed. And one of the leaders of the rebellion, Cruz Cabugá, decorated the walls of his house with portraits of French and American revolutionary heroes. In a symbolic gesture the revolutionaries of 1817 abandoned traditional protocol—instead of addressing each other as *Vossa Mercê* (Your Honor) or *Senhor* (Sir), they followed the example of French revolutionaries and used the expressions *vós* (you) and *patriota* (patriot).

By that time, however, the French Revolution belonged to history and the atmosphere in Europe had changed. After the Restoration, European governments interested in sweeping away the effects of the French Revolution had adopted counterrevolutionary policies. The Holy Alliance cautiously watched over Europe, ready to suppress any uprising. Crimes committed during the revolution had turned many people against revolutionary ideas and inclined them to reformist and conservative programs. But some who lived in Brazil in the early nineteenth century had continued to be stubbornly loyal to the ideals of the French Revolution. Although they had become more conservative and more afraid of mass movements, they had not given up their dreams of independence.

Imbued with revolutionary ideas, the Brazilian elites who conspired for independence in the late eighteenth century had created quite a number of secret societies. The Conjuração Bahiana, a conspiracy discovered in 1798 in Bahia, followed upon the creation in 1797 of a Masonic lodge: Os Cavaleiros da Luz (the Knights of the Light). Some of the men arrested in Pernambuco in 1817 were members of secret societies, and in 1818, John VI was informed that many important people in Rio de Janeiro—royal functionaries, merchants, planters, lawyers, professors, and priests—had connections with the Masonry. They constituted a powerful group and stoutly resisted the king's attempt to close their lodges. In 1821 they played an important role in politics and were ready to lead the movement for independence.

Although the influence of secret societies and liberal ideas on the revolutionary conspiracies is undeniable, one should not overestimate their importance. They seem to have played an important role only in 1821–22 and even then only a small minority belonged to secret societies. And only a few members of the elite were familiar with European authors, whom they read with more enthusiasm than judgement. The common man remained unmoved by theoretical speculation though he could be stirred by references to the "French principles," "pátria," and "freedom," expressions which seemed to have a magic effect upon the urban masses.

In addition to illiteracy, political indifference, and the deficient system of communication—all of which created obstacles to the spread of liberal ideas among the population—the very nature of these ideas imposed limits on their dissemination in Brazil. In Europe, liberalism had originally been a bourgeois ideology, an instrument in the struggle against the absolute power of kings, the privileges of the nobility, and the feudal institutions that inhibited economic development. But in Brazil, liberalism became the ideology of rural oligarchies, which found in the new ideas arguments they could use against the mother country. These men were primarily concerned with eliminating colonial institutions that restricted the landowners and merchants—the two most powerful groups in colonial society. When they struggled for freedom and equality, they were actually fighting to eliminate monopolies and privileges that benefited the mother country and to liberate themselves from commercial restrictions that forced Brazilians to buy and sell products through Portugal. Thus, during this period, liberalism in Brazil expressed the oligarchies' desire for independence from the impositions of the Portuguese Crown. The oligarchies, however, were not willing to abandon their traditional control over land and labor, nor did they want to change the traditional system of production. This led them to purge liberalism of its most radical tendencies.

The elites' commitment to slavery constituted a major obstacle to their full acceptance and implemention of liberal ideas. Since the eighteenth century, those who nurtured dreams of independence and conspired against the Portuguese government had confronted the problem of slavery. Serious talk of revolution was often stopped short by the fear of a slave rebellion. The revolutionary leaders were with few exceptions elitists and racists. But where would they find support for a conspiracy for independence if not among the blacks and mulattos who formed the majority of the Brazilian population? How would they control the masses of slaves and freedmen in a revolutionary situation? Should slaves be granted freedom? All of these questions were raised by the leaders of the Inconfidencia Mineira in 1789 and again in 1798 by some participants in the Conjuração Bahiana. The uneasiness of the white leaders in the face of the masses is most visible in the Conjuração Bahiana. Although most of the conspirators arrested in Bahia were mulattos and blacks—some free, some still enslaved—Cipriano Barata, a middle-class white and one of the heads of the conspiracy, wrote a letter to a friend advising him to "beware of this rabble of blacks and mulattos." Later, the leaders of the 1817 revolution in Pernambuco, anxious to gain the slaveowners' support, issued a proclamation to reassure them about their slaves: "Patriots," read the proclamation, "your property rights, even those that offend the ideal of justice, are sacred. The government will find the means to diminish the evil [slavery], but will not stop it by force."

Their distrust of the masses, their fear of a slave rebellion, and their desire to preserve the slave system led the elites to repudiate democratic procedures and to avoid mass mobilization. In 1821, those who struggled for independence sought the regent's support, hoping to gain independence without social turmoil. Considering the revolutionaries' commitment to slavery and their intention to exclude the majority of the population from the electoral process, their manifestos in favor of representative government, their speeches about the sovereignty of the people, and their designation of freedom and equality as inalienable human rights can only sound false and empty to modern ears.

Another peculiarity of Brazilian liberals during this period was their conciliatory attitude toward the Church and religion. In 1817 placards appeared in Recife showing such slogans as "Long live the country," "Long live the Virgin," "Long live the Catholic religion," and "Death to the aristocrats." These and the cheers to revolution and religion that could be heard in the streets suggest the revolutionaries' commitment to the Church and Catholicism. The participation of numerous priests in the conspiracy reinforces the impression. So many clergymen joined the 1817 rebellion in Pernambuco that the uprising came to be known as the Revolution of the Priests. When they were brought to trial, some priests were charged with using their churches to propagate subversive ideas. Others were accused of being Masons and of actively cooperating with the rebels. And certain churchmen, like the famous Friar Canéca, appeared in the court records as guerrilla leaders.

At first glance, it might seem difficult to explain the revolutionary tendency of the Brazilian clergy and their sympathetic attitude toward Freemasonry, which in Europe was the bulwark of the struggle against the Church. A closer analysis of the relationship between Church and State in Brazil reveals that the right of patronage granted by the pope to the Portuguese kings was the source of the clergy's hostility toward the system and explains their commitment to liberal ideas. As a consequence the anticlericalism and the secular tendencies typical of European liberalism were not to be found in Brazil at this point. Equally atypical was the role nationalist ideas played in Brazil. While in most European revolutions of the nineteenth century, liberal and nationalist ideas were closely associated in Brazil nationalist ideas found a less propitious ground. Nothing in the economic structure of the country furthered contact among the provinces. The internal market was insignificant, since most goods were shipped abroad and the communications network that linked the provinces was precarious and underdeveloped. Thus the conditions that led to national integration and inspired nationalist ideas in Europe were lacking in Brazil. It is not surprising, then, that most of the revolutionary movements before 1822 had a regional character and failed to develop national goals. The *inconfidentes* of 1789 talked about uniting Minas and São Paulo. The conspiracies of 1792 in Rio and 1798 in Bahia never spread beyond the limits of the two urban centers. The revolution of 1817 in Pernambuco, which followed a more ambitious plan, still recruited supporters only in a few northeastern provinces. And even in 1821, one year before the proclamation of independence, Brazilian representatives to the Portuguese Côrtes still made a point of presenting themselves as delegates from their provinces rather than from the colony. Because of these centripetal tendencies, many leaders of the 1822 movement feared that Brazil would follow the example of the Spanish colonies and split into several states after independence. So generalized was this opinion that in Portugal in 1822, plans to recolonize Brazil counted on the country's lack of unity. The maintenance of Brazil's territorial integrity after independence, then, cannot be attributed to a strong nationalist ideology; Brazilian elites simply recognized that the only way to assure the independent status of the nation was to eschew secession.

If there were no powerful nationalist ideas to promote national integration, there were definite and unifying anti-Portuguese tendencies in Brazil at the end of the colonial period. In spite of the fact that many Portuguese participated in the conspiracies and fought for independence, the majority of the revolutionaries were native Brazilians. And hostility against the mother country often expressed itself as hostility against the Portuguese. Even more curious, considering the underlying "racism" of the elite groups, is the fact that attacks against the Portuguese were sometimes voiced as racial antagonism between blacks and whites; in the words of a revolutionary in 1789, "We will soon throw out of Brazil these little whites from the mother country who wish to take over our land." In a memoir written in 1817, a conspicuous royalist observed that the "rabble" of mulattos, blacks, and the like, seduced by the word freedom, was not royalist and should be under constant surveillance. His impression was not unfounded; blacks and mulattos had several times expressed their animosity toward the Portuguese and white Brazilians and had shown their willingness to support revolutions. . . .

Lower-class blacks and mulattos saw independence as a step toward eliminating the racial discrimination that prohibited their appointment to administrative positions, barred their access to the University of Coimbra, and made the higher church positions inaccessible to them. Equal opportunity for all without regard to race or color was their primary aspiration. They also hoped to abolish class differences that separated men into rich and poor. And in liberalism they found the arguments they needed to justify their hopes. To these people the fight for independence was first of all a battle against whites and their privileges. As one of them put it, they would all be rich when privileges would be abolished and merit became the only criterion for promotion.

While the masses expressed their hostility against the Portuguese in racial terms, the white elite in general expressed fear of blacks and mulattos and would have endorsed the words of Carneiro de Campos, a high official in the administration, who wrote that "slaves and free coloreds were congenital enemies of the white man."

In spite of their mutual distrust and different goals, they joined together in their conspiracies and fought side by side for independence in the name of liberal ideals.

Most of the *inconfidentes* of 1789, for example, were landowners or high bureaucrats. But among them there were others of modest origins, petty functionaries, soldiers, muleteers, artisans, and servants. And two completely different groups participated in the Bahian conspiracy of 1798. The first was composed of "men of property and standing" educated in the Enlightenment tradition. The second group included slaves, freedmen, blacks, and mulattos recruited among the urban population, tailors, shoemakers, masons, hairdressers, soldiers, and peddlers.

The same combination of upper- and lower-class people characterizes the 1817 revolution in Pernambuco. Again the leaders were merchants, landowners, and royal functionaries from important families. At their trial, these men defended themselves by arguing that they could not have conspired against the government: they belonged to "the first and highest nobility of Pernambuco, and had been raised to respect the hierarchy of classes and orders." Their lawyer argued that these members of the elite had been forced to concede to the irresistible pressure of the masses. To present the elites as victims of mass rebellion was merely an expedient of the defense, but there is no doubt that in 1817, as in previous conspiracies, the common people had gladly joined with the revolutionary elite. The enthusiasm for "this damned freedom"—as counterrevolutionary documents called it—had spread among the urban masses of blacks and mulattos, although they seemed always more titillated by the idea of equality.

The behavior of the urban masses during the revolution of 1817 scandalized members of the elite who had not been carried away by revolutionary ideas. One of them, Cardoso, wrote to a friend that the "half-castes, mulattos, and creoles had become so daring that they declared all men equal, and boasted that they themselves would marry only white women of the best stock. Pharmacists, surgeons, and bloodletters gave themselves airs, and barbers refused to shave Cardoso, claiming that they were occupied in the service of their country. To his horror, Cardoso was forced to shave himself. Worse yet, the half-castes were familiar and disrespectful in manner. As he wrote to his friend, "Your Grace would not permit a half-caste to come up to you, hat on his head, and clapping you on the shoulder address you: 'Well met, patriot, how are you? How about giving me a smoke, or taking some of mine?' Such was the offer one of Brederodes' slaves made to Crown Judge Afonso! Fortunately," Cardoso concluded with evident satisfaction, "the half-caste received his well-deserved punishment. He has already been awarded five hundred lashes." Like many other conservatives, Cardoso was horrified to see Domingos José Martins, a well-established man and a leader of the 1817 revolution, walking arm in arm with members of the lower classes.

Before independence, the class and racial conflict latent in Brazilian society could often be disguised among the revolutionary ranks. Everyone was fighting for the same cause—to emancipate the colony from the mother country. Liberal formulas were at this stage sufficiently vague and abstract to encompass different aspirations and to create an illusory sense of unity. Besides, there were other mechanisms soothing class and racial tensions. People belonging to the lower classes—whites, blacks, or mulattos—were frequently linked to members of the elites through the system of clientele and patronage. And if patronage did not actually eliminate the lines of color and class, it did create an appearance of camaraderie and reciprocity that obscured social distinctions.

In spite of the mechanisms that contributed to solidarity among the revolutionaries, their goals, as we have seen, were often different if not contradictory. Slaves aimed at emancipation; free blacks and mulattos hoped to abolish racial discrimination and gain equality; upper-class white farmers and merchants wanted above all to free themselves from restrictions imposed by the mother country but were not inclined to emancipate their slaves or to make fundamental concessions to the poor. These contradictory interests came into open conflict after independence; earlier, different groups struggled side by side against the Portuguese government.

Until the beginning of the nineteenth century, every conspiracy failed. Those in Minas (1789), Rio de Janeiro (1792), and Bahia (1798) never progressed beyond the stage of plots and intrigues. The rebels were severely punished, the leaders condemned to death or exile. And the majority of the population remained indifferent to the events. In spite of growing discontent, nothing seemed to indicate that Portuguese control over Brazil would soon come to an end. One incident, however, accelerated the historical process—the invasion of the Iberian Peninsula by French troops and the consequent transfer of the Portuguese court to Brazil.

The location of the government center in the colony imposed fundamental changes on colonial policies. Brazilian ports were opened to all nations in 1808; Brazil became a kingdom united with Portugal in 1815; and new institutions were created to satisfy the needs of the imperial government. All these measures benefited the colony and hurt the mother country. And the most harmful measure of all, from the point of view of Portugal, was the adoption of free trade policies and the elimination of the commercial monopolies the Portuguese had formerly enjoyed.

Until 1808 the bulk of Portuguese trade was conducted with Brazil. Portugal was the distributor of colonial products in Europe and of European manufactures in Brazil. Outfitters, sailors, royal functionaries, and merchants all benefited from colonial trade. This profitable system broke down when Brazilian ports were opened. Worse yet, once in Brazil João VI granted preferential tariffs to England as compensation for the English help against the French. The Portuguese king tried to counteract the unpopular effects of his policies by granting his Portuguese subjects several privileges. He favored products transported in Portuguese ships as well as products that came from Portugal or the Portuguese empire. But this was of little use since Portuguese producers and merchants were not capable of competing in a free market. They could survive only as long as the system of monopolies and privileges was maintained. Without solving the problems of the Portuguese, the protective measures taken by the king aroused dissatisfaction among foreign merchants and Brazilians. Trying to satisfy conflicting interest groups, the king incurred the resentment of all. . . .

In Brazil, economic expansion after 1808 made the obsolescence of traditional institutions even more apparent. And in spite of censorship, publications denouncing the inefficiency of those institutions appeared one after another. Their main argument can be summarized in the words of Hipólito da Costa. In 1817, he wrote in the *Correio Braziliense*, a newspaper published in London, that a country on its way to becoming a great and civilized nation could not continue to endure a military government and colonial institutions that had been established when Brazilian settlements were mere garrison posts. Da Costa's opinion was corroborated by many travelers who visited the country in the first two decades of the nineteenth century. The colonists were obviously unhappy with the government. And the more they complained, the more discontented they became. They felt more alienated from and more eager to introduce changes in the administration. It is true that João VI had taken halting steps in that direction, but he had not gone as far as Brazilians wanted. The revolution of 1817 in Pernambuco was a symptom of these tensions. Repression could stop it but could not remove the causes of dissatisfaction. At any time revolutionary discontent could surface again, as it did in 1820, when the revolutionary tide that swept Europe reached Brazil.

In January of that year, Spain was shaken by a liberal revolution and João VI hastily passed several new laws intended to favor Portuguese merchants. He hoped with these measures to secure their support and to avoid repeating in Portugal the events in Spain. But in August 1820, there was an uprising in the city of Oporto. The revolutionaries demanded a constitution and the king's immediate return to Portugal.

These events had great repercussions in Brazil. Many people manifested their sympathy with the constitutionalist revolution. Portu-

guese and Brazilians, merchants and plantation owners, royal functionaries and military men supported the revolution for a variety of often
contradictory reasons and with predictably incompatible goals. Portuguese merchants, who identified themselves with the interests of the
mother country, supported the constitutionalist revolution in the hope
that the king would be forced by the Côrtes to reestablish the colonial
pact. They had the support of most military men and royal functionaries who were eager to return to Portugal. Plantation owners, foreign
merchants, and all the others, Portuguese or Brazilian, who had benefited from free trade, as well as royal functionaries and military men
who had invested money in Brazil or had established links with Brazilian families, saw the revolution as a liberal movement that would
put an end to absolutism and sweep away the remaining monopolies
and privileges. They believed that a constitutional government would
give them the opportunity to express their own interests in the Côrtes.
And they hoped to consolidate the privileges they had gained since the
Portuguese court had arrived in Brazil.

The contradiction between the two groups passed unnoticed at the
beginning. But it soon became clear that the revolution, which had
started in Portugal as a liberal revolution, now had as its main objective the annulment of liberal concessions made by João VI to Brazil.
This realization, however, was several months in coming. Meanwhile a
number of revolutionary juntas were formed. On 20 February 1821 a
military pronunciamento was followed by street demonstrations in Rio
de Janeiro. The main purpose of the demonstrations was to force the
king to accept the demands of the Portuguese Côrtes. João VI agreed to
swear allegiance to a still-to-be-written constitution and ordered the
municipal councils in Brazil to do the same. He called for the election
of Brazilian representatives to the Côrtes and decided, much against
his will, to return to Portugal, where a hostile and demanding convention awaited him. In April he left Brazil, leaving his son Pedro as
regent. . . .

While the majority of the population was unconcerned with politics,
a minority was determined to benefit from the political crisis, which
had given them an opportunity to be heard in the Portuguese Côrtes.
But they were quickly disappointed. The measures taken by the Côrtes
soon revealed that the Portuguese intended not only to restrict free
trade and reestablish the old monopolies and privileges, but also to
limit the colony's administrative autonomy. It was also clear that the
Côrtes were not willing to accept any compromise. The Brazilian delegates were greatly outnumbered by the Portuguese; only 50 of the
appointed 75 had arrived in Portugal, out of a total of 205 delegates.

They could do nothing to protect the colony's interests. Given these circumstances, the only sensible response was rebellion.

Leaflets denouncing the "recolonizing" intentions of the Côrtes and encouraging the people to support the cause of independence were posted around the city of Rio. From many parts of the country came petitions calling on the regent to disobey the Côrtes. . . . It was clear that the measures taken by the Côrtes—the last of which was an order for the prince to return to Portugal—had made it impossible for the Brazilian elites to reach the compromise they had hoped for at the beginning. They had dreamed of creating a dual monarchy, a system that would respect Brazilian autonomy, yet keep the two countries united. But the decrees abolishing administrative autonomy and limiting free trade had made this solution impossible. There was no alternative left to the Brazilian elites but to resist the orders. And the best way to minimize the effect of such disobedience on Portugal was to have the regent on their side. Even more important, with the prince's support they could hope to achieve political autonomy without mass mobilization. . . .

In June 1822 the Conselho de Procuradores, which the prince had created, recommended that he call a national convention. He accepted their suggestion immediately. A ruling of 19 June 1822 established eligibility requirements for the electorate. It gave the ballot to any male citizen, married or single, who was over twenty years of age and was not living with his parents. But it excluded from suffrage those whose income came from wage labor, with the exception of clerks in commercial firms, high-ranking employees of the royal household, and administrators of rural plantations and factories. It also denied the vote to members of religious orders, foreigners not yet naturalized, and criminals. Such legislation deprived the masses of the right to choose their representatives and gave all political power to the elites.

On 2 September 1822, the prince's wife Leopoldina presided over a meeting of the Council of State in Rio while the prince was traveling in São Paulo. She informed the councilors that the Côrtes intended to send troops to Brazil because it considered the regent and his advisors traitors and enemies of the Crown. It became clear then that the prince had only two options: to obey the Côrtes and return to Portugal in disgrace or to formalize Brazilian independence and remain in Brazil as King. José Bonifácio [his chief political advisor] wrote to him: "From Portugal we can expect only enslavement and horror. Come back and make a decision; irresolution and temperate measure cannot help. In view of this merciless enemy, one moment lost is a disgrace." Recognizing the inevitable, Pedro proclaimed Brazilian independence on

7 September 1822, while he was still in São Paulo. Once independence had been formally proclaimed, it was too late to back down. All the efforts of the Portuguese government to reverse the situation were frustrated. One after another, Portuguese attempts to get European support for their recolonizing project failed. The position of the British government was a decisive factor in consolidating Brazil's independence. Canning, the British minister, made it clear at his first meeting with the Portuguese foreign minister that Britain would not tolerate European military intervention in the New World. Any such action would force His Majesty to recognize the independence of the colony in question. Great Britain's strong position discouraged Portuguese plans to reconquer Brazil. England would later serve as mediator in Brazil's diplomatic efforts to obtain formal recognition of independence from Portugal.

32

A Wicked Revolution

Judgement in Bahia

Most of the movements of protest in late colonial Brazil—like independence itself—were devoid of revolutionary aims. They accepted social inequality, racial discrimination, and slavery, and focused their sights on political change and commercial reform. In Bahia in 1798, however, a conspiracy briefly surfaced that went beyond liberty and demanded equality. The actors were mainly poor people. They were artisans, many of them self-employed tailors; soldiers, most of them of the lowest rank; slaves and ex-slaves. All were fired by social anger, high food prices, and the ideas of the age. The majority of the conspirators were mulattos, with a few blacks and some whites. The whites, members of the elite, preached the primacy of reason, freedom of thought, political reform, and free trade. But the character of the conspiracy was set by mulatto artisans and soldiers, who were ready to use violence in pursuit of a new and democratic government: access to offices and higher military rank, independence from Portugal, abolition of slavery, and above all social and racial equality. The organization of the conspirators was weak, and their power nonexistent. But their revolutionary demands frightened the authorities and brought cruel retribution on their heads. The mulattos received no mercy, and between hangings, whippings, and imprisonment were taught a sharp lesson. The white participants were treated more leniently, for the Portuguese authorities knew that without the collaboration of the local elites they could not govern Brazil. The incident proved, first, that there existed an alternative model of revolution, recognized by Brazilians and Portuguese alike, against which reformist programmes as well as colonial government could be judged. Second, the movement confirmed that social

Translated by John Lynch from "A Inconfidência da Bahia em 1798," *Anais da Biblioteca Nacional do Rio de Janeiro*, 45 (1922–23), pp. 23–24, 54–59.

revolution of this kind was unlikely to succeed in Brazil; as soon as elite participants observed the radicalization of the popular sectors, they withdrew into the protection of the existing regime. The *Conjuração Bahiana* represented a revolution that never was.

PUBLIC DENUNCIATION SWORN BY JOAQUIM JOSÉ DA VEIGA, FREE MULATTO, MARRIED, BLACKSMITH BY TRADE, DOORKEEPER AT ST. BENEDICT'S, AGAINST A CERTAIN PERSON [JOÃO DE DEUS], MULATTO, OWNER OF A TAILOR'S SHOP IN A STREET TO THE RIGHT OF THE PALACE, AND AGAINST ALL THE OTHER PARTICIPANTS IN THE CONSPIRACY ORGANIZED BY HIM.

At five o'clock on the afternoon of 24 August [1798] the accuser was outside the Convent of Mercy with João de Deus, the mulatto tailor, who told him he had some business to discuss with him if he would come to his house. Veiga agreed to go at 7 o'clock the same night; he met the accused waiting in the doorway and was taken into the house. There were a number of other people inside, so João de Deus suggested they both go outside, which they did, and they found a place to talk in the Chapel of Our Lady of Succor, near the Sacristy. João de Deus then addressed Veiga as follows.

He said that Veiga looked like a Frenchman, to which the latter replied that this was not the case. But João de Deus continued: it was obvious that Veiga was clever and qualified for a matter that he wanted to discuss with him. It was important that all [Brazilians] become Frenchmen, in order to live in equality and abundance; for this purpose he had planned an agreement with two hundred or so people; he had already summoned them into an established party, and this party would organize a rebellion, by means of which they would achieve their aims. These were to sack the city, to force His Highness and Excellence the Governor to adhere to this same faction and to kill him if he resisted; at the same time to destroy all the officials, to attack the monasteries, to open their doors to those who wanted to leave, to plunder them of all their treasures, and to break the chains of prisoners and set them free. Thus they would reduce everything to a complete revolution, so that all might be rich and rescued from poverty, the difference between white, black, and brown would be brought to an end, and all would be regarded the same and admitted to offices and appointments without discrimination.

After this exhortation Veiga was asked to go on the following day at the time of the Angelus to the house of João de Deus, so that with other people who had already agreed and been invited for the same purpose they could proceed to settle the best methods and time to bring the projected revolution into effect. As Veiga was rightly frightened of such a revolution, which could only be the product of a deranged mind, he went early the following morning to the Colonel of the Artillery Regiment, Dom Carlos Balthazar da Silveira, and revealed everything he had heard. The Colonel advised him to guard his tongue and keep these outrageous proposals under cover, the better to investigate such treachery, and this he did. When he returned home the same morning, he learned that a black apprentice of João de Deus, whom he thought was a slave of Tabellião Bernardino de Senne e Araujo, had brought a message from the tailor that he should go immediately to his shop, where he encountered João de Deus, together with the youth who brought the message and two more artisans who were working there. João took him aside and told him that he had decided not to hold further meetings in his house of people who belonged to the projected party of rebellion, because they could easily be seen, and these frequent meetings of crowds of people could cause suspicion; therefore they would assemble in the field of the dike at Desterro [on the outskirts of Salvador]. The meeting was fixed for that night, and Veiga was to come to the house of João de Deus at the time of the Angelus, to set out from there with him and the others.

Thereupon Veiga sought out Lieutenant Colonel Alexandre Theotonio de Souza, who advised him that on no account should he discourage the said João; rather he should show willing to accompany him in his revolution, even offering to bring in more people to his party; this was the best way to discover all the participants. So the accuser returned a second time to the shop of João about two o'clock in the afternoon, where he met the same people, and following a few casual remarks João called him aside and said, "So are we ready for tonight's action?" Veiga replied, "Of course, I am ready, and as we need more men, either soldiers or civilians, I will bring them from my many acquaintances." João replied, "Bring a hundred, or two hundred, or as many as you think sufficient." With this assurance, Veiga withdrew.

PUBLIC DENUNCIATION SWORN BY CAPTAIN OF THE AUXILIARY REGIMENT
OF BLACKS, JOAQUIM JOSÉ DE SANTA ANNA, MARRIED, RESIDENT IN THE
STREET OF JOÃO PEREIRA, WITH A BARBER'S SHOP IN THE STREET OF
CORPO SANTO, AGAINST A CERTAIN MULATTO [JOÃO DE DEUS], WITH A
TAILOR'S SHOP IN THE STREET TO THE RIGHT OF THE PALACE, AND
AGAINST ALL THE OTHER PARTICIPANTS IN THE PROJECTED CONSPIRACY.

On Saturday 25 August about one o'clock in the afternoon the accuser was in his barber's shop in the street on the right of Corpo Santo, when the accused, João de Deus, approached and invited him to meet that same night in the field of the dike at Desterro, where he had arranged a meeting of more than two hundred people to organize an uprising and rebellion which they were planning to start in this city and its district. The intention was to establish a well-conceived system of liberty, and to destroy all the officials of the public, political, and economic administration which rules this continent under the salutary laws of His Most Faithful Majesty, whom God save for many years.

João began his diabolical and terrible attempt to entice Santa Anna by asking him how he fared with his [militia] regiment. The latter replied that all was well, in spite of the amount of work involved in participating in regimental manoeuvres; as his aim was to become a perfect officer and to serve satisfactorily, he was obliged to maintain frequent attendance at the barracks of the infantry regiments in order to improve himself in everything pertaining to military duties. At the same time, he continued, he felt extremely disappointed when he heard it said that a white Sergeant-Major [commanding officer] was being appointed for his Regiment, and if this were true he would certainly give up his great efforts. João de Deus replied that he should persevere, because he could become Colonel of the Second Regiment of the Line. Santa Anna answered that he thought this impossible. But the accused insisted that he should have no doubt, because things were changing in a direction Santa Anna did not imagine; that the day would soon come when he would see troops of the line with white, mulatto, and black commanding officers without distinction of racial category or qualification. To this Santa Anna replied that he could not hope to qualify so easily, it seemed impossible.

João de Deus again made answer, saying that there was a lot of powder and shot, and enough men to reduce the people of this city to equality, without distinction of racial category, as he had already said. The port, he continued, would be open and free to all foreign nations to come and trade, bringing cloth and every kind of merchandise to be exchanged for sugar, tobacco, and other products of the land, without need of Portugal, which was superfluous in matters of production. In support of this action, he said, there were many officers and soldiers among the troops of the line, who had been rewarded with advances of pay, and in addition to these there were many other people of substance. Even the Most Illustrious and Excellent Governor and Captain General of this Captaincy follows the party of rebellion, though secretly, for he has actually said, "What are they doing, these accursed people, that they have not already risen? How long are they going to wait?" Thereupon Santa Anna again expressed doubts, saying it was impossible to believe that the Governor would follow such a party or agree to its aims. But João replied that at the first outbreak of rebellion the Guard of the Palace and Person of the Governor would have to be attacked and the Governor himself arrested by subterfuge, and he would then issue all the necessary orders for the rest. Ministers were not necessary for the government of the people, and should therefore be immediately put to the knife, while merchants should be spared for the good of the public. At this point the Intendant General of Finance of Bahia happened to pass by the door of Santa Anna, who remarked on the fact, and the accused replied that this minister too had to be killed and relieved of the 60,000 cruzados he possessed.

João de Deus continued his exhortation. Their strength would be in the prison fortresses, and all the mulatto and black prisoners would be placed at liberty, and there would be no more slaves. In some plantations the slaves were already on the side of the rebellion. The convents and monasteries would be thrown open, and those who wanted to leave would be free to do so. Prisoners would be released and galley slaves freed, and everyone would be of the same party. He asked Santa Anna if he had at his disposition the arms of the soldiers of his company, and when the latter replied Yes, he asked him to persuade his men to join the rising, explaining to them everything he had said. He concluded by inviting Santa Anna to meet that night at his house, and from there they would all go to the field of the dike to see and admire the uniformed men who had joined the party of rebellion, to receive orders and instructions concerning the plans, and to learn the day and the hour (one o'clock at night) when they had to assemble with their people.

Final Judgement

ON 14 JUNE 1799 IN THE CITY OF SALVADOR DA BAHIA AT THE RESIDENCE OF THE SENIOR JUDGE OF THE CRIMINAL COURT, DR. MANOEL DE MAGALHAENS PINTO AVELAR DE BARBEDO, THE FOLLOWING SUMMARY OF LEGAL PROCEEDINGS AND CONCLUSIONS WERE MADE.

A number of wicked individuals of this city having planned and decided to organize a most abominable conspiracy, designed to raise the people, suborn them from their allegiance to the Supreme Power and high sovereignty of the monarch, and destroy the established form of government, replacing it by a base and independent democracy, they proceeded to consider the best means of accomplishing this detestable sedition, seeking to spread and communicate to the mass of the people the crazed message and poisonous doctrine with which they themselves were infected. They ceaselessly propagated and disseminated their own madness by persuasive tactics and the organization of secret meetings, attracting some wretches by the prospect of more relaxed customs, others by the offer of future promotion, and yet others by the rich plunder they expected to obtain from the sacking of the city, for they freely adopted the most barbarous and pernicious plans to burn the city, assassinate the government and the other authorities, raise the troops, and so achieve and perpetuate their abominable plot.

One of the principal chiefs of these wicked people was Luís Gonzaga das Virgens, a man of fanatical and insolent disposition, whose papers and writings show a refusal to tolerate differences in social conditions and inequality of wealth, which necessarily characterize civil society and which are balanced by reciprocal benefits and extensive rights. He dared to present to the government the audacious demands herein appended in which he developed the antisocial principles of absolute equality, subsequently promoted by the infamous conspiracy which he headed.

Enraged when the military promotion that he sought was blocked, Gonzaga was foolish and unscrupulous enough to denounce the holy religion and good government into which he was born, and sought to spread among the people of his faction the plague of his depraved ideas . . . above all to recommend to his confederates the illusion of a general equality without distinction of color and education. This was the doctrine he constantly taught, presenting it as the source of all happiness, the aim of the projected revolt.

While becoming leader and instigator of the proposed rebellion, Gonzaga began to frequent the house of the soldier Lucas Dantas, where he held numerous meetings to organize the project, for which he recruited the said Lucas Dantas together with Manuel de Santa Anna, a soldier of the Second Regiment of the Line. He initiated them in his system by introducing them to libertarian and seditious ideas, and then proceeded to exhort them to a concerted revolution. He persuaded them of the imaginary advantages of a regime of equality; this was the ultimate goal of his plans, a rash commitment that he never abandoned up to the time of his arrest. . . . He even went as far as forming a list of troops and their pay under his phantom government of equality, and another for those of his own regiment who showed themselves ready for immediate action.

[The accused were found guilty of actions calculated "to subvert public order," of encouraging others "to break the holy and sacred bonds of vassalage," and of committing "the horrible crime of high treason and lese-majesty." Luís Gonzaga das Virgens (soldier), Lucas Dantas (soldier), Manuel Faustino (tailor), and João de Deus (tailor), all poor mulattos, were condemned to death and hanged; their heads and hands were cut off and displayed, their possessions confiscated, and their houses demolished.]

Conclusion

FROM COLONY TO INDEPENDENCE

When the Spanish monarchy collapsed in 1808, the creoles could not allow the political vacuum to remain unfilled, with their lives and property at risk. They had to move quickly to anticipate anarchy and insubordination, convinced that if they did not seize the initiative, more dangerous forces would do so. In the critical period 1810 to 1814 absolute independence was not necessarily the first option. The broad river of creole opinion divided into many streams. Some kept their heads down and their ideas to themselves; others wanted a restoration of the Bourbons and a return to imperial unity; yet others sought the abatement of privilege and extension of opportunity. Even among the activists, many wanted no more than a transition to autonomy within a Spanish constitution, but the metropolis would not concede this. Americans soon found that Spanish liberals were no less imperialist than Spanish conservatives and that vacillation gained nothing. The lesson was learned quickly in the Río de la Plata; in Chile it was reinforced by the experience of harsh counterrevolution. And when counterrevolution prevailed, in Venezuela and New Granada as well as in Chile, the property of creole dissidents was targeted and the economy plundered for the royalist war effort. Creole moderates then joined creole revolutionaries because Spain offered no alternative to imperial government and high taxation.

The Spanish American revolutions were confronted by two enemies and an ambiguous ally—the armies of Spain, the royalist creoles, and popular insurgents. None of these forces alone could permanently impede the revolution, but in conjunction they could constitute a powerful restraint; and when the creoles' fear of the American populace caused them to prefer the protection of the Spanish army, independence could not make progress without external support. Some countries, such as the Río de la Plata and eventually Colombia, were in a position to provide support; others like Peru depended on receiving it. In Peru, where viceregal administration had the nerve and the means to govern effectively, and where the Indian masses were regarded as a greater menace than Spanish power, the creoles were slow to be convinced of the need for change, and liberation had to be imported by the armies of San Martín and Bolívar. In Mexico, on the other hand, the creole elite sought autonomy under a constitutional monarchy, but they were first defeated by the absolutists in 1808 and then overtaken by the insurgents in 1810. The popular rebellions led by the priests Miguel Hidalgo and José María Morelos caused a royalist reaction of extreme severity, which the creoles regarded as preferable to anarchy. Yet counterrevolution in turn dashed their hopes of reform and autonomy, and they grasped with relief the compromise offered by General Agustín de Iturbide: independence from Spain with some concession to reform but none to revolution. Everywhere, or almost everywhere, the struggle for independence was long and violent, and conditions favored the emergence of strong rather than liberal governments, in which executive power took precedence over congresses and constitutions.

The model of independence was political revolution, in which a national ruling class took power from the imperial rulers, with only marginal change in economic organization and social structure. This was true of Brazil no less than of Spanish America. The transfer of the Portuguese court from Lisbon to Rio de Janeiro in 1808 and the opening of the ports of Brazil to foreign trade dramatically reversed the role of colony and metropolis and freed Brazil of the dead weight of monopoly. But the Brazilian elite was still haunted by the social predicaments of the colony. The object, therefore, was to destroy the colonial system—insofar as it obstructed commercial opportunities and administrative autonomy—but to leave intact the plantation and mining economy, to maintain slavery and the existing order of society, and to preserve monarchy as the surest guarantee of stability.[1] In a country where free whites were heavily outnumbered by blacks and slaves, the leaders of independence feared the people and had no desire for equality or democracy. Independence under the protection of a prince rather than through popular mobilization was the preferred solution. They had a power base in the militia, which became the instrument by which landowners succeeded first in ending Portuguese rule, and then in defending the traditional social and political hierarchy against attacks from below.[2]

Brazilian independence contrasted sharply with that of Spanish America. Whereas by mid-century Spanish America was divided into seventeen different republics, Brazil retained its unity as one nation. Whereas Spanish Americans committed their government to personalist caudillos or authoritarian presidents, Brazil secured stability through constitutional monarchy. The difference can be explained in part by the existence in Brazil of a homogeneous elite, trained in civil law (often at Coimbra) and containing at its core a large number of bureaucrats and public employees, especially magistrates and judges. This gave the elite an ideological solidarity, and an awareness of the needs of state-building that was rare in Latin America.[3]

The monarchy in itself was not an agent of national unity, and Pedro I aroused mixed feelings: Was he really converted to constitutional ways? Was he totally disengaged from Portuguese interests? Political discontent was aggravated by economic recession and declining living standards, especially among the poor; soon it was claimed that independence had brought no benefits, except perhaps for the Portuguese, who still dominated commerce and remained a favored group. Hostility to Pedro reached a climax in April 1831 when an improbable alliance of popular sectors, liberal Brazilians, deputies, and the army confronted the monarch and forced him to abdicate in favor of his five-year-old son, who then became the emperor Pedro II. The abdication of the Portuguese prince in deference to his son, born and bred in Brazil, signified the Brazilianization of the monarchy and the final step in the country's political independence. The main beneficiaries of the new regime were the moderate liberals of the Brazilian elite, many of them from Rio, São Paulo, and Minas Gerais, who had been supporters of independence in 1822 and subsequently alienated by the absolutism of Pedro I. Their liberalism had few social implications. They belonged to the dominant class of landowners, slave owners, and bureaucrats, and were part of that national elite whose homogeneity gave Brazil its political culture in the nineteenth century, and whose preference for monarchy determined the form of government until 1889.

Spanish America rejected monarchy but otherwise made little change in the institutional structure. The leaders of independence began by demanding liberty and ended by seeking authority. Even Bolívar, republican though he was, insisted on a strong and centralized government. The Enlightenment had confirmed his attachment to reason and inspired his struggle for liberty and equality, but he had to employ his own intellectual resources to fashion an argument of colonial liberation, and then to find the appropriate limits for freedom and equality. In that process we can see traces of enlightened absolutism as well as of democratic revolution. Conscious of his compatriots' inexperience in

self-government and alarmed by the social conflicts that the wars unleashed, he sought to contain the forces of disorder by imposing a series
of authoritarian constitutions. Already in the Jamaica Letter of 1815 he
wrote, "Events in Tierra Firme have proved that wholly representative
institutions are not suited to our character, customs, and present knowledge."[4] Four years later, in his Angostura Address, he proclaimed, "Complete liberty and absolute democracy are but reefs upon which all republican hopes have foundered. . . . Let the legislature relinquish the
powers that rightly belong to the executive." On more than one occasion, in Venezuela, Peru, Ecuador, and Colombia, he was himself persuaded to become dictator in order to dispel anarchy or defeat the
Spanish enemy. But Bolívar's search for strong government outlived the
war. His final views were embodied in the Constitution that he wrote
for Bolivia in 1826, after the last Spanish army in South America had
been defeated. This document provided for a president with not only
life-long tenure but also with authority to choose his successor, thus
avoiding, he argued, the instability caused by frequent elections and
party government. This was the realistic Bolívar—his democratic
ideals tempered by experience of popular protest, race conflict, and
elite factionalism—the man who declared Spanish America to be ungovernable. The Bolivarian model of government appealed to the military but otherwise made few friends; it excluded too many vested
interests from political life and decisions to gain wide acceptance. The
civilian elites preferred more liberal constitutions, though these and
their authors were affected by that bias towards authority and centralism that was a feature of the republican as it had been of the colonial
state. Most of the Spanish American constitutions allowed the president extraordinary powers of intervention in time of crisis or rebellion,
and most defined the political nation in the narrowest of terms, establishing property and literacy qualifications for those entitled to stand
for election and even to vote.

Constitutions could not in themselves command respect, nor were
they the only focus of political allegiance. People looked to individual
leaders, to strong men to whom they were bound by personal ties of
kinship and obligation. Thus, the pioneers of independence—the intellectuals, bureaucrats, and professional politicians—soon gave way to
the caudillos, the chieftains whose rule was based on personal power
and control of local resources rather than on constitutional forms and
regulated succession. Caudillo prototypes could be observed at the end
of the colonial period, as land concentration and estate formation
pushed the dispossessed into bands under chieftains who would lead
them to plunder and subsistence. But caudillism was not characteristic

of the colonial state, which was a bureaucratic structure that left little space for the exercise of personal power. The caudillos were products of the wars of independence, which gave rural leaders the opportunity to become patriots and guerrillas and to enhance their legitimacy as republican heroes.[5] In the years around 1810 there was a progression from llanero or gaucho to vagrant, to bandit, to guerrilla fighter as local chieftains or new leaders sought to recruit followers by offering them first booty and then a political cause. These forces were not regular armies, nor were the caudillos always professional soldiers; the guerrillas came together under informal systems of allegiance from various interest groups whom the caudillos represented or could assemble, and they were not amenable to the discipline of army officers. Operating far from centers of government, the caudillos came to regard their particular sectors as personal battle fronts and, after the war, as independent fiefdoms. Caudillism was then perpetuated by postwar conflicts, between unitarists and federalists in Argentina, and between rival caudillos in Venezuela, between political factions in New Granada, and between regional interest groups in Central America. Spanish America was now the scene of a dual process, a militarization and a ruralization of power.

Militarization outlived the war of independence. In most countries the army of liberation survived, with its numerous officers, ill-paid troops, and *fuero militar*, and appeared now to act as an army of occupation in search of resources. Civilian politicians found the military difficult to control or to replace by national militias. Soldiers often resented civilians and claimed that the army was deprived of its just rewards. They also criticized the weakness of constitutional government and the frequent breakdown of law and order. Civilian rulers could not evade these challenges to their authority. In Chile the civilians imposed a strong presidential system and thus removed the pretext of weak government hitherto invoked by military dissidents. In Venezuela José Antonio Páez and his civilian allies kept the military establishment small and mobilized their own retainers when they needed to crush rebellions or enforce their authority. In Argentina Juan Manuel de Rosas had a power base in the military and militia; these were commanded by hand-picked officers. In New Granada the soldiers were integrated into civil society and encouraged to become peaceful constitutionalists. In all these countries the military were never completely dependent on an army career but often had landed estates or alternative occupations. This was one of the reasons why it was possible to assimilate them into the rest of society.

In Mexico, on the other hand, the military were professional officers, creoles who had been recruited initially into the Spanish army and then, transferring their allegiance, had led the movement of independence with the army intact. These regular officers needed the army and depended on a military career for they had no other; thus they identified with the military as a corporate group and fiercely defended their *fueros*. Unlike the other two power bases in Mexico, the Church and the landowners, the army did not possess an independent source of wealth; it relied upon impoverished and sometimes liberal governments for its income, and was therefore tempted to take short cuts to power and resources by periodically intervening in government. Similar circumstances could be found in Peru and Bolivia. Here too army personnel were in many cases royalist officers or their descendants; as professional military, they lacked independent means and sought to control the state in order to allocate resources in their own favor. Thus, there tended to be two forms of militarization: that in Mexico and Peru, where caudillos had a power base in regular army units but always had to negotiate their support; and that in countries where local caudillos depended not on professional armies but on rural militias or their own peons, both of them part of the hacienda structure.[6] In each case the performance of the postwar economies was critical.

Independence destroyed the colonial monopoly and opened the ports of Spanish America to the trade of the world. The local economies did not immediately respond to freedom. The wars were harmful to property and its owners; terror and insecurity caused a flight of labor and capital, which made it difficult to diversify the economy. Growth was further impeded by the absence, as yet, of foreign investment, while local owners of capital, the Church and merchants, had little inducement to invest in industry in the absence of a strong and protected market. The alternative was to allow British manufactures to supply national needs; and in the wake of British manufactures came British merchants and shippers, who filled the entrepreneurial vacuum left by Spain.

The basic economic institution, the hacienda, had acquired a new lease of life in the late colonial period. In Mexico population growth and mining boom were a stimulus to agriculture and encouraged haciendas to concentrate and extend their holdings, often at the expense of smaller farms. In Venezuela the planters of the center-north expanded into the llanos of the interior and gave impetus to the formation of great cattle ranches. In the Río de la Plata estancieros began to respond to export opportunities and land availability and took the first steps in the occupation of the pampas. Landowners survived the wartime disruption; their operations needed less capital than did mining and industry, and depended for their success on abundant land and cheap labor. Cattle ranching in Argentina and Venezuela could yield profits without great investment; here the liberalization of trade and access to stable markets were sufficient in themselves to stimulate growth. Tropical agriculture was less buoyant, and also faced international competition, but even so it found ways of surviving and expanding. Different economic sectors competed for influence, as they had done in the colonial period, but there was no longer a metropolis to arbitrate.

Policy was designed by the new rulers and interest groups who sought to make their particular center a new metropolis and reduce other regions to satellites of themselves. Capitals or ports such as Buenos Aires thus tried to monopolize the fruits of independence, interposing themselves as a controlling interest in national and overseas trade. The subregions protected their economies by insisting on various degrees of autonomy: Uruguay and Paraguay opted for complete independence of Buenos Aires; the interior provinces of Argentina chose the way of federalism. Venezuela and Ecuador seceded from Colombia in order to protect, among other things, their own economies. In Mexico, the artisan textile industry was initially less successful in protecting itself against the merchants of the capital who preferred to import British manufactures; in New Granada industry suffered a similar fate. The national economies, therefore, were divided originally by internal rivalries: between the center and the regions, between free trade and protection, between agriculturalists seeking export outlets and those who favored industry or mining. In the end the promoters of primary exports and cheap imports won the argument, and the British traders were waiting to take advantage. While trade was freer than before 1810 and the market less protected, customs duties were retained for revenue purposes as is the normal practice in societies where the elites refuse to pay income and property taxes.

The transition from colony to nation left its imprint on society. War and insecurity, the emergence of new leaders, the militarization of power, these were a shock to the colonial order and affected relations between social groups. Society could not be immune to the liberal and egalitarian ideas of the age, or to modes of thought that rejected discrimination and sought to harmonize social sectors in the interests of nation building. Legal differentiation between racial groups was now abolished, and republican constitutions declared all citizens equal before the law. But law was not the only agent of change; there was also a trend towards a class—as distinct from a caste—definition of society, as wealth eased the way to a person's progress, and status derived from income rather than legal classification.

Nevertheless, such social change as took place in Spanish America was marginal, not revolutionary. Land was a crucial issue in the wars of independence, and land was a prime source of wealth and power thereafter. The mining economies were damaged by warfare and the withdrawal of Spanish capital, and they were not an object of great interest to the new elites. Public office, of course, was one of the prizes of independence; creoles replaced Spaniards in the higher bureaucracy and found new opportunities in government and politics. But the urban elite was not a strong force in the new nations. The departure of the town-based Spaniards, the commercial influence of foreigners, and the political importance of the new power base, the hacienda, all combined to preclude the development of an urban plutocracy and to diminish the role of the cities. Political power would now be exercised by those who had economic power, and this was based on land. There was, therefore, a ruralization as well as a militarization of power, which represented a shift in the center of political gravity from the city to the countryside, from the intellectuals to the interest groups, from the bureaucrats to the rural militias, from the politicians to the caudillos.

Although the new elites abandoned the urban and bureaucratic state of the colonial regime, they continued to exploit the economic and social resources bequeathed by the colony. Haciendas and their owners were not always financially robust or able to exercise automatic social control, but land was the ultimate asset. And on the whole land remained in the hands of a relatively small group of creoles, often bound together by ties of family and kinship, which enabled them to dominate offices, resources, and labor. Many elite families naturally traced their ancestry to high colonial origins, not only as property owners but also as civil and military servants of the colonial state. But in the course of the wars the composition of the colonial elite was modified, as soldiers, merchants, and others who profited from the hostilities managed to turn themselves into landed proprietors. In Venezuela, where revolution and counterrevolution reduced the ranks of the colonial elite, many great estates passed into the possession of a new oligarchy, the victorious caudillos of independence, who frustrated Bolívar's plan to distribute land to the troops and perpetuated the extension of private property in land at the expense of common usages. Deprived of their traditional resources, the nomadic plainsmen were reduced to the status of ranch peons or reverted to banditry. In the pampas of Argentina a similar process could be observed. The merchants of Buenos Aires began to invest commercial capital in land, acquired vast territorial concessions from a compliant state, and added to them territory won during wars against the Indians. The estancieros thus inexorably tamed the gauchos and then hired them as ranch hands, tied to the estancias by anti-vagrancy laws and the threat of military conscription.

Control over labor was now virtually absolute. The slave trade, it is true, was abolished almost immediately throughout Spanish America, but abolition of slavery itself was a slow and partial process, except in those countries where it was already obsolete. The support of the Enlightenment for abolition was purely theoretical. From Montesquieu onwards the *philosophes* denounced slavery as useless and uneconomical as well as evil, but they did not make a crusade of abolition. The republican conspiracy of Gual and España in 1797 proposed that "slavery be immediately abolished as contrary to humanity," though it linked abolition with service in the revolutionary militia and with employment by the old master.[7] No doubt Bolívar was also aware of contemporary movements in England and France, inspired as they were by humanitarian and religious ideals, but the prime inspiration for his anti-slavery initiative seems to have been his innate sense of justice. He liberated his own slaves, first on condition of military service in 1814, when about fifteen accepted, then unconditionally in 1821 when over a hundred profited.[8] He urged legislators to decree abolition, but did not press the point because, it was alleged, he was reluctant to alienate the creole elite from the revolution. But Bolívar's final word on slavery is to be found in the constitution, which he regarded as Spanish America's last hope for peace and stability. The Bolivian Constitution declared slaves free; and, although proprietors contrived to evade his intentions, Bolívar's plea for absolute and unconditional abolition was uncompromising. Slavery, he declared, was the negation of all law, a violation of human dignity and of the sacred doctrine of equality, and an outrage to reason as well as to justice.[9] The Liberator's kinship with the age of revolution was unbroken. Yet the chronology of abolition was determined in practice by the number of slaves in a country, by their importance to its economy, and sometimes by arguments over compensation. Freedom for Venezuela's 40,000 slaves had to await 1854, when landowners appreciated that slaves were expensive and uneconomical workers, and that a cheaper labor force could be obtained by turning them into "free" peons tied to the estates by laws against vagrancy or by a coercive agrarian regime. Colombia, Peru, and Argentina also delayed abolition until the 1850s.

The Indians were losers from independence. In a formal sense they were emancipated, for they were now free citizens and released from payment of tribute and the obligation of forced labor. But Indians in Peru, Ecuador, and Bolivia did not automatically welcome the abolition of tribute in exchange for paying the same taxes as other citizens—for they saw tribute as a legal proof of their landholdings, from the surplus of which they paid their dues. And their land was now under threat: The liberals of post-independence regarded the Indians as an obstacle to national development, and believed that the autonomy that they had inherited from the colonial regime should be ended by integrating them into the nation. In Peru, Colombia, and Mexico the new legislators sought to destroy corporate entities in order to mobilize Indian lands and release Indian labor. The policy involved the division of communal lands among individual owners, theoretically among the Indians themselves, but in practice among their more powerful neighbors. The idea was not new; it had been a favorite subject of discussion among enlightened thinkers in the colonial period. In New Granada, Pedro Fermín de Vargas wanted to eliminate Indians by means of *mestizaje* and to create a reserve of producers or wage laborers: "It would be highly desirable that the Indians be extinguished, by miscegenation with the whites, declaring them free of tribute and other charges, and giving them private property in land."[10] In Mexico, Manuel Abad y Queipo advocated the abolition of the tribute and the division of Indian community lands among individuals, leaving only marginal land in common.[11] The Spanish Cortes of 1812 took up the idea, and in 1814 Viceroy Abascal produced a scheme, not implemented, to individualize community land in Peru.[12] Ten years later a similar plan by Bolívar was evidently drawn from the same common stock of liberal thinking, and the idea lived on in subsequent republican policy. The Indians, of course, had their own mechanisms of survival and could not be legislated out of existence. But their community lands were left without protection and eventually became one of the victims of land concentration and the export economy.

The revolution failed to reach out to Indians and slaves, even as it also stopped short of the mixed races. Since the middle of the eighteenth century the hopes of the pardos for advance had rested with the metropolis. It was Spanish policy that had first introduced a degree of social mobility against the protest and resistance of the creoles. Now the creoles were in power, the same families who had denounced the opening of doors to the pardos in the university, the Church, and civil and military office. For the mass of the pardos independence was, if anything, a regression. Political mobilization ended with the end of the war, and social mobility was thwarted by plutocratic prejudice and their own poverty. Yet their claims to education, office, and political rights could not be ignored, for in numbers alone they were indispensable to the whites in the wars of independence. In the army they qualified for promotion up to officer of middle rank. Finally they obtained legal equality—the new republican constitutions abolished all outward signs of racial discrimination and made everyone equal before the law. But this was the limit of equality, as many agencies of social mobility continued to be closed to pardos. In Venezuela the rules of university entrance were still restrictive: A certificate of *limpieza* (purity of blood) was demanded until 1822; after that, proof of legitimacy, relatively high entrance fees, and de facto discrimination all placed higher education beyond the reach of the majority of the people.[13]

The popular sectors in general were the outcasts of the revolution. In rural occupations they were subject to greater pressures, from land concentration, liberal legislation in favor of private property, and the renewed attack on vagrancy. In towns no doubt the retail and service sectors expanded with the expansion of international trade. But local industry suffered, or failed to develop. In Venezuela and Colombia, local industry declined, except in regional markets; in the Andean countries it survived only for local consumption; and in the Río de la Plata Britain supplied the popular market. Only in Mexico was industrial employment strong enough to enable artisans to become a significant part of the social structure and make an impact on politics. Elsewhere artisans were an unemployed or underemployed group; together with the rural poor, they were regarded as outside the political nation.

The new states were not necessarily nations. Although independence was won with the help of nationalist symbols and discourse, the emergence of nations lagged behind the creation of states. Creole nationality, as has been seen, predated independence and was to be found in a sense of loyalty to the *patria*, a growing consciousness of identity, and a conviction that Americans were denied equality with Europeans. The wars sharpened the distinction between Spaniards and Americans and for the first time gave American nationalism an exclusive character and political program. The first objective of nationalism, independence of outside power, was achieved by 1826. A second objective, national unity, was slower to develop and became in fact a cause of conflict among Americans themselves as new states sought to include within their frontiers all regions considered to belong to the nation—often against the resistance of smaller units claiming their own independence. But gradually national unity too was achieved, and the boundaries of the new Latin American states began to take shape.

The history of nationalism affords examples of a further process, in addition to independence and unity, namely that of nation building—the diffusion of national awareness downwards and outwards and the incorporation into the nation of all sectors of the people. Such an objective was absent from the policy of Latin America's new leaders. In

Brazil some 25 percent of the population were still slaves, automatically excluded from political life and bereft of any sense of nationality. Of the rest, the majority were debarred from political participation by lack of literacy and property qualifications. If to these social inequalities are added differences between regions and divisions between provinces, then it can be seen that Brazil still had a long way to go along the road of nation building.

In Spanish America creole views of nationality, like many of their ideas, were formed in the last decades of the colony, a time when the voices of Indians, pardos, and mestizos were raised with greater passion. The Andean insurgents of 1780 sought to give their movement a wider American identity. Túpac Amaru appealed to the creoles to join with the Indians "to destroy the Europeans," claiming to stand for "the defense, protection, and safeguard of the Spanish creoles, mestizos, zambos, and Indians, and for their tranquillity, because they are all fellow countrymen and compatriots . . . and all equal sufferers from the oppression and tyranny of the Europeans."[14] Such language reveals a strong sense of nationality and a desire to incorporate as many people as possible into the nation, barring only European Spaniards. But the appeal was rejected by the local elites. The leaders of independence offered liberation and citizenship to the Indians, usually with great eloquence, but in practice they sought to establish states that were predominantly creole in character, while the various ethnic majorities over whom they ruled retained their own ideas about the meaning of independence and its relevance to their lives. The new rulers defined the nation in an exclusive way to preserve the economic and social order that they had inherited from the colony, to monopolize the instruments of government, and to distance themselves from Indians, peasants, and urban populations. The majority of the people were disfranchised by literacy and property tests, and defense of the constitution became a process not of extending participation but of restricting it and preventing other social groups from joining the political nation. For many years to come, the states of Spanish America were creole, not national, states, and the forces of continuity and change remained in conflict.

Notes

INTRODUCTION

1. Baron de Montesquieu, *The Spirit of the Laws*, ed. Anne M. Cohlen and others (Cambridge, 1989), 396.

2. John Leddy Phelan, *The People and the King: The Comunero Revolution in Colombia, 1781* (Madison, Wisc. 1978), 20–26.

3. Juan Carlos Garavaglia and Juan Carlos Grosso, "Estado borbónico y presión fiscal en la Nueva España, 1750–1821," in Antonio Annino and others, eds., *America Latina: Dallo Stato Coloniale allo Stato Nazione (1750–1940)* 2 vols. (Milan, 1987), I: 78–97.

4. See Chapter 8.

5. See Chapter 6.

6. Michel Morineau, *Incroyables gazettes et fabuleux métaux. Les retours des trésors américains d'après les gazettes hollandaises (XVIe–XVIIIe siècles)* (Cambridge, 1985), 417–19, 438–40.

7. Richard J. Salvucci, *Textiles and Capitalism in Mexico: An Economic History of the Obrajes, 1539–1840* (Princeton, 1987), 153–60.

8. On survival of industry, see Chapter 6 and also John R. Fisher, Allan J. Kuethe, and Anthony McFarlane, eds., *Reform and Insurrection in Bourbon New Granada and Peru* (Baton Rouge and London, 1990), 160–62, 172–73. For Spanish policy, see Gil de Taboada to Pedro Lerena, 5 May 1791, *Colección documental de la independencia del Perú* 30 vols. (Lima, 1971–72), tomo XXII, 1: 23–24.

9. Quoted by Eduardo Arcila Farías, *Economía colonial de Venezuela* (Mexico, 1946), 315–19.

10. Miguel Izard, "Venezuela: Tráfico mercantil, secesionismo político e insurgencias populares," in Reinhard Liehr, ed., *América Latina en la época de Simón Bolívar* (Berlin, 1989), 207–25.

11. Quoted by Arcila Farías, *Economía colonial de Venezuela*, 368–69; see also P. Michael McKinley, *Pre-Revolutionary Caracas: Politics, Economy, and Society, 1777–1811* (Cambridge, 1985), 130–35.

12. Susan Migden Socolow, *The Merchants of Buenos Aires, 1778–1810: Family and Commerce* (Cambridge, 1978), 54–70, 124–35.

13. Carlos A. Mayo, "Landed but not Powerful: The Colonial Estancieros of

Buenos Aires (1750–1810)," *Hispanic American Historical Review,* 71 (1991): 761–79.

14. See Chapter 22.

15. Manuel José de Lavardén, *Nuevo aspecto del comercio en el Río de la Plata,* ed. Enrique Wedovoy (Buenos Aires, 1955), 130, 132, 185.

16. John R. Fisher, *Trade, War, and Revolution: Exports from Spain to Spanish America, 1797–1820* (Liverpool, 1992), 54–62.

17. Antonio García-Baquero González, *Comercio colonial y guerras revolucionarias* (Seville, 1972), 182–83.

18. See Chapter 28.

19. Manuel Ferrer Muñoz, "Guerra civil en Nueva España (1810–1815)," *Anuario de Estudios Americanos* 48 (1991): 391–434, esp. 394–95.

20. *Gaceta de Buenos Aires* [25 September 1810], in Naomi Goldman, *Historia y lenguaje: Los discursos de la Revolución de Mayo* (Buenos Aires, 1992), 33–34, 80.

21. See Chapter 25. For a modern, and different, view, see Mark A. Burkholder and D. S. Chandler, *From Impotence to Authority: The Spanish Crown and the American Audiencias, 1687–1808* (Columbia, Mo. 1977), 10–11, 74–75, 104–06.

22. *Esquisse Politique,* 236, and *La Paix et le bonheur,* 332–33, in Merle E. Simmons, *Los escritos de Juan Pablo Viscardo y Guzmán, Precursor de la Independencia Hispanoamericana* (Caracas, 1983).

23. Robert J. Ferry, *The Colonial Elite of Early Caracas: Formation and Crisis, 1567–1767* (Berkeley and Los Angeles, 1989), 241–45, 253–54.

24. Scarlett O'Phelan Godoy, *Rebellions and Revolts in Eighteenth Century Peru and Upper Peru* (Cologne, 1985), 241.

25. Eduardo Posada and P.M. Ibañez, eds., *Relaciones de mando. Memorias presentadas por los gobernantes del Nuevo Reino de Granada* (Biblioteca de Historia Nacional, 8, Bogotá, 1910), 113.

26. Quoted by Guillermo Céspedes del Castillo, *Lima y Buenos Aires. Repercusiones económicas y políticas de la creación del virreinato del Plata* (Seville, 1947), 123.

27. Burkholder and Chandler, *From Impotence to Authority,* 190–91.

28. Susan Migden Socolow, *The Bureaucrats of Buenos Aires, 1769–1810: Amor al Real Servicio* (Durham, N.C., 1987), 132.

29. Linda K. Salvucci, "Costumbres viejas 'hombres nuevos': José de Gálvez y la burocracia fiscal novohispana, 1754–1800," *Historia Mexicana* 33 (1983): 224–64; Jacques A. Barbier, *Reform and Politics in Bourbon Chile, 1755–1796* (Ottawa, 1980), 75, 190–94; Socolow, *The Bureaucrats of Buenos Aires,* 262–64.

30. See Chapter 3.

31. Juan Marchena Fernández, "The Social World of the Military in Peru and New Granada: The Colonial Oligarchies in Conflict, 1750–1810," in Fisher, Kuethe, and McFarlane, *Reform and Insurrection in Bourbon New Granada and Peru,* 54–95.

32. See Chapter 4.

33. Alberto Flores Galindo, *Aristocracia y plebe, Lima, 1760–1830* (Lima, 1984), 78–96.

34. See Chapter 15; and McKinley, *Pre-Revolutionary Caracas,* 116–19.

35. John R. Fisher, *Government and Society in Colonial Peru: The Intendant System, 1784–1814* (London, 1970), 87–99.

36. Enrique Florescano, *Precios del maíz y crisis agrícolas en México (1708–*

1810) (Mexico, 1969), 176–79; on inflationary trends, see David R. Brading, "Comments on 'The Economic Cycle in Bourbon Central Mexico: A Critique of the *Recaudación del diezmo líquido en pesos'*, by Ouweneel and Bigleveld," *Hispanic American Historical Review* 69 (1989): 531–38.

37. Enrique Tandeter and Nathan Wachtel, "Prices and Agricultural Production: Potosí and Charcas in the Eighteenth Century," in Lyman L. Johnson and Enrique Tandeter, eds., *Essays on the Price History of Eighteenth-Century Latin America* (Albuquerque, 1989), 201–76, esp. 256, 271–72.

38. Lyman L. Johnson, "The Price History of Buenos Aires During the Viceregal Period," ibid., 137–71, esp. 163–65.

39. Anthony McFarlane, "The 'Rebellion of the Barrios': Urban Insurrection in Bourbon Quito," *Hispanic American Historical Review* 69 (1989): 283–330. The rebellion in Paraguay from 1721—an expression of regional identity and of competition for resources between Jesuits and settlers—lies outside the sequence under discussion.

40. These are the conclusions of Eric Van Young, "Islands in the Storm: Quiet Cities and Violent Countrysides in the Mexican Independence Era," *Past and Present* no. 118 (1988): 130–55.

41. For a review of historiography and interpretation, see Steve J. Stern, "The Age of Andean Insurrection, 1743–1782: A Reappraisal," in Steve J. Stern, ed., *Resistance, Rebellion, and Consciousness in the Andean Peasant World, 18th to 20th Centuries* (Madison, Wisc. 1987), 34–93. See also Chapters 5 and 17.

42. John J. TePaske and Herbert S. Klein, *The Royal Treasuries of the Spanish Empire in America* Vol. 1, Peru, Vol. 2, Upper Peru (Bolivia) (Durham, N.C., 1982), 1: 196–208; 2: 390–403.

43. Manuel Lucena Salmoral, *El Memorial de don Salvador Plata. Los Comuneros y los movimientos antirreformistas* (Bogotá, 1982), 48–50. Plata, participant and chronicler of the *comuneros,* described these officials as "bárbaros," "personas vagas de Patria, y Padres desconocidos." See also Chapter 1, and Anthony McFarlane, "Civil Disorders and Popular Protests in Late Colonial New Granada," *Hispanic American Historical Review* 64 (1984): 17–54.

44. See Chapters 12 and 18. See also O'Phelan Godoy, *Rebellions and Revolts,* 266–67.

45. See Chapter 24 for Nariño's observation; on the viceroy's concern, see Pedro de Mendinueta, "Relación," 1803, in Posada and Ibañez, eds., *Relaciones de mando,* 476, 549.

46. Brian R. Hamnett, "Popular Insurrection and Royalist Reaction: Colombian Regions, 1810–1823," in Fisher, Kuethe, and McFarlane, eds., *Reform and Insurrection in Bourbon New Granada,* 292–326, esp. 309–12, 324–25.

47. For further discussion of social banditry and for bibliographical references, see John Lynch, *Caudillos in Spanish America, 1800–1850* (Oxford, 1992), 26–29. On the Peruvian bands, see Carmen Vivanco Lara, "Bandolerismo colonial peruano: 1760–1810," in Carlos Aguirre and Charles Walker, eds., *Bandoleros, abigeos y montoneros: Criminalidad y violencia en el Perú, siglos XVIII–XX* (Lima, 1990), 25–56. Also see Flores Galindo, *Aristocracia y plebe,* 139–48, 235.

48. Vivanco Lara, "Bandolerismo colonial peruano," 33–34, 49.

49. Ibid., 50.

50. Heraclio Bonilla, "Bolívar y las guerrillas indígenas en el Perú," *Cultura,*

Revista del Banco Central del Ecuador 6, 16 (1983): 81–95; Charles Walker, "Montoneros, bandoleros, malhechores: Criminalidad y política en las primeras décadas republicanas," *Pasado y Presente* 2 (1989): 119–37.

51. Stuart B. Schwartz, "The Formation of a Colonial Identity in Brazil," in Nicholas Canny and Anthony Pagden, eds., *Colonial Identity and the Atlantic World, 1500–1800* (Princeton, 1987), 15–50.

52. See Chapter 29.

53. See Chapter 32.

54. Quoted by Kenneth R. Maxwell, *Conflicts and Conspiracies: Brazil and Portugal, 1750–1808* (Cambridge, 1973), 222. See also Chapter 31.

55. R. R. Palmer, *The Age of the Democratic Revolution: A Political History of Europe and America, 1760–1800* 2 vols. (Princeton, 1959–64); E. J. Hobsbawm, *The Age of Revolution: Europe, 1789–1848* (London, 1962), 53.

56. John Lynch, *Simón Bolívar and the Age of Revolution* (Research Paper no. 10, Institute of Latin American Studies, London, 1983).

57. Miranda to Gual, 31 December 1799, *Archivo del General Miranda* 24 vols. (Caracas, 1929–50), 15: 404.

58. See Chapter 22.

59. See Chapter 23.

60. José M. Mariluz Urquijo, *El virreinato del Río de la Plata en la época del marqués de Avilés (1799–1801)* (Buenos Aires, 1964), 267.

61. See Chapters 1, 20, and 21. On the endurance of scholastic thought and the patrimonial structure, see Richard M. Morse, "Claims of Political Tradition," *New World Soundings: Culture and Ideology in the Americas* (Baltimore, 1989), 95–130.

62. See Chapter 27.

63. *The Second Treatise of Government*, 2: 102–03, 217, in John Locke, *Two Treatises of Government*, ed. Peter Laslett (Cambridge, 1989), 334–35, 419.

64. Montesquieu, *The Spirit of the Laws*, 328–29, 396.

65. *Gaceta de Buenos Aires* [13 November 1810], in Goldman, *Historia y lenguaje*, 37, 91.

66. "Manifiesto de José Angulo al Pueblo del Cuzco," [16 August 1814], in *Colección documental de la independencia del Perú*, vol. 3, *La revolución del Cuzco de 1814* (Lima, 1971), 211–15. See also Chapter 13.

67. *Common Sense*, in Thomas Paine, *Political Writings*, ed. Bruce Kuklick (Cambridge, 1989), 23, 37–38, 101.

68. *Rights of Man*, ibid., 140–41.

69. Manuel García de Sena, *La Independencia de la Costa Firme justificada por Thomas Paine treinta años ha*, ed. Pedro Grases (Caracas, 1949); see also Pedro Grases, *Libros y libertad* (Caracas, 1974), 21–26.

70. Abbé Raynal, *A Philosophical and Political History of the Settlement and Trade of the Europeans in the East and West Indies*, 6 vols., (Edinburgh, 1804), 16: 82, 83.

71. *Les trois âges des colonies* (Paris, 1801–2); see also D. A. Brading, *The First America: The Spanish Monarchy, Creole Patriots, and the Liberal State, 1492–1867* (Cambridge, 1991), 558–60.

72. See Chapter 27.

73. Goldman, *Historia y lenguaje*, 30–32.

74. Tulio Halperín Donghi, *Politics, Economics, and Society in Argentina in the Revolutionary Period* (Cambridge, 1975), 186–87.

75. Andrés Bello, *Resumen de la historia de Venezuela* [1810] (La Casa de Bello, Caracas, 1978), 45.

76. John Lynch, *The Spanish American Revolutions, 1808–1826* 2nd ed., (New York, 1986), 24–34; D. A. Brading, *The First America*, 379–81, 460–62, 480–83, 536–39. See also Chapter 25.

77. For further discussion of nationalism during and after independence, see Lynch, *Caudillos in Spanish America*, 132–68.

78. *Colección documental de la independencia del Perú*, 2, ii: 272; Alberto Flores Galindo, *Buscando un Inca: identidad y utopia en los Andes* (Lima, 1986), 126. See also Chapters 16 and 17.

79. José Santos Vargas, *Diario de un comandante de la independencia americana, 1814–1825*, ed. Gunnar Mendoza L. (Mexico, 1982), June 1816: 88.

80. Ibid., 30 December 1816: 118.

81. Simmons, *Los escritos de Viscardo*, 363, 366–67, 369, 376.

CHAPTER 2

1. We have borrowed the phrase from John J. TePaske, "The Collapse of the Spanish Empire," *Lex et Scientia: The International Journal of Law and Science* 10: 1–2 (January-June 1974): 34–46.

CHAPTER 3

1. [A quotation from the legislation of Henry III mentioned above. *Ed.*]

2. [The calculation is certainly too high. Equally, the comments on miscegenation are not an adequate record of fact or perceptions. *Ed.*]

CHAPTER 4

1. [Special militia commanders appointed for New Granada in 1773. *Ed.*]

2. [Alejandro O'Reilly, field marshal in the Spanish army; his reorganization of the defenses and militias of Cuba in 1763 to 1765 became a model for military reform elsewhere in Spanish America. *Ed.*]

3. [The Spanish regular army in America comprised (1) fixed (*fijos*) or permanent garrisons recruited mainly in America, and (2) rotating Spanish battalions sent from the peninsula to key positions. *Ed.*]

4. [Viceroy Francisco Gil y Lemos, in the name of economy, severely curtailed military expenditure in New Granada from 1789. *Ed.*]

CHAPTER 7

1. ["Distributional factors" mean the distribution of agricultural property and product among different regions (horizontal), and among class and ethnic groups (vertical). *Ed.*]

CHAPTER 14

1. [A modern calculation would give a population of about 6 million; the 1,097,928 whites formed only 18 percent of the whole, Indians 60 percent, castas 22 percent, blacks and mulattos 10 percent. *Ed.*]

CHAPTER 16

1. [Spanish-born merchants and leading citizens of Arequipa. *Ed.*]

CHAPTER 17

1. [The author distinguishes local rebellion from "a full scale insurrection of regional or supraregional proportions" (p. 11). *Ed.*]

CHAPTER 18

1. [See Chapter 1. *Ed.*]

CHAPTER 19

1. William B. Taylor, *Drinking, Homicide, and Rebellion in Colonial Mexican Villages* (Stanford, 1979), 115–16, 124, 146.

CHAPTER 21

1. [A more appropriate date for the abolition of slavery in Argentina and Uruguay is 1853. *Ed.*]

CHAPTER 25

1. [Modern research gives a figure even lower than this, not more than 15,000. *Ed.*]
2. The publication of both the Flora of New Spain and the Flora of Santa Fe de Bogota is expected with impatience. The latter is the fruit of 40 years' researches and observations by the celebrated Mutis, one of the great botanists of the age.
3. [Modern estimates would suggest a Venezuelan population of less than 800,000. *Ed.*]

CHAPTER 27

1. [Fray Servando Teresa de Mier Noriega y Guerra. *Ed.*]

CHAPTER 28

1. [In fact there were less than 15,000 peninsulares in a total population of 6 million, of whom 1 million were whites. *Ed.*]
2. Of the 170 viceroys appointed to America up to 1813 only four had been born there, and these happened to be the sons of Spanish officials.
3. Of 706 bishops in all America up to 1812 105 were creoles, though few of these were appointed to major sees.

CONCLUSION

1. See Chapters 29 and 31.

2. F. W. O. Morton, "The Military and Society in Bahia, 1800–1821," *Journal of Latin American Studies* 7 (1975): 249–69.

3. José Murilo de Carvalho, *A construção da ordem: A elite política imperial* (Rio de Janeiro, 1980), and the same author's "Political Elites and State Building: The Case of Nineteenth-Century Brazil," *Comparative Studies in Society and History* 24 (1982): 378–99.

4. See Chapter 27.

5. Lynch, *Caudillos in Spanish America*, 35–83.

6. Frank Safford, "Politics, Ideology and Society in Post-Independence Spanish America," in Leslie Bethell, ed., *The Cambridge History of Latin America* 3 Vols. (Cambridge, 1985), 3: 347–421, esp. 380–81.

7. Pedro Grases, *La conspiración de Gual y España y el ideario de la independencia* (Caracas, 1949), 175–76.

8. Simón Bolívar, *Decretos del Libertador* 3 vols., ed. Vicente Lecuna (Caracas, 1961) 1: 55–56.

9. Message to Congress of Bolivia, 25 May 1826, Simón Bolívar, *Obras completas* 2d ed., 3 vols. (Havana, 1950), 3: 768–69.

10. Pedro Fermín de Vargas, *Memoria sobre la población del Reino*, in Rafael Gómez Hoyos, *La revolución granadina de 1810: Ideario de una generación y de una época, 1781–1821*, 2 vols. (Bogotá, 1962), 1: 282.

11. See Chapter 14.

12. Timothy E. Anna, *The Fall of the Royal Government in Peru* (Lincoln, Nebr., 1979), 62–63.

13. Ildefonso Leal, *Historia de la Universidad de Caracas (1721–1827)* (Caracas, 1963), 332–38.

14. "Edicto para la provincia de Chichas," [23 December 1780], *Colección documental de la independencia del Perú*, 2, ii: 374–5. See also Introduction and Chapter 16.

Glossary of Spanish and Portuguese Terms

abogado lawyer or attorney
aduana customs; customs house
aguardiente liquor, spirits
alcabala sales tax
alcalde mayor district officer, comparable to a *corregidor*
alcalde ordinario a leading member of a cabildo; magistrate
arroba measure of weight: 25 pounds
audiencia high court of justice with administrative functions
aviador financier
bando decree
cabildo town council
cabildo abierto a cabildo augmented with selected citizens for an
  extraordinary meeting
cacique Indian chieftain
caboclo (Brazil) of mixed white and Amerindian descent
câmara (Brazil) town council
castas people of black or mixed descent
caudillo leader, whose rule is based on personal power
cédula royal decree issued by council
cédula de gracias al sacar a royal decree granting an exemption
chacra small farm
chapetón South American nickname for peninsular Spaniard
cholo mestizo (Peruvian)
chorrillos domestic textile workshop
compadre godfather
consulado merchant guild and commercial court
consolidación sequestration of funds of pious foundations for remission to Spain
côrtes (Port.) parliament

corregidor   district officer with administrative and judicial authority

criollo   creole, a Spaniard born in America

cura   parish priest; priest with a specific benefice or living

curaca   see *kuraka*

derrama   (Brazil)   capitation tax

efectos de Castilla   imported goods

efectos de la tierra   locally produced goods

estancia   large cattle ranch; *estanciero,* owner of an estancia

fanega   grain measure: about 1.5 bushels

forasteros   Indians living in a community outside their original kin group

fuero   right, privilege, immunity, conferred by membership of profession or community

gañanes   rural wage laborers

gachupines   nickname in Mexico for European-born Spaniards

gente decente   respectable people

garrucha   torture rack, pulley

hacendado   owner of hacienda

hacienda   large landed estate

inconfidência   (Port.)   disloyalty, conspiracy

infame   infamous, vile

kuraka   Andean ethnic chief

llanos   plains (*llaneros* plainsmen)

letrado   law graduate, lawyer

Mesa do Bem Comum   (Brazil)   commercial association

mestizo   of mixed white and Indian descent

mita   Quechua word, meaning "turn": forced labor recruitment of Indians in rotation, especially for work in the silver mines of Potosí

natural, naturales   a native of a given place, one born there

obrajes   workshop, especially textile; *obrajero,* owner of obraje

originario   Indian still living with original kin group

pacto colonial   the colonial relationship: in return for protection, the colonies exported to Spain precious metals and raw materials and imported manufactured goods

palenque   community of runaway slaves, possibly defended by palisades

pampa   plains, prairie; in Andes, a grassy plateau

pardo   mulatto, of mixed white and black descent

peninsular   Spaniard born in Spain

peso   unit of currency: in eighteenth century the *peso de a ocho reales* equalled 272 maravedís

porteño   of Buenos Aires, inhabitant of Buenos Aires

pueblo   people; common people; village

plaza   in administrative context, a post or appointment

radicado   having local roots or interests

real   standard silver coin: equaled 34 maravedís

regidor   member of a *cabildo*, town councillor

reinóis   persons born in the kingdom of Portugal

repartimiento (reparto) de mercancías   forced sale of goods to Indians

resguardos   reservations, Indian community lands

revisita   inspection of a province for register of tribute payers

seismaria   (Brazil) land grant, holder of land grant

tocuyo   coarse cotton cloth

togado   lawyer, judge

trapiche   sugar mill; ore crusher

visita   official inspection of a colonial administration carried out by a special commissioner called a *visitador*

yanacona   Indian laborer removed from his community and bound to a Spanish master

zambo   of mixed black and Indian descent

Select Bibliography

GENERAL

Bethell, Leslie, ed. *The Cambridge History of Latin America*. 3 vols. Cambridge, 1984–85. The relevant chapters of volume three are republished in *The Independence of Latin America* (Cambridge, 1987).
Fisher, John R., Allan J. Kuethe, and Anthony McFarlane, eds. *Reform and Insurrection in Bourbon New Granada and Peru*. Baton Rouge, 1990.
Flores Galindo, Alberto, ed. *Independencia y revolución (1780–1840)*. 2 vols. Lima, 1987.
Halperín Donghi, Tulio. *Reforma y disolución de los imperios ibéricos, 1750–1850*. Madrid, 1985.
Humphreys, R. A. *Tradition and Revolt in Latin America*. London, 1969.
Lynch, John. *The Spanish American Revolutions, 1808–1826*. 2d ed. New York, 1986.

I. IMPERIAL RECOVERY: FROM CONSENSUS TO CONTROL

Archer, Christon I. *The Army in Bourbon Mexico, 1760–1810*. Albuquerque, 1977.
Barbier, Jacques A. *Reform and Politics in Bourbon Chile, 1755–1796*. Ottawa, 1980.
Brown, Kendall W. *Bourbons and Brandy: Imperial Reform in Eighteenth-Century Arequipa*. Albuquerque, 1986.
Burkholder, Mark A., and D. S. Chandler. *From Impotence to Authority: The Spanish Crown and the American Audiencias, 1687–1808*. Columbia, Mo., 1977.
Campbell, Leon G. *The Military and Society in Colonial Peru, 1750–1810*. Philadelphia, 1978.
Farriss, N. M. *Crown and Clergy in Colonial Mexico, 1759–1821: The Crisis of Ecclesiastical Privilege*. London, 1968.
Fisher, John R. *Government and Society in Colonial Peru: The Intendant System 1784–1814*. London, 1970.
Garavaglia, Juan Carlos, and Juan Carlos Grosso. "Estado borbónico y presión

fiscal en la Nueva España, 1750–1821." In Antonio Annino and others, eds. *America Latina: Dallo Stato coloniale allo Stato nazione (1750–1940)*. 2 vols. Milan, 1987, I, 78–97.

Hamnett, Brian R. *Politics and Trade in Southern Mexico, 1750–1821*. Cambridge, 1971.

Kuethe, Allan J. *Cuba, 1753–1815: Crown, Military, and Society*. Knoxville, Tenn., 1986.

———. *Military Reform and Society in New Granada, 1773–1808*. Gainesville, Fla., 1978.

Lynch, John. *Spanish Colonial Administration, 1782–1810: The Intendant System in the Viceroyalty of the Río de la Plata*. London, 1958.

Marchena Fernández, Juan. *Oficiales y soldados en el ejército español en América*. Seville, 1983.

McFarlane, Anthony. *Colombia before Independence: Economy, Society, and Politics under Bourbon Rule*. Cambridge, 1993.

Socolow, Susan Migden. *The Bureaucrats of Buenos Aires, 1769–1810: Amor al Real Servicio*. Durham, N.C., 1987.

Wortman, Miles L. *Government and Society in Central America, 1680–1840*. New York, 1982.

2. THE COLONIAL ECONOMY: GROWTH AND CRISIS

Assadourian, Carlos Sempat. *El sistema de la economía colonial*. Lima, 1982.

Brading, D. A. *Haciendas and Ranchos in the Mexican Bajío: León, 1700–1860*. Cambridge, 1978.

———. *Miners and Merchants in Bourbon Mexico, 1763–1810*. Cambridge, 1971.

Buechler, Rose Marie. *The Mining Society of Potosí, 1776–1810*. Syracuse, N. Y., 1981.

Fisher, John R. *Commercial Relations between Spain and Spanish America in the Era of Free Trade, 1778–1796*. Liverpool, 1985.

———. *Silver Mines and Silver Miners in Colonial Peru, 1776–1824*. Liverpool, 1977.

——— *Trade, War, and Revolution: Exports from Spain to Spanish America, 1797–1820*. Liverpool, 1992.

Florescano, Enrique. *Precios del maíz y crisis agrícolas en México (1708–1810)*. Mexico, 1969.

García-Baquero González, Antonio. *La Carrera de Indias: Suma de la contratación y Océano de negocios*. Seville, 1992.

——— *Comercio colonial y guerras revolucionarias*. Seville, 1972.

Jacobsen, Nils, and Hans-Jürgen Puhle, eds. *The Economies of Mexico and Peru during the Late Colonial Period, 1760–1810*. Berlin, 1986.

Johnson, Lyman L., and Enrique Tandeter, eds. *Essays on the Price History of Eighteenth-Century Latin America*. Albuquerque, 1990.

Ortiz de la Tabla, Javier. *Comercio exterior de Veracruz, 1778–1821: Crisis de dependencia*. Seville, 1978.

Salvucci, Richard J. *Textiles and Capitalism in Mexico: An Economic History of the Obrajes, 1539–1840*. Princeton, 1987.

Tandeter, Enrique. *Coercion and Market: Silver Mining in Colonial Potosí, 1692–1826*. Albuquerque, 1993.

Tandrón, Hurberto. *El real consulado de Caracas y el comercio exterior de Venezuela.* Caracas, 1976.

Taylor, William B. *Landlord and Peasant in Colonial Oaxaca.* Stanford, 1972.

Van Young, Eric. *Hacienda and Market in Eighteenth-Century Mexico: The Rural Economy of the Guadalajara Region, 1675–1820.* Berkeley and Los Angeles, 1981.

3. COLONIAL SOCIETY: CONTINUITY AND CONFLICT

Anna, Timothy E. *The Fall of the Royal Government in Mexico City.* Lincoln, Nebr., 1978.

Bonilla, Heraclio, and others. *La Independencia en al Perú.* 2d ed. Lima, 1981.

Ferry, Robert J. *The Colonial Elite of Early Caracas: Formation and Crisis, 1567–1767.* Berkeley and Los Angeles, 1989.

Flores Galindo, Alberto. *Aristocracia y plebe, Lima, 1760–1830.* Lima, 1984.

Izard, Miguel. *El miedo a la revolución: La lucha por la libertad en Venezuela (1777–1830).* Madrid, 1979.

Ladd, Doris M. *The Mexican Nobility at Independence, 1780–1826.* Austin, 1976.

Lucena Salmoral, Manuel. *Vísperas de la independencia americana: Caracas.* Madrid, 1986.

McKinley, P. Michael. *Pre-Revolutionary Caracas: Politics, Economy, and Society, 1777–1811.* Cambridge, 1985.

Socolow, Susan Migden. *The Merchants of Buenos Aires, 1778–1810: Family and Commerce.* Cambridge, 1978.

4. POPULAR PROTEST

Aguirre, Carlos and Charles Walker, eds. *Bandoleros, abigeos y montoneros: Criminalidad y violencia en el Perú, siglos XVIII–XX.* Lima, 1990.

Hamnett, Brian R. *Roots of Insurgency: Mexican Regions, 1750–1824.* Cambridge, 1986.

McFarlane, Anthony. "Civil Disorders and Popular Protests in Late Colonial New Granada," *Hispanic American Historical Review* 64 (1984): 17–54.

O'Phelan Godoy, Scarlett. *Rebellions and Revolts in Eighteenth Century Peru and Upper Peru.* Cologne, 1985.

Perez, Joseph. *Los movimientos precursores de la emancipación en Hispano-américa.* Madrid, 1977.

Phelan, John Leddy. *The People and the King: The Comunero Revolution in Colombia, 1781.* Madison, Wisc., 1978.

Stern, Steve J., ed. *Resistance, Rebellion, and Consciousness in the Andean Peasant World, 18th to 20th Centuries.* Madison, Wisc., 1987.

Taylor, William B. "Banditry and Insurrection: Rural Unrest in Central Jalisco, 1790–1816." In Friedrich Katz, ed. *Riot, Rebellion, and Revolution: Rural Social Conflict in Mexico.* Princeton, 1988.

———. *Drinking, Homicide, and Rebellion in Colonial Mexican Villages.* Stanford, 1979.

Van Young, Eric. "Islands in the Storm: Quiet Cities and Violent Countrysides in the Mexican Independence Era," *Past and Present* 118 (1988): 130–55.

5. IDEAS AND INTERESTS

Barbier, Jacques A. and Allan J. Kuethe. *The North American Role in the Spanish Imperial Economy, 1760–1819.* Manchester, 1984.

Chiaramonte, José Carlos, ed. *Pensamiento de la Ilustración: Economía y sociedad iberoamericanas en el siglo XVIII.* Caracas, 1979.

Collier, Simon. *Ideas and Politics of Chilean Independence, 1808–1833.* Cambridge, 1967.

Goldman, Naomi. *Historia y Lenguaje: Los discursos de la Revolución de Mayo.* Buenos Aires, 1992.

Goldman, Naomi, and others. *Imagen y recepción de la Revolución Francesa en la Argentina.* Buenos Aires, 1990.

Liss, Peggy K. *Atlantic Empires: The Network of Trade and Revolution, 1713–1826.* Baltimore and London, 1983.

Lynch, John. *Simón Bolívar and the Age of Revolution.* Research Paper no. 10, Institute of Latin American Studies. London, 1983.

Morse, Richard M. "Claims of Political Tradition," *New World Soundings: Culture and Ideology in the Americas.* Baltimore, 1989.

Simmons, Merle E. *Los escritos de Juan Pablo Viscardo y Guzmán.* Caracas, 1983.

Stoetzer, O. Carlos. *The Scholastic Roots of the Spanish American Revolution.* New York, 1979.

6. INCIPIENT NATIONALISM

Brading, D. A. *The First America: The Spanish Monarchy, Creole Patriots, and the Liberal State, 1492–1867.* Cambridge, 1991.

———— *The Origins of Mexican Nationalism.* Cambridge, 1985.

————. *Prophecy and Myth in Mexican History.* Cambridge, 1984.

Buisson, Inge, and others, eds. *Problemas de la formación del estado y de la nación en Hispanoamérica.* Bonn, 1984.

Canny, Nicholas and Anthony Pagden, eds. *Colonial Identity and the Atlantic World, 1500–1800.* Princeton, 1987.

7. BRAZIL: FROM COLONY TO EMPIRE

Alden, Dauril, ed. *Colonial Roots of Modern Brazil.* Berkeley, 1973.

Dias Tavares, Luis Henrique. *História da sedição intendada na Bahia em 1798: A "conspiração do alfaiates".* São Paulo, 1975.

Mota, Carlos Guilherme. *Atitudes de inovação no Brasil, 1789–1801.* Lisbon, n.d.

———— *Nordeste 1817.* São Paulo, 1972.

Jobson de A. Arruda, José. *O Brasil no comércio colonial.* São Paulo, 1980.

Maxwell, Kenneth R. *Conflicts and Conspiracies: Brazil and Portugal, 1750–1808.* Cambridge, 1973.

Murilo de Carvalho, José. *A construção da ordem: A elite política imperial.* Rio de Janeiro, 1980.

Novais, Fernando A. *Portugal e Brasil na crise do antigo sistema colonial (1777–1808).* São Paulo, 1979.

Prado, Caio, Jr. *The Colonial Background of Modern Brazil.* Berkeley and Los Angeles, 1967.

Ramos, Donald. "Social Revolution Frustrated: The Conspiracy of the Tailors in Bahia, 1798." *Luso-Brazilian Review* 13 (1976): 74–90.

Russell-Wood, A. J. R., ed. *From Colony to Nation: Essays on the Independence of Brazil.* Baltimore and London, 1975.

Viotti da Costa, Emilia. *The Brazilian Empire: Myths and Histories.* Chicago, 1985.

Index